A BLACK PHILADELPHIA READER

T0244303

A Black Philadelphia Reader

African American Writings About
the City of Brotherly Love

EDITED BY LOUIS J. PARASCANDOLA

The Pennsylvania State University Press
University Park, Pennsylvania

Library of Congress Cataloging-in-Publication Data

Names: Parascandola, Louis J., 1952– editor.
Title: A Black Philadelphia reader : African American writings about the city of
    brotherly love / edited by Louis J. Parascandola.
Other titles: African American writings about the city of brotherly love
Description: University Park, Pennsylvania : The Pennsylvania State
    University Press, [2024] | Includes bibliographical references and index.
Summary: "A collection of historical and literary depictions of Philadelphia by
    Black native Philadelphians and those with a significant link to the city"—
    Provided by publisher.
Identifiers: LCCN 2024007446 | ISBN 9780271097312 (paperback)
Subjects: LCSH: African Americans—Pennsylvania—Philadelphia—History. |
    African Americans—Civil rights—Pennsylvania—Philadelphia—History. |
    American literature—Pennsylvania—Philadelphia—African American
    authors—History and criticism. | African Americans—Pennsylvania—
    Philadelphia—Literary collections. | Philadelphia (Pa.)—Race
    relations—History. | LCGFT: Literature.
Classification: LCC F158.9.B53 B53 2024 | DDC 974.8/1100496073—dc23/eng/
    20240315
LC record available at https://lccn.loc.gov/2024007446

10 9 8 7 6 5 4 3 2 1

The Pennsylvania State University Press is a member of the Association of
University Presses.

It is the policy of The Pennsylvania State University Press to use acid-free paper.
Publications on uncoated stock satisfy the minimum requirements of American
National Standard for Information Sciences—Permanence of Paper for Printed
Library Material, ANSI z39.48–1992.

To Philadelphia

CONTENTS

MAP

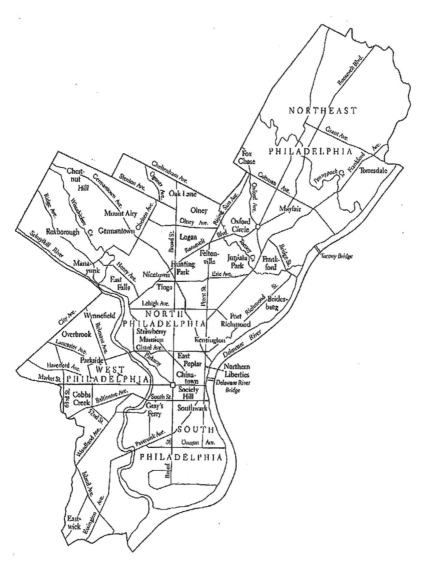

The Neighborhoods of Philadelphia, 1940. From *Philadelphia Stories: A Photographic History, 1920–1960*, by Frederic M. Miller, Morris J. Vogel, and Allen F. Davis, page 4. Used by permission of the Temple University Press. © 2008 by Temple University Press. All Rights Reserved.

ACKNOWLEDGMENTS

Writing a book can often seem like a solitary experience. Yet upon reflection one realizes how many people actually contributed in one way or another. I would like to thank some of those people below, whose help and encouragement aided me in completing this book.

I thank my undergraduate and graduate classes at Long Island University, Brooklyn, whose interest and enthusiasm helped sustain me.

Several of my graduate students, some research assistants, aided me, particularly Tiani Kennedy, who read and commented on much of the manuscript.

I thank my colleagues and especially my chairs at LIU, Vidhya Swaminathan, Leah Dilworth, and Deborah Mutnick, for their support. In addition, I thank LIU for providing some needed travel funds and for granting a sabbatical, which made much of the writing possible.

My initial editor, Kathryn Bourque Yahner, and her able assistant, Maddie Caso, had unfailing faith in this project. I would also like to thank managing editor Alex Ramos, copyeditor Dana Henricks, and associate director Jennifer Norton, as well as Jon Gottshall for his help in getting the cover art; and the rest of the staff at Penn State University Press for their help and support. In addition, I thank the anonymous reviewers of the manuscript whose suggestions, sometimes criticisms, helped make this a better book.

Thanks to artist Jess X. Snow and the people at Mural Arts Philadelphia for permission to use the cover mural.

To complete this project, I needed the help of numerous publishers and their representatives. Without their permissions, this book would never have appeared. Many went out of their way to help me find copyright holders, especially for overseas rights, and to keep down fees. Among those I wish to thank included Raian Khan (Farrar, Straus, & Giroux), Christopher Wait (New Directions), Lisa C. Moore (for Joseph Beam's estate), Jill Dougan (Beacon), old friend Fred Courtright (The Permissions Company), Yessenia Santos (Simon & Schuster), Maile Beal (Carol Mann Agency), Christopher Aguirre (Penguin Random House), Peter London (HarperCollins), Wendy Appelle (Wylie Agency), Jordan Stepp and Elizabeth Adams (University of

Georgia Press), Audrey Crooks (Trident), Lori Anderman (Farrar, Straus, & Giroux), Eileen O'Malley (University of Pittsburgh Press), Robert Hershon (Hanging Loose Press), Sherri Marmon (Penguin Random House), Sam Moore (Penguin Random House), Laura Forker (Penguin Random House UK), Malav Kanuga (Common Notions), Pam McMillan (Canongate, UK), and The Hachette Book Group. Several of the writers themselves granted me permission and offered me support. These include Warren Longmire, Yvonne, Lorene Cary, Diane McKinney-Whetstone, Sonia Sanchez, and David Bradley. I thank them all.

On a more personal level, I wish to thank my ever-reliable family members. John, as usual, has been a great source of support and encouragement, reading parts of the manuscript and offering helpful suggestions. The Nero family again has provided comfort and support. My wife, Shondel Nero, of course, was a sounding board for this project. We made several educational and entertaining trips to Philly. Her love and support got me through the occasional hurdles of working on this project.

Finally, I would like to thank the people of Philadelphia, who always offered a welcoming hand. This book is dedicated to Philadelphia.

NOTE ON THE TEXTS

This anthology is a collection of Black Philadelphia writers on their city. Having been born there, such as Mae Cowdery or Don Bolton, is not enough. They did not have to be born there (John Edgar Wideman and David Bradley, for example, were not), but they needed to have lived there for several years or to have resided there (such as Harriet Jacobs) during a significant event in their lives. Therefore, for instance, Ta'Nehisi Coates's novel *The Water Dancer* did not qualify. The final selection of authors/works included was made difficult, especially in the twenty-first century, by the sheer abundance of talented writers.

The selections are arranged chronologically to provide a historical perspective and to make the development of views clearer. Alternate tables of contents by genre, theme, and geographic area are provided for those who want to read the works in such fashion.

In the case of longer works, such as novels or lengthy essays, excerpts are provided, using sections dealing with the city. I hope people are intrigued enough to read some of them in their entirety. They will not be disappointed. Every effort has been made to choose selections that are independent in their own right. Material that has been omitted is marked by three asterisks (***).

Some explanatory notes for the selections, marked by endnote numbers, are provided at the end of each entry to explain material that might not be readily understood by the general reader.

Works have been taken from many sources, all with their own editorial styles. I have kept the original spellings except for a very few silent corrections of obvious typing errors or places that might be confusing to the reader. I use Black and African American interchangeably. In trying to adhere to the original intent of the authors, I have retained the usage of material and language that could be considered objectionable by some.

Introduction

The common date given for the settlement of Philadelphia is 1682, when William Penn established a Quaker colony, providing it with a name that means "one who loves his brother." Penn intended an idyllic "greene country towne," one that was well ordered, with large open spaces within its twelve hundred acres. It "was the first major American town to be planned."[1] Penn envisioned his "towne" as a place of freedom, particularly in terms of religion. As with a certain amount of history, much of this is myth. The land, of course, had been settled by the Lenape Indians long before the Europeans arrived. Additionally, Penn's "greene country towne" soon became a highly congested city, plagued by disease, crime, and fires. Its vaunted freedom was largely limited to White Protestants, and its "brotherly love" certainly did not extend to most immigrants, to non-Christians, or, in particular, to its Black residents.

Blacks have been at the center of Philadelphia's history since before it was even known by that name. More than two thousand Blacks lived in the area once called New Sweden between 1638 and 1655. The fledgling colony encompassed parts of western Delaware and parts of Pennsylvania that now include Philadelphia. One of the most famous of these settlers was Antoni Swart (Black Anthony), a West Indian who arrived in the colony in 1639 aboard a Swedish vessel. Though initially enslaved, records indicate he eventually became free and was employed by Governor Johan Printz.[2]

The history of Black Philadelphians has been one fraught with both great promise and shattered dreams from its beginnings until today. Philadelphia was, as historian Gary Nash observes, "created in an atmosphere of growing Negrophobia"; still, despite ongoing racial prejudice, "it continues to this day to be one of the vital urban locations of black Americans."[3] It is this paradoxical condition that is the most characteristic dynamic of the city's relationship with its Black citizens. One facet of this relationship has been constant: whether African Americans have thrived here or suffered egregious oppression, they have never remained silent, never letting anyone else define their situation for them. They have always voiced their own opinions about their condition in their city through fiction, poetry, plays, essays, diaries, letters, or memoirs. The city has been blessed with a number of significant authors, ranging, among others, from Richard Allen to W. E. B. Du Bois to Jessie Fauset to Sonia Sanchez to John Edgar Wideman to Lorene Cary. In addition, there have been numerous lesser known but also forceful figures as well, including the enslaved people Alice and Cato, who were only known by those names. Whether they were native sons and daughters or spent significant time in the city or were there only long enough to experience the city in an impactful moment, Philadelphia has touched them all deeply. This anthology is a documentation of and a tribute to their collective voice. The focus here is not just on writers with a Philadelphia connection but on the authors' views on the city itself. The hope is to provide a wide variety of Black perspectives on the city.

There is something special about what leading African American intellectual W. E. B. Du Bois once labeled "the Philadelphia Negro." One reason for this uniqueness is the city's relationship to its Black inhabitants, in part caused by their intertwined, virtually symbiotic, history. No other major Northern city in the country has had such a long connection with African Americans, one forged in the seventeenth century, and Blacks have never stopped coming. They first settled largely in what are now called the Old City and Center City, where some Blacks still live. They have since scattered throughout the city, sometimes by choice but often by necessity and force, today mostly residing in Northern and Western Philadelphia. Migration patterns have changed over the years, as in other cities, but the Black population in the city has rarely declined and has often increased in number. Philadelphia was, as of 2020, the sixth-largest metropolis in the nation,[4] and Blacks make up more than 40 percent of the population there, more than the percentage of any of the other top ten cities in the country.[5]

Philadelphia has a vibrant and culturally rich history, offering enormous promise to its inhabitants since its beginnings. It was founded with the premise of religious freedom and steeped in the radical independence movement that created this country. The city was settled by Quakers, perhaps the religious group that, in popular opinion if not always in fact, has most vociferously been associated with opposition to slavery.[6] The "peculiar institution" was, in fact, almost nonexistent there by the early years of the nineteenth century. Philadelphia was the center of the Underground Railroad, with such legendary conductors as William Still. As the closest major city situated above the Mason-Dixon line, symbolically separating the North from the South, many fugitives from enslavement passed through Philadelphia. Some moved on, but a large number stayed, as the city seemed like the promised land for many African Americans. This is the powerful narrative of the city's history that still holds true for numerous people today when they think of Philadelphia.

There is also something unique about the Black experience in this city. Blacks have had a nominal freedom throughout most of their existence in Philadelphia, yet when we look under the surface, Philadelphia's treatment of African Americans has hardly been benign. The city has held out promises, but unfortunately many of these promises were not kept. Philadelphia may be situated in the North, but as Sonia Sanchez so eloquently writes in her poem "elegy (For MOVE and Philadelphia)," in many ways "philadelphia / [is] a disguised southern city." There were Quakers, many of whom were abolitionists and worked for the Underground Railroad, but there were many others of the faith who were slaveholders, including the colony's founder, William Penn. And even if the city was replete with abolitionists, it did not ensure that they viewed African Americans as equals. Blacks were, in fact, disfranchised from the vote in 1838, never to regain it until the ratification of the Fifteenth Amendment in 1870. Although the city was the center of the antislavery movement, not all of its White residents opposed slavery, and even if they did, the Fugitive Slave Acts of 1793 and 1850 hampered efforts to keep Blacks out of bondage. Before and after the Civil War, as demonstrated throughout this text, the city experienced a series of violent racial conflicts and has continue to practice an ugly pattern of segregation in housing, transportation, education, and employment, severely limiting the prospects of improvement for its Black citizens. There is a long history of racial injustice practiced by Philadelphia's police as well as Black residents being ignored, at best, by the city government.

Many enslaved people wrote about their desire to come to Philadelphia in search of freedom, including Henry "Box" Brown, who literally mailed himself from Richmond, Virginia, to Philadelphia in 1849. Another famous fugitive, Harriet Jacobs, in a section from *Incidents in the Life of a Slave Girl* (1860), voices her ambivalent feelings about the city's promises and its frequent failure to live up to its storied history as a center of freedom. After escaping slavery, Jacobs writes of her initial evening in Philadelphia, a city where many enslaved people tasted the air of freedom for the first time: "That night I sought my pillow with feelings I had never carried to it before. I verily believed myself to be a free woman." However, the next morning, she got on a city rail car and faced segregation, immediately disabusing her of any idealistic views of the city and of life in the North. Jacobs's experience typified that of many Black Philadelphians, both before and after her time.

In the face of often open hostility, one may question why African Americans continued to come to the city and why they remained after arriving. Historian Julie Winch states a possible reason why those early Black residents kept coming: "The place of refuge that beckoned many black Pennsylvanians [and others]—those legally free and those running away in search of freedom—was Philadelphia. Urban life offered anonymity and economic opportunity, and the city's growing network of black churches, schools, and social organizations held the promise of a vibrant community life."[7] Winch's apt suggestion of such a promise—if often undelivered—may give good reason why African Americans came to Philadelphia in the eighteenth and nineteenth centuries, but what about twentieth- and twenty-first-century people with many more options of where to live? After all, there is no city in the nation that better epitomizes the lofty promises of the country's founding of establishing liberty and equality for all yet also depicts too well the chief flaw of the grand American experiment: the unjust treatment of its poor and its non-White inhabitants.

Black Philadelphians have suffered from an almost overarching segregation throughout the city's history, yet like most people they take a fierce pride in their place of abode. Journalist and activist Charles D. Ellison poetically captures the spirit and vitality of the city and of its Black population in his essay "Philadelphia, Where Blackness Transcends": "There are no boundaries to the blackness of Philly, the blackness that empowers you, protects you and never leaves. The blackness that brings you home and loves you back." Although Ellison is playing on a 1997 tourism marketing slogan, "Philadelphia, the Place that Loves You Back," the city's Black residents do create their own form of empowerment.[8] They are the ones that love and support one another; it is certainly not the amorphous city, often an antagonist to their hopes and dreams. Philadelphia largely remains Black people's city, and they claim it proudly, protesting vigorously and making it known loudly when it commits one of its many offenses against them.

This anthology offers a composite portrait of the city, one that displays both the promises and pitfalls Philadelphia holds forth for its Black residents—their joys when its promises are fulfilled, but also their lamentations when they are repeatedly denied liberty and justice. Their writings are collected and arranged chronologically from 1781 to 2019 to give a sense of the city's often troubled relationship with African Americans. The authors comment on numerous topics, most making evident the racial prejudice that has often dogged African Americans living in Philadelphia. These include areas such as public health, the justice system, transportation, and how they result in racial and gender inequality. However, the writers also often focus on love, part of the city's name, made famous in the sculpture by Robert Indiana that has become one of the most iconic landmarks of the city.[9] Love is omnipresent in this anthology—not necessarily love between partners but more often the love of family and community. It is this sense of love that provides the most hope for the city to fulfill its long delayed promises to its Black inhabitants.

This book is divided into four sections: the beginnings of Black settlement in Philadelphia until 1849, the pre–Civil War years until 1949, the rally and decline from 1950 to 1999, the beginning of the twenty-first century and beyond. The discussion of these periods and the writers included attempts to supply an overview of Black literary Philadelphia as well as some context of their history in the city. Thus, the anthology includes not only literary works but also significant historical documents concerning the Black presence in Philadelphia. The time covered in each of the four sections gets increasingly shorter as the book progresses. This is due largely to the burgeoning number of important Black literary writers and writings about the city over the past seventy-five years or so. Not surprisingly, as the Black population has increased in recent years, the number of works depicting the city have increased exponentially. The book tries to give a representative balance of Black writings about Philadelphia historically while also reflecting the increasing importance of the city in literary representation.

Section 1, "Early Black Settlement Until the Pre–Civil War Years (Beginnings–1849)," provides an overview of the Black presence in the city from its founding through the turbulent years leading up to the Civil War. This section demonstrates the generally ambivalent relationships between Black and White Philadelphians. On the one hand, several eighteenth-century Quaker abolitionists attempted to separate the city from the system of slavery. This early activism was continued by such institutions as the Society for the Relief of Free Negroes Unlawfully Held in Bondage (1775). After the Revolution the group added even more forceful language to the title, The Pennsylvania Society for Promoting the Abolition of Slavery. Its members included Benjamin Franklin and the prominent physician Benjamin Rush.[10] The city soon became a center of progressive ideas for the gradual abolition of slavery even while often maintaining the inferiority of Blacks.

The city also drew an African American population, which had an important impact on Philadelphia's history. In 1787, Black ministers Absalom Jones and Richard Allen formed the Free African Society and established fledgling African American churches. The two also played a prominent role as participants and documenters of the devastating yellow fever epidemic of 1793. Jones and Allen, and others, like the wealthy Black businessman, James Forten, also penned a number of pamphlets condemning the slave trade and calling for an abolition to slavery. Examples of the writing of such pioneering crusaders are included in the first section of this book.

While Blacks made some social and cultural gains during the early decades of the nineteenth century, as reflected in the essays by William Whipper and Joseph Willson, they also suffered setbacks. Perhaps the most significant was being disfranchised from the right to vote. James Forten's son-in-law Robert Purvis wrote forcefully but unsuccessfully about this injustice in his *Appeal of Forty Thousand Citizens, Threatened with Disfranchisement, to the People of Philadelphia* (1838).

The second section, covering the pre–Civil War years to 1949, demonstrates the rapid growth of the city beginning in the time leading up to the war between the states. Frank J. Webb, in his early novel *The Garies and Their Friends* (1857), writes of the roiling tensions between the races that culminated in the horrendous race riots that engulfed the city in the 1830s. Nevertheless,

Philadelphia has remained a beacon of hope and freedom for Black Americans. This more optimistic view of the city only increased as it became a center of the Underground Railroad, ushering escaped slaves into a new life in the North. William Still and contemporary fiction writer Lorene Cary (in the third section) exemplify in their writings the treacherous life of the conductors and the fugitives who pursued this treacherous journey to freedom.

Once in the city, however, Blacks soon learned of the prejudice they frequently were forced to endure on the street cars (William Still's *A Brief Narrative of the Struggle for the Rights of the Colored People of Philadelphia in the City Railway Cars*) and in their impoverished living conditions (Fanny Jackson Coppin's "Christmas Eve Story"). The most extensive view of the lives of African Americans living in the city in this era, of course, is W. E. B. Du Bois's landmark sociological tract *The Philadelphia Negro* (1899), providing an in-depth look into how Blacks lived in a small area of South Philadelphia.

This section also shows the continued expansion of the Black population and the problems they often faced. It includes another Black intellectual giant, Alain Locke, whose brief piece celebrates Philadelphia's Black creative talent, which is demonstrated in selections from two leading members of the New Negro Movement of the early decades of the twentieth century, Jessie Fauset and Alice Dunbar-Nelson.

The third section (1950–99) also displays the continuing racial tension as Blacks began to spread beyond their early base into formerly "White" neighborhoods, as seen in William Gardner Smith's *South Street* and in David Bradley's novel of the same name. The most emblematic example of racial violence is the harrowing bombing of the anarchist Black group MOVE's headquarters by the police in 1985, powerfully portrayed in works by Sonia Sanchez and John Edgar Wideman. Another scourge during this period is the tragic cost of human life because of drug wars, palpably rendered in the excerpt from Alexs Pate's novel, *Losing Absalom*.

Authors such as Bebe Moore Campbell, Toni Cade Bambara, and Diane McKinney-Whetstone not only display the dark side of Philadelphia but also speak of the strong sense of community. Their writings remind us that despite the troubles Black Philadelphians face, they have a tenacity of spirit that helps them to survive their often troubling living experiences.

The final section treats the present century. Mumia Abu-Jamal provides a useful history of the often disturbing relationship between Philadelphia's

White inhabitants and its Black citizens in his essay "A Panther Walks in Philly." Major Jackson looks at one of the major plagues in Black communities across the nation starting in the 1980s, the use of crack cocaine, in his poem "Euphoria" from his collection *Leaving Saturn*. Meanwhile, Asali Solomon's short story "Secret Pool" exposes the continuing signs of racism that exist in even the most seemingly innocuous pockets of the city.

As in the other sections, however, there are moments of celebration of Black life in the city. Sonia Sanchez writes of the many murals throughout the city in "10 Haiku (for Philadelphia Murals)." Yolanda Wisher demonstrates the vibrancy in South Philadelphia in "5 South 43rd Street, Floor 2." And Ross Gay encapsulates the life-generating quality of Black residents through his poem "To the Fig Tree on 9th and Christian."

This brief introduction has touched on many important subjects that will be revisited and explored further in the longer historical introductions to each of the four major chronological divisions in the book and to the individual introductions to each of the pieces included. It is hoped that this information and the selections themselves will provide greater insight into the complex relationship between Blacks and Philadelphia.

NOTES

1. Simon, *Philadelphia*, 3.
2. National Park Service, "Anthony Swart."
3. Nash, *Forging Freedom*, 2; Trotter and Smith, *African Americans in Pennsylvania*, 44–72.
4. World Population Review.
5. US Census, "Philadelphia City, Pennsylvania."
6. See, for example, Carey, *From Peace to Freedom*, and Jordon, *Slavery and the Meetinghouse*.
7. Winch, "Making and Meaning," 130.
8. Dilworth, "Philadelphia," *Encyclopedia of Greater Philadelphia*.
9. Mires, "LOVE (Sculpture)."
10. Otter, *Philadelphia Stories*, 4–5.

BIBLIOGRAPHY

Carey, Brycchan. *From Peace to Freedom: Quaker Rhetoric and the Birth of American Antislavery, 1658–1761*. New Haven: Yale University Press, 2012.
City of Philadelphia. Coronavirus Disease. https://www.phila.gov/programs /coronavirus-disease-2019-covid-19/.
Dilworth, Richardson. "Philadelphia, the Place that Loves You Back." *Encyclopedia of Greater Philadelphia*. https://philadel phiaencyclopedia.org/themes /philadelphia-the-place-that-loves-you -back/.
Mires, Charlene. "LOVE (Sculpture)." *Encyclopedia of Greater Philadelphia*. https://phila delphiaencyclopedia.org/essays/love -sculpture.
Jordan, Ryan P. *Slavery and the Meetinghouse: The Quakers and the Abolitionist Dilemma, 1820–1865*. Bloomington: Indiana University Press, 2007.

Nash, Gary B. *Forging Freedom: The Formation of Philadelphia's Black Community 1720–1840*. Cambridge: Harvard University Press, 1988.

———. "Slaves and Slave-Owners in Colonial Philadelphia." In Trotter and Smith, *African Americans in Pennsylvania*, 44–72.

National Park Service. "Anthony Swart." https://www.nps.gov/people/anthony-swart.htm.

Otter, Samuel. *Philadelphia Stories: America's Literature of Race and Freedom*. Oxford: Oxford University Press, 2010.

Simon, Roger D. *Philadelphia: A Brief History*. Revised and updated edition. Philadelphia: Temple University Press, 2017.

Trotter, Joe William, Jr. and Eric Ledell Smith, eds. *African Americans in Pennsylvania: Shifting Historical Perspectives*. Philadelphia: Pennsylvania Historical and Museum Commission and The Pennsylvania University Press, 1997.

US Census. "Philadelphia City, Pennsylvania." Quick Facts. https://www.census.gov/quickfacts/fact/table/philadelphiacitypennsylvania/PST045222.

Winch, Julie. "The Making and Meaning of James Forten's *Letters from a Man of Colour*." *William and Mary Quarterly* 64, no. 1 (2007): 129–38.

World Population Review. https://worldpopulationreview.com.

Early Black Settlement Until the Pre–Civil War Years (Beginnings–1849)

Blacks have long been a presence in the Delaware Valley, particularly in the area later known as Philadelphia, having largely been brought over as enslaved people by the early Swedish and Dutch settlers. In fact, they lived in the area at least forty years earlier than what is normally considered the founding of the city itself by the Quakers in 1682. Blacks immediately became an integral part of the community, and by 1700, about 10 percent of White Philadelphians owned slaves. Pennsylvania did not have a plantation economy as did many other states, so most enslaved people worked in the commercial sector in such fields as livestock, agriculture, domestic service, or in the maritime industries. Although enslaved individuals generally did not have as harsh an existence as those in the South, they still were in bondage. Most attempted to retain as much of their African culture as possible and to form families.[1]

Although Quakers generally opposed slavery, they permitted the institution, particularly in the early years of the colony's settlement when they were hoping to populate it.[2] By 1710, the percentage of slaves among the general population rose to 17 percent, and over the next fifty or sixty years, the number of slaves increased rapidly, particularly in the 1750s and '60s, depending in part upon the number of indentured servants that were available from Europe. In raw numbers, the zenith occurred during the 1760s when slaves were owned by about 20 percent of households and made up some 8 percent of the city's total population. This number dropped off considerably by the 1770s in part because of opposition by abolitionists such as Dr. Benjamin Rush and

Anthony Benezet, who took on the task of educating young Blacks.[3] Many, but not all, Quakers, examining their faith, had abandoned the institution by this time, but the decrease in enslaved people was due not only to religious reasons but also to economics. Passage of a 1773 resolution raising the taxes on the importation of slaves made ownership too costly for all but the wealthiest owners.[4]

Though they may have had nominal freedom, manumitted African Americans often lacked possessions, education, and economic resources; in addition, African Americans were subject to special rules. Sexual intermingling or marriage to those of different races was subject to punishment, at a harsher rate for Blacks than Whites. Blacks who were deemed "slothful" could be bound out as labor until they were twenty-four if a male and twenty-two if a female. Furthermore, those who harbored runaways would be severely punished.[5]

During the Revolutionary War years, many White Philadelphians feared a possible insurrection by those who were enslaved. Owners who fled the city often took the enslaved with them or sent them to be safeguarded outside Philadelphia. The British and their Hessian allies did occupy the city in late 1776 and offered freedom to enslaved Blacks who were willing to fight on the side of the British. James Forten, a free Black fighting for the Americans, refused release as a prisoner of war rather than betray the young nation. Enslaved people weighed the risks and rewards of attempting to gain their freedom or to remain in bondage; it is estimated that by 1783, about eight hundred enslaved Philadelphians had attained their liberty during the years of the Revolution while about four hundred remained in bondage.[6]

By the early 1790s, Philadelphia saw an increase in its Black population, most of whom were free. The city, in fact, had the largest number of free Blacks in the nation. Many White Philadelphians were alarmed by what they considered "a city swarming with dark-hued, impoverished, and criminal persons," even though newly arrived Irish immigrants were generally the most destitute of the city's dwellers.[7] However, an incident soon occurred that would make these Whites largely dependent upon their African American neighbors, the yellow fever epidemic of 1793.

At the time of the epidemic, Philadelphia was the capital of the country and the largest city in the nation. It was "also the intellectual, commercial, and medical center, the seat from which the nation's leading politicians, physicians, and businessmen influenced culture, policy, and trade."[8] When the fever broke out, Mayor Matthew Clarkson asked for volunteers to combat it; only African Americans Richard Allen, Absalom Jones, William Gray, and the members of their organization, the Free African Society, volunteered to assist Dr. Benjamin Rush. These Blacks worked heroically as carriers of the sick, as nurses, as gravediggers. When they learned that they were not immune to the disease, as they were led to believe, many of them continued their work despite the danger.[9] While there was momentary goodwill given them by White Philadelphians, this soon dissipated when Blacks asked for modest remuneration for supplies needed to help the sick. Publisher Mathew Carey led the charge against them by issuing his own distorted account of the illness.[10] Jones and Allen's firsthand account of the disease, *Narrative of the Proceedings of the Black People, During the Late Awful Calamity in Philadelphia*, corrects Carey's mistaken record. John Edgar Wideman provides a modern fictional rendering of this incident in the excerpt from his novel *The Cattle Killing*, (1990) included in section 3.

In the early decades of the nineteenth century, Blacks began to exert their force as a community. Jones and Allen both led African American churches with expanding congregations—Jones the African Episcopal Church and Allen the African Methodist Episcopal Church. Many, often led by the churches, did not forget those African Americans still in chains, as is witnessed by the petition against the slave trade authored by Jones, Allen, and others in 1799, *Petition of the People of Color and Freemen of Philadelphia—Against the Slave Trade to the Coast of Guinea*. Another example of Black Philadelphian activism against the slave trade is Russell Parrott's *An Oration on the Abolition of the Slave Trade* (1814). Parrott tells the enslaved that "you have secured to yourself a band of citizens, who will not forsake you in the hour of danger, whose bosoms are ready to be bared for your service, and whose blood will cheerfully flow in your defence."[11]

During this period, the enslaved population of the city dwindled; by the 1820 census, there were only three listed, while more than 7,500 free Blacks were counted.[12] The increase in both the free Black and immigrant White population to the city frequently led to quarrels over jobs, particularly since people were often competing for the same unskilled positions. As the city expanded, wealth disparity within the race also increased. Black poverty increased markedly after the War of 1812, and with it criminal activities committed by African Americans grew. Blacks represented a widely disproportionate amount of the inmate population, although they were generally imprisoned for lesser offenses than Whites.

On the other hand, the population of African Americans of means was also growing. These somewhat better off Blacks created several Masonic lodges to demonstrate their respectability, often putting them at odds with their more "backward" brethren who had migrated from the South. Many Whites began to grow resentful of the small but growing Black middle class, such as sailmaker James Forten, who became active in the city's politics, as is evidenced in his *Letters from a Man of Colour* (1813). At either end of the spectrum, however, Blacks were generally looked down on by White Philadelphians. Things reached the point that some Black leaders, including Paul Cuffe, and for a brief time Forten, proposed repatriating African Americans to Africa. The vast majority of Philadelphia's Black population, however, maintained little interest in such a plan, and it was soon abandoned.[13] James Forten and Russell Parrott's *To the Humane and Benevolent Inhabitants of the City and County of Philadelphia* (1817) demonstrates one forceful example of the resistance to such colonization plans.

By 1830, the city was almost 10 percent Black, with a population of about fifteen thousand people.[14] There were attempts to improve conditions for African Americans and Black leaders such as James Forten, James Cornish, and Robert Purvis headed a growing number of benevolent associations, churches, and cultural organizations for the Black population. The importance of such organizations cannot be overestimated. As one White Philadelphian stated, "They have been the means of turning the attention of this friendly people, in some measure, to a dependence on themselves and given them some juster notions of their own importance."[15] This emerging Black middle class was now demonstrating "that they expected to be treated as befitted their status, not their race."[16] The significance of institutions for Black self-improvement is reflected in writings such as William Whipper's *An Address Delivered in Wesley Church on the Evening of June 12, Before the Colored Reading Society of Philadelphia, for Mental Improvement* (1828). Whipper also cofounded the American Moral Society in 1835 to further cultivate the intellect and morals of African Americans, and he, Forten, and Purvis led annual conventions for the Improvement of Free People of Colour. Whipper says in his *Address* that such improvement is necessary not only for the good of the individual but to emancipate "our brethren from universal thralldom." Moreover, as critic Samuel Otter observes, the conventions (five of the first six were held in Philadelphia) "were a venue for grappling with the challenges faced by African Americans, free and enslaved, as well as a response to heightening northern repression."[17] For other examples of essays preaching the need for moral improvement, see Prince Saunders's *An Address, Delivered at Bethel Church, Philadelphia; on the 30th of September, 1818* and William Watkins's *Address Delivered Before the Moral Reform Society in Philadelphia, August 8, 1836.* Both are contained in Dorothy Porter's *Early Negro Writing, 1760–1837* (Boston: Beacon, 1971).

The city was also the center of the abolitionist movement. The American Anti-Slavery Society was established there in 1833, and the Pennsylvanian Anti-Slavery Society began in 1837, yet the city was far from united on the issue of slavery. In fact, most Philadelphians opposed abolition. Even the Quakers were divided on the issue, particularly after the Hicksite-Orthodox Separation in 1827, splitting the group into two sects, with the Hicksite Quakers being more opposed to slavery. The Unitarian Church was also divided, with many of its members abandoning the church when its most prominent minister voiced his opposition to slavery in 1839.[18] Black women also raised their voices in opposition to slavery with, for example, Charlotte Forten (wife of James Forten) and her three daughters, Harriet, Sarah, and Margaretta, playing prominent roles in the racially integrated Philadelphia Female Anti-Slavery Society.[19]

The racial tensions boiled over in blatant examples of prejudice in the 1830s, from the presentation of minstrel shows to discrimination in jobs and housing. Many Whites particularly resented the relative financial and social stability of the Black community near Bethel Church in Spring Garden (Center City). They also feared possible "amalgamation" or race mixing as Whites and Blacks intermingled more frequently, and they especially disliked that some Blacks and their White allies dared to raise their voices publicly and in print against Whites.[20] Racial prejudice led to the disfranchisement of Blacks in 1838, as exemplified in Robert Purvis's *Appeal of Forty Thousand Citizens, Threatened with Disfranchisement, to the People of Pennsylvania* (1838).

Numerous racial riots manifested throughout the 1830s and 1840s. In 1834 there was a skirmish between working-class Black residents on Cedar Street (now South Street) above Seventh. Many Black residences were burned by the angry mob. Perhaps the most significant of the riots occurred in 1838, when the newly built Pennsylvania Hall in the northeastern section of the city was razed by an angry anti-Black mob, which was aroused by a meeting there of the Anti-Slavery Convention of American Women and other abolitionist activities. A crowd of up to thirty thousand protesters was involved. Other riots occurred in 1842 and 1849, largely in the Cedar Street area.[21] White novelists such as George Lippard in *The Quaker City* (1845) and *The Killers* (1849) and John Beauchamp Jones in *The City Merchant* (1851) give their perspective on the riots, while an excerpt from Frank Webb's novel *The Garies and Their Friends* provides an example by a Black writer on the destructiveness of life and property in African American communities (see section 2). "The graphic riot scenes at the center of *The Garies and Their Friends* do not," in the words of Samuel Otter, "tear the novel open, rending its mannered surfaces and revealing hidden brutality. Instead, they offer a spectacular enactment of the violence in everyday life that has been on display, in the South and in the North, from the beginning of the narrative."[22] The racial riots of the 1830s and '40s set the tone for Black-White relationships in Philadelphia leading into the years preceding the Civil War.

NOTES

1. Nash, *Forging*, 8–13.

2. Dunn and Dunn, "Founding," 30–31.

3. Saunders, *100 Years After Emancipation*, 34–35.

4. Nash, "Slaves and Slave-Owners," 44–45; Simon, *Philadelphia*, 13–15.

5. Gross, *Colored Amazons*, 29; Nash, *Forging*, 35.

6. Nash, *Forging*, 48–55, 65.

7. Nash, *Forging*, 102, 172–73.

8. Bishop, "Rhetoric and Identity," 63.

9. Finger, *Contagious City*, 127–30; Espinosa, "Question of Racial Immunity," 429.

10. Miller, "Federal City," 187.

11. Newman, Rael, and Lapsansky, *Pamphlets of Protest*, 78.

12. Richardson, "Athens of America," 254.

13. Nash, *Forging*, 212–23, 233–45.

14. Lapsansky, "'Since They Got Those Separate Churches,'" 96.

15. Quoted in Nash, *Forging*, 211.

16. Winch, "Making and Meaning," 136.

17. Otter, *Philadelphia Stories*, 108.

18. Wainwright, "Age of Nicholas Biddle," 296–97.

19. Sumler-Lewis, "Forten-Purvis Women," 281–88.

20. Lapsansky, "'Since They Got Those Separate Churches,'" 100–107.

21. Wainwright, "Age of Nicholas Biddle," 293–96; Otter, *Philadelphia Stories*, 131–57.

22. Otter, *Philadelphia Stories*, 244.

BIBLIOGRAPHY

Bishop, Jacqueline. "Rhetoric and Identity in Absalom Jones and Richard Allen's *Narrative of the Proceedings of the Black People, During the Late Awful Calamity in Philadelphia.*" *Pennsylvania Magazine of History and Biography* 125, nos. 1/2 (January–April 2001): 61–90.

Dunn, Mary Maples, and Richard S. Dunn. "The Founding, 1681–1701." In Weigley, *Philadelphia*, 1–32.

Espinosa, Mariola. "The Question of Racial Immunity to Yellow Fever in History and Historiography." *Social Science History* 38, nos. 3/4 (Fall/Winter 2014): 437–53.

Finger, Simon. *The Contagious City: The Politics of Public Health in Early Philadelphia.* Illustrated ed. Ithaca: Cornell University Press, 2012.

Gross, Kali N. *Colored Amazons: Crime, Violence, and Black Women in the City of Brotherly Love, 1880–1910.* Illustrated edition. Durham: Duke University Press, 2006.

Lapsansky, Emma Jones. "'Since They Got Those Separate Churches': Afro-Americans and Racism in Colonial Pennsylvania." In Trotter and Smith, *African Americans in Pennsylvania,* 96–120.

Miller, Richard G. "The Federal City, 1783–1800." In Weigley, *Philadelphia,* 155–207.

Nash, Gary B. *Forging Freedom: The Formation of Philadelphia's Black Community, 1720–1840.* Cambridge: Harvard University Press, 1988.

———. "Slaves and Slave-Owners in Colonial Philadelphia." In Trotter and Smith, *African Americans in Pennsylvania,* 44–72.

Newman, Richard, Patrick Rael, and Philip Lapsansky, eds. *Pamphlets of Protest: An Anthology of Early African-American Protest Literature, 1790–1860.* New York: Routledge, 2001.

Otter, Samuel. *Philadelphia Stories: America's Literature of Race and Freedom.* New York: Oxford University Press, 2010.

Richardson, Edgar J. "The Athens of America, 1800–1825." In *Philadelphia: A 300-Year History,* edited by Russell F. Weigley, 208–57. New York: W. W. Norton, 1982.

Saunders, John A. *100 Years After Emancipation (History of the Philadelphia Negro) 1787 to 1963.* F.R.S. Publishing, 1963.

Simon, Roger D. *Philadelphia: A Brief History.* Revised and updated ed. Philadelphia: Temple University Press, 2017.

Sumler-Lewis, Janice. "The Forten-Purvis Women of Philadelphia and the American Anti-Slavery Crusade." *Journal of Negro History* 66, no. 4 (Winter 1981–82): 281–88.

Trotter, Joe William, Jr. "Introduction: Pennsylvania's African American History: A Review of the Literature." In Trotter and Smith, *African Americans in Pennsylvania,* 1–39.

Trotter, Joe William, Jr. and Eric Ledell Smith, eds. *African Americans in Pennsylvania: Shifting Historical Perspectives.* Pennsylvania Historical and Museum Commission and The Pennsylvania University Press, 1997.

Wainwright, Nicholas B. "The Age of Nicholas Biddle, 1815–1841." In Weigley, *Philadelphia,* 258–306.

Weigley, Russell F., ed. *Philadelphia: A 300-Year History.* New York: W. W. Norton, 1982.

Winch, Julie. "The Making and Meaning of James Forten's *Letters from a Man of Colour.*" *William and Mary Quarterly* 64, no. 1 (2007): 19–38.

Cato and Petitioners, "Letter of Cato and Petition by 'The Negroes Who Obtained Freedom by the Late Act,'" *The Freeman's Journal* (September 21, 1781)

In 1780, the Pennsylvania legislature passed "An Act for the Gradual Abolition of Slavery." By this piece of legislation, Pennsylvania became the first state in the American Revolution era to free slaves in stages. Those born after the act's passage were still required to serve their mothers' masters for at least twenty-eight years to be freed; however, if slaveholders failed to register their slaves by November 1, 1780, the enslaved person would be emancipated, freeing some people. Immediately after the law was passed, there was a fierce blowback from conservative legislators, who attempted to repeal it. A group of formerly enslaved people soon petitioned the Pennsylvania Assembly to reject this repeal. Their petition was published in a Philadelphia African American newspaper, the *Freeman's Journal*. Also published was a single-authored letter from a newly freed person, Cato, who eloquently made the case that repealing the law would violate the principles of the "Christian gentlemen" who had written the original act. The pleas of Black Philadelphians and their allies were successful, and the act was never repealed. We do not know if Cato was the real name of the letter writer or a pseudonym, taken perhaps from *Cato's Letters*, a series of 144 essays published from 1720 to 1723 by British authors John Trenchard and Thomas Gordon under the name Cato, the opponent of Julius Caesar. *Cato's Letters*, highly popular in the United States, condemned the British political system, accusing it of corrupt and tyrannical actions.

⁓

Mr. PRINTER.

I am a poor negro, who with myself and children have had the good fortune to get my freedom, by means of an act of assembly passed on the first of March 1780, and should now with my family be as happy a set of people as any on the face of the earth, but I am told the assembly are going to pass a law to send us all back to our masters. Why dear Mr. Printer, this would be the cruelest act that ever a sett of warthy [*sic*] good gentlemen could be guilty of. To make a law to hang us all, would be *merciful*, when compared with this law, for many of our masters would treat us with unheard of barbarity, for daring to take the advantage (as we have done) of the law made in our favor.—Our lots in *slavery* were hard enough to bear: but having tasted the sweets of *freedom*, we should now be miserable indeed.—Surely no christian gentlemen can be so cruel! I cannot believe they will pass such a law.—I have read the act which made me free, and I always read it with joy—and I always dwell with particular pleasure on the following words, spoken by the assembly in the top of the said law: "We esteem it a particular blessing granted to us, that we are enabled this day to add one more step to universal civilization, by removing as much as possible the sorrows of those, who have lived in *undeserved* bondage, and from which, by the assumed authority of the kings of Great-Britain, no effectual legal relief could be obtained." See it was the king of Great-Britain that kept us in slavery before.—Now surely, after saying so, it cannot be possible for them to make slaves of us again—nobody, but the king of England can do it—and I sincerely pray, that he may never have it in his power.—It cannot be, that the assembly will take from us the liberty they have given, because a little further they go on and say, "we conceive ourselves, at this particular period, extraordinarily called upon, by the blessings which *we* have received, to make manifest the sincerity of our professions and to give a substantial proof of our gratitude." If after all this, *we*, who by virtue of this very law (which has those very words in it which I have copied,) are now enjoying the sweets of that "substantial proof of gratitude" I say if we should be plunged back into slavery, what must we think of the meaning of all those words in the beginning of the said law, which seem to be a kind of creed respecting slavery? but what is most serious than all, what will our great father think of such doings? But I pray that he may be pleased to tern the hearts of the honorable assembly from this cruel law; and that he will be pleased to make us poor blacks deserving of his mercies.

CATO

A Correspondent informs us that a petition is about to be presented to the assembly by the negroes who obtained freedom by the late act, praying to be heard by counsel; and as they presented a petition to the house some time ago, on the subject of preserving their liberty, he has requested us to publish it. The following he says is a pretty exact copy:

To the honourable the Representatives of the
Freemen of the State of Pennsylvania,
We are fully sensible, that an address from persons of our rank is wholly unprecedented, and we are fearful of giving offence in the attempt: but touched in the most sensible manner, by a dread of being deprived that liberty which we have obtained under the late law, we venture to appear before you. In the act which gave us our freedom, we read with gratitude and joy these admirable sentiments contained in the preamble a part of which we beg leave to repeat. It begins with these pathetic words: "When we contemplate our abhorrence of that condition, to which the army and tyranny of Great Britain were exerted to reduce us: when we look back on the variety of dangers to which we have been exposed, and how miraculously our wants in many instances have been supplied, and our deliverances wrought, when even hope and human fortitude had become unequal to the conflict, we are unavoidably

led to a serious and grateful sense of the manifold blessings which we have undeservedly received from the hand of that being, from whom every good and perfect gift cometh. Impressed with these ideas, we conceive that it is our duty, and we re[j]oice that is in our power, to extend a portion of that freedom to others, which hath been extended to us, and a release from that state of thralldom, to which we ourselves were tyrannically doomed, and from which we have now every prospect of being speedily relieved," & c. We your petitioners are a few amongst the great number in this state, who have derived freedom from that clause which directs all slaves to be registered by a certain day, of which we have obtained certificated from the clerk of the sessions.

Just emerging from a state of hereditary slavery, and enjoying the sweets of that freedom so forceably described in the preamble, it is with the utmost poignancy of grief, that we are informed your honourable house are about to pass a law to return us to our late masters, and allow them a still further time for registering us as slaves. Whilst it pleased the great author of our beings to continue us in slavery, we submitted to our hard lot, and bore it with habitual patience, but rescued from our misery, and tasting the sweets of that liberty, for the defense of which this whole continent is now involved in war, we shall deem our selves the most wretched of the human race, if the proposed act should take place. Raised to the pinnacle of human happiness by a law unfought and unexpected by us, we find ourselves p[l]unged into all the horrors of hateful slavery; made doubly irksome by the small portion of freedom we have already enjoyed. Not having by any act of ours deprived ourselves of the common rights of mankind, we were happy to find the house sympathing [sic] in our distress, and declaring that we had hitherto "lived in undeserved bondage" & c. "We cannot therefore persuade ourselves to believe that this honorable house, possessed of such sentiments of humanity and benevolence, will pass an act to make slaves of those whom they have freed by law; and to whom they have restored" [sic] the common blessings "they were by nature entitled to." We fear we are too bold, but our all is at stake. The grand question of slavery or liberty, is too important for us to be silent—it is the momentous person of our lives, if we are silent this day, we may be silent for ever; returned into slavery we are deprived of even the right of petition-ing and this emboldens us to grasp the present moment, and to pray on behalf of ourselves and a number of our unhappy colour, that this house will not pass the bill. And we further pray that you may long possess that heart felt peace and joy, which will ever arise in the humane breast, when successfully employed in the relief of misery and distress.

Fearful of the danger and delay, we have not allowed ourselves time to collect the names of others within this city, whose cases are similar to ours; but on the feelings of the honorable house, and not on our numbers do we build our hopes.

BIBLIOGRAPHY

Kaplan, Sidney, and Emma Nogrady Kaplan. *The Black Presence in the Era of the American Revolution*. Rev. ed. Amherst: University of Massachusetts Press, 1989.

"Letter of Cato and Petition by 'The Negroes Who Obtained Freedom by the Late Act.'" https://www.pbs.org/wgbh/aia/part2/2h73.html.

Nash, Gary B. *Forging Freedom: The Formation of Philadelphia's Black Community, 1720–1840*. Cambridge: Harvard University Press, 1988.

Absalom Jones and Richard Allen, *Narrative of the Proceedings of the Black People, During the Late Awful Calamity in Philadelphia in the Year 1793; And a Refutation of Some Censures Thrown upon Them in Some Late Publications* (1794)

The Reverend Absalom Jones was born an enslaved person in Sussex County, Delaware, in 1746. Jones taught himself to read before being sold when he was sixteen and brought to Philadelphia. After being manumitted in 1784, he became the lay minister at St. George's Methodist Episcopal Church. Because of racial prejudice faced within the church, he and Richard Allen formed the First African Church in 1792. He worked with Allen to fight the yellow fever epidemic in 1793. That same year he was part of a group that wrote a petition against the Fugitive Slave Act. Jones became the first African American priest to be installed in the Episcopal Church in 1802, and he continued his work on behalf of social justice until his death in 1818.

Bishop Richard Allen was born in Philadelphia in 1760 as an enslaved person and grew up on a plantation in Delaware. Encouraged by his owner, Stokely Sturgis, Allen attended meetings of the Methodist Church. He joined the church when he was seventeen and purchased his freedom by 1783. He became a preacher at St. George's Methodist Episcopal Church in 1786. He, along with

Absalom Jones, was unhappy with the treatment of Black members in the church, who faced segregation. The two men formed the Free African Society in 1787. In 1794 in Philadelphia, he founded and opened the African Methodist Episcopal (AME) Church, which was the first independent Black denomination established in the United States. The building where the church stands, at 419 South 6th Street in Spring Garden (Center City), is known as the Mother Bethel African Methodist Episcopal Church, and it is the oldest piece of real estate in the country that has been owned continuously by African Americans. In 1816, five Black Methodist congregations united and elected Allen as their first bishop. He continued to preach, as well as to operate as a member of the Underground Railroad along with his wife, Sarah, until his death in 1831.

Narrative of the Proceedings of the Black People, During the Late Awful Calamity in Philadelphia in the Year 1793 (1794), written by Allen and Jones, describes the heroic role played by Blacks during the yellow fever epidemic of 1793. The two men volunteered the services of the Free African Society to treat the sick, to carry out the dead, to dig graves, and to bury the victims. Blacks had been told that they were immune to the disease, but as the White doctor Benjamin Rush, who was in charge, lamented, "The Negroes are everywhere submitting to the disorder."[1] Rush had done his best to combat the illness, and like Allen, he contracted the disease; however, despite his attempts, the limited understanding of the disease, thought to be best treated by bleeding and purging the victim (with "calomel," mercurous chloride), often worsened the situation, leading to a death toll of more than five thousand people. Despite the efforts of African Americans to help save Philadelphia from even further death and destruction, publisher Mathew Carey issued *A Short Account of the Malignant Fever* (1793), accusing some Blacks of trying to gain exorbitant profits from their efforts. Although he singled out Jones and Allen for praise, Carey stated that some African Americans "extorted two, three, four, and even five dollars a night for attendance, which would have been well paid by a single dollar. Some of them were even detected in plundering the houses of the sick."[2] This proved too much for Allen and Jones to bear, and they responded to Carey's malicious charges in *Narrative of the Proceedings of the Black People*, "the first African American polemic in which black leaders sought to articulate black community anger and directly confront an accuser."[3]

———

In consequence of a partial representation of the conduct of the people who were employed to nurse the sick in the late calamitous state of the city of

Philadelphia, we were solicited by a number of those who feel themselves injured thereby, and by the advice of several respectable citizens, to step forward and declare facts as they really were; seeing that from our situation, on account of the charge we took upon us, we had it more fully and generally in our power to know and observe the conduct and behaviour of those that were so employed.

Early in September, a solicitation appeared in the public papers, to the people of colour, to come forward and assist the distressed, perishing, and neglected sick; with a kind of assurance, that people of our colour were not liable to take the infection; upon which we and a few others met and consulted how to act on so truly alarming and melancholy an occasion. After some conversation, we found a freedom to go forth, confiding in him who can preserve in the midst of a burning fiery furnace, sensible that it was our duty to do all the good we could to our suffering fellow mortals. We set out to see where we could be useful. The first we visited was a man in Emsley's alley, who was dying, and his wife lay dead at the time in the house. There were none to assist but two poor helpless children. We administered what relief we could, and applied to the overseers of the poor to have the woman buried. We visited upwards of twenty families that day—they were scenes of woe indeed! The Lord was pleased to strengthen us, and remove all fear from us, and disposed our hearts to be as useful as possible.

In order the better to regulate our conduct, we called on the mayor next day, to consult with him how to proceed, so as to be most useful. The first object he recommended was a strict attention to the sick, and the procuring of nurses. This was attended to by Absalom Jones and William Gray; and in order that the distressed might know where to apply, the mayor advertised the public that upon application to them they would be supplied. Soon after, the mortality increasing, the difficulty of getting a corpse taken away was such, that few were willing to do it, when offered great rewards. The black people were looked to. We then offered our services in the public papers, by advertising that we would remove the dead and procure nurses. Our services were the production of real sensibility;—we sought not fee nor reward, until the increase of the disorder rendered our labour so arduous that we were not adequate to the service we had assumed. The mortality increasing rapidly, obliged us to call in the assistance of five[i] men in the awful charge of interring

i. Two of whom were Richard Allen's brothers.

the dead. They, with great reluctance, were prevailed upon to join us. It was very uncommon, at this time, to find any one that would go near, much more, handle, a sick or dead person.

Mr. Carey, in page 106 of his third edition, has observed, that, "for the honor of human nature, it ought to be recorded, that some of the convicts in the gaol, a part of the term of whole confinement had been remitted as a reward for their peaceable, orderly behavior, voluntarily offered themselves as nurses to attend the sick at Bush-hill; and have, in that capacity, conducted themselves with great fidelity, &c." Here it ought to be remarked (although Mr. Carey hath not done it) that two thirds of the persons, who rendered these essential services, were people of colour, who, on the application of the elders of the African church (who met to consider what they could do for the help of the sick) were liberated, on condition of their doing the duty of nurses at the hospital at Bush-hill; which they as voluntarily accepted to do, as they did faithfully discharge, this severe and disagreeable duty.—May the Lord reward them, both temporally and spiritually.

When the sickness became general, and several of the physicians died, and most of the survivors were exhausted by sickness or fatigue; that good man, Dr. Rush, called us more immediately to attend upon the sick, knowing that we could both bleed.; he told us that we could increase our utility by attending to his instructions, and accordingly directed us where to procure medicine duly prepared, with proper directions how to administer them, and at what stages of the disorder to bleed; and when we found ourselves incapable of judging what was proper to be done, to apply to him, and he would, if able, attend them himself, or send Edward Fisher, his pupil, which he often did; and Mr. Fisher manifested his humanity by an affectionate attention for their relief. This has been no small satisfaction to us; for we think that when a physician was not attainable, we have been the instruments in the hands of God, for saving the lives of some hundreds of our suffering fellow mortals.

We feel ourselves sensibly aggrieved by the censorious epithets of many who did not render the least assistance in the time of necessity, yet are liberal of their censure of us, for the prices paid for our services, when no one knew how to make a proposal to any one they wanted to assist them. At first we made no charge, but left it to those who served in removing their dead, to give what they thought fit. We set no price until the reward was fixed by those we had served. After paying the people we had to assist us, our compensation was much less than many will believe.

We do assure the public that *all* the money we received for burying, and for coffins which we ourselves purchased and procured, has not defrayed the expense of wages which we had to pay those whom we employed to assist us.

***

That some extravagant prices were paid we admit; but how came they to be demanded? the reason is plain. It was with difficulty persons could be had to supply the wants of the sick as nurses; applications became more and more numerous, the consequence was, when we procured them at six dollars per week, and called upon them to go where they were wanted, we found they were gone elsewhere; here was a disappointment. Upon inquiring the cause, we found they had been allured away by others who offered greater wages, until they got from two to four dollars per day. We had no restraint upon the people. It was natural for people in low circumstances to accept a voluntary, bounteous reward; especially under the loathsomeness of many of the sick, when nature shuddered at the thoughts of the infection, and the task assigned was aggravated by lunacy, and being left much alone with them. Had Mr. Carey been solicited to such an undertaking, for hire, Query[4]— what would *he* have demanded? But Mr. Carey, although chosen a member of that band of worthies who have so eminently distinguished themselves by their labours for the relief of the sick and helpless; yet, quickly after his election, left them to struggle with their arduous and hazardous task, by leaving the city. 'Tis true Mr. Carey was no hireling, and had a right to flee, and upon his return, to plead the cause of those who fled; yet, we think, he was wrong in giving so partial and injurious an account of the black nurses; if they have taken advantage of the public distress, is it any more than he hath done of its desire for information? We believe he has made more money by the sale of his "Scraps" than a dozen of the greatest extortioners among the black nurses. The great prices paid did not escape the observation of that worthy and vigilant magistrate, Matthew Clarkson, mayor of the city, and president of the committee. He sent for us, and requested we would use our influence to lessen the wages of the nurses. But on informing him of the cause, i.e., that of the people over-bidding one another, it was concluded unnecessary to attempt any thing on that head; therefore it was left to the people concerned. That there were some few black people guilty of plundering the distressed we acknowledge; but in that they only are pointed out, and made mention of, we esteem partial and injurious. We know as many whites who were guilty of it; but this is looked over, while the blacks are held up to censure. Is it a greater crime for a black to pilfer than for a white to privateer?

***

The public were informed that in the West-Indies and other places where this terrible malady had been, it was observed that the blacks were not affected with it. Happy would it have been for you, and much more so for us, if this observation had been verified by our experience.

When the people of colour had the sickness and died, we were imposed upon and told it was not with the prevailing sickness, until it became too notorious to be denied, then we were told some few died, but not many. Thus were our services extorted *at the peril of our lives.* Yet you accuse us of extorting *a little money from you.*

The bill of mortality for the year 1793, published by Matthew Whitehead and John Ormrod, clerks, and Joseph Dolby, sexton, will convince any reasonable man that will examine it, that as many coloured people died in proportion as others. In 1792, there were 67 of our colour buried, and in 1793, it amounted to 305; thus the burials among us have increased more than fourfold, was not this in a great degree the effects of the services of the unjustly vilified black people?

Perhaps it may be acceptable to the reader to know how we found the sick affected by the sickness. Our opportunities of hearing and seeing them have been very great. They were taken with a chill, a head-ach, a sick stomach, with pains in their limbs and back. This was the way the sickness in general began; but all were not affected alike, some appeared but slightly affected with some of those symptoms, what confirmed us in the opinion of a person being smitten was the colour of their eyes. In some it raged more furiously than in others. Some have languished for seven and ten days, and appeared to get better the day, or some hours before they died, while others were cut off in one, two, or three days; but their complaints were similar. Some lost their reason, and raged with all the fury madness could produce, and died in strong convulsions; others retained their reason to the last, and seemed rather to fall asleep than die. We could not help remarking that the former were of strong passions, and the latter of a mild temper. Numbers died in a kind of dejection, they concluded they must go, (so the phrase for dying was), and therefore in a kind of fixed determined state of mind went off.

It struck our minds with awe, to have application made by those in health, to take charge of them in their sickness, and of their funeral. Such applications have been made to us; many appeared as though they thought they must die and not live; some have lain on the floor to be measured for their coffin and grave. A gentleman called one evening to request a good nurse might be got for him when he was sick, and to superintend his funeral, and gave particular directions how he would have it conducted. It seemed a surprising circumstance; for the man appeared at the time to be in perfect health; but calling, two or three days after, to see him, found a woman dead in the house, and the man so far gone, that to administer any thing for his recovery was needless—he died that evening. We mention this as an instance of the dejection of despondence, that took hold on the minds of thousands, and are of opinion, that it aggravated the case of many; while others who bore up cheerfully, got up again, that probably would otherwise have died.

When the mortality came to its greatest stage, it was impossible to procure sufficient assistance; therefore many whose friends, and relations had left them, died unseen, and unassisted. We have found them in various situations, some lying on the floor, as bloody as if they had been dipt in it, without any appearance of their having had, even a drink of water for their relief; others laying on a bed with their clothes on, as if they had came in fatigued, and lain down to rest; some appeared, as if they had fallen dead on the floor, from the position we found them in.

Truly our task was hard, yet through mercy, we were enabled to go on.

NOTES

1. Quoted in Nash, *Forging Freedom*, 124.
2. Quoted in Otter, *Philadelphia Stories*, 32.
3. Lapsansky, "'Abigail, a Negress,'" 61.
4. Quere: (Latin), I want (to know).

BIBLIOGRAPHY

Bacon, Jacqueline. "Rhetoric and Identity in Absalom Jones and Richard Allen's *Narrative of the Proceedings of the Black People, During the Late Awful Calamity in Philadelphia*." *Pennsylvania Magazine of History and Biography* 125, nos. 1/2 (January–April 2001): 61–90.

Estes, J. Worth, and Billy G. Smith. *A Melancholy Scene of Devastation: The Public Response to the 1793 Yellow Fever Epidemic*. Canton, MA: Science History Publications, for the College of Physicians of Philadelphia and the Library Company of Philadelphia, 1997.

Finger, Simon. *The Contagious City: The Politics of Public Health in Early Philadelphia*. Ithaca: Cornell University Press, 2012.

Howell, Ricardo. "Mother Bethel AME Church: Congregation and Community." *Encyclopedia of Greater Philadelphia*. https://philadelphia encyclopedia.org/essays/mother -bethel-ame-church-congregation-and -community-2/.

Lapsansky, Phillip. "'Abigail, a Negress':
  The Role and the Legacy of African
  Americans in the Yellow Fever
  Epidemic." In Estes and Smith,
  Melancholy Scene of Devastation, 61–78.
Nash, Gary B. *Forging Freedom: The Formation
  of Philadelphia's Black Community
  1720–1840*. Cambridge: Harvard
  University Press, 1988.

Otter, Samuel. *Philadelphia Stories: America's
  Literature of Race and Freedom*. Oxford:
  Oxford University Press, 2010.
Rush, Benjamin. *An Account of the Bilious
  Remitting Yellow Fever as It Appeared in
  the City of Philadelphia in the Year 1793*.
  2nd ed. Philadelphia: Thomas Dobson,
  1794.

Absalom Jones and Others, *Petition of the People of Color and Freemen of Philadelphia—Against the Slave Trade to the Coast of Guinea (1799)*

In 1797, former slaves from North Carolina, liberated by their Quaker masters, were threatened with being sent back into slavery since the state did not recognize manumission. Although they then resided in Philadelphia, their freedom was threatened by the passage of the first Fugitive Slave Act (1793), which allowed for the return of formerly enslaved people to their owners. As historian Gary Nash describes it, "These laws provided what amounted to hunting licenses for anyone with sufficient force at his disposal to seize the hundreds of manumitted slaves living in North Carolina and sell them back into bondage."[1] The laws extended the reign of slavery from the South to the North since the freedom of Blacks there was now also in jeopardy. The men, with allies such as Absalom Jones, wrote a petition in vain against slavery. Two years later, two of these men, along with sixty-eight other free Blacks, headed by Jones and Richard Allen, submitted a second petition to condemn the slave trade and to advocate for the gradual emancipation of African Americans as well as condemning the Fugitive Slave Act. The controversial proposal died in committee, whose members were persuaded by James Madison's argument that the petition on behalf of enslaved people had no merit. Still, antislavery advocates were encouraged that the decision was made on legal grounds.[2] Regardless, the document remains one of the first important pieces of writing by Black Americans, working together with their Quaker allies, requesting their liberty. Jones also wrote, among other pieces, the powerful "A Thanksgiving Sermon" (January 1, 1808) advocating abolition (http://anglicanhistory.org/usa/ajones/thanksgiving1808.html).

⸻

To the President, Senate, and House of Representatives of the United States—
The Petition of the People of Colour, Freemen within the City, and Suburbs
of Philadelphia:

Humbly Sheweth[3]
That thankful to God our Creator and the Government under which we live,
for the blessing and benefit extended to us in the enjoyment of our natural
right to Liberty, and the protection of our Persons and property from the
oppression and violence which so great a number of like colour and National
Descent are subjected; we feel, ourselves bound from a sense of these blessings to continue our respective allotments, and to lead honest and peaceable
lives, rendering due submission to the Laws, and exciting and encouraging
each other thereto, agreeable to the uniform advice of our real friends of every
denomination.—Yet, while we feel impressed with grateful sensations for the
Providential favours we ourselves enjoy, we cannot be insensible of the conditions of our afflicted Brethren, suffering under curious circumstances in
different parts of these States; but deeply sympathizing with them, we are
incited by a sense of Social duty and humbly conceive ourselves authorized
to address and petition you in their behalf, believing them to be objects of
representations in your public Councils, in common with ourselves and every
other class of Citizens within the Jurisdiction of the United States, according to the declared design of the present Constitution, formed by the General
Convention and ratified by the different States, as set forth in the preamble
thereto in the following words—viz.—"We the People of the United States
in order to form a more perfect union, establish justice, insure domestick
tranquility, provide for the Common Defence, and to secure the blessings of
Liberty, to ourselves and posterity, do ordain & c."—We apprehend this
solemn Compact is violated by a trade carried on in clandestine manner to
the Coast of Guinea, and another equally wicked practised openly by Citizens of some of the Southern States upon the waters of Maryland and
Delaware: Men sufficiently callous as to qualify, for the brutal purpose, are
employed in kidnapping those of our Brethren that are free, and purchasing
others of such as claim a property in them; thus these poor helpless victims
like droves of Cattle are seized, fettered, and carried into places provided for
this most horrid traffic, such as dark cellars and garrets, as is notorious at
Northwestfork, Chester-town, Eastown, and divers other places. After a

sufficient number is obtained, they are forced on board vessels, crowded under hatches, and without the least commiseration, left to deplore the sad separation of the dearest ties in nature, husband from wife, and Parents from children thus pack'd together they are transported to Georgia and other places and there inhumanely exposed to sale: Can any Commerce, trade, or transaction, so detestably, shock the feelings of Man, or degrade the dignity of his nature equal to this, and how increasingly is the evil aggravated which practised in a Land, high in profession of the benign doctrines of our blessed Lord who taught his followers to do unto others as they would they should do unto them!—Your petitioners desire not to enlarge though volumes might be filled with the sufferings of this grossly abused class of the human species (700,000 of whom it is said are now in unconditional bondage in these United States) but, conscious of the rectitude of our motives in a concern so nearly affecting, and so essentially interesting to the real welfare of this Country, we cannot but address you as Guardians of our Civil rights, and Patrons of equal and National Liberty, hoping you will view the subject in an impartial and unprejudiced light.—We do not ask for:—the immediate emancipation of all, knowing, that the degraded state of many and their want of education, would greatly disqualify for such a change; but humbly desire, you may exert every means in your power to undo the heavy burdens, and prepare the way for the oppressed to go free, that every yoke may be broken.

The Law not long since enacted Congress called the Fugitive Bill, is, in its execution found to be attended with circumstances peculiarly hard and distressing for many of our afflicted Brethren in order to avoid the barbarities wantonly exercised upon them, or thro fear of being carried off by those Men-stealers, have been forced to seek refuge by flight; they are then hunted by armed Men, and under colour of this law, cruelly treated, shot, or brought back in chains to those who have no just claim upon them.

In the Constitution, and the Fugitive bill, no mention is made of Black people or Slaves—therefore if the Bill of Rights, or the declaration of Congress are of any validity, we beseech that we as men, may be admitted to partake of the Liberties and unalienable Rights therein held forth firmly believing that the extending of Justice and equity to all Classes, would be a means of drawing down, the blessing of Heaven upon this Land, for the Peace and Prosperity of which, and the real happiness of every member of the Community, we fervently pray—

NOTES

1. Nash, *Forging Freedom*, 186.
2. Wood, "A 'Class of Citizens,'" 131.

3. Sheweth: (archaic) to show humbly.

BIBLIOGRAPHY

Bragg, George F. *History of the Afro-American Group of the Episcopal Church*. Baltimore: Church Advocate Press, 1922.
Nash, Gary B. *Forging Freedom: The Formation of Philadelphia's Black Community, 1720–1840*. Cambridge: Harvard University Press, 1988.

White, Deborah Gray. *Freedom on My Mind: A History of African Americans*. 2 vols. Boston: Bedford / St. Martins, 2013.
Wood, Nicholas P. "A 'Class of Citizens': The Earliest Black Petitioners to Congress and Their Quaker Allies." *William and Mary Quarterly* 74, no. 1 (January 2017): 109–44.

Alice, from Thomas Isaiah's *Eccentric Biography: Memoirs of Remarkable Female Characters, Ancient and Modern* (1804)

This entry was not actually written by the enslaved woman named Alice (also known as "Old Alice," "Black Alice," or "Alice of Dunk's Ferry"). Rather, it is a sketch of her contained in a work called *Eccentric Biography: Memoirs of Remarkable Female Characters, Ancient and Modern* (1804), written by Thomas Isaiah. Alice was born in Philadelphia about 1686 and spent the first ten years of her life there. Afterward, she frequently returned to the city from her nearby residence in the area now known as Bucks County.

Alice was a remarkable woman, not only for her long life, estimated at more than one hundred years, but for her skills in a variety of fields, including fishing. She worked as a ferry operator who transported passengers across the Delaware River from Bensalem, Pennsylvania. Her memories of her early life in Philadelphia serve as a window for us, as it did for the descendants of the early settlers, to the city's development from a forest into an urban area. Alice was a well-known figure by the time of her death in 1802. Despite Isaiah's sometimes condescending tone about Alice, he has given us a glimpse into slave life in colonial Philadelphia. It allows a perspective of the city not generally seen when reading the works written by the city's founders such as William Penn and Benjamin Franklin.

A female slave, and native of America. She was born in Philadelphia, of parents who came from Barbadoes, and lived in that city until she was ten years old, when her master removed her to Dunk's Ferry, in which neighborhood she continued to the end of her days. She remembered the ground on which Philadelphia stands, when it was a wilderness, and when the Indians (its chief inhabitants) hunted wild game in the woods, while the panther, the wolf, and the beasts of the forest were prowling about the wigwams and cabins in which they lived. Being a sensible intelligent woman, and having a good memory, which she retained to the last, she would often make judicious remarks on the population and improvements of the city and country, hence her conversation became particularly interesting, especially to the immediate descendants of the first settlers, of whose ancestors she often related acceptable anecdotes. She remembered William Penn, the proprietor of Pennsylvania, Thomas Story,[1] James Logan,[2] and several other distinguished characters of their day. During a short visit which she paid to Philadelphia last fall, many respectable persons called to see her, who were all pleased with her innocent cheerfulness, and that dignified deportment, for which (though a slave and uninstructed) she was ever remarkable. In observing the increase of the city, she pointed out the house next to the episcopal church, to the southward, in Second street, as the first brick building that was erected in it; and it is more than probable she was right, for it bears evident signs of antiquity. The first church, she said, was a small frame that stood where the present building stands, the ceiling of which she could reach with her hands from the floor. She was a worthy member of the episcopal society, and attended their public worship as long as she lived. Indeed, she was so zealous to perform this duty in proper season, that she was often met on horseback, in a full gallop, to church, at the age of 95 years. The veneration she had for the bible induced her to lament that she was not able to read it; but the deficiency was in part supplied by the kindness of many of her friends, who, at her request, would read it to her, when she would listen with great attention, and often make pertinent remarks. She was temperate in her living, and so careful to keep to the truth, that her veracity was never questioned; her honesty was also unimpeached, for such was her master's confidence in it, that she was trusted at all times to receive the ferriage money, for upwards of forty years. This extraordinary woman retained her hearing to the end of her life, but her sight began to fail gradually in her ninety-sixth year, without any visible cause than from old age. At one hundred she became blind so that she could not see the sun at noon day. Being habituated from her childhood to constant employment, her kindly master excused her from her usual labor; but s[h]e could not be idle, for she afterwards devoted her time to fishing, at which she was very expert, and even at this late period, when her sight had so entirely left her, she would frequently row herself out into the middle of the stream, from which she seldom returned without a handsome supply of fish for her master's table.—About the one hundred and second year of her age, her sight gradually returned, and so far, that she could perceive objects moving before her, though she could not distinguish persons. Before she died, her hair became perfectly white, and the last of her teeth dropt sound from her head at the age of 116 years. At this age she died, (1802) at Bristol, in Pennsylvania.

NOTES

1. Story was an English-born converted Quaker who was a friend of William Penn. He was the first recorder for Philadelphia in 1700. He was also a preacher and was known for his sermons.

2. Logan was born in Ireland. He held many positions in Philadelphia, including serving as mayor in 1723. He was a founder of the Academy of Philadelphia (the origins of the University of Pennsylvania).

BIBLIOGRAPHY

"Alice." The Library Company of Philadelphia. https://www.librarycompany.org /extraordinarywoman/5.1.htm.
Blockson, Charles. "Alice of Dunk's Ferry." In Notable Black American Women, book 2, edited by Jessie Carney Smith, 1. Detroit: Gale, 1996.
Comegno, Carol. "Life of Enslaved Ferry Operator Honored." Courier Post, June 19, 2015. https://www.courierpostonline .com/story/news/local/south-jersey /2015/06/19/alice-ferry-beverly /29013911/.
Isaiah, Thomas. Eccentric Biography: Memoirs of Remarkable Female Characters, Ancient and Modern. Boston: B & J. Homans, 1804.
Kaplan, Sidney, and Emma Nogrady Kaplan. The Black Presence in the Era of the American Revolution. Rev. ed. Amherst: University of Massachusetts Press, 1989.

John Joyce, *Confession of John Joyce, Alias, Davis, Who Was Executed on Monday, the 14th of March, 1808, for the Murder of Mrs. Sarah Cross* (1808)

Criminal narratives have had a longstanding appeal to readers, dating back at least as far as the Newgate Prison stories of eighteenth-century England of which Jack Sheppard's tale is just one example. Reverend Richard Allen hoped to capitalize on the popularity of such narratives by acting as amanuensis for the confessions of both John Joyce and his "accomplice," Peter Mathias. Allen published these stories to provide a moral lesson and to help dispel the notion that Blacks were intent on murdering Whites. The crimes were supposedly caused by moral flaws of the perpetrators rather than out of racial hatred; however, the narratives also contributed to the stereotype of Black criminality. The Confessions include a sermon by Allen against immoral behavior, a summary of newspaper accounts of the trial, and a report from the judge. Joyce's narrative follows a standard pattern in criminal literature of crime, justice/punishment, and moral redemption through God's forgiveness.

Joyce was born into slavery in Maryland, but after serving in the United States Navy, he lived a hardscrabble life in Philadelphia, drifting along in a life of crime. He moved to several locations, fleeing from crimes he had committed and being fired from jobs after committing thefts while employed. While lodging with Mrs. Sarah Cross, he decided to kill the woman for her money and possessions. Although he committed the murder himself, he recruited his friend Peter Mathias to help dispose of the evidence. Once caught, Joyce insisted that Peter was innocent of the murder, but he, too, was sentenced to die. It is left uncertain how much Mathias, who did not confess to the murder, contributed to the crime, but it is noteworthy that Joyce pled for his innocence. Thus, he felt guilt not only for the death of Sarah Cross but also for that of Mathias as well.

—

Confession.

I, JOHN JOYCE, alias DAVIS (about 24 years of age,) was born at West River, state of Maryland, a slave in the service of Sarah Saunders, I left her about 9 years and an half since, to go into the service of the United States.

My parents were piously inclined. My uncle had religious meetings held at his house—my father is living in Maryland—I was depraved in my morals, and never belonged to any religious society.—On parting with my mother, after giving me much good advice, she observed, "she was afraid I would be hanged one day or another."

Went to Boston, and from thence went on board the ship Boston, M'Neal commander, on a cruise to the Straits. I continued in service about 7 years, during which period I sailed with Commodore Preble, Captain Chauncey, Captain Cox, and Commodore Barron. I returned to the city of Washington—and lived there about twelve months in the family of Dr. John

Bullus, married an hired woman in the family, and had by her 2 children (and two by other women.) I went out to sea again on a cruise to the Straits, and returned with Captain Decatur in the Congress to Washington. While absent on this voyage, my wife was unfaithful to me, and cohabited with another man in consequence of which I left her. The first crime against the laws of my country, was the stealing on an horse at Washington, from Lawrence Hays, about eighteen months ago, on which I came up to Philadelphia, and sold him to a white man, by the name of—, for eighteen dollars. I boarded with Margaret Tucker, a black woman in Fourth below South-streets, about a week, and then hired with Adam Guyer, to keep horses, and take care of his stable, corner of Filbert and Eleventh-streets, where I staid near two months. I then hired as a servant of Dr. B—'s in Sansom-street, where I continued about two months. I then went to live with Mr. W—, in Second between Vine and Race-streets, as a coachman, where I staid about two months, during which period I drove Mr. W—twice to Lancaster, to visit his son-in-law Mr. R—. While at Lancaster the last time, I entered the house adjoining Mr. R—'s and stole a watch, which being missed by the owners who suspected me as the thief, they sent one of the Lancaster stage drivers to Mr. W—to demand the watch which I gave up. In consequence of this transaction, Mr. W—turned me away: from thence I went to live with David Kennedy, in Lætitia Court,[1] as a waiter in the tavern, with whom I lived about two months; the cause of my leaving his service, was my going out to a dance late at night, and leaving the door open. While I lived at Mr. Kennedy's, I became acquainted with Mrs. Cross, who kept a shop in Blackhorse-alley, being frequently sent there on errands. After leaving Mr. Kennedy's I engaged with Mrs. Scott, to drive her carriage, the day on which, in the evening, I perpetrated the horrid crime for which I am condemned to die. On Friday the 18th December last, early in the evening, I went down to the house of Peter Mathias or Matthews, to Fifth below Small-street: while there, I conceived the plan of the murder, but did not relate it to Peter, at that, or any other time, and he (Peter) is innocent. I asked Peter to go with me up to Kennedy's, to receive money due me for wages. Peter declined, saying "he was engaged that evening to play for a dance." I prevailed upon him to accompany me, by promising him as much or more money than he could get by playing the fiddle: I then saw a rope, or clothes line, which I told Hester Cook (the woman of the house with whom Peter lived,) that I wanted, and of which I cut off a part and took with me. Leaving the house with Peter, we went together to a shop in Shippen-street,[2] and I bought an half pint of gin, the most of which I drank myself; and from thence proceeded toward Lætitia Court. While walking up Front-street, saw some wood which had been sawed, and took a small stick of it in my hand and carried it with me. We went to another shop in Market near Water street, & I got a gill[3] of gin; & from thence, I and Peter went to Lætitia Court to Mr. Kennedy's, I looked in the window and saw Cyrus Porter, a black man who was a waiter at nights, and assisted me while I lived there. I then asked Peter to go with me to Mrs. Cross, in Blackhorse-alley: I bought half a dozen apples, gave Peter a part, and he eat his at the counter. While conversing with Mrs. Cross, she observed to me, that, "I had left my place," (Mr. Kennedy's.) She asked Peter to "come by the stove and warm himself." I felt tempted to commit the act. Peter was desirous to go, and proposed it, I asked what is your hurry? Peter then went out of the house. I called after him to tarry a little, and I would go along with him in a few minutes. The door was shut too by Peter. I then, holding the stick in my hand, felt strongly tempted to perpetrate the horrid act: I struck her on the head with the stick, she cried out "Lord, John, what did you do that for," and fell to the floor. I then took the rope out of my pocket, made a noose in it, put it round her neck, and drew it tight. I then took the candle, and went up stairs to look for the money. Under the pillow, between the bed and sacking bottom,[4] I found a handkerchief containing a purse of dollars and a crown or two, and another containing gold and some silver, which I took, and came down stairs, and found in the drawer of the counter, a small purse with silver and small change, and took that also. Peter then came to the door, to see if I was ready to go, and let him in. On Peter's coming in, and seeing the situation of Mrs. Cross, lying on the floor, he said, "Lord! John, what have you been about? Have you killed the woman?" To which I replied, "no, she is not dead." Then a little girl came in, and asked for a penny's worth of liquorice [sic]. No reply was made to her. The door was then shut and locked by me.

I asked Peter and the girl to go up stairs to help me tie up the bed. The girl held the candle. I took the bed down stairs, put it out of doors, and left it in the alley. Coming down stairs, I demanded of the little girl whether she knew me? She said no, I asked her if she would go with me? She replied "yes." I came out of the house with a bundle of clothes, and a looking glass, at the same time held the girl by the hand, and came into Second-street, she then cried out "murder." I let go of her hand, and I and Peter ran up Second to

Market street, and up Market to Fifth streets, and down Fifth to Peter's house: found there Hester Cook, with whom Peter lived. I sat down, and put the looking glass on the table. Peter put the bundle down. I then took the money out of my pocket, and told Peter to count it. Peter did so and it was put in the purse again. I then requested Hester Cook to take the money and the clothes, and put them away for me, which she did, by putting them in a trunk. After a short pause, I asked Peter what he would drink. Each gave a quarter of a dollar, and sent Hester Cook for a quart of brandy, which she brought. Two women of colour who lived up stairs came down (they are of loose character.) I asked them to drink; but I did not drink myself. I then went with Peter to Margaret Tucker's; Peter went from there to Jenny Miller's in Pine Alley, where he had been engaged to play the fiddle that evening.

While I was at Margaret Tucker's, Hester Cook came there after me, and shortly after, (about 10 o'clock) the Watchmen came in, apprehended me, and brought me to prison.

In a conversation with Mr. Allen, prior to his making this Confession, he (John) enquired, "whether any thing could be done for that innocent man, Peter." He said, "three things[5] laid heavy on his mind: he had murdered that Old Lady, and was the cause of the death of that innocent man." Mr. Allen demanded, "how he (Peter) could be innocent? Was he not consulted in the plot? Was he not present when you struck Mrs. Cross with the stick, and put the rope round her neck?" to which he replied, "No my dear Mr. Allen, he is clear of it as G-d is himself. The poor Old Woman, was snatched off in her sins, with scarce time to say, Lord have mercy on me; but we, miserable sinners, have time to repent. It is better with Peter, than with ME, for he is innocent, and I am the guilty wretch." On being again questioned by Mr. Allen, whether "Peter was present when he struck the woman, or when he put the rope round her neck," he replied, "No, he was not."

JOHN X [his mark] JOYCE

NOTES

1. Laeticia Court: named after William Penn's daughter. Located in the Old City.

2. Shippen Street: now Bainbridge Street near Independence Hall in the Old City (City Center).

3. Gill: a quarter of a pint.

4. Sacking bottom: a rectangle of sail cloth with eyelets to correspond to the pegs in the sail.

5. Three things: there seem to be two things troubling him, his murder of the old lady and his insistence on Peter's innocence.

BIBLIOGRAPHY

Cohen, Daniel. *Pillars of Salt, Monuments of Grace: New England Crime Literature and the Origins of American Popular Culture, 1674–1860.* Amherst: University of Massachusetts Press, 2006.

Joyce, John. *Confession of John Joyce, Alias, Davis, Who Was Executed on Monday, the 14th of March, 1808, for the Murder of Mrs. Sarah Cross.* Philadelphia: Printed for the benefit of Bethel Church, 1808.

Documenting the American South. https://docsouth.unc.edu/neh/joyce /menu.html.

Newman, Richard S. *Freedom's Prophet: Bishop Richard Allen, the AME Church, and the Black Founding Fathers.* New York: New York University Press, 2008.

Otter, Samuel. *Philadelphia Stories: America's Literature of Race and Freedom.* Oxford: Oxford University Press, 2010.

James Forten, from *Letters from a Man of Colour, on a Late Bill Before the Senate of Pennsylvania* (1813)

James Forten was a sailor, sailmaker, businessman, and abolitionist born a free person in Philadelphia in 1766. Forten's family was impoverished after his father died, and young James left school when he was nine years old to work full-time. As a teen he fought in the Revolutionary War and became a prisoner of war. He refused an offer to be released if he switched sides, saying, "I am here a prisoner for my country. *I never, Never, shall prove a traitor to her interest.*"[1] He maintained this patriotic zeal even after realizing how badly the nation had treated African Americans.

After the war's end, Forten used his skills as a sailmaker and business-man to accumulate a fortune, which he utilized to oppose slavery. In 1801, Forten wrote to the members of the Pennsylvania Abolition Society that he and those like him, freeborn, educated, and affluent, were "attached to our race by the Tie of Sympathy."[2] By 1830, however, conditions for Blacks in Philadelphia continued to deteriorate. There were several violent riots, and in 1838 a new constitution was ratified that disfranchised African Americans. Though aged and unwell, in 1838 Forten helped fund the American Moral Reform Society to try to ameliorate the situation. He died in 1842, but during his lifetime Forten had proven himself to be a debater and polit-ical theorist of considerable skill.[3] His desire for social justice continued in his progeny, such as his three daughters Harriet, Margaretta, and Sarah, his son James Jr., his son-in-law Robert Purvis, and his granddaughter Charlotte Forten Grimké.

What occasioned Forten's *Letters from a Man of Colour* (1813) was a bill advocating closing Pennsylvania's borders to Black migrants, particularly escaped slaves. The bill had failed once to become a law, but Forten wrote his brief pamphlet in hopes of ensuring it was not reintroduced. Forten wrote the first letter to thank those who rejected the initial bill, and he praised Philadelphians for the rights they had afforded their Black population. Forten expanded on this in his anonymous pamphlet, which expounded on his belief that all Americans deserved equal treatment. In the fifth and final letter, Forten laments the restrictions that have been placed on Black citizens of the city by this recent bill. The legislation, among other things, restricted the right of free movement by Blacks and allowed police to arrest any African American who could not produce a letter of registration and even allowed for the possibility of their sale into slavery.

The bill that Forten railed against eventually failed, but not because Forten had changed the hearts of White legislators. Other petitions restricting Blacks were proposed again within a short period. Nevertheless, as historian Julie Winch states about him, in this short pamphlet Forten poses important questions for the nation: "What this black veteran of the American War of Independence had written as the nation grappled with the consequences of that independence was a passionate plea for equal rights, a fervent appeal to America to live up to what he firmly believed was its founding promise."[4]

—

LETTER 1.

O Liberty! thou power supremely bright,
Profuse of bliss and pregnant with delight,
Perpetual pleasures in thy presence reign,
And smiling Plenty leads thy wanton train

ADDISON[5]

We hold this truth to be self-evident, that GOD created all men equal, and is one of the most prominent features in the Declaration of Independence, and in that glorious fabric of collected wisdom, our noble Constitution. This idea embraces the Indian and the European, the Savage and the Saint, the Peruvian and the Laplander, the white Man and the African, and whatever measures are adopted subversive of this inestimable privilege, are in direct violation of the letter and the spirit of our Constitution, and become subject to the animadversion[6] of all, particularly those who are deeply interested in the measure.

These thoughts were suggested by the promulgation of a late bill, before the Senate of Pennsylvania, to prevent the emigration of people of colour into this state. It was not passed into a law at this session and must in consequence lay over until the next, before when we sincerely hope, the white men whom we should look upon as our protectors, will have become convinced of the inhumanity and impolicy of such a measure, and forbear to deprive us of those inestimable treasures, Liberty and Independence. This is almost the only state in the Union wherein the African have justly boasted of rational liberty and the protection of the laws, and shall it now be said they have been deprived of that liberty, and publicly exposed for sale to the highest bidder? Shall colonial inhumanity that has marked many of us with shameful stripes, become the practice of the people of Pennsylvania, while Mercy stands weeping at the miserable spectacle? People of Pennsylvania, descendants of the immortal Penn, doom us not to the unhappy fate of thousands of our countrymen in the Southern States and the West Indies; despise the traffic in blood, and the blessing of the African will forever be around you. Many of us are men of property, for the security of which, we have hitherto looked to the laws of our blessed state, but should this become a law, our property is jeopardized, since the same power which can expose to sale an unfortunate fellow creature, can wrest from him those estates which years of honest industry have accumulated. Where shall the poor African look for protection, should the people of Pennsylvania consent to oppress him? We grant there are a number of worthless men belonging to our colour, but there are laws of sufficient rigour for their punishment, if properly and duly enforced. We wish not to screen the guilty do not permit the innocent to suffer. If there are worthless men, there are also men of merit among the African race, who are useful members of Society. The truth of this let their benevolent institutions and the numbers clothed and fed by them witness. Punish the guilty man of colour to the utmost limit of the laws, but sell him not to slavery! If he is in danger of becoming a public charge prevent him! If he is too indolent to labour for his own subsistence, compel him to do so; but sell him not to slavery. By selling him you do not make him better, but commit a wrong, without benefiting the object of it or society at large. Many of our ancestors were brought here more than one hundred years ago; many of our fathers, many of ourselves, have fought and bled for the independence of our country. Do not then expose us to sale. Let not the spirit of the father behold the son robbed of that liberty which he died to establish, but let the motto of our legislators, be "The Law knows no distinction."

These are only a few desultory remarks on the subject and intend to succeed this effervescence of feeling, by a series of essays, ending to prove the impolicy and unconstitutionality of the law in question.

For the present, I leave the public to the consideration of the above observations, in which I hope they will see so much truth, that they will never consent to sell to slavery.

LETTER V.

A few more remarks upon the bill which has been the subject of my preceding numbers, shall conclude these Letters, which have been written in my own cause as an individual, and my brethren as a part of the community. They are the simple dictates of nature and need no apology. They are not written in the gorgeous style of a scholar, nor dressed in the garments of literary perfection. They are the impulse of a mind formed, I trust, for feeling, and smarting under all the rigours which the bill is calculated to produce.

By the third section of this bill, which is its peculiar hardship, the police officers are authorized to apprehend any black, whether a vagrant or a man of reputable character, who cannot produce a Certificate that he has been registered. He is to be arrayed before a justice, who thereupon is to commit him to prison! The jailor is to advertise a Freeman, and at expiration of six months, if no owner appears for this degraded black, he is to be exposed to sale, and if not sold to be confined at hard labour for seven years! Man of feeling,[7] read this!—No matter who, no matter where. The Constable, whose antipathy generally against the black is very great, will take every opportunity of hurting his feelings! Perhaps, he sees him at a distance and having a mind to raise the boys in hue and cry against him, exclaims, "Halloa! Stop the Negro?" The boys, delighting in the sport immediately begin to hunt him, and immediately from a hundred tongues, is heard the cry—"Hoa, Negro, where is your certificate!" Can any thing be conceived more degrading to humanity! Can anything be done more shocking to the principal of Civil Liberty!—A person arriving from another state, ignorant of the existence of such a law, may fall a victim to its cruel oppression. But he is to be advertised, and if no owner appears—How can an owner appear for a man who is free and belongs to no one!—If no owner appears, he is exposed for sale!—Oh, .

inhuman spectacle: found in no unjust act convicted of no crime, he is barbarously sold like the produce of the soil, to the highest bidder, or what is still worse, for no crimes, without the inestimable privilege of a trial by his peers, doomed to the dreary walls of a prison for the term of seven tedious years! My God, what a situation is his. Search the legends of tyranny and find no precedent. No example can be found in all the reigns of violence and oppression, which have marked the lapse of time. It stands alone. It has been left for Pennsylvania, to raise her ponderous arm against liberties of the blacks, whose greatest boast has been, that he resided in a State where Civil Liberty, and sacred Justice were administered alike to all.—What must be his reflections now, that the asylum he left for emancipation has been destroyed, and he is left to suffer like Daniel[8] of old, with no one but his God to help him! Where is the bosom that does not have a sigh for his fall, unless it be callous to every sentiment of humanity and mercy?

The fifth section of this bill, is also peculiarly bare, inasmuch as it prevents freemen from living where they please—Pennsylvania has always been a refuge from slavery, and to this state the Southern black, when freed, has flown for safety. Why does he this! When masters in many of the Southern states, which they frequently do, free a particular black, unless that black leaves the state in so many hours any person resident of the said state, can have him arrested and again sold to Slavery:—The hunted black is obliged to flee or remain and be again a slave. I have known persons of this description sold three times after being first emancipated. Where shall he go? Shut every state against him, and like Pharoah's kine,[9] drive him into the sea.—Is there no spot on earth that will protect him! Against their inclination, his ancestors were forced from their homes by trades in human flesh, and even under such circumstances, the wretched offspring are denied the protection you afforded to brutes.

It is in vain that we are forming societies of different kinds to ameliorate the condition of our unfortunate brethren, to correct their morals and to render them not only honest but useful members of society. All our efforts by this bill, are despised and we are doomed to feel the lash of oppression:— As well may we be outlawed, as well may the glorious privileges of the Gospel, be denied us, and all endeavours used to cut us off from happiness hereafter as well as here!—The case is similar, and I am much deceived if this bill does not destroy the morals it is intended to produce.

I have done. My feelings are acute, and I have ventured to express them without intending either accusation or insult to any one. An appeal to the heart is my intention, and if I have failed, it is my great misfortune, not to have laid a power of eloquence sufficient to convince. But I trust the eloquence of nature will succeed, and the law-givers of this happy Commonwealth will yet remain the Black's friend, and the advocates of Freemen, is the sincere wish of every freemen.

NOTES

1. Quoted in Winch, "Making and Meaning," 132.

2. Quoted in Winch, "Making and Meaning," 133.

3. Winch, *Gentleman of Color*, 151.

4. Winch, "Making and Meaning," 129.

5. Joseph Addison, a British author, lived from 1672 to 1719. The quotation is from the play *Cato, a Tragedy*, written in 1712 and first performed in 1713.

6. Animadversion: criticism.

7. Man of feeling: Henry Mackenzie, a Scottish author, wrote the sentimental novel, *A Man of Feeling*, in 1771.

8. Daniel: In Daniel (Book 6), the biblical figure is thrown into a den of lions but is saved by his God.

9. Pharoah's kine: ill favored, cows in Genesis 41:2–7.

BIBLIOGRAPHY

Douty, Esther M. *Forten the Sailmaker: Pioneer Champion of Negro Rights*. Chicago: Rand McNally, 1968.

Forten, James. *An Address Delivered Before the Ladies' Anti-slavery Society of Philadelphia, On the Evening of the 14th of April*. Philadelphia: Merrihew and Gunn, 1836.

Newman, Richard. "Not the Only Story in 'Amistad': The Fictional Joadson and the Real James Forten." *Pennsylvania History: A Journal of Mid-Atlantic Studies* 67, no. 2 (2000): 218–39.

Winch, Julie. *A Gentleman of Color: The Life of James Forten*. Oxford: Oxford University Press, 2002.

———. "The Making and Meaning of James Forten's *Letters from a Man of Colour*." *William and Mary Quarterly* 64, no. 1 (2007): 129–38.

James Forten and Russell Parrott, *To the Humane and Benevolent Inhabitants of the City and County of Philadelphia, Address Delivered August 10, 1817* (1817)

James Forten and Russell Parrott (1791–1824) were among the prominent Black Philadelphians who often spoke out on issues of concern to the African American community. Forten and Parrott were both members of, the

Philadelphia African Institution, which advocated the abolition of slavery, an issue both often wrote and spoke about. For more on Forten, see the introduction to *Letters from a Man of Colour* (1813).

Parrott was a member of the Saint Thomas Episcopal Church, where he eventually became an assistant to the pastor. In 1814, Parrott gave "An Oration on the Abolition of the Slave Trade." In his speech, he gave support for those still enslaved. His address was later revised and published by the African Benevolent Societies. In his address, Parrott singled out Benjamin Rush for praise in his support of African Americans. And he also praised Pennsylvania for its forward thinking: "Philadelphia, first in virtue, first in patriotism, to the wisdom of thy councils, and the firmness of thy magistrates, we are indebted for the privileges we now enjoy."[1]

Parrott also was involved in a number of activities involving Black Philadelphians; for example, he helped organize Blacks in resisting a possible British occupation of the city during the War of 1812. Parrott, as leader of the African Literary Society, was also an advocate of furthering Black education, and he helped open the first African American school in Philadelphia in 1822.

Parrott did support some efforts to resettle Blacks in Africa, such as those espoused by the mixed-race American Paul Cuffe, who hoped to settle Sierra Leone. However, he maintained that many such plans, such as one proposed by the American Colonization Society, largely led by White abolitionists, were often based more on greed than on altruism. The address Parrott and Forten gave in 1817, *To the Humane and Benevolent Inhabitants of the City and County of Philadelphia*, was very tactfully but forcefully delivered. The authors challenged the plan set forth, to send Blacks to Liberia, which was proposed by some of their own allies, in a very respectful manner. However, they maintained that Blacks had earned the right to full American citizenship because of their labors and it was not to their advantage to be denied their benefits by being sent to Africa. Parrott and Forten also feared that slaveholders would likely send the most recalcitrant of their enslaved Blacks, leaving behind only the most submissive. Additionally, they were concerned that the loss of some better-off African Americans would lead to a diminution of the cause for those left behind and weaken the cause for the eventual abolition of slavery. This would be particularly galling coming from Philadelphia, "where the voice of the suffering sons of Africa was first heard." Eventually, the deportation of Blacks back to Africa, to Forten and Parrott, could lead to the expulsion of any Blacks whom Whites chose to exclude from the United States.

The free people of color, assembled together, under circumstances of deep interest to their happiness and welfare, humbly and respectfully lay before you this expression of their feelings and apprehensions.

Relieved from the miseries of slavery, many of us by your aid, possessing the benefits which industry and integrity in this prosperous country assures to all its inhabitants, enjoying the rich blessings of religion, by opportunities of worshipping the only true God, under the light of Christianity, each of us according to his understanding; and having afforded to us and to our children the means of education and improvement; we have no wish to separate from our present homes, for any purpose whatever. Contented with our present situation and condition, we are not desirous of increasing their prosperity but by honest efforts, and by the use of those opportunities for their improvement, which the constitution and laws allow to all. It is therefore with painful solicitude, and sorrowing regret, we have seen a plan for colonizing the free people of color of the United States on the coast of Africa, brought forward under the auspices and sanction of gentlemen whose names give value to all they recommend, and who certainly are among the wisest, the best, and the most benevolent of men, in this great nation.

If the plan of colonizing is intended for our benefit, and those who now promote it will never seek our injury, we humbly and respectfully urge, that it is not asked for by us; nor will it be required by any circumstances, in our present or future condition, as long as we shall be permitted to share the protection of the excellent laws and just government which we now enjoy, in common with every individual of the community.

We, therefore, a portion of those who are the objects of this plan, and among those whose happiness, with that of others of our color, it is intended to promote, with humble and grateful acknowledgments to those who have devised it, renounce and disclaim every connexion with it; and respectfully but firmly declare our determination not to participate in any part of it.

If this plan of colonization now proposed, is intended to provide a refuge and a dwelling for a portion of our brethren who are now held in slavery in the south, we have other and stronger objections to it, and we entreat your consideration of them.

The ultimate and final abolition of slavery in the United States by the oper-ation of various causes is, under the guidance and protection of a just God, progressing. Every year witnesses the release of numbers of the victims of oppression, and affords new and sage assurances that the freedom of all will be in the end accomplished. As they are thus by degrees relieved from bondage, our brothers have opportunities for instruction and improvement; and thus they become in some measure fitted for their liberty. Every year, many of us have restored to us by the gradual, but certain march of the cause of abolition—parents, whom we have long been separated—wives and children whom we had left in servitude—and brothers, by blood as well as in early sufferings, from whom we had been long parted.

But if the emancipation of our kindred shall, when the plan of coloniza-tion shall go into effect, be attended with transportation to a distant land, and shall be granted on no other condition; the consolation for our past sufferings and of those of our color who are in slavery, would continue to be, afforded to us and to them; will cease for ever. The cords, which now connect them with us, will be stretched by the distance to which their ends will be carried, until they break; and all the sources of happiness, which affection and connexion and blood bestow, will be ours and theirs no more.

Nor do we view the colonization of those who may become emancipated by its operation among our southern brothers, as capable of producing their happiness. Unprepared by education and a knowledge of the truths of our blessed religion for their new situation, those who will thus become colonists will themselves be surrounded by every suffering which can afflict the mem-bers of the human family.

Without arts, without habits of industry, and unaccustomed to provide by their own exertions and foresight for their wants, the colony will soon become the abode of every vice, and the home of every misery. Soon will the light of Christianity, which now dawns among that portion of our species, be shut out by the clouds of ignorance, and their day of life be closed, without the illuminations of the gospel.

To those of our brothers who shall be left behind, there will be assured perpetual slavery and augmented sufferings. Diminished in numbers, the slave population of the southern states, which by its magnitude alarms its proprietors, will be easily secured. Those among their bondsmen who feel that they should be free, by rights which all mankind have from God and from nature, and who thus may become dangerous to the quiet of their masters, will be sent to the colony, and the tame and submissive will be retained, and subjected to increased rigor. Year after year will witness these means to assure safety, and submission among their slaves, and the southern masters will colonize only those whom it may be dangerous to keep among them. The bondage of our brothers will thus be rendered perpetual.

Should the anticipations of misery and want among the colonists, which with great deference we have submitted in your better judgment, be realized, to emancipate and transport to Africa will be held forth by slaveholders as the worst and heaviest of punishments; and thus will be threatened and successfully used to enforce increased submission to their wishes, and subjection to their commands.

Nor ought the sufferings and sorrows which must be produced by an exercise of the right to transport and colonize such only of their slaves as may be selected by the slaveholders, escape the attention and consideration of those whom with all humility we now address. Parents will be torn from their children—husbands from their wives—brothers from brothers—and all the heart-rending agonies which were endured by our forefathers when they were dragged into bondage from Africa will be again renewed, and with increased anguish. The shores of America will, like the sands of Africa, be watered by the tears of whose who will be left behind. Those who shall be carried away will roam childless, widowed, and alone, over the burning plains of Guinea.

Disclaiming, as we emphatically do, a wish or desire to interpose our opinions and feelings between all plans of colonization, and the judgment of those whose wisdom as far exceeds ours as their situations are exalted above ours; we humbly, respectfully, and fervently intreat and beseech your disapprobation of the plan of colonization now offered by 'the American Society for colonizing the free people of color of the United States.'—Here, in the city of Philadelphia, where the voice of the suffering sons of Africa was first heard; where was first commenced the work of abolition, on which heaven has smiled, for it could have had success only from the Great Maker; let not a purpose be assisted which will stay the cause of the entire abolition of slavery in the United States, and which may defeat it altogether; which proffers to those who do not ask for them what it calls benefits, but which they consider injuries; and which must insure to the multitudes whose prayers can only reach you through us, misery, sufferings, and perpetual slavery.

NOTE

1. Quoted in Newman, Rael, and Lapsansky,
Pamphlets of Protest, 78.

BIBLIOGRAPHY

Kershen, Lois. "Parrott, Russell." In *Encyclopedia
of African American History, 1619–1895:
From the Colonial Period to the Age of
Frederick Douglass*, edited by Paul
Finkelman, 75–79. Oxford: Oxford
University Press, 2009.
Newman, Richard, Patrick Rael, and Philip
Lapsansky, eds. *Pamphlets of Protest: An
Anthology of Early African-American*

Protest Literature, 1790–1860. New York:
Routledge, 2001.
Rezek, Joseph. "The Orations on the Abolition of
the Slave Trade and the Uses of Print in
the Early Black Atlantic." *Early American
Literature* 45, no. 3 (2010): 655–82.
Winch, Julie. *A Gentleman of Color: The Life of
James Forten*. Oxford: Oxford University
Press, 2002.

William Whipper, from *An Address Delivered in Wesley Church on the
Evening of June 12, Before the Colored Reading Society of Philadelphia, for
Mental Improvement* (1828)

William Whipper was born in Dunmore Township, Lancaster County, Pennsylvania, in 1804, to a White father and an enslaved mother. Whipper moved
to Philadelphia in the 1820s and became a successful businessman, establishing a lumberyard with his partner Stephen Smith. He used his wealth to
further the temperance and antislavery movements, and he cofounded the
American Moral Reform Society in 1835. The society "planned to emphasize
education, temperance, economy, and universal liberty."[1]

Whipper worked for social justice on several fronts. He was a devout Christian, believing the answer to violence was benevolence and acceptance of all
people regardless of race. In fact, he often eschewed references to racial des-
ignation, arguing, as critic Samuel Otter writes, "that such distinctive
nomenclature perpetuated the tropes of racism." Such thinking often put him
outside the mainstream of most Black leaders, who felt he was too idealistic
and visionary.[2] Whipper not only fought for African Americans through his
writings; he was also a member of the Underground Railroad, aiding hundreds of slaves on the path to freedom from his home in Columbia,
Pennsylvania. In 1837, Whipper published "An Address on Non-Resistance to

Offensive Aggression" in the *Colored American*, advocating for nonviolent opposition to slavery.

Black Philadelphians had been advocating for the creation of cultural institutions to help uplift Blacks by improving their moral character as is demonstrated in such works as Prince Saunders's *An Address before the Pennsylvania Augustine Society* (1818). Whipper developed this idea further in *An Address Delivered in Wesley Church on the Evening of June 12, Before the Colored Reading Society of Philadelphia*. He maintained that "lower class" African Americans needed to be saved from moral degeneration through education. He made a connection between slavery and the debased conditions of Black people and maintained the best way to improve their condition was to be made "superior in morals" to White people. At that point they would be better respected and accepted by the rest of society. Education, Whipper notes, is particularly important for Blacks who have often been denied the skills of reading and writing. In Whipper's advocation of a reading society, it is also important to note that the cost of books was beyond many people at the time, although the city was fortunate to already have the Library Company of America, founded by Benjamin Franklin in 1731. Whipper's optimism about the possibility for reform radically changed after the riots of the 1830s, the disfranchisement of African American men in Philadelphia in 1838, and the passage of the Fugitive Slave Act. This change of heart is evidenced in such essays as "Our Elevation" (1839) and "Appeal to the Colored Citizens of Philadelphia" (1848).[3] Whipper lived his final years in Philadelphia.

The full text of this address is available in Dorothy Porter's *Early Negro Writing, 1760–1837* (Boston: Beacon, 1971).

⁓

Friends and Fellow Citizens—

If it be useful to cherish moral and intellectual improvement, the occasion which has called us together is one of high interest. The establishment of a literary institution, whether we consider it as connected with the progress of science in times past, or associated with its future advancement, is an event which we cannot regard with feelings of indifference.

But sincerely do I regret that the task of awakening these reflections in your minds had not devolved on some one more competent to do justice to the important subject from which they spring. To my fellow members belonging to this institution I have made sufficient apology for my inadequacy, without transgressing on your patience at present.

I am well aware that the age in which we live is fastidious in its taste. It demands eloquence, figure, rhetoric, and pathos; plain, honest, common sense is no longer attracting. No: the orator must display the pomp of words, the magnificence of the tropes and figures, or he will be considered unfit for the duties of his profession.

But I pretend to none of these. Such high-wrought artificial lectures, however, are like beautiful paint upon windows, they rather obscure the light of the sun. Truth should always be exhibited in such a dress as may be best suited to than adapt the state of the audience, accompanied with every principle of science and reason.

In establishing a new institution, respect for public opinion requires us to make our motives understood. This is the golden age of Literature; men studious of change are constantly looking for something new, and no sooner has the mind become gratified than new means of gratification is sought for. The Literature of the day is accommodating itself to the public taste, and brings in regular succession the condensed learning of past ages; and all the erudition of the present. We shall make no pretentions to concentrate learning, or display erudition, ours will be a humbler task, but not the less important, and we humbly hope not the less useful.

1st. This society shall be known and distinguished by the name of *The Colored Reading Society for Mental Improvement*. 2ndly. All persons initiated into this Society shall become members in the same mode as is customary in all benevolent institutions, with the same strictness and regard to the moral qualifications as is necessary in all institutions to secure their welfare. 3rdly. Every person on becoming a member of this institution, shall pay into the hands of the Treasurer his initiation fee and monthly dues. 4thly. All monies received by this Society (with the exception of wood, light, rent, & c.) is to be expended in useful books, such as the Society may from time to time appropriate. 5thly. All books initiated into this Society shall be placed in the care of the Librarian belonging to said institution, and it shall be his duty to deliver to said members alternately, such books as they shall demand, with strict regard that no member shall keep said book out of the library longer than one week, without paying the fine prescribed in the constitution, unless an apology for sickness or absence: those shall be the only excuses received. 6thly. It shall be the duty of this Society to meet once a week to return and receive books, to read and express whatever sentiments they may have conceived if they think proper, and transact the necessary business relative to this institution. 7th and lastly. It shall be our whole duty to instruct and assist each other in the improvement of our minds, as we wish to see the flame of improvement spreading amongst our brethren and friends; and the means prescribed shall be our particular province. Therefore we hope that many of our friends will avail themselves of the opportunity of becoming members of this useful institution.

I feel as though your minds have already become acquainted with the subject, as the necessity of the case demands the greatest attention. If there be any who doubt the usefulness and utility of this institution to be conducive of much to the public, I refer them to the most learned gentlemen of our city, or to our coloured brethren in the state of New York, who have established a reading room long ago, much to their credit be it said. It is a new era in the affairs of our state (transacted by men of colour) and consequently must meet with those trials and difficulties which commonly attend the origin of new institutions.

I make no doubt but at this moment there may be many objections made by some of you. It may be said that it has not had its origin amongst the most noble, the most opulent, or literate. To this I will agree, for had they used their talents, and influence, this might have been accomplished long ago. In establishing this institution, for the avowed purpose of spreading useful knowledge, we do not expect to escape the shafts of calumny and opposition.

Indeed we would rather count than shun the contest, as the very sparks which may be elicited by the clashing of our weapons will in some measure tend to dissipate the surrounding darkness, and thus facilitate the progress of those who are in search of the reality of our sentiments.

Another objection—That to acquire the necessities of life, men's occupations will deprive them of the liberty of spending a few hours in a week to the improvement of their minds. To them I will answer—What occupation is within the boundary of our city that some of those who have been engaged in have not been seen once, twice, or three times a week, spending their time and money within the walls of a public house, when they might have been better employed? And it is bold in me to assert that some of our most classic young men spend much of their time in public houses. Yes; men capable of doing justice to the subject I am rather abusing, and displaying themselves, and developing their profound talents, over the full-flowing bowl; and it is a fact that the most important literature amongst us is discussed in these evening conventions. This may be for want of a public institution. I cannot say but I fear, that the cup of intemperance will overtake many, do they not resist those baneful attractions.

I do not expect that any thing I have said, or will say, will have any tendency to bring about a new state of affairs. If I have digressed too far, I hope my sentiments will meet with a public refutation, that this force of truth may be the result. I have said no more than is said by almost every reflecting man on the same occasion. The only difference is that their channel of communication is private, while mine is public.

It would not have been my intention here to have aimed the blow at the learned; to all classes of citizens it is equally productive of the same ill consequences. But as the world in general are taught to expect something of the highest order from minds richly furnished with education, our respect and social happiness depend much on their conduct and outward performances.

The station of a scholar highly versed in classic lore (with the exception of a Christian preacher) is indeed higher than any other occupied by man. The purity of principle and integrity of life required to fill its several stations as it should be filled, the weighty and important duties it imposes and the magnitude of objects which must ever be in view, entitles it to this superiority. It is their particular province to instruct the unenlightened, to comfort the disconsolate, and to awaken hope in the breasts of the despondents; to convince the faithless, to check those who are rushing onward to ruin, to suppress the ebullition of lawless passion, and to invigorate reason, to put the blasphemer to shame, and in fact every duty that is characteristic in the history of civilized man, should shine conspicuously in them. It is required of them that their lives be pure as the precepts they inculcate, and that humility, self-denial, and every other virtue should ever remain as brilliant stars in their characters. Their situation is one of danger, as well as of difficulty. The ignorant and depraved by whom they are surrounded, and whose eyes are intently fixed on their steps, are ever busy with their fame, seeking with malicious industry to find something in their lives injurious to their profession, and to cast a reproach upon literature.

By such the smallest error of their judgments will be magnified into a wilful perversion of truth; and the most trifling deviation from the path of moral rectitude, into a grossly criminal violation of virtue. Their zeal will be called bigotry—their liberality want of devotion—their firmness obstinacy—and their independence and ambition thirst for power.

In order that we may become acquainted with the transacting of public affairs, it requires our strictest attention to study, or the young and rising generation that are receiving the advantages of a liberal education will look back on the present state of Science amongst us, and will speak of our times as the day of small things, in stronger and juster language than any in which we can depict the poverty of science in the days of our fathers, when they were bound by the galling chains of slavery, and the lights of knowledge not permitted to enter their beclouded minds.

The post rings incessantly in our ears of the progress of education amongst all classes; Sir Franceis [sic] Burdett cries up the march of mind; Mr. Brougham tells us the Schoolmaster is abroad; Mr. Peel boasts of the improvement of the age, and while all these have been going on it is time for us to be up and a-doing.

Perhaps I have said too much about [the] necessity of obtaining a liberal education, and not enough about its advantages when attained. It is here my design to make a few remarks. I do not mean however to detain you with trite remarks on this subject, but shall feebly offer you my views respecting a learned education.

1st. The first object of education is to exercise, and by exercising to improve the faculties of the mind. Every faculty we possess is improveable by exercise. This is a law of nature. The acquisition of knowledge is not the only design of a liberal education; its primary design is to discipline the mind itself, to strengthen and enlarge its powers, to form habits of close and accurate thinking, and to acquire a facility of classifying and arranging, analyzing and comparing our ideas on different subjects. Without this preparatory exercise, our ideas will be superficial and obscure, and all the knowledge we acquire will be but a confused mass thrown together without arrangement, and incapable of useful application.

For this purpose, the course of study pursued in most of the Seminaries is well adapted. The study of the languages under the directions of a careful instructor is admirably calculated to call forth the energies of the youthful minds, to fix the attention, to strengthen the memory, and to form habits of analyzing, comparing, abstracting, and correct reasoning.

The advantage of which we are speaking, is that which distinguishes the real scholar no less than the extent of his knowledge, and so great is it that if there were no other advantage to be derived from a liberal education, this alone would compensate for all the time and labour employed in acquiring it. But this is not all the diligent student in the mean time acquires.

2nd. Another important object of education, viz: Useful knowledge. In studying the dead languages, the student acquires a knowledge of the principles of grammar, the philosophy of language, and becomes more thoroughly acquainted with his own. The authors which are studied are valuable on their own account, and the students, by going to the fountains themselves, attain advantages not to be derived from translation. A fund of ideas is acquired on a variety of subjects; the taste is greatly improved by conversing with the best models; the imagination is enriched by the fine scenery with which the classics abound; and an acquaintance is formed with human nature, together with the history, customs and manners of antiquity. Without some knowledge of the ancient classics it is impossible to see the beauty and understand many of the illusions of our best English writers, who imbibed the spirit and were formed on the model of the ancients. In addition to all this we may add the advantage of being able to read the sacred oracles of God in the languages in which they were originally written.

***

We will here conclude our remarks on this part of our subject, and I shall feebly attempt to exhibit to you, that notwithstanding the regular mode and system of instruction, we every day view a different mode of application; we see one man a divine, another a lawyer, another a physician, &c. These are professions which are necessary to be filled, while among the most learned and enlightened statesmen that our country can boast of, we see them advocating a cause that they and their fathers groaned under a little more than half a century ago, and burst the bands of colonial bondage, and that is slavery. The wise and patriotic legislature of South Carolina, at their last convention, assembled for the purpose of discussing such questions as would be most conducive to the welfare of state, the benefit of their constituents; and to raise themselves into responsibility, passed a law that under the penalty of fine and disgraceful stripes,[4] any white or black teaching a man of colour how to read or write. Amongst these dreadful catalogues of wrongs, we find the name of Col. D. of South Carolina (whose name shall shine bright in the history of infamy) is such a lover of his country, and the cause of injured humanity, that he has preferred to see this country drenched in blood—yea, even to a dissolution of the union, rather than see slavery banished from its soil. The Hon. J.R. of Virginia has declared that no man east of the Potomac has any right to meddle with the cause of slavery. Such philanthropists as these we cannot find in the wide extended range of creation; no, it's impossible to find its parallel; superstition and Gothic darkness would have startled at measures like these, as too base and wretched even for their gloomy policy.

And yet these avowed advocates of slavery, would wish to be classed amongst the religious, the moral, and the honest, &c, but I deny them the privilege, for there is not a slaveholder under the canopy of heaven possesses one of these titles, or else I am mistaken in the articles of justice. Where is the slaveholder who professes to love his God that has not a lie in his mouth when he says that he does unto others as he would that they should do unto him. Or in point of morality, can he say that he treats his slaves and their posterity in the same way that he would wish them to treat him and his posterity? And until there is a law enacted that will not correct the holder of stolen goods, as well as the thief, the slaveholder cannot be an honest man. Yet the dishonest slaveholders bear the name of honest upright men—men in whom the affairs of state are at pledge. Yes, and I am sorry to say, that the seat of our national government contains a majority of these misanthropes, who every day are heard exclaiming against oppressions in their conventions, and developing the same to an enlightened community on paper. We see them rejoicing in the convention of '76, that ever-memorable epoch in the annals of the nation, when their fathers declared themselves free from British tyranny— when they threw off the yoke of colonial oppression, in words as strong as it is in the power of language to express, which was "to live free or die."

Yet these wise men, who hate the very idea, form, and name of slavery as respects themselves, are holding and dooming an innocent posterity (connected to themselves in all the sublime qualities of man, differing only in the colour of their skin, which is the natural production of a tropical climate) to slavery in their own country—on their own farms—and at their own firesides, in a bondage ten times as severe as the one already mentioned, that their fathers denounced as being too ignominious to be borne by man. Yes, a race of beings only doomed to be inhabitants of this soil, by the injustice and dishonesty of their fathers who purloined our ancestors from their own country. Oh! horrible spectacle! Oh! for an asylum to hide the knowledge of such barbarity and injustice.

May the letter and spirit of the constitution of the United States stare them in their faces—May the unalienable rights of man stand as a mirror for them to view their words, until they are ashamed of their deeds; and if not, they may see their children rise up and set the example for their fathers to look upon, ere the cold messenger of death shall summon them before a just God, where master and slave will be equal, and each judged according to their deeds. May they move on the cause of emancipation, ere the spirits of just men, such as the venerable Franklin, and immortal Rush, rise up and warn them of their awful judgement.

***

If climate and natural scenery have a powerful effect in forming the intellectual character of a nation, surely we have much to hope from them, and much to encourage us to action, while the literary spirit of our country is still awake. A day or in an hour may sweep away a throne, but years must elapse ere any sensible change be produced on literature. It is a cause we all ought to be deeply engaged in; it is the pillars of this empire, and the basis on which the whole superstructure of our liberty and happiness depends.

It is the hope of benefitting our condition, that has encouraged us to commence the present undertaking. It is not a spirit of rivalry or competition that has brought this institution before the public. We occupy a field till now unappropriated, and which has hitherto been regarded too limited to justify such an attempt. It is an humble hope of contributing something to the advancement of science generally amongst our brethren, as well as of elevating its character in this City, that has called us to the enterprise. And, if it should be our fortune to lay the foundation only, of an institution which shall hereafter become commensurate with the demands of this great metropolis, and the improvement of science through the country, we shall feel that we have done an honour to the undertaking, and discharged a duty that we owe to our fellow citizens. And who knows but it may be reserved to this institution to make some discovery in philosophy which shall commence a new era in science, or furnish the world with something of magnificent worth, which now eludes the power of the universe. Who can say that it is not reserved for some member of this institution to be the happy discoverer of the solvents of the stone? Who knows but some bold and fortunate genius, who shall have his zeal first kindled in this institution, may be destined, while climbing up the rocky mountains, or exploring the vale of the Mississippi, to discover a plant or a mineral which shall prove a cure for hydrophobia, or a remedy for consumption? or find out on the shaking prairie of Louisiana, or at the mouth of the Mobile, the true nature of miasmata[5] and its operations on the human body?

Who knows but this institution may be destined to produce a Wilberforce, a Jay, or a Clarkson,[6] or give to the world a Franklin, a Rush, or a Wistar?[7] Who knows but talent (who knows no man by the colour of his skin) may not bestow her treasures on some one of our brethren (who may yet belong to this institution), that from this noble seat of wisdom, he shall adorn the brows of this great empire?

My friends, you carry with you my best wishes for your welfare; may your earthly comforts remain unsullied; and when done with time, may you be admitted to still higher posts in heaven.

NOTES

1. Bell, "American Moral Reform Society," 34.

2. Otter, *Philadelphia Stories*, 108–10.

3. Otter, *Philadelphia Stories*, 113–17.

4. Stripes: marks from whippings.

5. Miasmata: an obsolete medical theory that certain diseases such as cholera or the Black Death were caused by miasma, or noxious air, caused by rotting organic matter.

6. Thomas Clarkson (1760–1846) was a leading British abolitionist.

7. Wistar: probably Caspar Wistar (1761–1818), but it could also be other members of the prominent Philadelphian family, including Caspar's brother (John anglicized the name by using "e" instead of the English "a"), or Thomas Wister, an advocate for abolition and prison reform.

BIBLIOGRAPHY

Bacon, Jacqueline, and Glen McClish. "Reinventing the Master's Tools: Nineteenth-Century African-American Literary Societies of Philadelphia and Rhetorical Education." *Rhetoric Society Quarterly* 30, no. 4 (Autumn 2000): 19–47.

Bell, Howard H. "The American Moral Reform Society, 1836–1841." *Journal of Negro Education* 27, no. 1 (Winter 1958): 34–40.

Foner, Philip Sheldon. *History of Black Americans, From the Emergence of the Cotton Kingdom to the Eve of the* Compromise of 1850. Westport, CT: Greenwood, 1983.

McCormick, Richard P. "William Whipper: Moral Reformer." *Pennsylvania History: A Journal of Mid-Atlantic Studies* 43, no. 3 (1976): 23–46.

Otter, Samuel. *Philadelphia Stories: America's Literature of Race and Freedom*. Oxford: Oxford University Press, 2010.

Pease, Jane H., and William H. Pease. "Negro Conventions and the Problem of Black Leadership." *Journal of Black Studies* 2, no. 1 (September 1971): 29–44.

Richard Allen, from *The Life, Experience, and Gospel Labours of the Rt. Rev. Richard Allen. To Which Is Annexed the Rise and Progress of the African Methodist Episcopal Church in the United States of America. Containing a Narrative of the Yellow Fever in the Year of Our Lord 1793: With an Address to the People of Colour in the United States* (1833)

Allen's autobiography, *The Life, Experience, and Gospel Labours*, was published posthumously in 1833. Two of the most important segments from his narrative are included in this anthology. The first one describes the incident that pushed Allen and Jones to break away from St. George's Church. The African American parishioners were told they had to remove themselves from their usual place to pray and to move to a separate section of the church. Rather than suffer such indignation, the Black church members decided to start their own institution, the African Methodist Episcopal Church, and collected money to buy a lot for building, which would become Mother Bethel. The other section, written by Richard Allen and Absalom Jones, describes the heroic role played by Blacks during the yellow fever epidemic of 1793 and has been provided earlier in this anthology.

A number of us usually attended St. George's Church in Fourth street, and when the coloured people began to get numerous in attending the church, they moved us from the seats we usually sat on, and placed us around the wall, and on Sabbath morning we went to church and the sexton stood at the door, and told us to go in the gallery. He told us to go, and we would see where to sit. We expected to take the seats over the ones we formerly occupied below, not knowing any better. We took those seats. Meeting had begun, and they were nearly done singing, and just as we got to the seats, the elder said, "let us pray." We had not been long upon our knees before I heard considerable scuffling and low talking. I raised my head up and saw one of the trustees, H—M—, having hold of the Rev. Absalom Jones, pulling him up off of his knees, and saying, "You must get up—you must not kneel here." Mr. Jones replied, "wait until prayer is over." Mr. H—M—said, "no, you must get up now, or I will call for aid and force you away." Mr. Jones said, "wait until prayer is over, and I will get up and trouble you no more." With that he beckoned to one of the other trustees, Mr. L—S—to come to his assistance. He came, and went to William White to pull him up. By this time prayer was over, and we all went out of the church in a body, and they were no more plagued with us in the church. This raised a great excitement and inquiry among the citizens, in so much that I believe they were ashamed of their conduct. But my dear Lord was with us, and we were filled with fresh vigour to get a house erected to worship God in. Seeing our forlorn and distressed situation, many of the hearts of our citizens were moved to urge us forward; notwithstanding we had subscribed largely towards finishing St. George's Church, in building the gallery and laying new floors, and just as the house was made comfortable, we were turned out from enjoying the comforts of worshiping therein. We then hired a store room, and held worship by ourselves. Here we were pursued with threats of being disowned, and read publicly out of meeting if we did continue to worship in the place we had hired; but we believed the Lord would be our friend. We got subscription papers out to raise money to build the house of the Lord. By this time we had waited on Dr. Rush and Mr. Robert Ralston,[1] and told them of our distressing situation. We considered it a blessing that the Lord had put it into our hearts to wait upon those gentlemen. They pitied our situation, and subscribed largely towards the church, and were very friendly towards us, and advised us how to go on. We appointed Mr. Ralston our treasurer. Dr. Rush did much for us in public by his influence. I hope the name of Dr. Benjamin Rush and Mr. Robert Ralston will never be forgotten among us. They were the two first gentlemen who espoused the cause of the oppressed, and aided us in building the house of the Lord for the poor Africans to worship in. Here was the beginning and rise of the first African church in America. But the elder of the Methodist church still pursued us. Mr. J—M—called upon us and told us if we did not erase our names from the subscription paper, and give up the paper, we would be publicly turned out of meeting. We asked him if we had violated any rules of discipline by so doing. He replied, "I have the charge given to me by the Conference, and unless you submit I will read you publicly out of meeting." We told him we were willing to abide by the discipline of the Methodist church, "and if you will show us where we have violated any law of discipline of the Methodist church, we will submit; and if there is no rule violated in the discipline, we will proceed on." He replied, "we will read you all out." We told him if he turned us out contrary to rule of discipline, we should seek further redress. We told him we were dragged off of our knees in St. George's Church, and treated worse than heathens; and we were determined to seek out for ourselves, the Lord being our helper. He told us we were not Methodists, and left us. Finding we would go on in raising money to build the church, he called upon us again, and wished to see us all together. We met him. He told us that he wished us well, and that he was a friend to us, and used many arguments to convince us that we were wrong in building a church. We told him we had no place to worship; and we did not mean to go to St. George's Church any more, as we were so scandalously treated in the presence of all the congregation present; "and if you deny us your name, you cannot seal up the scriptures from us, and deny us a name in heaven. We believe heaven is free for all who worship in spirit and truth." And he said, "so you are determined to go on." We told him—"yes, God being our helper." He then replied, "we will disown you all from the Methodist connexion." We believed if we put our trust in the Lord, he would stand by us. This was a trial that I never had to pass through before. I was confident that the great head of the church would support us. My dear Lord was with us. We went out with our subscription paper, and met with great success. We had no reason to complain of the liberality of the citizens. The first day the Rev. Absalom Jones and myself went out we collected three hundred and sixty dollars. This was the greatest day's collection that we met with. We appointed a committee to look out for a lot—the Rev. Absalom Jones, William Gray, William Wilcher, and myself. We pitched upon a lot at the corner of Lombard and Sixth streets. They authorized me to go and agree for it. I did accordingly. The lot belonged to Mr. Mark Wilcox. We entered into articles of agreement for the lot. Afterwards the committee found a lot in Fifth street, in a more commodious part of the city, which we bought; and the first lot they threw upon my hands, and wished me to give it up. I told them they had authorized me to agree for the lot, and they were all well satisfied with the arrangement I had made, and I thought it was hard that they should throw it upon my hands. I told them I would sooner keep it myself than to forfeit the arrangement I had made. And so I did.

NOTE

1. Robert Ralston: a Philadelphia philanthropist and merchant who made a fortune working with the East India Company. He lived from 1761 to 1836.

BIBLIOGRAPHY

Allen, Richard. *The Life, Experience, and Gospel Labours*. Philadelphia: Martin & Boden, 1833. Documenting the American South. https://docsouth.unc.edu/neh/allen/allen.html.

George, Carol V. R. *Segregated Sabbaths: Richard Allen and the Emergence of Independent Black Churches, 1760–1840*. Oxford: Oxford University Press, 1973.

Nash, Gary B. *Forging Freedom: The Formation of Philadelphia's Black Community, 1720–1840*. Cambridge: Harvard University Press, 1988.

Newman, Richard S. *Freedom's Prophet: Bishop Richard Allen, the AME Church, and the Black Founding Fathers*. New York: New York University Press, 2008.

Otter, Samuel. *Philadelphia Stories: America's Literature of Race and Freedom*. Oxford: Oxford University Press, 2010.

Wesley, Charles H. *Richard Allen, Apostle of Freedom*. 2nd ed. Washington, DC: Associated Publishers, 1969.

Robert Purvis, from *Appeal of Forty Thousand Citizens, Threatened with Disfranchisement, to the People of Pennsylvania* (1838)

Robert Purvis was a free-born Black of mixed race born in Charleston, South Carolina, in 1810. He spent most of his life in Philadelphia, where he helped found the American Anti-Slavery Society and the Library Company of Colored People. He also served as president of the biracial Pennsylvania Anti-Slavery Society between 1845 and 1850. He married Harriet Davy Forten, daughter of the prominent Black Philadelphia leader James Forten in 1832. Purvis worked for the Underground Railroad, and he estimated he helped some nine thousand enslaved people gain freedom by hiding them on his Byberry Hall estate, which is still standing on 3003 Byberry Road in Northeast Philadelphia. Purvis died in 1898.

Purvis wrote *Appeal of Forty Thousand Citizens, Threatened with Disfranchisement, to the People of Pennsylvania* in the *Colored American Magazine* (1838) in response to the decision of the Pennsylvania "Reform Convention" to disfranchise African Americans after some Whites had become resentful of perceived Black wealth. As Eric Ledell Smith points out, "The reputation of Philadelphia's African Americans gave rise to the erroneous perception that they were better off than they really were."[1] Purvis's fears about disfranchisement were first aroused by the insertion of the word "white" prior to "freemen" as a qualification for voting. Purvis's *Appeal* countered White stereotypes by pointing out the many contributions Blacks had made to the economic health, culture, and general well-being of Philadelphia. Despite Purvis's meticulous statistical analysis, the vote on Black disfranchisement was ratified by 113,971 to 112,759—on October 9, 1838.

FELLOW CITIZENS:—We appeal to you from the decision of the "Reform Convention," which has stripped us of a right peaceably enjoyed during forty-seven years under the Constitution of this commonwealth. We honor Pennsylvania and her noble institutions too much to part with our birthright, as her free citizens, without a struggle. To all her citizens the right of suffrage is valuable in proportion as she is free; but surely there are none who can so ill afford to spare it as ourselves.

Was it the intention of the people of this commonwealth that the Convention to which the Constitution was committed for revision and amendment, should tear up and cast away its first principles? Was it made the business of the Convention to deny "that all men are born equally free," by making political rights depend upon the skin in which a man is born? Or to divide what our fathers bled to unite, to wit, TAXATION and REPRESENTATION? We will not allow ourselves for one moment to suppose, that the majority of the people of Pennsylvania are not too respectful of the rights and too liberal towards the feelings of others, as well as too much enlightened to their own interests, to deprive of the right of suffrage a single individual who may safely be trusted with it. And we cannot believe that you have found among those who bear the burdens of taxation any who have proved, by their abuse of the right, that it is not safe in their hands. This is a question, fellow citizens, in which we plead *your* cause as well as our own. It is the safeguard of the strongest that he lives under a government which is obliged to respect the voice of the weakest. When you have taken from an individual his right to vote, you have made the government, in regard to him, a mere despotism; and you have taken a step towards making it a despotism for all.—To your women and children, their inability to vote at the polls may be no evil, because they are united by consanguinity and affection with those who can do it. To foreigners and paupers the want of the right may be tolerable, because a little time or labor will make it theirs. They are candidates for the privilege, and hence substantially enjoy its benefits. But when a distinct class of the community, already sufficiently the objects of prejudice are wholly, and for ever, disfranchised and excluded, to the remotest posterity, from the possibility of a voice in regard to the laws under which they are to live—it is the same thing as if their abode were transferred to the dominions of the Russian autocrat, or the Grand Turk. They have lost their check upon oppression, their wherewith to buy friends, their panoply of manhood; in short, they are thrown upon the mercy of a despotic majority, Like every other despot, this despot majority, will believe in the mildness of its sway; but who will the more willingly submit to it for that?

To us our right under the Constitution has been more precious, and our deprivation of it will be the more grievous, because our expatriation has come to be a darling project with many of our fellow citizens. Our abhorrence of a scheme which comes to us in the guise of Christian benevolence, and asks us to suffer ourselves to be transplanted to a distant and barbarous land,[2] *because we are a "nuisance" in this*, is not more deep and thorough than it is reasonable. We love our native country, much as it has wronged us; and in the peaceable exercise of our inalienable rights, we will cling to it. The immortal

Franklin, and his fellow laborers in the cause of humanity, have bound us to our homes here with chains of gratitude. We are PENNSYLVANIANS, and we hope to see the day when Pennsylvania will have reason to be proud of us, as we believe she has none to be ashamed! Will you starve our patriotism? Will you cast our hearts out of the treasury of the commonwealth? Do you count our enmity better than our friendship?

***

Are we to be disfranchised, lest the purity of the *white* blood should be sullied by an intermixture with ours? It seems to us that our white brethren might well enough reserve their fear, till we seek alliance with them. We ask no social favors. We would not willingly darken the doors of those to whom the complexion and features, which our Maker has given us, are disagreeable. The territories of the commonwealth are sufficiently ample to afford us a home without doing violence to the delicate nerves of our white brethren, for centuries to come. Besides, we are not intruders here, nor were our ancestors. Surely you sought to bear us as unrepiningly the evil consequences of your fathers' guilt, as we those of our fathers' misfortunes. Proscription and disfranchisement are the last things in the world to alleviate these evil consequences. Nothing, as shameful experience has already proved, can so powerfully promote the evil which you profess to deprecate, as the degradation of our race by the oppressive rule of yours. Give us that fair and honorable ground which self-respect requires to stand on, and the dreaded amalgamation, if it take place at all, shall be by your own fault, as indeed it always has been. We dare not give full vent to the indignation we feel on this point, but we will not attempt wholly to conceal it.

We ask a voice in the disposition of those public resources which we ourselves have helped to earn; we claim a right to be heard, according to our numbers, in regard to all those great public measures which involve our lives and fortunes, as well as those of our fellow citizens; we assert our right to vote at the polls as a shield against that strange species of benevolence which seeks legislative aid to banish us—and we are told that our white fellow citizens cannot submit to an *intermixture of the races!* Then let the indentures, title-deeds, contracts, notes of hand, and all other evidences of bargain, in which colored men have been treated as *men*, be torn and scattered on the winds. Consistency is a jewel. Let no white man hereafter ask his colored neighbor's *consent* when he wants his property or his labor, lest he should endanger the Anglo-Saxon purity of his descendants! Why should not the same principle hold good between neighbor and neighbor, which is deemed necessary, as a fundamental principle, in the Constitution itself? Why should you be ashamed to act in private business, as the Reform Convention would have you act in the capacity of a commonwealth? But, no! we do not believe our fellow citizens, while with good faith they hold ourselves bound by their constraints with us, and while they feel bound to deal with us only by fair contract, will ratify the arbitrary principle of the Convention, howmuchsoever they may prefer the complexion in which their Maker has pleased to clothe themselves.

We would not misrepresent the motives of the Convention, but we are constrained to believe that they have laid our rights a sacrifice on the altar of slavery. We do not believe our disfranchisement would have been proposed, but for the desire which is felt by political aspirants to gain the favor of the slaveholding States. This is not the first time that northern statesmen have "bowed the knee to the dark spirit of slavery," but it is the first time that they have bowed so low! Is Pennsylvania, which abolished slavery in 1780, and enfranchised her tax-paying colored citizens in 1790, now in 1838, to get upon her knees and repent of her humanity, to gratify those who disgrace the very name of American Liberty, by holding our brethren as goods and chattels? We freely acknowledge our brotherhood to the slave, and our interest in his welfare. Is this a crime for which we should be ignominiously punished? The very fact that we are deeply interested for our kindred in bonds, shows that we are the right sort of stuff to make good citizens of. Were we not so, we should better deserve a lodging in your penitentiaries than a franchise at your polls.

***

We take our stand upon that solemn declaration, that to protect inalienable rights "governments are instituted among men, deriving their JUST POWERS from the CONSENT of the governed," and proclaim that a government which tears away from us and our posterity the very power of CONSENT, is a tyrannical usurpation which we will never cease to oppose. We have seen with amazement and grief the apathy of white Pennsylvanians while the "Reform Convention" has been perpetrating this outrage upon the good old principles of Pennsylvania freedom. But however others may forsake these principles, we promise to maintain them on *Pennsylvania soil*, to the last man. If this disfranchisement is designed to uproot us, it shall fail. Pennsylvania's fields, valleys, mountains, and rivers; her canals, railroads, forests, and mines; her domestic altars, and her public, religious and benevolent institutions; her

Penn and Franklin, her Rush, Rawle,[3] Wistar, and Vaux;[4] her consecrated past and her brilliant future, are as dear to us as they can be to you. Firm upon our Pennsylvania BILL OF RIGHTS, and trusting in a God of Truth and Justice, we lay our claim before you, with the warning that no amendments of the present Constitution can compensate for the loss of its foundation principle of equal rights, nor for the conversion into enemies of 40,000 friends.
In behalf of the Committee,

ROBERT PURVIS, *Chairman*

NOTES

1. Smith, "End of Black Voting Rights," 283.
2. Barbarous land: Liberia.
3. William Rawle (1759–1836) was an American lawyer. He was an abolitionist and the first president of the Pennsylvania Abolition Society.
4. Roberts Vaux (1786–1836) was an American lawyer, jurist, abolitionist, and philanthropist.

BIBLIOGRAPHY

Bacon, Margaret Hope. *But One Race: The Life of Robert Purvis*. Albany: SUNY Press, 2007.

Newman, Richard, Patrick Rael, and Phillip Lapsansky, eds. *Pamphlets of Protest: An Anthology of Early African American Protest Literature 1790–1860*. New York: Routledge, 2001.

Otter, Samuel. *Philadelphia Stories: America's Literature of Race and Freedom*. Oxford: Oxford University Press, 2010.

Price, Edward. "The Black Voting Rights Issue in Pennsylvania, 1780–1900." *Pennsylvania Magazine of History and Biography* 100, no. 3 (July 1976): 356–73.

Reader, David. "Appeal of 40,000 Citizens." *Greater Philadelphia Encyclopedia*. https://philadelphiaencyclopedia.org/essays/appeal-of-forty-thousand-citizens.

Smith, Eric Ledell. "The End of Black Voting Rights in Pennsylvania: African Americans and the Pennsylvania Constitutional Convention of 1837–1838." *Pennsylvania History: A Journal of Mid-Atlantic Studies* 65, no. 3 (Summer 1988): 279–99.

Winch, Julie. *Philadelphia's Black Elite: Activism, Accommodation, and the Struggle for Autonomy, 1787–1848*. Philadelphia: Temple University Press, 1998.

Joseph Willson, from *Sketches of the Higher Classes of Colored Society in Philadelphia* (1841)

The author of *Sketches of the Higher Classes of Colored Society in Philadelphia* was simply given as "A Southerner" when it first appeared. The real author, Joseph Willson, was indeed born in the South and described himself as an outsider to Philadelphia; however, he and his family moved north in the decades before the Civil War. Willson was about sixteen when he arrived in Philadelphia in 1833, from Augusta, Georgia, so by the time he wrote *Sketches* in 1841, he had lived in the city long enough to make some pointed observations about its Black inhabitants. Willson lived in what is now the neighborhood of Spring Garden. Joseph and his family lived there for fifteen years, one of the few Black families in the area at the time.[1]

There may not have been many Black inhabitants in Willson's neighborhood, but there were plenty at the time in Philadelphia and the larger Philadelphia County, some 14,500, "one of the largest concentrations of African Americans anywhere in the United States."[2] While the African Americans Willson met growing up in Georgia were largely enslaved, he quickly realized that those living in Philadelphia were a diverse group. The majority were poor, but others, such as Robert Purvis and James Forten, were people of considerable wealth. Most of the people in what Willson considered the higher class were solidly middle class, the main qualification being that they were homeowners,[3] working as ship caulkers, milliners, builders, shoemakers, furniture makers, caterers, ministers—all occupations that required a certain amount of skill. Still, Willson's higher class made up no more than 5 percent of the city's Black population.[4]

By the mid-1830s, Philadelphia's Black community was suffering from racial oppression. There were several riots, as portrayed, for example, in Frank Webb's novel *The Garies and Their Friends*, and Blacks were eventually disfranchised in 1838 as lamented by Robert Purvis in his *Appeal*. Willson tried to counter White stereotypes of African Americans as being of one large mass, mostly living in squalor. As he says in the preface to *Sketches*, his two goals were "first, to remove some of the unfounded prejudice from without; and secondly, to correct certain abuses which are known to exist among themselves." He maintained that the poor behavior of some Blacks in the higher classes, particularly their immorality and in-fighting, contributed to their negative image.

Though Willson may have considered himself an outsider, he was fairly well off, and part of the better class of which he writes. He stayed in the Philadelphia vicinity until 1854, moving to Moyamensing Township, adjacent to the Cedar (South) Street areas after his mother's death in 1847.[5] Then he moved to Cleveland before finally migrating to Indianapolis, where he died in 1895.

Julie Winch provides a full text of the essay with an excellent introduction and notes.

—

FROM CHAPTER 1

Taking the whole body of the colored population in the city of Philadelphia, they present in a gradual, moderate, and limited ratio, almost every grade of character, wealth, and—I think it not too much to add—of education. They are to be seen in ease, comfort and the enjoyment of all the social blessings of this life; and, in contrast with this, they are to be found in the lowest depths of human degradation, misery, and want. They are also presented in the intermediate stages—sober, honest, industrious and respectable—claiming "neither poverty nor riches,"[6] yet maintaining, by their pursuits, their families in comparative ease and comfort, oppressed neither by the cares of the rich, nor assailed by the deprivation and suffering of the indigent. The same in these respects that may be said of any other class of people, may, with the utmost regard to truth, be said of them.

They have their churches, school-houses, institutions of benevolence, and others for the promotion of literature; and if I cannot include scientific pursuits, it is because the avenues leading to and upholding these, have been closed against them. There are likewise among them, those who are successfully pursuing various branches of the mechanic arts: tradesmen and dealers of various descriptions, artists, clergymen, and other professional gentlemen; and, last of all, though not the least, men of fortune and gentlemen of leisure.

Their churches embrace nearly all the Christian denominations, excepting the papal, and those which may be considered *doubtful*, as I am not aware that there is any Universalists' society among them. Whether this arises from a determination to keep on the sure side here, and enjoy the benefit of others' doubts, if realized, hereafter, it has never occurred to me, till now, to inquire! The Methodists are by far the most numerous, and next to these, in numerical order, may be named the Presbyterians, Baptists and Episcopalians. There is in existence, I believe, a Unitarian society; but their house of worship, for the want of competent support, has, for some time past, been relinquished.

Mutual Relief Societies are numerous. There are a larger number of these than of any other description, in the colored community. They are generally well sustained, to the great advantage of those who compose them. There are also one or more others, strictly devoted to objects of outdoors benevolence. The last mentioned are chiefly composed of females.

I pass by here the several literary associations, proposing to make them a distinct subject in another place.

In addition to the public, or common schools supported by the commonwealth—for the continuance, and prosperity of which, much interest and solicitude has of late been manifested—there are also three or four private schools, male and female, conducted by colored teachers. The great facilities afforded by the first mentioned of these, has had the effect greatly to decrease the numbers in the private schools; nevertheless, the latter class still present a favorable condition—particularly the female—from the superior excellence of their government, and attention to the general deportment of the pupils.

FROM CHAPTER III

The higher classes of colored society in Philadelphia, are amenable to a liberal share of animadversion, on account of the numerous divisions which exist among them. However they may appear to the eye of the casual observer to be resolved into one unbroken link, yet, he who is acquainted with their social relations, well knows that this seeming unity is quite contrary to the actual existence, and true state of things, in this respect. There are numerous distinct social circles, even among those equally respectable and of equal merit and pretensions, every way; and if these were confined within proper and legitimate limits—as each has the undoubted right to choose his or her private friends—there is certainly nothing in the fact to excite surprise or call forth censure. But they are not thus confined. They are carried into most of the relations of life, and in some cases are kept up with the most bitter and relentless rancor—arising, however, in such extreme cases, from ancient feuds or personal disagreements, which have descended perhaps from father to son, and so been perpetuated! I do not intend to represent, that there is always an open hostility kept up; it may appear dormant for the while, but favored by the time and the occasion and often when the occasion would seem loudly to forbid, it seldom fails to develope [sic] its existence. It is the personification of true revenge,

> "—patient as the watchful alchymist,
> Sagacious as the blood-hound on the scent,
> Secret as death."

Secret—until the opportunity offers of making its victims feel its presence. But where those personal dislikes or hates do not exist—when the social springs solely from the exercise of the unquestionable right, to choose one's private associations and companions—the case is widely different; and in all other relations, they meet each other on terms of apparent amity and good will.

The separations, however, in all cases, are seen to produce rivalry between the different circles; and in settling the claim to precedence and superiority, the character and reputation of one or the other of the parties, is almost sure to suffer, that being the first thing aimed at. An effort of this description, when set on foot, involves the basest of means for carrying it forward, and frequently nothing is left undone that malignant mischief can invent, for destroying the peace, happiness, and success of any one party or individual, who or which may become obnoxious to another.

The chief causes which lead to divisions of the society of the colored classes, are, in turn, the very result of these divisions. They are not to be found in any real pride of self-conceited superiority, for they well know that any pretension of this kind, founded otherwise than in personal good qualities, would never avail them aught beyond their own immediate pale, and among those who know them, would be laughed to scorn. They lie deeper or nearer the surface, as the reader pleases. There is an unhappy disposition, untiring and ever constant, to detract the one from the merits of the other; and if possible to thwart every plan or scheme, by which a few may be benefitted, unless it is made more than obvious, that all may equally partake of such benefit. The motto is changed from "live, and let live," to "let *me* live *first*, and you afterwards." This reprehensible disposition, it may be truly said, is carried into nearly all the relations of life. The more determined in its practice, will disregard every honorable consideration, whenever they set themselves about to arrest the career of some one of their acquaintances who may appear to be more successful in some particular department than themselves. Instead of following the example of their more industrious neighbors—of letting the good fortune of these furnish a motive to their own laudable exertions— their first efforts are directed to discredit and to destroy. Thus, because they either will not, nor cannot move themselves, they need stand ready to grasp, and to hold back, all those who would advance. In this way many lose more time—waste more anxiety—than would be required to make them all they could reasonably wish to be. And what are the means of success, usually resorted to in such cases? Falsehood the most vile, slander, the most opprobrious, hypocrisy, violated faith, social traitorism,—these, with their sub-divisions and concomitants, furnish the chief weapons for keeping up the odious strife.

The influence of such a course of conduct upon those who are subject to its operation, is easily perceptible. Suspicion and distrust very naturally usurp the place of confidence—without mutual reliance the one upon the integrity of the other, no circle of society can long exist together in unbroken harmony. Division after division, must necessarily be the consequence, upon the discovery of each new conspiracy, by any aggrieved party; for surely no person of common sense, would a second time repose full confidence in those who, without provocation, had, by the use of the basest of means, shown themselves so eminently unworthy of it. And such discoveries, unfortunately, are too frequently made—quite too frequent, for the general good and improvement of colored society!

Those who are always the greatest sufferers from the shafts of envy and malice, aimed at their destruction, are those young ladies who are so *unfortunate*—so it may be regarded in many instances!—as to become objects of jealousy to their associates. Be the cause of offence real or imagined, and never so trifling—and though the newly appointed victim may have had no direct agency in producing it—still it makes no difference with her inexorable persecutors. The late, perhaps, bosom friend, is now an object of aversion in the circle of her sex in which lately she moved and appeared to be esteemed, and must fare according to the usage which, with them, in such cases governs. This not being the kindest or most sisterly, is not always to be coveted!

This insecurity in the conduct of the young ladies toward each other, is remarkable in various other ways, and to an extent almost incredible. If a young man makes his appearance in society, whose position and prospects render him worthy of being sought for as a prize, by any or all of the marriag[e]able ladies of a circle, you may rest assured that if he chooses at all, the one so decided upon will be marked out by her companions—her dear, confidential friends!—as one whose character must speedily be blackened, in order, if possible, to prevent any consummated results! They may probably first "sound" (as the vulgar phrase goes) the young lady on the subject—first "feel her pulse well"—and if they find she is likely to make a "case" of the gentleman's proposal, they will leave nothing available untried to make a *case* of her!

Suppose those who engage in such crusades are successful in their design, what but a fiendish satisfaction, can it afford? The satisfaction of having been

instrumental in destroying, perhaps, for ever the happiness of a fellow creature!—that fellow creature an innocent young lady!—that young lady late
you proclaimed your friend! Is there any thing in nature more heartless and
inhuman?

It is known that young men!—start not reader! it is known that those
who *call* themselves MEN, have been engaged in similar noble exploits against
innocence and virtue!—but for the honor of our common nature, they are
passed by!

***

Another bad feature in the circles of the higher classes of colored society, is that which requires of those who obtain admission in any particular
one, a total surrender of their independence to the whims or caprices of
the majority who compose it. In fact one must make up his mind to be governed entirely by their feelings—their affections and aversions;—love those
whom they love—hate those whom they hate—slander those whom they
slander—and laud those whom they speak well of. Any exhibition of the
right of opinion, in such matters, is very apt to beget for him who had the
boldness to show it, the indifference of the other members of the circle—
excite in their bosoms suspicions of his attachment to them—and thereupon
he is very apt to find his society suddenly "cut," before, perhaps, he is fully
aware of the cause! It may be, however, that they have "searched the scriptures" for this rule of their government and are determined to consider all
who are "not with them," to the utmost extent required, as being decidedly
"against them."

Although I have here spoken in terms of general application, in recounting some of the more prominent vices, that are in practice among the higher
classes of colored society, yet I would by no means have it understood that
they are all equally vulnerable in this respect. There are exceptions—honorable exceptions—in the ranks of both male and female. There are young
ladies, whose virtues, purity of mind and strict moral worth, render them in
no wise amenable to my censures,—who are as incapable of the practices
adverted to, as any to be found in any other division of society;—but whose
misfortune it is to be brought in[to] social contact with those to whom this
exception cannot justly apply.

Those therefore whom it will fit, will readily recognise [*sic*] the garment—
and it is hoped will endeavor to repair it;—and such as it would illy become,
will concur heartily in the most unlimited denunciation of its wear.

The vices of the higher classes in all countries, are no less those of the better informed, and more wealthy portion of those who form the subject of these sketches. The vulgar and indecent practices which obtain foothold among them, and which would perhaps for ever soil the fame of any one of the plain, unostentatious, unpretending members of pleb[e]ian society in the estimation of his associates, are by them termed "fashionable foibles," and he or she who is not an adept in such matters, is looked upon as a "simpleton," or a "flat"; or is otherwise regarded in the light that one would be who should appear in a ball-room and offer to lead in the dance, with brogans[7] upon his feet—a grossly ignorant and unfashionable fellow! It is not of course for the want of education or of better information, but in truth the very possession of these, which they consider—conjoined with wealth—confers upon them the privilege of establishing and adhering to just whatever regulations and practices, under the name of "fashion," their corrupt fancies may lead them to. So with many of those at whose vices I have aimed. Their demeanor in the eyes of the world is by no means in consonance with such conduct.[i] They are as fully sensible of the importance of "keeping up appearances," as any that can be named, and are as equally successful in maintaining them.

i. Let it be here distinctly understood, that I deign not to impute any greater criminality or grosser immorality, than has been distinctly designated.

NOTES

1. Winch, *Elite of Our People*, 5.
2. Winch, *Elite of Our People*, 5.
3. Otter, *Philadelphia Stories*, 125.
4. Winch, *Elite of Our People*, 41.

5. Otter, *Philadelphia Stories*, 124.
6. "Poverty nor riches": Proverbs 30:8.
7. Brogans are heavy, ankle-high shoes or boots.

BIBLIOGRAPHY

Berlin, Ira. *Slaves Without Masters: The Free Negro in the Antebellum South*. New York: New Press, 1976.
Litwak, Leon. *North of Slavery: The Negro in the Free States, 1790–1860*. Chicago: University of Chicago Press, 1961.
Otter, Samuel. *Philadelphia Stories: America's Literature of Race and Freedom*. Oxford: Oxford University Press, 2010.

Winch, Julie, ed. and intro. *The Elite of Our People: Joseph Willson's Sketches of Black Upper-Class Life in Antebellum Philadelphia*. University Park: Pennsylvania State University Press, 2000.

The Pre–Civil War Years Through World War II (1850–1949)

Black leaders visiting the city in the years leading up to the Civil War were often critical of the treatment of the Black residents, most of whom lived in the Fifth Ward, in the heart of the city. Author William Wells Brown in 1854 described Philadelphia by saying, "Colorphobia is more rampant here than in the pro-slavery, negro-hating city of New York."[1] The prejudice and racial violence probably were major reasons why the Black population, 19,833 in 1840, decreased a bit by 1850, unlike the White population, which grew tremendously. Despite these factors, the Black population in the city was still about 7 percent of the total population, the largest percentage of any Northern city at the time.[2]

Philadelphians reflected the growing division within the country. Although many White Philadelphians were not overly sympathetic to the plight of Blacks, they were not generally supportive of the 1850 Fugitive Slave Act, requiring Whites to help slave catchers return allegedly escaped slaves to their owners. Enforcement of the act was a spark uniting many Philadelphians of all races. Frances Ellen Watkins Harper reflects her repugnance for the act and her support for those who aided the fugitives in her letter "An Appeal for the Philadelphia Rescuers" (1860). Philadelphia was a magnet for runaway fugitives seeking freedom; consequently, the Black population increased in the 1850s in part due to the number of runaway slaves. By 1860, there were also more than 22,000 free Blacks living in the city.[3]

The city was the center of the Underground Railroad. William Still was a member of the Pennsylvania Anti-Slavery Society and became a leading conductor. His account of some of the attempts of enslaved people to find freedom is narrated in *The Underground Railroad: A Record of Facts, Authentic Narratives, Letters, & c.* Once these fugitives arrived in the city, however, they did not always find the freedom and refuge they sought. Harriet Jacobs, as indicated above, in her narrative from *Incidents in the Life of a Slave Girl*, reveals the mixed feelings she had about the city. In addition, as stated earlier, while White Philadelphians may not have been happy to turn escaped slaves over to slave catchers, they were not eager to fight for their freedom, either. There was resistance to what many Whites saw as a war being fought over Black freedom. As was stated in one piece of doggerel, Philadelphians had "a willingness to fight with vigor / For loyal rights, but not the nigger."[4]

With such a mood, it is not surprising that Abraham Lincoln barely carried the city in the 1860 election.[5] By the early years of the Civil War, conditions had even worsened for Blacks. Most White Philadelphians did not want to fight what they felt was a war for Black freedom, which fueled anger at African Americans. Frederick Douglass wrote in February 1862, "There is not perhaps anywhere to be found a city in which prejudice against color is more rampant than in Philadelphia."[6] It was only Confederate general Robert E. Lee's incursion into Pennsylvania itself that aroused them against the South. Emilie Davis's *Diaries* gives a good sense of how ordinary Black Philadelphians lived their lives during the war years.

African American soldiers from the city, however, more than did their part in the war.[7] In 1862, a group of wealthy White Philadelphians established the Union League, pressing for African Americans to be able to fight in the war. In 1863, Blacks could enlist, and with the aid of Frederick Douglass and other Black leaders, the Union Army was able to establish eleven Black regiments in Philadelphia.[8] Almost eleven thousand African Americans enlisted even though they had to join for at least three years and accept lower pay. African American troops from the Philly area trained at Camp William Penn and fought in numerous battles, including the Richmond-Petersburg Campaign and the Appomattox Campaign.[9]

The post–Civil War years did not bring about a necessary healing but often created additional fissures. As historian Roger Lane points out, these years solidified the concept of two Philadelphias, one White and one Black. The standard of living for White residents generally improved as the city enjoyed a period of "unparalleled prosperity."[10] The city itself thrived as such important urban institutions as the Art Museum (1877), the Free Library (1891), and the nation's first zoo (1874)—opened within Fairmount Park— were all established. However, for most African American residents, segregation and declining lifestyles continued, despite their service to the nation during the Civil War and the city's newfound prosperity.

African Americans had limited choices in housing, education, and transportation. They were largely confined to certain areas of the city, most frequently in the Center City section between Spruce and Fitzwater Streets, west of Seventh Street. Despite a state Supreme Court ruling in 1887 that discrimination in restaurants and hotels was illegal, the practice continued. The same was also true in education, where most African Americans were sent to second-tier elementary and high schools. Blacks were systematically discriminated against in the public school system until 1881, and after that a de facto segregation continued. As for advanced education, there were only a handful of graduates from the city's private and public institutions. Even the charity wards and prisons were segregated.[11] Blacks were not allowed to ride on the city's streetcars during and immediately after the war, a segregation that William Still argued against in his *A Brief Narrative of the Struggle for the Rights of the Colored People of Philadelphia in the City Railway Cars* (1867). A Black-led protest movement finally led to the end of segregation on the railway the same year as Still's narrative.

New antidiscriminatory legislation did not lessen prejudice. After the passage of the Fourteenth Amendment in 1870, it was necessary for federal troops to be called in to allow Blacks their legal right to vote. Octavius Catto, an African American leader advocating for Black suffrage, was killed for his actions in 1871 after advocating for reform.[12] While Catto's murderers were never brought to justice, his funeral was attended by representatives across the country and brought a moment of calm to the city.[13] However, Blacks continued to be confined to the lowest-paying jobs. Roger Simon writes that "in 1880, 60 percent of black men and 90 percent of black women were employed as domestics or service workers, compared with about 30 percent of immigrants and less than 10 percent of native-born whites."[14] Black women in particular, lured by what they saw as the freedom of factory work rather than domestic service, often found themselves "subject to an intricate matrix of exclusion and exploitation."[15] The famous *Plessy v. Ferguson* decision in 1896 brought matters to a low point by legalizing segregation.

Despite the problems they faced, Blacks kept coming to the city and made their own achievements. To combat segregation, African Americans learned to depend on each other more. Black lodges, fraternal organizations, loan associations, and cultural groups flourished. Because of discrimination against Blacks in medical care, Black Philadelphian doctor Nathan F. Mossell led a group of Blacks that created the Frederick Douglass Memorial Hospital (located at 15th and Lombard Streets) in 1895. And to help counter the prejudice they faced in the press, Christopher Perry started the *Philadelphia Tribune* in 1884, the oldest continuously operated Black newspaper established in the country.[16]

There were also economic and social gains for African Americans during this era. Though much of the Black population was poor, as W. E. B. Du Bois documents in his groundbreaking study *The Philadelphia Negro* (1899), there was a growing number of wealthy African Americans, as many as three thousand, most living along Lombard Street in South Philadelphia, including a small number of doctors and lawyers.[17] Still, this minimal advancement did not meet the expectations of African Americans who after the war hoped for substantial improvement in their lives. As Du Bois observed, "After the war and Emancipation great hopes were entertained by the Negroes for rapid advancement, and nowhere did they seem better founded than in Philadelphia."[18] However, the crumbling row houses, deteriorating services, and abject poverty many Blacks endured in Philadelphia's Seventh Ward, which Du Bois studied and where he resided, horrified him. What also discouraged him was the lack of hope of advancement for most of these people.

Philadelphia's African American population more than doubled between 1900 and 1920, up to 134,000 inhabitants.[19] With this growth, tensions between Whites and Blacks increased over housing and jobs. African Americans began to move from their base in South Philadelphia to areas in the north and west sections of the city, raising the ire of many Whites living in those parts of the city. In 1918, Whites stoned the house of a Black woman who had moved into a previously Whites-only section of the city. A riot broke out lasting two days, injuring and even killing both Blacks and Whites. The violence led to the creation of the Colored Protective Association.[20] This African American expansion led many White Philadelphians to begin their flight to nearby Bucks, Montgomery, and Delaware counties, a pattern that would continue for ensuing decades.[21]

The major force impacting both Black and White Philadelphians in this period was World War I. The decline in foreign immigrants and the increased need for workers because of the war helped lead to what was known as the Great Migration. According to the 1910 Census, 89 percent of Blacks lived in the South.[22] Once World War I began, African American migrated in droves to Northern cities such as Philadelphia. They came with the hope of getting jobs and to escaping discrimination and threats of violence in the South, as well as to gaining educational opportunities and personal freedoms they lacked back home; however, most had limited job skills and struggled once they arrived, and their expectations were not met.[23]

African Americans also were directly involved in the war itself. Many Black civilians donated to relief agencies, conserved food, and volunteered at recreational centers and at military hospitals both at home and abroad. Many, of course, served in the nation's armed forces. Unfortunately, these Black soldiers were often denied the equipment and medical care afforded to Whites. As a result, African American Philadelphians formed the Crispus Attucks Circle for War Relief, which helped establish Mercy Hospital, located on Broad Street, to treat Black soldiers. The hospital, opened in 1919, not only treated African American patients but also trained Black medical staff and personnel.[24]

The 1920s saw a continued expansion of the Black population in Philadelphia, particularly in the area near Girard College on Diamond Street and Twenty-Ninth in North Philadelphia; parts of West Philadelphia also saw growth. Many Blacks worked in railway maintenance or in the service industry, or as trash collectors or street cleaners. During the decade, the Black population in the city increased to almost 220,000.[25] Despite this growth in the African American population, conditions for them remained largely unchanged. Philadelphia was a city still suffering from a split in the job and housing markets, which was largely determined by race and ethnicity. New Black migrants from the South, and the influx of European immigrants, particularly the Irish, added to the toxicity. The Ku Klux Klan heightened the level of racism even further; there were some 300,000 KKK members in the Pennsylvania chapter by the mid-1920s.[26]

Despite these challenges, a Black social and cultural movement was awakening in the city. Although New York City was the center of the New Negro Movement or so-called Harlem Renaissance, there was a thriving arts community in Philadelphia as well. Among the members of the city's literary Beaux Arts Club were Germantown-born poet/artist Mae Cowdery and poet / social worker Evelyn Crawford Reynolds. The major venue for young Black Philadelphia writers in this period was *Black Opals* (1927–28), cofounded by Philadelphians Arthur Huff Fauset and poet/teacher Nellie Bright, who were both published in it. Philadelphian Alain Locke wrote an enthusiastic welcoming of the periodical entitled "Hail Philadelphia." The best known of these writers was Jessie Fauset, a graduate of Cornell University and the long-time literary editor of the National Association for the Advancement of Colored People's (NAACP's) magazine, *The Crisis*.[27]

Any advances that may have occurred in the 1920s came to an immediate halt when the Great Depression began in 1929. Philadelphia was hit hard, especially in the African American community, where "the unemployment rate exceeded 50 percent."[28] Alice Dunbar-Nelson's sketch, "By Paths in the Quaker City," portrays the pluckiness of the city's inhabitants despite the rampant poverty; however, racial tensions simmered over scarce housing, jobs, and city resources.

Perhaps even more concerning than the dire economy was the housing situation. In December 1936, two aging row houses collapsed in a Black South Philadelphia neighborhood, killing six people. Pictures of the devastation shocked even the mayor, S. Davis Wilson. African American residents formed a Tenants League to put pressure on the city to improve conditions. The biggest obstacle in creating better housing for Blacks was not money but concern by Whites over where to construct it. None of them wanted it to be constructed in their neighborhood. Finally, to ease the dreadful housing crisis, the Philadelphia Housing Authority in 1937, using federal funds, ordered the construction of three essentially segregated large housing projects: Tasker Homes (in South Philadelphia, and almost exclusively for Whites) and two for Blacks, the James Weldon Johnson Homes and the Richard Allen Homes (both in North Philadelphia). The city, however, put up obstacles for potential tenants. Single women, for example, were discriminated against when applying for apartments.[29] Government administrators of the homes, wishing to limit crowding, also barred extended family members from living with their relatives, even for short times. This broke often vital financial and communal links between families. Many other Blacks had their own objections, such as not liking the idea of being further segregated and being isolated from jobs and good schools. Furthermore, many residents disliked the stigma of poverty that increasingly grew around the projects. Some may wonder, then, why Blacks would choose to live in such conditions. Du Bois succinctly replied to this question: "The answer is, they do not." However, with few other options, thousands of African Americans moved to the buildings.[30]

During the war years, Philadelphians of all colors were largely support- ive of Franklin D. Roosevelt. It was felt he brought prosperity to the nation, and the demand for machinery to fuel the military helped revive the city's economy. In addition, unemployment was negligible because of the man- power shortage. African Americans also did well by the Works Progress Administration, where they secured some 10 percent of the jobs, though they composed less than 8 percent of the city's population. In 1944, however, racial quarrels emerged as many unions excluded Blacks.[31] The Philadelphia Trans- portation Company hired African Americans to work as conductors and motormen, inciting White workers, who went on strike, resulting in all public transportation being halted. White gangs looted Black neighborhoods. After four days, the army was called in, and five thousand soldiers were ordered to ride the trolley cars to keep the peace in the city.[32] The local branch of the NAACP and the newly formed Fellowship Committee, a coalition of reli- gious and civic groups, helped to end the strike and to prevent racial violence,[33] but the tensions continued.

NOTES

1. Quoted in Weigley, Border City, 386.
2. Geffen, "Industrial Development," 353.
3. Hershberg, "Free Blacks," 111.
4. Quoted in Weigley, Border City, 406.
5. Simon, Philadelphia, 45.
6. Quoted in Weigley, Border City, 386.
7. Saunders, 100 Years After Emancipation, 52–81.
8. Tremel, "Union League," 14.
9. Holness, "United States Colored Troops"; Weigley, Border City, 411.
10. Lane, Roots of Violence, 12–13.
11. Lane, Roots of Violence, 14–16.
12. Willis, Cecil's City, 38–40.
13. Smith, "Murder of Octavius Catto."
14. Simon, Philadelphia, 63–64.
15. Gross, Colored Amazons, 46.
16. Saunders, 100 Years After Emancipation, 146–68.
17. Burt and Davies, "Iron Age," 491–93.

18. Katz and Sugrue, W. E. B. Du Bois, 1–24.
19. Abernethy, "Progressivism," 531; Wolfinger, Philadelphia Divided, 12–13.
20. Downs, "Philadelphia in World War I"; Vincent, "Philadelphia Race Riot," 319–24.
21. Abernethy, "Progressivism," 531–32.
22. Miller, "Black Migration," 316.
23. Wilkerson, Warmth of Other Suns, 260–65; Great Migration (website); Gross, Colored Amazons, 44–46.
24. Moniz, "How Black Philadelphians Fought."
25. Dudden, "City Embraces 'Normalcy,'" 388.
26. Wolfinger, Philadelphia Divided, 12–27.
27. Collins, "Black Opals," 133; West, "Philadel- phia and the Harlem Renaissance," 261–64.
28. Simon, Philadelphia, 75.
29. Levenstein, Movement Without Marches, 96–102.

30. Wolfinger, *Philadelphia Divided*, 59–68.
31. Wolfinger, *Philadelphia Divided*, 40–48.

32. Tinkcom, "Depression and the War," 642–44; Simon, *Philadelphia*, 79.
33. "Civil Rights in a Northern City."

BIBLIOGRAPHY

Abernethy, Lloyd M. "Progressivism, 1905–1919." In Weigley, *Philadelphia*, 524–65.

Burt, Nathaniel, and Wallace E. Davies. "The Iron Age, 1876–1905." In Weigley, *Philadelphia*, 471–523.

"Civil Rights in a Northern City: Philadelphia." https://northerncity.library.temple.edu/exhibits/show/civil-rights-in-a-northern-cit.

Collins, Kathleen. "Black Opals." In *Encyclopedia of the Harlem Renaissance*, edited by Cary D. Wintz and Paul Finkleman. 2 vols. New York: Taylor & Francis, 2004.

Downs, Jacob. "Philadelphia in World War I." *Greater Philadelphia Encyclopedia*.

Dudden, Arthur P. "The City Embraces 'Normalcy,' 1919–1929." In Weigley, *Philadelphia*, 566–600.

Geffen, Elizabeth M. "Industrial Development and Social Crisis, 1841–1854." In Weigley, *Philadelphia*, 307–62.

The Great Migration (website). https://greatmigrationphl.org/.

Gross, Kali N. *Colored Amazons: Crime, Violence, and Black Women in the City of Brotherly Love, 1880–1910*. Illustrated edition. Durham: Duke University Press, 2006.

Hershberg, Theodore. "Free Blacks in Antebellum Philadelphia." In *The Peoples of Philadelphia: A History of Ethnic Groups and Lower-Class Life, 1790–1940*, edited by Allen F. Davis and Mark H. Haller, 111–33. Philadelphia: Temple University Press, 1973.

Holness, Lucien. "United States Colored Troops." *Encyclopedia of Greater Philadelphia* https://philadelphiaencyclopedia.org/essays/united-states-colored-troops/.

Katz, Michael B., and Thomas J. Sugrue, eds. and intro. *W. E. B. Du Bois, Race and the City: "The Philadelphia Negro" and Its Legacy*. Philadelphia: University of Pennsylvania Press, 1998.

Lane, Roger. *Roots of Violence in Black Philadelphia, 1860–1900*. Cambridge: Harvard University Press, 1986.

Levenstein, Lisa. *A Movement Without Marches: African American Women and the Politics of Poverty in Postwar Philadelphia*. Chapel Hill: University of North Carolina Press, 2009.

Miller, Fredric. "The Black Migration to Philadelphia: A 1924 Profile." *Pennsylvania Magazine of History and Biography* 108, no. 3 (July 1984): 315–50.

Moniz, Amanda B. "How Black Philadelphians Fought for Soldiers During World War I." National Museum of American History, November 8, 2018. https://americanhistory.si.edu/blog/crispus-attucks-circle.

Saunders, John A. *100 Years After Emancipation (History of the Philadelphia Negro) 1987 to 1963*. N.p.: F. R. S. Publishing, 1963.

Simon, Roger D. *Philadelphia: A Brief History*. Revised and updated ed. Philadelphia: Temple University Press, 2017.

Smith, Aaron X. "Murder of Octavius Catto." *Encyclopedia of Greater Philadelphia* https://philadelphiaencyclopedia.org/essays/murder-of-octavius-catto/.

Tinkcom, Margaret B. "Depression and the War, 1929–1946." In Weigley, *Philadelphia*, 601–48.

Tremel, Andrew T. "The Union League, Black Leaders, and the Recruitment of Philadelphia's African American Civil War Regiments." *Pennsylvania History: A Journal of Mid-Atlantic Studies* 80 (Winter 2013): 13–36.

Trotter, Joe William, Jr. and Eric Ledell Smith, eds. *African Americans in Pennsylvania: Shifting Historical Perspectives*. Pennsylvania Historical and Museum Commission and The Pennsylvania University Press, 1997.

Vincent, V. P. "The Philadelphia Race Riot of 1918." In Trotter and Smith, *African Americans in Pennsylvania*, 316–29.

Weigley, Russell F. "The Border City in the Civil War, 1854–1865." In Weigley, *Philadelphia*, 363–416.

———. *Philadelphia: A 300-Year History*. New York: W. W. Norton, 1982.

West, Sandra L. "Philadelphia and the Harlem Renaissance." In *Encyclopedia of the Harlem Renaissance*, edited by Aberjhani and Sandra L. West, 261–64. New York: Facts on File Publishing, 2003.

Wilkerson, Isabel. *The Warmth of Other Suns: The Epic Story of America's Great Migration*. New York: Vintage, 2010.

Willis, Arthur C. *Cecil's City: A History of Blacks in Philadelphia, 1638–1979*. New York: Carlton Press, 1990.

Wolfinger, James. *Philadelphia Divided: Race and Politics in the City of Brotherly Love*. Chapel Hill: University of North Carolina Press, 2007.

Frank J. Webb, from *The Garies and Their Friends* (1857)

Frank Webb was born in Philadelphia in 1828. He is best known for *The Garies and Their Friends*, one of the earliest novels to be written by an African American. He also wrote two novellas and several poems and editorials. Webb was born to two free Black parents; his mother was an illegitimate child fathered by one-time American Vice President Aaron Burr. In 1845 he married Mary Espartero, an actress known for her dramatic readings, particularly from Harriet Beecher Stowe's *Uncle Tom's Cabin*. Her readings led to a tour of England and France in 1856–58 that Webb joined. Because of Mary's poor health, the couple moved to Jamaica in 1858, but Mary died there in 1859. Webb, however, continued to live on the island until 1869, when he returned to the United States. Shortly before his return, he married Mary Rosabelle Rodgers, the daughter of a Jamaican merchant. In later years, the couple lived in Washington, DC, and Galveston, Texas, where he died in 1894.

The Garies and Their Friends is set in Philadelphia in the 1830s and '40s, and, as Werner Sollors points out in his introduction to Webb's writings, the book is "a suspenseful Philadelphia novel that seethes with city life; a book of social critique and political protest that confronts the reader with a sharply drawn exposé on Philadelphia's system of color discrimination in the pre–Civil War period."[1] The novel takes us on a tour of Black Philadelphia from "the streets of nineteenth-century coloured South Philadelphia . . . [to] the fancier outlying areas at Winter Street near Logan Square [the northwestern part of Center City], where the Garies settle."[2]

The novel is set in one of the darkest periods in the city's history for African Americans. There were several race riots in Philadelphia, including one where White rage over the abolition movement led to the burning of

Pennsylvania Hall. In addition, Blacks were disfranchised in 1838, as was mentioned in the pamphlet by Robert Purvis. While recent actions such as this disfranchisement and the passage of the Fugitive Slave Act of 1850 are never overtly mentioned, they are "omnipresent" in the book.[3] The novel, set in this not-too-distant past, follows the lives of Clarence Garie, a Georgia slaveholder, his slave/common-law wife, Emily, and their two children, also named Clarence and Emily. Because their union is illegal in Georgia, they migrate to Philadelphia, where they are befriended by the Ellises, a free Black couple and their children. The most famous scene in the novel is a race riot, a blending of several historical riots in Philadelphia that occurred in 1834, 1838, 1842, and 1849. During the riot, the Ellises are able to defend their home, but unfortunately the Garies are unable to do so, and both the father and the pregnant mother die as their horrified children stand by helplessly. The novel concludes in New York City where the offspring of the two families meet various fates. Fittingly, the two families are united through the marriage of young Emily Garie and the Ellises' son Charlie. While this seems to promise a happy ending, "the sequence of episodes in the book leaves open the question of whether the future will repeat or diverge from the Philadelphia pattern of regressive advance."[4]

CHAPTER 21 "MORE HORRORS."

Unaware of the impending danger, Mr. Garie sat watching by the bedside of his wife. She had been quite ill; but on the evening of which we write, although nervous and wakeful, was much better. The bleak winds of the fast approaching winter dealt unkindly with her delicate frame, accustomed as she was to the soft breezes of her Southern home.

Mr. Garie had been sitting up looking at the fires in the lower part of the city. Not having been out all that day or the one previous, he knew nothing of the fearful state into which matters had fallen.

"Those lights are dying away, my dear," said he to his wife; "there must have been quite an extensive conflagration." Taking out his watch, he continued, "almost two o'clock; why, how late I've been sitting up. I really don't know whether it's worth while to go to bed or not. I should be obliged to get up again at five o'clock; I go to New York to-morrow, or rather to-day; there are some matters connected with Uncle John's will that require my personal attention. Dear old man, how suddenly he died."

"I wish, dear, you could put off your journey until I am better," said Mrs. Garie, faintly; "I do hate you to go just now."

"I would if I could, Emily; but it is impossible. I shall be back to-morrrow, or the next day, at farthest. Whilst I'm there, I'll—"

"Hush!" interrupted Mrs. Garie, "stop a moment. Don't you hear a noise like the shouting of a great many people."

"Oh, it's only the firemen," replied he; "as I was about to observe—"

"Hush!" cried she again. "Listen now, that don't sound like the firemen in the least." Mr. Garie paused as the sound of a number of voices became more distinct.

Wrapping his dressing-gown more closely about him, he walked into the front room, which overlooked the street. Opening the window, he saw a number of men—some bearing torches—coming rapidly in the direction of his dwelling. "I wonder what all this is for; what can it mean," he exclaimed.

They had now approached sufficiently near for him to understand their cries. "Down with the Abolitionist—down with the Amalgamationist! give them tar and feathers!"

"It's a mob—and that word Amalgamationist—can it be pointed at me? It hardly seems possible; and yet I have a fear that there is something wrong."

"What is it, Garie? What is the matter? asked his wife, who, with a shawl hastily thrown across her shoulders, was standing pale and trembling by the window.

"Go in, Emily, my dear, for Heaven's sake; you'll get your death of cold in this bleak night air—go in; as soon as I discover the occasion of the disturbance, I'll come and tell you. Pray go in." Mrs. Garie retired a few feet from the window and stood listening to the shouts in the street.

The rioters, led on evidently by some one who knew what he was about, pressed forward to Mr. Garie's house; and soon the garden in front was filled with the shouting crowd.

"What do you all want—why are you on my premises, creating this disturbance?" cried Mr. Garie.

"Come down and you'll soon find out. You white livered Abolitionist, come out damn you! we are going to give you a coat of tar and feathers, and your black wench nine-and-thirty. Yes, come down—come down!" shouted several, "or we will come up after you."

"I warn you," replied Mr. Garie, "against any attempt at violence upon my person, family, or property. I forbid you to advance another foot upon the premises. If any man of you enters my house, I'll shoot him down as quick as I would a mad dog."

"Shut up your gap; none of your cussed speeches," said a voice in the crowd: "if you don't come down and give yourself up, we'll come in and take you—that's the talk, ain't it boys?" A general shout of approval answered this speech, and several stones were thrown at Mr. Garie, one of which struck him on the breast.

Seeing the utter futility of attempting to parley with the infuriated wretches below, he ran into the room, exclaiming, "Put on some clothes, Emily! shoes first—quick—quick, wife!—your life depends upon it. I'll bring down the children and wake the servants. We must escape from the house—we are attacked by a mob of demons. Hurry, Emily! do, for God sake!"

Mr. Garie aroused the sleeping children, and threw some clothes upon them, over which he wrapped shawls or blankets, or whatever came to hand. Rushing into the next room, he snatched a pair of loaded pistols from the drawer of his dressing-stand, and then hurried his terrified wife and children down the stairs.

"This way, dear—this way!" he cried, leading on toward the back door; "out that way through the gate with the children, and into some of the neighbour's houses. I'll stand here to keep the way."

"No, no, Garie," she replied, frantically; "I won't go without you."

"You must!" he cried, stamping his foot impatiently; "this is no time to parley—go, or we shall all be murdered. Listen, they've broken in the door. Quick—quick! go on"; and as he spoke, he pressed her and the children out of the door, and closed it behind them.

Mrs. Garie ran down the garden, followed by the children; to her horror, she found the gate locked, and the key nowhere to be found.

"What shall we do?" she cried. "Oh, we shall all be killed!" and her limbs trembled beneath her with cold and terror.

"Let us hide in here, mother," suggested Clarence, running toward the wood-house; "we'll be safe in there."

Seeing that nothing better could be done, Mrs. Garie availed herself of the suggestion and when she was fairly inside the place, fell fainting upon the ground.

As she escaped through the back door, the mob broke in at the front, and were confronting Mr. Garie, as he stood with his pistol pointed at them, prepared to fire.

"Come another step forward and I fire!" exclaimed he, resolutely; but those in the rear urged the advance of those in front, who approached cautiously nearer and nearer their victim. Fearful of opening the door behind him, lest he should show the way taken by his retreating wife, he stood uncertain how to act; a severe blow from a stone, however, made him lose all reflection, and he immediately fired. A loud shriek followed the report of his pistol, and a shower of stones was immediately hurled upon him.

He quickly fired again, and was endeavouring to open the door to effect his escape, when a pistol was discharged close to his head and he fell forward on the entry floor lifeless.

All this transpired in a few moments, and in the semi-darkness of the entry. Rushing forward over his lifeless form, the villains hastened upstairs in search of Mrs. Garie. They ran shouting through the house, stealing everything valuable that they could lay their hands upon, and wantonly destroying the furniture; they would have fired the house, but were prevented by McClosky, who acted as leader of the gang.

For two long hours they ransacked the house, breaking all they could not carry off, drinking the wine in Mr. Garie's cellar, and shouting and screaming like so many fiends.

Mrs. Garie and the children lay crouching with terror in the wood-house, listening to the ruffians as they went through the yard cursing her and her husband and uttering the direst threats of what they would do should she fall into their hands. Once she almost fainted on hearing one of them propose opening the wood-house, to see if there was anything of value in it—but breathed again when they abandoned it as not worth their attention.

The children crouched down beside her—scarcely daring to whisper, lest they should attract the attention of their persecutors. Shivering with cold they drew closer around them the blanket with which they had been providentially provided.

"Brother, my feet are *so* cold," sobbed little Em. "I can't feel my toes. Oh, I'm so cold!"

"Put your feet closer to me, sissy," answered her brother, baring himself to enwrap her more thoroughly; "put my stockings on over yours;" and, as well as they were able in the dark, he drew his stockings on over her benumbed feet. "There, sis, that's better," he whispered, with an attempt at cheerfulness, "now you'll be warmer."

Just then Clarence heard a groan from his mother, so loud indeed that it would have been heard without but for the noise and excitement around the house—and feeling for her in the dark, he asked, "Mother, are you worse? are you sick?"

A groan was her only answer.

"Mother, Mother," he whispered, "do speak, please do!" and he endeavored to put his arm around her.

"Don't dear—don't," said she faintly, "just take care of your sister—you can't do me any good—don't speak, dear, the men will hear you."

Reluctantly the frightened child turned his attention again to his little sister; ever and anon suppressed groans from his mother would reach his ears—at last he heard a groan even fierce in its intensity; and then the sounds grew fainter and fainter until they entirely ceased. The night to the poor shivering creatures in their hiding place seemed interminably long, and the sound of voices in the house had not long ceased when the faint light of day pierced their cheerless shelter.

Hearing the voices of some neighbours in the yard, Clarence hastened out, and seizing one of the ladies by the dress, cried imploringly. "Do come to my mother, she's sick."

"Why, where did you come from, child?" said the lady, with a start of astonishment. Where have you been?"

"In there," he answered, pointing to the wood-house. "Mother and sister are in there."

The lady, accompanied by one or two others, hastened to the wood-house.

"Where is she?" asked the foremost, for in the gloom of the place she could not perceive anything.

"Here," replied Clarence, "she's lying here." On opening a small window, they saw Mrs. Garie lying in a corner stretched upon the boards, her head supported by some blocks. "She's asleep," said Clarence. "Mother—Mother," but there came no answer. "MOTHER!" said he, still louder, but yet there was no response.

Stepping forward, one of the females opened the shawl, which was held firmly in the clenched hands of Mrs. Garie—and there in her lap partially covered by her scanty nightdress, was discovered a new-born babe, who with its mother had journeyed in the darkness, cold, and night, to the better land, that they might pour out their woes upon the bosom of their Creator.

The women gazed in mournful silence on the touching scene before them. Clarence was on his knees, regarding with fear and wonder the unnatural stillness of his mother—the child had never before looked on death, and could not recognize its presence. Laying his hand on her cold cheek, he cried, with faltering voice, "Mother, can't you speak?" but there was no answering light in the fixed state of those glassy eyes, and the lips of the dead could not move. "Why don't she speak?" he asked.

"She can't, my dear; you must come away and leave her. She's better off, my darling—she's dead."

Then there was a cry of grief sprung up from the heart of that orphan boy, that rang in those women's ears for long years after; it was the first outbreak of a loving childish heart pierced with life's bitterest grief—a mother's loss.

The two children were kindly taken into the house of some benevolent neighbour, as the servants had all fled none knew whither. Little Em was in a profound stupor—the result of cold and terror, and it was found necessary to place her under the care of a physician.

After they had all gone, an inquest was held by the coroner, and a very unsatisfactory and untruthful verdict pronounced—one that did not at all coincide with the circumstances of the case, but such a one as might have been expected where there was a great desire to screen the affair from public scrutiny.

NOTES

1. Sollors, introduction to *Fiction, Essays, Poetry*, 4.

2. Sollors, introduction to *Fiction, Essays, Poetry*, 6–7.

3. Otter, *Philadelphia Stories*, 238.

4. Otter, *Philadelphia Stories*, 264.

BIBLIOGRAPHY

Gardner, Eric. "'A Gentleman of Superior Cultivation and Refinement': Recovering the Biography of Frank J. Webb." *African American Review* 35, no. 2 (Summer 2001): 297–308.

Henry, Katherine. "Garies (The) and Their Friends." *Encyclopedia of Greater Philadelphia*. https://philadelphia encyclopedia.org/essays/garies -the-and-their-friends/.

Hershberg, Theodore. "Free Blacks in Antebellum Philadelphia." In *The Peoples of Philadelphia: A History of Ethnic Groups and Lower-Class Life, 1790–1940*, edited by Allen Freeman Davis and Mark H. Haller, 111–33. Philadelphia: University of Pennsylvania Press, 1973.

Lapsansky, Phillip S. "Afro American: Frank J. Webb and His Friends." *Annual Report of the Library Company of Philadelphia for the Year 1990* (1991), 27–43.

Maillard, Mary. "'Faithfully Drawn from Real Life': Autobiographical Elements in Frank J. Webb's *The Garies and Their*

Friends." *Pennsylvania Magazine of History and Biography* 137, no. 3 (July 2013): 261–300.

Sollors, Werner. Introduction to *Fiction, Essays, Poetry*, by Frank J. Webb. New Milford, CT: Toby Press, 2004.

Otter, Samuel. *Philadelphia Stories: America's Literature of Race and Freedom*. Oxford: Oxford University Press, 2010.

Webb, Frank J. *Fiction, Essays, Poetry*. Edited and with an introduction by Werner Sollors. New Milford, CT: Toby Press, 2004.

Frances Ellen Watkins Harper, "An Appeal for the Philadelphia Rescuers," *Weekly Anglo-African* (June 23, 1860)

Poet, fiction writer, essayist, and lecturer Frances Ellen Watkins was born in Baltimore, Maryland, in 1825 to free African American parents. She was one of the most significant Black women authors in the nineteenth century: the first African American woman to publish a short story ("The Two Offers," 1859), one of the first to write a novel (*Iola Leroy*, 1892), and also the author of one of the most famous abolitionist poems ("Bury Me in a Free Land," 1857). She had an active role in many abolitionist, temperance, and women's rights organizations. She married Fenton Harper in 1860, but he died four years later. Harper moved around for much of her early life, first coming to Philadelphia in 1853, where she worked for the Underground Railroad. In 1870, she settled at 1006 Bainbridge Street in the Bella Vista area of South Philly and remained there until she died in 1911. Her Bella Vista home is now a National Historic Landmark.

Harper's "Appeal" appears in the form of a letter to the editor of the *Weekly Anglo-African* newspaper. She had long resisted the Fugitive Slave Act (1850), ordering Northerners to assist slavecatchers to return Blacks accused of being runaway slaves. Frances Smith Foster, in a footnote reproducing the piece, states that the letter likely refers to "the capture of Moses Horner, a fugitive slave. A group of the Philadelphians failed in their rescue attempt, and ten of the rescuers, nine blacks and one white, were jailed."[1]

—

Mr. Editor:—I saw in a late number of your paper an appeal from one of the Philadelphia rescuers, and I would ask through the columns of your paper if this appeal does not find a ready and hearty response in the bosom of every hater of American despotism? Shall these men throw themselves across the track of the general government and be crushed by that mo[n]strous Jugger-naut of organized villainy, the Fugitive Slave Law, and we sit silent, with our hands folded, in selfish inactivity? It is not enough to express our sympathy by words; we should be ready to crystalize it into actions. I am not content with simply offering them pecuniary assistance from my limited resources; I would call on others to aid these men in their hour of trial. Let the day-laborer bring his offering, and our men of wealth be ready with their contributions. Let the hands of toil release their hold upon their hard-won earnings, feeling that there is no poverty like the poverty of meanness, no bankruptcy like that of a heart bankrupt in just, kind, and generous feelings.

Brethren and sisters of the East and West, will you not rally around these men? Their's [sic] is a common cause; they bear a common standard. Do not stop to cavil and find fault by saying they were rash and imprudent, and engaged in a hopeless contest. Their ears were quicker than ours; they heard the death-knell of freedom sound in the ears of a doomed and fated brother, and to them they were clarion sounds, rousing their souls to deeds of noble daring—trumpet tones, inciting them to brave and lofty actions.

And now shall these men stand alone? Are we not all ready to contribute means and money to defray the expences of their trial—not as a matter of charity, but as a memorial of their services and a token of our gratitude? And let me, in conclusion, ask our young men and maidens, our pastors and people, to unite in giving a tangible expression to their sympathy by sustaining these men, with the consciousness that it is a privilege to do the humblest deed for freedom.

NOTE

1. Foster, *Brighter Coming Day*, 52.

BIBLIOGRAPHY

Alexander, Kerri Lee. "Frances Ellen Watkins Harper." National Women's History Museum. https://www.womenshistory.org/education-resources/biographies/frances-ellen-watkins-harper.

Bilbija, Marina. "The Anglo-African Newspaper." Oxford Bibliographies. https://doi.org/10.1093/obo/9780190280024-0003.

Boyd, Melba. *Discarded Legacy: Politics and Poetics in the Life of Frances E. W. Harper, 1825–1911*. Detroit: Wayne State University Press, 1995.

Field, Corinne T. "Frances E. W. Harper and the Politics of Intellectual Maturity." In *Toward an Intellectual History of Black Women*, edited by Mia Bay, Farah J. Griffin, Martha S. Jones, and Barbara D. Savage, 110–26. Chapel Hill: University of North Carolina Press, 2015.

Foster, Frances Smith, ed. *A Brighter Coming Day: A Frances Ellen Watkins Reader*. New York: Feminist Press 1990.

McKnight, Utz. *Frances E. W. Harper: A Call to Conscience*. Boston: Polity, 2020.

Harriet Jacobs, from *Incidents in the Life of a Slave Girl: Written by Herself* (1861)

Harriet Jacobs was born as an enslaved person in 1813 in Edenton, North Carolina. Harriet's relatively benevolent mistress, Mary Hornblow, taught Jacobs to read. When her mistress died in 1825, she was bequeathed to three-year-old Mary Norcom while the child's father, Dr. James Norcom, and his wife Maria became her de facto masters. Harriet (writing under the pseudonym Linda Brent) spent years trying to avoid the clutches of Dr. Norcom, who desired her sexually, and escape the jealousy of his wife. Much to the anger of Dr. Norcom, Jacobs had two children by a White congressman. Becoming increasingly desperate to avoid Norcom, Jacobs hid in a crawl space in her grandmother's home for seven years before fleeing to the North in 1842. Her first place of refuge there was in Philadelphia. Jacobs had mixed feelings about the city. She went to bed thinking for the first time she was "a free woman." She soon realizes, however, that this "freedom" comes with a sense of inequality. This is driven home the next day when she goes on public transportation in the city; she sees that Blacks are forced by segregation to ride in a "large, rough car." She also realizes that because of the Fugitive Slave Act, her own freedom can be taken away from her. The mixed feelings that Jacobs experienced were similar to many Black visitors to and residents of Philadelphia. Jacobs's *Incidents* took several years to be published, partly because for many years people disputed whether the events in it actually occurred, and also because of the sexual matters discussed in it. Now, after Frederick Douglass's *Narrative* (1845), it is probably the most famous of the many American slave narratives.

─

CHAPTER XXXI: "INCIDENTS IN PHILADELPHIA"

I had heard that the poor slave had many friends at the north. I trusted we should find some of them. Meantime, we would take it for granted that all were friends, till they proved to the contrary. I sought out the kind captain,[1] thanked him for his attentions, and told him I should never cease to be grateful for the service he had rendered us. I gave him a message to the friends I had left at home, and he promised to deliver it. We were placed in a row-boat, and in about fifteen minutes were landed on a wood wharf in Philadelphia. As I stood looking round, the friendly captain touched me on the shoulder, and said, "There is a respectable-looking colored man behind you. I will speak to him about the New York trains, and tell him you wish to go directly on." I thanked him, and asked him to direct me to some shops where I could buy gloves and veils. He did so, and said he would talk with the colored man till I returned. I made what haste I could. Constant exercise on board the vessel, and frequent rubbing with salt water, had nearly restored the use of my limbs. The noise of the great city confused me, but I found the shops, and brought some double veils and gloves for Fanny² and myself. The shopman told me they were so many levies.³ I had never heard the word before, but I did not tell him so. I thought if he knew I was a stranger he might ask me where I came from. I gave him a gold piece, and when he returned the change, I counted it, and found out how much a levy was. I made my way back to the wharf, where the captain introduced me to the colored man, as the Rev. Jeremiah Durham, minister of Bethel church. He took me by the hand, as if I had been an old friend. He told us we were too late for the morning cars to New York, and must wait until the evening, or the next morning. He invited me to go home with him, assuring me that his wife would give me a cordial welcome; and for my friend he would provide a home with one of his neighbors. I thanked him for so much kindness to strangers, and told him if I must be detained, I should like to hunt up some people who formerly went from our part of the country. Mr. Durham insisted that I should dine with him, and then he would assist me in finding my friends. The sailors came to bid us good by. I shook their hardy hands, with tears in my eyes. They had all been kind to us, and they had rendered us a greater service than they could possibly conceive of.

I had never seen so large a city or been in contact with so many people in the streets. It seemed as if those who passed looked at us with an expression of curiosity. My face was blistered and peeled, by sitting on deck, in wind and sunshine, that I thought they could not easily decide to what nation I belonged.

Mrs. Durham met me with a kindly welcome, without asking any questions. I was tired, and her friendly manner was a sweet refreshment. God bless her! I was sure that she had comforted other weary hearts, before I received her sympathy. She was surrounded by her husband and children, in a home made sacred by protecting laws. I thought of my own children, and sighed.

After dinner Mr. Durham went with me in quest of the friends I had spoken of. They went from my native town, and I anticipated much pleasure in looking on familiar faces. They were not at home, and we retraced our steps through streets delightfully clean. On the way, Mr. Durham observed that I had spoken to him of a daughter I expected to meet; that he was surprised, for I looked so young he had taken me for a single woman. He was approaching a subject on which I was extremely sensitive. He would ask about my husband next, I thought, and if I answered him truly, what would he think of me? I told him I had two children, one in New York the other at the south. He asked some further questions, and I frankly told him some of the most important events of my life. It was painful for me to do it; but I would not deceive him. If he was desirous of being my friend, I thought he ought to know how far I was worthy of it. "Excuse me, if I have tried your feelings," said he. "I did not question you from idle curiosity. I wanted to understand your situation, in order to know whether I could be of any service to you, or your little girl. Your straight-forward answers do you credit; but don't answer everybody so openly. It might give some heartless people a pretext for treating you with contempt."

That word *contempt* burned me like coals of fire. I replied, "God alone knows how I suffered; and He, I trust, will forgive me. If I am permitted to have my children, I intend to be a good mother, and to live in such a manner that people cannot treat me with contempt."

"I respect your sentiments," said he. "Place your trust in God, and be governed by good principles, and you will not fail to find friends."

When we reached home, I went to my room, glad to shut out the world for a while. The words he had spoken made an indelible impression upon me. They brought up great shadows from the mournful past. In the midst of my meditations I was startled by a knock at the door. Mrs. Durham entered, her face all beaming with kindness, to say that there was an anti-slavery friend down stairs, who would like to see me. I overcame my dread of encountering strangers, and went with her. Many questions were asked concerning my experiences, and my escape from slavery; but I observed how careful they all were not to say any thing that might wound my feelings. How gratifying this was, can be fully understood only by those who have been accustomed to be treated as if they were not included within the pale of human beings. The anti-slavery friend had come to inquire into my plans, and to offer assistance, if needed. Fanny was comfortably established, for the present, with a friend of Mr. Durham. The Anti-Slavery Society agreed to pay her expenses to New York. The same was offered to me, but I declined to accept it; telling them that my grandmother had given me sufficient to pay my expenses to the end of my journey. We were urged to remain in Philadelphia a few days, until some suitable escort could be found for us. I gladly accepted the proposition, for I had a dread of meeting slaveholders, and some dread also of railroads. I had never entered a railroad car in my life, and it seemed to me quite an important event.

That night I sought my pillow with feelings I had never carried to it before. I verily believed myself to be a free woman. I was wakeful for a long time, and I had no sooner fallen asleep, than I was roused by fire-bells. I jumped up, and hurried on my clothes. Where I came from, every body hastened to dress themselves on such occasions. The white people thought a great fire might be used as a good opportunity for insurrection, and that it was best to be in readiness; and the colored people were ordered out to labor in extinguishing the flames. There was but one engine in our town, and colored women and children were often required to drag it to the river's edge and fill it. Mrs. Durham's daughter slept in the same bed with me, and seeing that she slept through all the din, I thought it was my duty to wake her. "What's the matter?" said she, rubbing her eyes.

"They're screaming fire in the streets, and the bells are ringing," I replied.

"What of that?" said she, drowsily. "We are used to it. We never get up, without the fire is very near. What good would it do?"

I was quite surprised that it was not necessary for us to go and help fill the engine. I was an ignorant child, just beginning to learn how things went on in great cities.

At daylight, I heard women crying fresh fish, berries, radishes, and various other things. All this was new to me. I dressed myself at an early hour, and sat at the window to watch that unknown tide of life. Philadelphia seemed to me a wonderfully great place. At the breakfast table, my idea of going out to drag the engine was laughed over, and I joined in the mirth.

I went to see Fanny, and found her so well contented among her new friends that she was in no haste to leave. I was also very happy with my kind hostess. She had had advantages for education, and was vastly my superior. Every day, almost every hour, I was adding to my little stock of knowledge. She took me out to see the city as much as she deemed prudent. One day she took me to an artist's room, and showed me the portraits of some of her children. I had never seen any paintings of colored people before, and they seemed to me beautiful.

At the end of five days, one of Mrs. Durham's friends offered to accompany us to New York the following morning. As I held the hand of my good hostess in a parting clasp, I longed to know whether her husband had repeated to her what I had told him. I supposed he had, but she never made any allusion to it. I presume it was the delicate silence of womanly sympathy.

When Mr. Durham handed us our tickets, he said, "I am afraid you will have a disagreeable ride; but I could not procure tickets for the first class cars."

Supposing I had not given him money enough, I offered more. "O, no," said he, "they could not be had for any money. They don't allow colored people to go in the first-class cars."

This was the first chill to my enthusiasm about the Free States. Colored people were allowed to ride in a filthy box, behind white people, at the south, but there they were not required to pay for the privilege. It made me sad to find how the north aped the customs of slavery.

We were stowed away in a large, rough car, with windows on each side, too high for us to look out without standing up. It was crowded with people, apparently of all nations. There were plenty of beds and cradles, containing screaming and kicking babies. Every other man had a cigar or pipe in his mouth, and jugs of whiskey were handed round freely. The fumes of the whiskey and the dense tobacco smoke were sickening to my senses, and my mind was equally nauseated by the coarse jokes and ribald songs around me. It was a very disagreeable ride. Since that time there has been some improvement in these matters.

NOTES

1. Kind captain: the ship captain, a Southerner, who piloted Jacobs to freedom in Philadelphia.

2. Fanny: Jacobs's friend, another fugitive.
3. Levies: A levy is a coin worth between eleven and twelve and a half cents.

BIBLIOGRAPHY

Braxton, Joanne M. "Harriet Jacobs' 'Incidents in the Life of a Slave Girl': The Re-definition of the Slave Narrative Genre." *Massachusetts Review* 27, no. 2 (Summer 1986): 379–87.
Doherty, Thomas. "Harriet Jacobs' Narrative Strategies: 'Incidents in the Life of a Slave Girl.'" *Southern Literary Journal* 19, no. 1 (Fall 1986): 79–91.
Foster, Frances Smith. *Written by Herself: Literary Production by African American Women, 1746–1892.* Bloomington: Indiana University Press, 1993.
Garfield, Deborah M., and Rafia Zahar, eds. *Harriet Jacobs and "Incidents in the Life of a Slave Girl": New Critical Essays.* Cambridge: Cambridge University Press, 1996.
Jacobs, Harriet. *Incidents in the Life of a Slave Girl: Text, Contexts, Criticism.* Edited by Nellie Y. McKay and Francis Smith Foster. New York: W. W. Norton, 2001.

Yellin, Jean Fagan. "'Written by Herself': Harriet   *Literature* 53, no. 3 (November 1981):
    Jacobs' Slave Narrative." *American*   479–86.

Emilie Davis, from Diaries (1863–65)

Emilie Davis (1839–1889) was born a free Black woman in Philadelphia. She attended the Institute for Colored Youth, worked as a seamstress, and was a member of the Ladies' Union Association of America, which raised funds and collected supplies for Black Union troops as well as petitioning against streetcar segregation in the city. She also belonged to numerous church groups. Davis lived in Center City (in the Seventh Ward) with her brother Elijah, Sarah (his wife), Elwood, (the couple's son), and Elizabeth and Thomas Davis. She was living on her own by 1863, and in 1866 she married George Bustill White, a barber descended from a prominent Black Philadelphia family.

Davis kept three separate diaries (only discovered within the past thirty years), one each for the years 1863, 1864, and 1865. She made brief entries, many times running them together over several days at a time. Her diaries give us a rare insight into the life of a free Black woman in Philadelphia during the most turbulent years of the nation's history. As Judith Giesberg points out, "The real significance of the diary is that it allows us to see how the Civil War was lived as part of everyday life, folded between Emilie's sewing and her attendance at church and school, shopping and socializing, worrying and rejoicing."[1] Davis combines both personal and public events, recording tragic accounts from her life, such as the death of family members or friends, as well as major national events, including the death of President Abraham Lincoln. She also records happier moments, such as attending lectures by Black luminaries, including Frederick Douglass or Frances Ellen Watkins Harper, or concerts by Elizabeth Taylor Greenfield (the Black Swan) or Thomas Higgins. These are interwoven with national events of great concern, including her reaction to the Emancipation Proclamation, the taking of Richmond, and the end of the war. Through Davis's pithy accounts of her activities, whether ordinary daily events or ones of national import, we learn about the way residents of the Northern city with the largest population of free Black people (some twenty-two thousand) lived their lives during this time of crisis.

Judith Giesberg and the rest of her team provide a text of the full diaries with copious annotations. Davis's original spelling from the diaries has been retained.

—

1863
Thursday, January 1, 1863.
    To-day has bin a memorable day and I thank god i have bin sperd to see it the day was religously observed all the churches were open we had quite a Jubilee² in the evenin I went to Joness to a Party had a very pleasent time

Friday 2
    Beutiful day Nellie³ was up and spent Part of the day reading was here Nellie had an engagement and had to go home i stoped home a few minutes the girls were

Saturday 3
    all there very Pleasant this morning buisey all day reading and his were her [here] to service I went down home to see if father had begun and was coming away when

Sunday, January 4, 1863.
    he cam i was delighted to see him I did not go to church in the morning very good Discours in the afternoon Dave was down we had a full choir bible class at gertrudes very interresting
                                   ***
Friday [July] 31
    to day is the eventful day they begin to Draft⁴ in the seventh ward Alfred⁵ and EJ⁶ are both drafted Mary⁷ is quite worried I hope he will not have

Saturday, August 1
    to go Elijah is over the Mrs. Seward was buried yesterday Elijah got a [...] and we all would I stoped up to hazards
                                   ***
Sunday [November] 1
    lovely day I went to church in the morning heard a very good sermon stoped at mrs gibbs and at millses I spent the rest of my time with mary she is very ill

Monday 2

very fine day I went down to see mary found her very ill in truley helpless stoped over home and told sarah in the afternoon Nell came up for me
May was diei

Tuesday, November 3, 1863.

ng [dying] I went down and staid with her she died last night about 7
oclock she died very calm she was ready Alfred did not get to see her very
long all day cleaning up the house

Wednesday 4

mary J and I poor Mary is to be buried to day no work of Alfred Poor little
Frank is left an orphan Mr Gibbs attended the funral Frank went home

Thursday 5

and fixed the thinghs Nell mrs sisco and [...] And ther mother were there
I went to hazards to day they seem to simpythize with me I have

Friday, November 6, 1863.

bin so very busy since I came up here I have hardly had time to think Mary
Sue was in yesterday I was down home a little while to day Frank seems to be

Saturday 7

quite contented John came home he came running in here yesterday I
was delighted to see him Nell and went up to the doctors this morning he
was not ther

***

Sunday [November] 29

very dull morning I went to church heard quite a good sermon [...] out
Bible class at Whites very good turn out Mr bustil[8] came home with me Cristy

Monday, November 30, 1863.

went with Mary Clay very cold Nell was up here in the after noon we went
down to school found Mr lively waiting for us hannah

Tuesday, December 1

brown was there P meeting at Mrs turners after meeting we stoped at
bustils had quite a Pleasant chat

Wednesday 2

Cristy still Teaching I do not know how to treat him I certainly do not feel the same towards him nell was up this evening

Thursday, December 3, 1863.

Thursday very Pleasant Nell Mrs Jordan and I went out shopping nell bought herself a
coat we went up to harrises then paid several other visits

Friday 4

in the evening we went to hear Fred Duglass yesterday I Paid a visit to the White house I have bin so busy I have not had time to write

***

Memoranda

Wednesday [June] the 17th 1863 will be remembered by a great many of our People nearly all of our best young men left for the war but happily returned the next day un harmed

Sarah Thomas was married on last Saturday the 20th of June

Monday the 29th the most exciting day ever witness by having Refugees line the streets from all the towns this side of

Memoranda

Harrisburg and even from Harrisburg

The riot[9] in New York comenced on Monday the 13th contnued over five days the Colored People suffrd most from the mob

1864

November, Tuesday, 8, 1864.

rainy angain to day to day is the great election i think lincoln will gain the day i did not go to meeting for fer [fear] something might happeen

***

Wednesday [December], 7.

very Stormy vincent gave me coupel of tickets and for Nell we went to the Celabraion it certainly was a very grand afair the singing and speaking was exellent

1865
Monday [April], 3

beutiful day i have bin quite busy all day in the afternoon i went down to Ellens to rejoce over the great newes Richmond has fallen

Thursday, April 4, 1865.

the city is wild with excitement flags are flying everywere busy day i have bin running errands in the evening i went to meeting at mrs gibbs

***

Friday [April] 14

to day is the day we Celebrate the soldiers Parrade a flag was presented to the reggiment by the banneker very Plesent it every body seemed to have a holidy

Saturday 15

very sad newes was received this morning of the murder of the President the city is in deep mourning we had a meeting of the association

***

Wednesday [December] 20

Cold i received very sad news today my Dear Brother Alfred Died at 10 oclock To Day I am so Sorry i Did not get to see him

Thursday, December 21, 1865.

before he Died very Cold to Day i started for harrisburg this after noon found father nell and the rest of the family i had a very sad journey

Friday 22

Very Cold this Day i have looked forward to with Dead [dread] Poor Alfred was buried this afternoon no one but him that knows all things knew my feeling

***

Sunday [December], 31

very cloudy this morning i went to s church very few out mr weaver spoke for us i stoped at mary's after church she looks quite comical sailing around this year closes with many changes who knows what the next year will be i feel vey thankfull that i am alive and well Nell and mary are bothe sick vincent spent Part of the evening with me we went to watch meeting

Miscellaneous

Jan 1 1865 mr gibbs Preached his farewell sermon to day his text was from 2v of acts 32 verse and now brethren i commend you to god A grand reception was given on the 11th of Jan for mr pierson the antislavery sufferer vincent went to harrisburg on the 7th of Feb to attend the convention Feeb 20th 1865

John Simson has at last enlisted mary is quite distessed mary S maried [. . .] the 9th 1865 an eventful wedding mr gibbs married them

Miscellaneous

March 19 mr gibbs Preached a very impressive sermon from the text the kings bussiness

requires hast som [. . .]

April 14, 1865 The President Was assasinated by Som Confederate villain at the theathre

die Saturday morning the 15 the city is in the Deepest sorrow

These are strang times The body of the President Passed through on the 22 of april Dec

[. . .] 1865 Sues boy born this afternoon i was there in the afternoon after church

all is well that ends well
485 york avenue
439 north fourth st

NOTES

1. Giesberg, *Emilie Davis's Civil War*, 5.

2. Jubilee: day of Emancipation, January 1, 1863, after the Emancipation Proclamation freed enslaved people in Southern states.

3. Nellie: likely Emilie's close friend.

4. The draft was deeply unpopular in Philadelphia. Whites rioted against it.

5. Alfred was Emilie's brother. He served in the US Navy.

6. EJ. Elijah, another brother, was a waiter.

7. Mary was Alfred's wife.

8. Possibly George Bustill White, Emilie's future husband. They were married on December 13, 1866.

9. The New York draft riots from July 13 to July 16, 1863.

BIBLIOGRAPHY

The Emilie Davis Diaries. Emilie Davis diaries, Collection 3030, The Historical Society of Pennsylvania. https://libraries.psu .edu/about/collections/emilie-davis -diaries.

Giesberg, Judith. *Army at Home: Women and the Civil War on the Northern Home Front.* Chapel Hill: University of North Carolina Press, 2012.

Giesberg, Judith, et al., eds. *Emilie Davis's Civil War: The Diaries of a Free Black Woman in Philadelphia, 1863–1865.* University

Park: Pennsylvania State University Press, 2014.

Whitehead, Karsonya Wise. *Notes from a Colored Girl: The Civil War Pocket Diaries of Emilie Frances Davis.* Columbia: University of South Carolina Press, 2014.

Octavius Catto, *Our Alma Mater: An Address Delivered at Concert Hall on the Occasion of the Twelfth Annual Commencement of the Institute for Colored Youth, May 10th, 1864* (1864)

Octavius Catto was born a free person of mixed race in Charleston, South Carolina, in 1839. He and his family moved first to Baltimore and then Philadelphia when he was a child. His father, William Catto, had been born enslaved but was manumitted and became a prominent Presbyterian minister. Octavius was well educated, first attending the Vaux Primary School and then Lombard Grammar School, both segregated institutions. After attending an all-White school in New Jersey in 1854, he became a student in a rigorous Philadelphia school, the Institute for Colored Youth (ICY), run by Quakers. The school was founded in Philadelphia at 9th and Bainbridge in 1837 and is now located in Delaware County, Pennsylvania, and called Cheyney University. In 1859, Catto was hired to teach math and English at ICY. In 1869, he was selected to be principal of the school's male division.

Catto gave his speech *Our Alma Mater* at the twelfth commencement of the Institute for Colored Youth. He began his address in a fairly typical fashion, speaking about the educational goals and values the school espoused. He went on to praise the successes of the small number of graduates the school had produced, at the same time calling for a larger facility to allow for more students. But then Catto went beyond the topic of the school itself, making a plea for equal rights that undoubtedly made many of the White patrons of the school uncomfortable. He spoke of the need for more Black teachers to teach the students. He went on to make a call for action, that "educated colored people like himself, . . . teach the newly freed slaves."[1]

In addition to his interest in education, Catto pursued a number of other causes on behalf of African Americans. He encouraged Black Philadelphians to fight for the Union cause during the Civil War. In concert with Frederick

Douglass and others, Catto raised eleven regiments of Black soldiers in the Philadelphia area. Although he was commissioned as a major, Catto never fought in the war. When the war ended, he worked vigorously for the ratification of the Fifteenth Amendment, giving Black men the right to vote. He also fought to desegregate the Philadelphia trolley car system, leading protests and writing petitions.

In addition to operating in the political sphere, Catto took a great interest in sports, particularly cricket and baseball. He was one of the founders of the Pythian Base Ball Club of Philadelphia. Although the Pythians were rejected in their bid to enter the Pennsylvania Base Ball Association, they did play against a White team in 1869, the first baseball game played between the races.

On October 10, 1871, on his way to vote, after an altercation with a White mob that tried to prevent him from voting, Catto was shot and killed. His killer was never convicted of either assault or murder. Though he was much respected during his lifetime and his funeral well attended with full military honors, Catto's grave was neglected for a number of years. This was corrected in 2007 when a headstone was erected at his burial site in Eden Cemetery. A bronze statue of him was installed in front of Philadelphia's City Hall in 2017, the first public monument in the city honoring an individual African American.

—

Ladies and Gentlemen:

The brief part which we may occupy of this evening's passage will not permit, nor does the intelligence of the audience here assembled require us to enter into any argument for the establishment of the highly important utility of Education.

Fortunately, from the enlightenment of the age in which we live, the past achievements of educated minds in the world's history are so plainly evident and immensely valuable, that he who in these halcyon days of intellectual progress invites the attention of an assemblage to the subject of Popular Education, has his cardinal principles as readily accepted as are the axioms and postulates of mathematical science. And even now,—in the midst of an internal revolution,—while our country's energies are being severely taxed to exhibit her resources in those arts and sciences which are not in the curriculum of institutions similar to the one under whose auspices we have been called together,—it is wise to pause and remember, that the principles of right, equity, and justice; the very ideas of an improved civilization, more benign and general in its diffusion; the very moral conception of individual and mutual rights of property, contract and government, upon which the people of the North justify their attitude in the present conflict, have never been more successfully and generally promulgated than through the teachings of the School. And we venture the belief, that had there been, through the Southern part of this country, a system of education for the masses, irrespective of class or color exhibiting in its energy one half of the zeal which has, within those States, been exerted to keep the conscience unenlightened and the understanding uninstructed,—we to-night would not be found at the crisis of a civil war.

It was a true estimate of the potent influence which education would wield in the politics of the State and in the councils of the Church, that created, as schools began to be multiplied in Europe, a lively interest in those respective bodies for the establishment and perpetuity of educational institutions.

Aristotle, in the spirit of a true philosopher and wise statesman, held, that "the most effective way of preserving a State, is to bring up the citizens in the spirit of the Government; to fashion, and, as it were, cast them in the mould of the Constitution."[2]

Martin Luther, passing in the midst of the clashing Modes of the Reformation,—with the spirit of a zealous churchman—urged that "it is a grave and serious thing, affecting the interest of the Kingdom of Christ, and of all the world, that we apply ourselves to the work of aiding and instructing the young."

The wisdom and value of those opinions are evidenced in the immense debt which those Churches and States that lead the civilized world, owe to their educated men, and by the honorable rivalry which has subsequently existed between the political economist and the religious sect for the direction of the educational systems of their countries.

In Prussia, the State gained the advantage; and, consequently, there is no country in Europe in which educated men join so numerously in the intelligent administration of the Government.

In England, the Church secured the management of the educational system. And to-night, England in all her glory, the enlightenment of her Christianity, the purity of her morals, the researchers of her sciences, the application of her wisdom, and the spirit of her just laws, is not more indebted to the influence of her Church than is the English Church to the genius and talents of her Christian scholars.

In our country this rivalry has been compromised. The State may, for any special purpose, establish such schools as it deems proper. The Church, too, is granted the same privileges. But by far the greater number of schools,— we refer to those under the system called Public,—are established and governed by neither Church nor State, being left entirely to the control of the people. This system, though liable to many abuses, is probably the best yet devised. Besides these public institutions, supported by direct taxation, there is a numerous class founded and cherished by benevolent and philanthropic individuals. Such is the institution which convenes us now, and of which we purpose to give a synoptical[3] history.

The original fund upon which the institute was founded, came like many other goodly gifts for the amelioration of the colored man's unfortunate condition in this country, from a member of the Society of Friends: a people whose proverbial sympathy and charity for the oppressed, whose consistent opposition to ignorance, intemperance, war, and slavery, have rendered their name inseparable from our heartfelt gratitude and respect. The honor of first conceiving the feasibility and utility of such an institution belongs to Richard Humphreys[4] of Philadelphia. It was he who left the first fund of ten thousand dollars for the establishment. When the legacy came under the guidance of the Society in 1837, it had amounted to thirteen thousand three hundred and twelve dollars. Up to the time of the second meeting of the Society in 1838, the fund had been increased by individual donations to sixteen thousand two hundred and ninety dollars.

With this sum as a basis, the "Institute for Colored Youth" procured its charter from the Legislature of Pennsylvania in the year 1842.

Its primary objects are the education and improvement of colored youths, male and female, "to act as teachers and instructors in the different branches of school learning, or in the mechanic arts and agriculture."

The corporation, according to a provision of the charter, consists only of members of the Society of Friends.

The government of the affairs and the control of the funds of the institute are committed to a "Board of Managers," consisting of fifteen members, these managers being members of, and receiving their appointment from the corporation.

Shortly after this charter of the institute had been secured, an additional sum of eighteen thousand, five hundred dollars, which had been devised for educational purposes by another Friend, was granted to the corporation and increased the school fund to thirty-four thousand seven hundred and ninety dollars. This amount was, in turn, increased by subscriptions at various times from members of the Society of Friends until the aggregate school fund reached sixty-four thousand dollars.

At this stage in the history of the fund, the Board of Managers considered it wise to erect buildings for the permanent establishment and location of the Institute; and those on Lombard Street, in which, the school is now taught, were erected in 1851.

There are now in the school four departments. One High, and one Preparatory School, for each sex. There are six teachers, all colored, employed within the Institute.

Three of the teachers are graduates of the Institution.

The course of study is similar to that pursued in high schools, including an acquaintance with Latin, Greek, Geometry, and the Trigometries.

Connected with the Institute are a public reading room and library containing over two thousand volumes selected with care from the various fields of literature.

The average attendance of pupils is a little above one hundred.

Text-books and all privileges of the Institute are free of charge to those regularly admitted.

There have been graduated from the school twenty-seven scholars; which number is to be increased tonight by the presentation of the Diploma to nine others who have completed the required course of study.

Probably, there is no better way of judging the worth of the Institute than by glancing at the positions the graduates hold in the sphere of usefulness to their fellow-men, and the amount of intelligently directed labor they may be performing, to contradict the aspersions which have been cast upon the people with whom they are identified.

The first graduate, J. E. Glasgow, Jr., of the class of 1856, entered the University of Edinburgh and pursued his studies with distinguished success. He won a prize in every examination which his class entered, and shortly before his death, which took place on the near approach of his graduating, he bore away the second prize for excellence in Mathematics. This was no light achievement in one of the best Universities in Europe, and among the noblest youth of Scotland.

Two graduates are now pursuing a course at the Penn Medical University[5] in this city, and sixteen others have been engaged in teaching; three of whom are now in public schools in our own city.

One in the seventh section, having raised without aid from any source, a school, large and prosperous enough to be entered among the public schools of her section of the city. The other two are severally in the twelfth and twenty-fourth school sections.

And here we might consistently ask that the liberal spirit and manly example of the Boards in the section just referred to, may be followed by others to whom the appointment of teachers for colored schools is delegated.

It is at least unjust to allow a blind and ignorant prejudice to so far disregard the choice of parents and the will of the colored tax-payers, as to appoint over colored children White teachers, whose intelligence and success, measured by the fruits of their labors, could neither obtain nor secure for them positions which we know would be more congenial to their tastes.

Besides these graduates then employed in teaching, three are now performing the duties of office clerks in this city; and one other, the pioneer from our ranks, is engaged in the commendable task of instructing the Freed children at Norfolk in Virginia.

Thus have we enumerated those who are contributing by their positions to establish the good which was primarily hoped in the beginning of the Institute.

About two years ago, the Managers, constantly regarding the interest and welfare of the school, called the attention of its friends to the advantages which would result from more ample and convenient accommodations, in a location less noisy and surrounded by influence of a more moral tendency.

Two members of the Society of Friends at once offered the Board of Managers five thousand dollars apiece, if twenty thousand additional could be raised by the Board.

The executors of the late Josiah Dawson,[6] having previously given five thousand dollars to the Institute, promised five thousand more, on condition that the Managers would collect the remaining ten thousand. Both of these generous proposals were accepted, and very shortly after, by private contributions from Friends, the total sum of thirty thousand dollars was secured. This amount, with six thousand for a similar purpose already in the hands of the treasurer, gave the Board a new building fund of thirty-six thousand dollars. Thus we have been brought to the present epoch in our Institute's history.

Of the amount recently raised for the erection of the new buildings, ten thousand dollars have been expended for the purchase of a fine lot, seventy-seven by one hundred and forty feet, on Shippen Street, above Ninth. The site is peculiarly well adapted to the purpose for which the wise choice of this Board selected it. It fronts opposite Ronaldson's Cemetery on one side, and the three other sides being so situated that no buildings may closely approach them,—it possesses all that could be desired for the conveniences of a healthy ventilation. The ample depth of the grounds will allow the main building a situation so far back from Shippen Street as to secure the recitations from the ordinary noise of common throughfares, and at the same time provide liberal yards for the erection of the modern appliances for gymnastic exercises. The accommodations for pupils, library and reading room are to be on a more extensive basis than we now enjoy; and the erection of a laboratory for the more successful instruction in the practical science, is a part of the plan of the building.

Indeed, we may readily perceive the intention of the Board to make this a first class Institute, to rank its course of instruction among the best of our Normal Schools.[7] For this noble determination on their part, not only the colored people themselves should be grateful and their friends well pleased; but for which every man who admires the spirit of disinterested benevolence and unostentatious charity which their labors exhibit, should rejoice and feel encouraged.

But there is a broader view of the Institute's history than that which simply regards its efforts upon the individual scholar.

You will pardon us, if we briefly, and as we think very naturally and consistently turn to a few thoughts touching the part which this and other similar institutions are destined to play is determining the future condition of the colored American.

If we were asked to point to one of the most prominent features by which the history of the colored man's struggles in this country shall be defined, we would direct your attention to that brave vessel returning from one of the West India Islands, freighted with native-born black citizens of the United States. Let it be recorded to the credit of Mr. Lincoln as the purest act which his administration has thus far performed for justice to the colored American. Let the statesman regard it as the jeweled hand of the President lifting the dark veil of the golden Future.[8] Let the nation accept it as the voice of God, declaring that He has made of one blood all nations to dwell upon the face of this country.

How much of the course of this terrible revolution remains yet to be run, or how many political evolutions our Government may yet be forced to make, no man can foresee. But it must be the most superficial view, indeed, which concludes that any other condition than a total change in the status which the colored man has hitherto had in this country, must of necessity grow out of the conflicting theories of the parties to whose lands this question is at present committed. There must come a change, one now in process of completion, which shall force upon this nation, not so much for the good of the black man, as for its own political and industrial welfare, that course which Providence seems wisely to be directing for the mutual benefit of both peoples.

Those millions of human beings now scattered through the Southern country must eventually come forth into the sunlight of Freedom, and what a field will there then be opened for the benevolence of the wealthy, and the labors of the educated colored man! Truly, the harvest will be great and the laborers comparatively few.

Those people will need among them Christian missionaries, intelligent teachers and laborers, to direct them to that course of life and in those modes of industry which have always in the world's history contributed so much for peoples similarly situated. It is for the purpose of promoting, as far as possible, the preparation of the colored man for the assumption of the new relations with intelligence and with the knowledge which promises success that the Institute feels called upon at this time to act with more energy and on broader scale than has hitherto required. It is just here that its claims are worthiest of consideration. It is the duty of every man, to the extent of his interests and means, to provide for the immediate improvement of the four or five millions of ignorant and previously dependent laborers who will be thrown upon society in the reorganization of the Union.

It is for the good of the Nation that every element of its population be wisely instructed in the advantages of a Republican Government, that every element of its people, mingled though they be, shall have a true and intelligent conception of the allegiance due to the established powers.

Now this cannot be done in any other way than by properly educating the masses in the South; then these States will, indeed, be regenerated and the elements of their population be made ministering agents for the profit of the whole Nation and the lasting security of the Government.

Such we believe to be the philosophy of the relations which the colored man will hold to this country. Then will he be enjoying intelligently the franchises of the citizen, understanding the system and spirit of the laws that govern his country, entering knowingly into the development of her physical resources and the cultivation of his own moral and intellectual gifts. For though born in ignorance and liable to fall in a competition with the intelligent foreigner and migrating Northerner as they go southward,—yet he has within him an aspiration and a capability to rise by faith, labor, and perseverance to a respectable place among his competitors. All that he asks is, that there shall be no unmanly quibbles about intrusting to him any positions of honor or profit for which his attainments may fit him. And that which is committed to him as a *man*, he will perform as no other than a *man* could perform.

Then when the day of his disabilities shall have passed, his memory will cling with pleasure, and his heart throb deep with gratitude to those men, who, like the managers and donors of this our Alma Mater, will have contributed so vastly to a "consummation so devoutly wished."[i][9]

Their sufferings on the voyage, and after they had reached the island, were beyond description. The attention of the President having been called to their condition, he despatched Mr. D. C. Donohue of Indiana, to examine the case. On receiving a report of their sufferings, the President directed that they be returned to the United States, and the ship Martin C. Day was sent to the island, during February, and yesterday returned with three hundred and sixty-eight of the original number. "It is to be hoped that is experience will teach us the folly of attempting to depopulate the country of its valuable labor."—*Philadelphia Press*, March 22, 1864.

i. In April last, four hundred and twenty colored colonists were embarked from Fortress Monroe, under a contract with Messrs. Forbes and Tuckerman of New York, for the Isle of Avache.

NOTES

1. Biddle and Dubin, *Tasting Freedom*, 310–11.

2. From Aristotle's *Politics*.

3. Synoptical: a summary.

4. Richard Humphreys: a silversmith who later became a philanthropist, leaving funds to establish the Institute for Colored Youth.

5. Penn Medical University: the oldest medical school in the United States, founded in 1765.

6. Josiah Dawson married into the wealthy Elfreth family.

7. Normal Schools: institutions that train students to become teachers.

8. Golden Future: Lincoln's failed attempt to resettle freed slaves in Central America and the Caribbean after the Civil War. Many Blacks did not see this as a benevolent act.

9. Paul S. Forbes and Charles K. Tuckerman were entrepreneurs engaged by Abraham Lincoln to establish a colony of formerly enslaved people on the Haitian island Île à Vache in 1862.

BIBLIOGRAPHY

Biddle, Daniel R., and Murray Dubin. *Tasting Freedom: Octavius Catto and the Battle for Equality in Civil War America*. Philadelphia: Temple University Press, 2010.

Silcox, Harry C. "Nineteenth Century Philadelphia Black Militant: Octavius V. Catto (1839–1871)." *Pennsylvania History: A Journal of Mid-Atlantic Studies* 44, no. 1 (January 1977): 53–76.

Smith, Aaron X. "Murder of Octavius Catto." *Encyclopedia of Greater Philadelphia*. https://philadelphiaencyclopedia.org /essays/murder-of-octavius-catto/.

Waskie, Andy. "Biography of Octavius V. Catto: Forgotten Black Hero of Philadelphia." General Meade Society. https://general meadesociety.org/octavius-catto -biography.

William Still, from *A Brief Narrative of the Struggle for the Rights of the Colored People of Philadelphia in the City Railway Cars* (1867)

William Still was born a free Black in Burlington, New Jersey, in 1821. He moved to Philadelphia in 1844 and in 1847 began working as a clerk for the Pennsylvania Society for the Abolition of Slavery. Soon he became a leader in the Philadelphia Vigilance Committee, serving as the nerve center of the Underground Railroad. Though he had little formal education, Still taught himself to read and write. He became a leading businessman working in real estate and in the stove and coal industries. In addition to being an abolitionist, Still was a strong advocate for universal suffrage, and he fought for equal treatment of all people.

Still wrote his *Brief Narrative of the Struggle for the Rights of the Colored People of Philadelphia in the City Railway Cars* in response to the segregated transportation system in the city. The pamphlet grew from a newspaper letter and article Still wrote in 1859. The railway cars did not allow Blacks to ride within them, so they had to stand on platforms outside the doors, causing a dangerous and humiliating experience. This was the case no matter the weather and regardless of the social status or gender of the person, things that especially irked him. Still also points out what W. E. B. Du Bois would elaborate on in *The Philadelphia Negro*: that Blacks were no longer isolated in one or two wards of the city, and that the streetcars needed to address this. As their population spread out over the city, as Geoff Zylstra observes, "African Americans demanded access to the streetcar both because it was critical to their mobility in a growing industrial city and because they desired freedom and equality, things they associated with rail technology."[1]

My first newspaper article appeared in the *North American and United States Gazette* in the year above [1859] alluded to. The extract taken therefrom will show whether I advocated the rights of the masses or only a few. It literally reads thus:

COLORED PEOPLE AND THE CARS.

To the Editor of the North American and United States Gazette:

Sir:—As a colored man, and constant reader of your paper, allow me a brief corner in your columns to make a few remarks on the sore grievance of genteel colored people in being excluded from the city passenger railroad cars, except they choose to "stand on the front platform with the driver."

However long the distance they may have to go, or great their hurry, however unwell or aged, genteel or neatly attired—however hot, cold or stormy the weather—however few in the cars, as the masses of the colored people now understand it, they are unceremoniously excluded.

Of course my own humble opinion will weigh but little with yourself and readers (being, as I am, of the proscribed class)—as to whether it is a loss or a gain to railroad companies, thus to exclude colored people. Nevertheless, pardon me for saying that this severe proscription, for some unaccountable reason, is carried to an extent in Philadelphia unparalleled in any of the leading cities of the Union. This is not imagination or an exaggerated assertion.

In New Orleans, colored people—slaves as well as free—ride in all the city cars and omnibuses. In Cincinnati, colored women are accommodated in the city omnibuses, but colored men are proscribed to a certain extent. In Chicago it may be safely said that not the slightest proscription exists in the public conveyances of that flourishing city. In New York, Brooklyn,[2] &c., (except on one or two of the New York city passenger lines,) there is not the slightest barrier to any persons riding, on account of complexion. There is no obstruction in the way of colored persons in any of the Boston cars or omnibuses.

I need not allude to the cities of minor importance, whether favorable or unfavorable, North or South. Sufficient are the facts in the examples of the cities already alluded to, to make it a very painfully serious inquiry with intelligent colored people, why it is so in Philadelphia, the city of "Brotherly Love," so noted as the bulwark of the "Religious Society of Friends, commonly called Quakers," so noted as one of the leading cities in the Union, in great religious and benevolent enterprises, so pre-eminently favorable to elevating the heathen in Africa, while forgetful of those in their very precincts—those who are taxed to support the very highways that they are rejected from.

But, doubtless, on a hurried consideration of the claims of the colored people, serious objections would be found by railroad boards and others, under the erroneous impression that the vicinity of St. Mary,[3] Bedford,[4] Seventh and Lombard[5] streets, &c., furnishes a sample of the great body of colored people residing in Philadelphia.

I beg, Mr. Editor, to respectfully add, that the inhabitants of this ill-fated region are by no means a fair sample of the twenty thousand colored people of Philadelphia. The gulf between this degraded class and the great mass of industrious colored people, is well nigh as marked as was the gulf between Dives and Lazarus,[6] in the parable; as I shall attempt to demonstrate here, besides volunteering further to prove, by ocular testimony, if any of your readers choose to condescend to accompany me to parts and places where the decent portions of colored people reside; to the eighteen or twenty colored churches, with their Sabbath schools; to at least twenty day schools, of a public and private character; to the dozens of beneficial societies, united for the mutual support of their sick and disabled members; to the neat and genteely furnished three-story brick houses, owned, occupied, and paid taxes for, almost entirely by colored people—on Rodman street, Ronaldson street,[7] and Washington street; to observe the extent of valuable property owned on South and Lombard streets (in the most respectable part of those streets); to examine some of the stores (they may not be large) kept by colored men; (of which more will be said presently) to pass those living in respectable houses elegantly furnished, houses alone worth from five to ten thousand dollars; likewise leaving out the many in various other parts of the city, where industrious, sober and decent people live and own considerable real estate. I think abundant evidence may be found in the directions alluded to, to convince the most prejudiced against the colored man, that he is by no mean[s] so sadly degraded and miserably poor as the public have generally been led to suppose, from all that has been said of him in connection with the degraded localities alluded to before.

I hardly know an anti-slavery paper in the country into which this article was not copied and commended. And, if I mistake not, it was the first newspaper article that found its way into any of the daily papers of Philadelphia on the subject of our grievance.

***

In the winter of 1864 the following letter appeared in the morning *Press* of this city, and I merely give it in this connection to show the spirit in which I advocated the cause, and the effect it produced.

THE PASSENGER CARS AND COLORED CITIZENS.
To the Editor of the Press:

Sir: Please permit me to state through the columns of your liberal journal a matter of very serious public grievance, which colored people generally are daily subjected to, and which, as an individual, I experienced to-day to a degree that I shall not attempt to fully describe, although I feel I shall never forget it.

Briefly, the circumstances were these: Being under the necessity of going out to Camp William Penn[8] to-day, on business, I took the North Pennsylvania Railroad, and reached the ground about 11 o'clock. Remembering that pressing duties required my presence at my store by a certain hour in the early part of the afternoon, I promptly attended to my business at the camp, but as I could not return by the way I came without waiting two and a half hours for the down train, I concluded that I would walk over to Germantown, and come to the city by the 1 o'clock steam cars. Accordingly, I reached Germantown, but too late for the train by about five minutes, as the cars had just gone. To wait another hour I felt was out of the question; hence, I decided to take the city passenger cars. Soon one came along with but few passengers in it, and into it I walked with a man who had been to the camp with me (but fortunately he happened to be of the approved complexion), and took a seat. Quickly the conductor approached me and I tendered him the fare for us both (the man alluded to being in my employment). The conductor very cordially received the money, but before he took time to hand me the change that was due to me, invited me to "step out on the platform." "Why is this?' I remarked. "It is against the rules," he added. "Who objects?" I inquired. "It is the aristocracy," he again added. "Well, it is a *cruel rule!* and I believe this is the only city of note in the civilized world, where a decent colored man cannot be allowed to ride in a city passenger car. Even the cars which were formerly built in Philadelphia for New Orleans were not devoid of accommodations for colored people inside," I continued. ["]And now, with regard to the aristocracy, I do not believe the blame rests with them; for I happen to be one of a committee who some time back brought this question before the public in the shape of a petition, and it was very freely signed by hundreds of the most respectable citizens; by leading clergymen, lawyers, doctors, editors, merchants, etc,. amongst whom were Bishop Potter, Hon. Horace Binney, etc., and some of the railway presidents besides." Of course, the conductor declared that he had no objections himself, but continued to insist that it was "the rules."

"Who is the President of this road?"

After pausing for a moment (what he meant I know not), he answered by saying he believed his name was "Mr. Whartman."

"A former President," I remarked, declared to a committee that "no such rules had ever been made on this road."

I told him that I paid taxes, etc., but of course it was of no avail.

Riding on the platform of a bitter cold day like this I need not say is almost intolerable, but to compel persons to pay the same as those who enjoy comfortable seats inside by a good fire, seems quite atrocious.

Yet I felt, under the circumstances, compelled to submit to the wrong, for the sake of arriving at my place of business in due time. But before I arrived at my destination it began to snow, which, as I was already thoroughly chilled with the cold, made the platform utterly intolerable; hence, I concluded to walk the rest of the distance, and accordingly got off, feeling satisfied that no where in Christendom could be found a better illustration of Judge Taney's decision in the Dred Scott case,[9] in which he declared that "black men have no rights which white men are bound to respect," than are demonstrated by the "rules" of the passenger cars of the City of Brotherly Love.

The Judge's decision and the "rules" have harassed me every moment since. I try to think of cannibals in heathen lands and traitors in the South, and wrongs generally, but it is all to no purpose—this car inhumanity sticks to me.

"But this is only an individual case, hence but a trifling matter," you may think, Mr. Editor. Far from it, sir. Every colored man, woman, and child of the 25,000 inhabitants of this city, many of whom are tax payers, and as upright as any other class of citizens, are daily liable to this treatment. The truth is, so far as my case is concerned, I fared well, compared with the treatment some have received. A long catalogue of injuries and outrages could be recounted, but suffice it to remind your readers of only one or two instances:

A venerable old minister of the Gospel, in going from here to his home at Frankford, one dark, cold, and rainy night last winter, while occupying the only place on the platform assigned for colored people, was killed. Who has forgotten this fact?

One more instance, and I will relieve you. One evening, in going home from a lecture, two elegantly-dressed women stepped into a car, and took seats. The conductor courageously brought the rules forward, and one of them instantly stepped out, while the other remained. The car was stopped and the conductor seized her, and actually, by physical force, thrust her out of the car. The father of this young woman pays several hundred dollars taxes annually; keeps his horse and carriage, and lives as nicely as most respectable citizens. But the God-given hue of the skin of his daughter rendered her obnoxious to the rules of the railway company, and she had to meekly submit to the outrage.

Respectfully,
Wm. Still

Philadelphia, Dec. 11, 1863.

This little incident, which I had no idea would create an interest outside of Philadelphia, to my great surprise was copied in many papers through the country, and likewise found its way into the columns of the *London Times.*

NOTES

1. Zylstra, "Whiteness, Freedom, and Technology," 680.

2. Brooklyn was not consolidated into New York City until 1898.

3. St. Mary's Street was in the Seventh Ward. It, like other streets mentioned, were in some of Philadelphia's worst slums.

4. Bedford Street (now Wildey Street) ran from Frankford Avenue to Columbia Avenue.

5. Parts of Seventh and Lombard were also in the Seventh Ward.

6. Dives and Lazarus (Luke 16:19–31): Dives is not an actual name but is used to describe a rich man. After he dies, he suffers in torment in the afterlife because of his sinful life, whereas a good man, Lazarus, who was a beggar when alive, is comforted.

7. Ronaldson Street (now South Delhi Street) is the area in which abolitionist William Still lived.

8. Camp William Penn: a Union Army training camp located in Cheltenham Township, Pennsylvania, from 1863 to 1865. Over eleven thousand African American soldiers were trained there.

9. Dred Scott case: also known as *Dred Scott v. Sandford*. Scott, an enslaved person, was taken by his owner from Missouri, a slave state, to several free states. In 1846, Scott sued for his freedom on the grounds that he had been residing in free states. When the case was finally decided in 1854, Chief Justice Roger Taney ruled against Scott, deciding that all people of African descent, free or enslaved, were not

United States citizens and therefore had no right to sue in American courts. Scott was eventually freed by his owner in 1857, but he died in 1858 from tuberculosis.

BIBLIOGRAPHY

Diemer, Andrew K. *Vigilance: The Life of William Still: Father of the Underground Railroad.* New York: Alfred A. Knopf, 2022.

Foner, Philip S. "The Battle to End Discrimination Against Negroes in Philadelphia Against Negroes on Philadelphia Streetcars, Part I." *Pennsylvania History A Journal of Mid-Atlantic Studies* 40, no. 3 (July 1973): 261–92.

———. "The Battle to End Discrimination Against Negroes in Philadelphia Against Negroes on Philadelphia Streetcars, Part II." *Pennsylvania History: A Journal of Mid-Atlantic Studies* 40, no. 4 (October 1973): 354–79.

Zylstra, Geoff D. "Whiteness, Freedom, and Technology: The Racial Struggle over Philadelphia's Streetcars, 1859–1867." *Technology and Culture* 52, no. 4 (October 2011): 678–702.

William Still, from *The Underground Railroad: A Record of Facts, Authentic Narratives, Letters, & c.* (1872)

Still is best known for his book *The Underground Railroad*. He took copious notes on the numerous men and women who passed through the Philadelphia station while he was working there. The case of Henry Box Brown may be the most famous escape recorded by Still. Brown, considered to be a piece of property, gained his freedom by making himself into a parcel, one to be mailed from Richmond, Virginia, to Philadelphia. The fact that he was willing to endure being shipped in a box "two feet eight inches deep, two feet wide, and three feet long" shows his desperation to escape slavery. To him, Philadelphia represented freedom, the Promised Land. Yet Still rather blasély remarks of this extraordinary escape that "in point of interest, however, his case is no more remarkable than many others. Indeed, neither before nor after escaping did he suffer one-half what many others have experienced."

One who may have suffered more than Brown is Jane Johnson. Still writes of her situation, which is also fictionalized by Lorene Cary in her novel *The Price of a Child*, an excerpt of which is included in section 3 of this anthology. Still relates the story of how Johnson and two of her sons gain their freedom after meeting members of the Underground Railroad in Philadelphia. Despite their aid, Johnson exerted agency for her freedom. She told Black people she desired her freedom and stated, "I went away of my own free will." Johnson testified in New York on behalf of Passmore Williamson, a White abolitionist who helped lead her to freedom. He had been imprisoned for aiding her, but Johnson's brave testimony, risking her own freedom, helped gain his release from prison after three months. Williamson was thereafter treated as a hero by members of the abolitionist movement.

Among other duties devolving on the Vigilance Committee when hearing of slaves brought into the State by their owners, was immediately to inform such persons that as they were not fugitives, but were brought into the State by their masters, they were entitled to their freedom without another moment's service, and that they could have the assistance of the Committee and the advice of counsel without charge, by simply availing themselves of these proffered favors.

Many slave-holders fully understood the law in this particular, and were also equally posted with regard to the vigilance of abolitionists. Consequently they avoided bringing slaves beyond Mason's and Dixon's Line in traveling North. But some slave-holders were not mindful of the laws, or were too arrogant to take heed, as may be seen in the case of Colonel John H. Wheeler, of North Carolina, the United States Minister to Nicaragua. In passing through Philadelphia from Washington, one very warm July day in 1855, accompanied by three of his slaves, his high official equilibrium, as well as his assumed rights under the Constitution, received a terrible shock at the hands of the Committee. Therefore, for the readers of these pages, and in order to completely illustrate the various phases of the work of the Committee in the days of Slavery, this case, selected from many others, is a fitting one. However, for more than a brief recital of some of the more prominent incidents, it will not be possible to find room in this volume. And, indeed, the necessity of so doing is precluded by the fact that Mr. Williamson in justice to himself and the cause of freedom, with great pains and singular ability, gathered the most important facts bearing on his memorable trial and imprisonment, and published them in a neat volume for historical reference.[1]

In order to bring fully before the reader the beginning of this interesting and exciting case, it seems only necessary to publish the subjoined letter, written by one of the actors in the drama, and addressed to the New York Tribune, and an additional paragraph which may be requisite to throw light on a special point, which Judge Kane[2] decided was concealed in the "obstinate" breast of Passmore Williamson, as said Williamson persistently refused before the said Judge's court, to own that he had a knowledge of the mystery in question.

After which, a brief glance at some of the more important points of the case must suffice.

Letter Copied from the New York Tribune

Philadelphia, Monday, July 30, 1855.

As the public have not been made acquainted with the facts and particulars respecting the agency of Mr. Passmore Williamson and others, in relation to the slave case now agitating this city, and especially as the poor slave mother and her two sons have been so grossly misrepresented, I deem it my duty to lay the facts before you, for publication or otherwise, as you may think proper.

On Wednesday afternoon, week, at 4-½ o'clock, the following note was placed in my hands by a colored boy whom I had never before seen, to my recollection:

"Mr. Still—*Sir*. Will you come down to Bloodgood's Hotel[3] as soon as possible—as there are three fugitive slaves here and they want liberty. Their master is here with them, on his way to New York."

The note was without date, and the signature so indistinctly written as not to be understood by me, having evidently been penned in a moment of haste.

Without delay I ran with the note to Mr. P. Williamson's office, Seventh and Arch, found him at his desk, and gave it to him, and after reading it, he remarked that he could not go down, as he had to go to Harrisburg that night on business—but he advised me to go, and to get the names of the slave-holder and the slaves, in order to telegraph to New York to have them arrested there, as no time remained to procure a writ of habeas corpus here.

I could not have been two minutes in Mr. W's office before starting in haste for the wharf. To my surprise, however, when I reached the wharf, there I found Mr. W., his mind having undergone a sudden change; he was soon on the spot.

I saw three or four colored persons in the hall at Bloodgood's, none of whom I recognized except the boy who had brought me the note. Before having time for making inquiry, some one said they had gone on board the boat. "Get their description," said Mr. W. I instantly inquired of one of the colored persons for the desired description, and was told that she was "a tall, dark woman, with two little boys."

Mr. W. and myself ran on board of the boat, looked among the passengers on the first deck, but saw them not. "They are up on the second deck," an unknown voice uttered. In a second we were in their presence. We approached the anxious-looking slave-mother with her two boys on her left-hand; close on her right sat an ill-favored white man having a cane in his hand which I took to be a sword-cane. (As to its being a sword-cane, however, I might have been mistaken.)

The first words to the mother were: "Are you traveling?" "Yes," was the prompt answer. "With whom?" She nodded her head toward the ill-favored man, signifying with him. Fidgeting on his seat, he said something, exactly what I do not now recollect. In reply I remarked: "Do they belong to you, Sir?" "Yes, they are in my charge," was his answer. Turning from him to the mother and her sons, in substance, and word for word, as near as I can remember, the following remarks though calmly addressed by the individuals who rejoiced to meet hem on free soil, and who felt unmistakably assured that they were justified by the laws of Philadelphia as well as the Law of God, in informing them of their rights.

"You are entitled to your freedom according to the laws of Pennsylvania, having been brought into the State by your owner. If you prefer freedom to slavery, as we suppose everybody does, you have the chance to accept it now. Act calmly—don't be frightened by your master—you are as much entitled to your freedom as we are, or as he is—be determined and you need have no fears but that you will be protected by the law. Judges have time and time again decided cases in this city and State similar to yours in favor of freedom! Of course, if you want to remain a slave with your master, we cannot force you to leave; we only want to make you sensible of your rights. *Remember, if you lose this chance you may never get such another,*" etc.

***

"*State of New York, City and County of New York.*

"Jane Johnson being sworn, makes oath and says—

"My name is Jane—Jane Johnson; I was the slave of Mr. Wheeler of Washington: he bought me and my two children, about two years ago, of Mr. Cornelius Crew, of Richmond, Va.; my youngest child is between six and seven years old, the other being between ten and eleven; I have one other child only, and he is in Richmond; I have not seen him for about two years; never expect to see him again; Mr. Wheeler brought me and my two children to Philadelphia, on the way to Nicaragua, to wait on his wife; I didn't want to go without my two children, and he consented to take them; we came to Philadelphia by the cars; stopped at Mr. Sully's, Mr. Wheeler's father-in-law, a few moments; then went to the steamboat for New York at 2 o'clock, but were too late; we went into Bloodgood's Hotel, Mr. Wheeler went to dinner; Mr. Wheeler had told me in Washington to have nothing to say to colored persons, and if any of them spoke to me, to say I was a free woman traveling with a minister; we staid at Bloodgood's till 5 o'clock; Mr. Wheeler kept his eye on me all the time except when he was at dinner; he left his dinner to come and see if I was safe, and then went back again; while he was at dinner, I saw a colored woman and told her I was a slave woman, that my master had told me not to speak to colored people, and that if any of them spoke to me to say that I was free; but I am not free; but I want to be free; she said: 'poor thing, I pity you': after that I saw a colored man and said the same thing to him, he said he would telegraph to New York, and two men would meet me at 9 o'clock and take me with them; after that we went on board the boat, Mr. Wheeler sat beside me on the deck; I saw a colored gentleman come on board the boat, he beckoned to me; I nodded my head, and could not go; Mr. Wheeler was beside me and I was afraid; a white gentleman then came and said to Mr. Wheeler, "I want to speak to your servant, and tell her of her rights'; Mr. Wheeler rose and said, 'If you have anything to say, say it to me—she knows her rights'; the white gentleman asked me if I wanted to be free; I said 'I do, but I belong to this gentleman and I can't have it'; he replied, 'Yes, you can, come with us, you are as free as your master, if you want your freedom come now; if you go back to Washington you may never get it'; I rose to go, Mr. Wheeler spoke, and said, 'I will give you your freedom,' but he had promised it before, and I knew he would never give it to me; the white gentleman held out his hand and I went toward him; I was ready for the word before it was given me; I took the children by the hands, who both cried, for they were frightened, but both stopped when they got on shore; a colored man carried the little one, I led the other by the hand. We walked down the street till we got to a hack;[4] nobody forced me away; nobody pulled me, and nobody led me; I went away of my own free will; I always wished to be free and meant to be free when I came North; I hardly expected it in Philadelphia, but I thought I should get free in New York; I have been comfortable and happy since I left Mr. Wheeler, and so are the children; I don't want to go back; I could have gone in Philadelphia if I had wanted to; I could go now; but I had rather die than go back. I wish to make this statement before a magistrate, because I understand that Mr. Williamson is in prison on my account, and I hope the truth may be of benefit to him."

NOTES

1. Historical reference: Passmore Williamson published his *Case* in 1856.

2. Judge Kane: Judge John K. Kane served Williamson with a writ of habeas corpus under the Fugitive Slave Act of 1850 to turn over Jane Johnson and her children. Williamson claimed not to know where they were, so Kane charged him with contempt of court and sentenced him to ninety days in prison. The case established a legal precedent.

3. Bloodgood's Hotel: 10 Walnut Street and Delaware Avenue in Penn's Landing.

4. Hack: short for hackney carriage, an early form of transportation; similar to a modern taxi for hire.

BIBLIOGRAPHY

Diemer, Andrew. *Vigilance: The Life of William Still: Father of the Underground Railroad.* New York: Alfred A. Knopf, 2022.

Gara, Larry. "William Still and the Underground Railroad." *Pennsylvania History: A Journal of Mid-Atlantic Studies* 28, no. 1 (January 1961): 33–44.

Hall, Stephen G. "To Render the Private Public: William Still and the Selling of 'The Underground Rail Road.'" *Pennsylvania Magazine of History and Biography* 127, no. 1 (January 2003): 35–55.

Kashatus, William C. *William Still: The Underground Railroad and the Angel at Philadelphia.* Notre Dame: University of Notre Dame Press, 2021.

Okur, Nilgun Anadolu. "Underground Railroad in Philadelphia, 1830–1860." *Journal of Black Studies* 25, no. 5 (May 1995): 537–57.

Still, William. *The Underground Railroad: A Record of Facts, Authentic Narratives, Letters, & c.* Philadelphia: Porter & Coates, 1872.

Turner, Diane D. "William Still's National Significance." Temple University Libraries. http://stillfamily.library .temple.edu/exhibits/show/william -still/historical-perspective/william -still---s-national-sig.

Fanny Jackson Coppin, "Christmas Eve Story," *The Christian Recorder* (December 1880)

Fanny Jackson Coppin was born into slavery in Washington, DC, in 1837. Coppin's freedom was purchased when she was twelve by her aunt, and she moved to New Bedford, Massachusetts, to live with another aunt. While in New Bedford, she gained employment as a domestic in the home of the aristocrat George Henry Calvert, and went to public school and also had a private tutor. Coppin was admitted to the Rhode Island State Normal School at Bristol, and after excelling there, she attended Oberlin College. Upon her graduation in 1865, Coppin took a position at the Institute for Colored Youth (ICY, now Cheyney University), where she would remain for thirty-seven years, becoming principal in 1869. She was the first African American woman to hold such a position. She wrote of her experiences there in *Reminiscences of a School Life and Hints on Teaching* (1913).

In 1881, she married the Reverend Levi Jenkins Coppin, who became editor of the *AME Review* in 1887, a position he held until 1896. At that point, he became the pastor of the AME Church (Mother Bethel), where he remained until 1900, whereupon he accepted a position as a bishop in South Africa. Coppin retired from her position at ICY in 1902 and joined her husband in South Africa. Exhausted by her work with ICY and the AME and her time in South Africa, Coppin and her husband returned to the United States in 1904, where she remained until she died in Philadelphia in 1913.

While Coppin is primarily thought of as an educator, she was also a fighter on behalf of the rights of women and the poor. While at the Institute of Colored Youth, she eliminated tuition. She also contributed many articles advocating for social change to periodicals. She worked tirelessly as president of the Women's Home and Foreign Missionary Society of the AME Church. In 1888, she was a delegate and speaker at a conference in London on the Protestant Missions of the World.

Coppin's advocacy for social justice is evidenced in her "Christmas Eve Story," published in the *Christian Recorder*, the organ for the AME Church. The short piece, written in the style of a fairy tale, has a serious message: to remember the many urban poor who suffer while Christians celebrate their Savior's birth. Though no specific city is mentioned in the tale, the children described in it were like many of those Coppin encountered in the slums of Philadelphia, where many Blacks resided in poor alleys. As historian Bettye Collier-Thomas notes, "The references to Acorn Alley and the almshouse suggest a large city, most likely Philadelphia, where Fanny Jackson Coppin resided."[1]

⁓

Once upon a time, there was a little girl named Maggie Devins, and she had a brother named Johnny, just one year older than she. Here they both are. Now if they could they would get up and make you a bow. But dear me! We all get so fastened down in pictures that we have to keep as quiet as mice, or we'd tear the paper all to pieces. I'm going to tell you something about this little boy and girl, and perhaps some little reader will remember it. You see how very clean and neat both of them look. Well, if you had seen them when

Grandma Devins first found them you never would have thought that they could be made to look as nice as this. Now hear their story:

Last Christmas Eve while Grandma Devins was sitting by her bright fire there was a loud knock at the door, and upon opening it, she found a policeman who had in his arms two children who were nearly dead.

"I come, mum," he said, "to ask you, if you will let these poor little young ones stay here to-night in your kitchen; their mother has just died from the fever. She lived in an old hovel around in Acorn Alley, and I'm afraid to leave the young ones there to-night, for they're half starved and half frozen to death now. God pity the poor, mum, Good pity the poor, for it's hard upon them, such weather as this."

Meanwhile, Grandma Devins had pulled her big sofa up to the fire and was standing looking down upon the dirty and pinched little faces before her. She didn't say anything, but she just kept looking at the children wiping her eyes and blowing her nose. All at once she turned around as if she had been shot; she flew to the pantry and brought out some milk which she put on the fire to boil. And very soon she had two steaming cups of hot milk with nice biscuit broken into it, and with this she fed the poor little creatures until a little color came into their faces, and she knew that she had given them enough for that time.

The policeman said he would call for the children in the morning and take them to the almshouse. The fact is the policeman was a kindhearted man, and he secretly hoped that he could get someone to take the children and be kind to them.

As soon as Maggie and Johnny had their nice warm milk they began to talk. Johnny asked Grandma Devins if she had anybody to give her Christmas presents, and Grandma said, "no." But Maggie spoke up and said her mamma told her before she died that God always gave presents to those who had no one to give them any. And throwing her arms around Grandma's neck she said, "God will not forget you, dear lady, for you've been so good to us." Like a flash of light it passed through Grandma Devins' mind that God had sent her these children to be her Christmas gift. So she said at once:

"Children, I made a mistake. I *have* had a Christmas present."

"There," said Maggie, "I knew you would get one; I knew it."

When the policeman came in the morning his heart was overjoyed to see the "young ones," as he called them, nicely washed and sitting by the fire bundled up in some of Grandma Devins' dresses. She had burnt every stich of the dirty rags which they had on the night before. So that accounted for their being muffled up so.

"You can go right away, policeman; these children are my Christmas gift, and please God I'll be mother and father both to the poor little orphans."

A year had passed since then, and she says that Johnny and Maggie are the best Christmas gifts that any old woman ever had. She has taught Maggie to darn and sew neatly, and one of these days she will be able to earn money as a seamstress. Have you noticed her little needle-case hanging against the wall? Do you see the basket of apples on one side? Johnny was paring them when Maggie asked him to show her about her arithmetic, for Johnny goes to school, but Maggie stays at home and helps Grandma. Now as soon as Grandma comes back she is going to make them some mince pies for Christmas. Johnny will finish paring his apples, while Maggie is stoning[2] the raisins. Oh! What a happy time they will have to-morrow. For I will whisper in your ear, little reader, that Grandma Devins is going to bring home something else with her other than raisins. The same kindhearted policeman who I told you about in the beginning, has made Johnny a beautiful sled, and painted the name "Hero" on it. Grandma has bought for Maggie the nicest little hood and cloak that ever you saw. Is that not nice? I guess if they knew what they're going to get they wouldn't sit so quietly as we see them; they'd jump up and dance about the floor, even if they tore the paper all to pieces. Oh! Let every little girl [and boy] thank our heavenly father for the blessed gift of His dear Son on the first Christmas Day, eighteen hundred and eighty years ago.

NOTES

1. Collier-Thomas, *Treasury of African American Christmas Stories*, 22.

2. Stoning the raisins: removing the seeds.

BIBLIOGRAPHY

Collier-Thomas, Bettye, ed. *A Treasury of African American Christmas Stories*. Boston: Beacon Press, 2018.

Perkins, Linda M. *Fanny Jackson Coppin and the Institute for Colored Youth, 1865–1902.* New York: Garland, 1987.

———. "Fanny Jackson Coppin." In *Notable Black American Women*, edited by Jessie Carney Smith, 224–28. Detroit: Gale, 1991.

W. E. B. Du Bois, from *The Philadelphia Negro: A Social Study* (1899)

William Edward Burghardt Du Bois was born in 1868, in Great Barrington, Massachusetts. Du Bois did not grow up in privilege. His was one of the few Black families in their community, and Du Bois's father deserted the family when his son was only two; however, Du Bois's intellect and determination enabled him to overcome these obstacles. He graduated from Fisk University, went on for a master's degree from Harvard, studied at the University of Berlin, and graduated with a PhD from Harvard in 1895, the first African American to do so. After being refused a position at the University of Pennsylvania because of his race, Du Bois took a teaching position at Atlanta University from 1897 to 1914.

Du Bois wrote many important works, including *The Suppression of the African Slave Trade* (1896), which addressed the question of why the slave trade was created, and urged Blacks to study their true history. Additionally, he published the collection of essays *The Souls of Black Folk* (1903), where his theory of "double consciousness" is posited, that a Black person "ever feels his twoness—an American, a Negro, two souls, two thoughts, two unreconciled strivings; two warring ideals in one dark body, whose dogged strength alone keeps it from being torn asunder." He also published *Black Reconstruction in America* (1935), which he considered his greatest work. In it he counters much of the propaganda of Whites about Black people. He praises the skill and courage of Blacks living in this important period after the Civil War. In addition to his sociological writings, Du Bois also wrote several novels, including *The Quest of the Silver Fleece* (1911), which advances his belief that "all art is propaganda"[1] and should also be used in the cause of racial uplift.

Du Bois was the leading Black intellectual of the twentieth century. He countered Booker T. Washington's accommodationist philosophy that Blacks should accept lesser treatment from Whites for a time and wait for equality. Instead of working in trades and staying in the South as Washington proposed, Du Bois envisioned a skilled, highly educated Talented Tenth of Black intellectuals who would lead the race. Du Bois also challenged the beliefs of Black separatists such as Marcus Garvey who wanted to establish communities apart from Whites; instead, he favored a policy of assimilation. This belief led Du Bois to help establish first the Niagara Movement and then the National Association for the Advancement of Colored People (NAACP) with its organ

The Crisis magazine. Du Bois eventually became bitter at the lack of progress made by Blacks in America and grew more openly Marxist in his beliefs. He expatriated himself to Ghana in 1961 and died there in 1963.

The Philadelphia Negro is a sociological examination of Philadelphia's Seventh Ward, the boundaries of which ran north-south from Spruce to South Street and east-west from Seventh Street to the Schuylkill River. The ward was a racially and socially diverse area that historically contained the earliest Black community in Philadelphia. It housed almost ten thousand Blacks, about a quarter of the city's African American population in 1890. It also had a disproportionate amount of the city's crime and poverty and included the most squalid sections of the city. For more than a year, Du Bois lived in the ward, within the poorer section surrounding College Settlement on Saint Mary Street. His purpose in conducting the study, a meticulous investigation including thousands of interviews, was to demonstrate that the abysmal conditions in the ward were due to environmental factors and not those of heredity. At this stage of Du Bois's early career, written during the Progressive Era, he was still optimistic that society could be shaped for the better. By 1927, his views had changed and Du Bois would declare that Philadelphia is "the best place to discuss race relations because there is more race prejudice here than in any other city in the United States."[2]

~

FROM CHAPTER 2 "THE PROBLEM"

4. The Negro Problems of Philadelphia.—In Philadelphia, as elsewhere in the United States, the existence of certain peculiar social problems affecting the Negro people are plainly manifest. Here is a large group of people—perhaps forty-five thousand, a city within a city—who do not form an integral part of the larger social group. This in itself is not altogether unusual; there are other unassimilated groups: Jews, Italians, even Americans; and yet in the case of the Negroes the segregation is more conspicuous, more patent to the eye, and so intertwined with a long historic evolution, with peculiarly pressing social problems of poverty, ignorance, crime and labor, that the Negro problem far surpasses in scientific interest and social gravity most of the other race or class questions.

The student of these questions must first ask, What is the real condition of this group of human beings? Of whom is it composed, what sub-groups and classes exist, what sort of individuals are being considered? Further, the student must clearly recognize that a complete study must not confine itself to the group, but must specifically notice the environment: the physical environment of city, sections and houses, the far mightier social environment—the surrounding world of custom, wish, whim, and thought which envelops this group and powerfully influences its social development.

Nor does the clear recognition of the field of investigation simplify the work of actual study; it rather increases it, by revealing lines of inquiry far broader in scope than first thought suggests. To the average Philadelphian the whole Negro question reduces itself to a study of certain slum districts. His mind reverts to Seventh and Lombard streets and to Twelfth and Kater streets of to-day, or to St. Mary's in the past. Continued and widely known charitable work in these sections makes the problem of poverty familiar to him; bold and daring crime too often traced to these centres has called his attention to a problem of crime, while the scores of loafers, idlers and prostitutes who crowd the sidewalks here night and day remind him of a problem of work.

All this is true—all these problems are there and of threatening intricacy; unfortunately, however, the interest of the ordinary man of affairs is apt to stop here. Crime, poverty and idleness affect his interests unfavorably and he would have them stopped; he looks on these slums and slum characters as unpleasant things which should in some way be removed for the best interests of all. The social student agrees with him so far, but must point out that the removal of unpleasant features from our complicated modern life is a delicate operation requiring knowledge and skill; that a slum is not a simple fact, it is a symptom and that to know the removable causes of the Negro slums of Philadelphia requires a study that takes one far beyond the slum districts. For few Philadelphians realize how the Negro population has grown and spread. There was a time in the memory of living men when a small district near Sixth and Lombard streets comprehended the great mass of the Negro population of the city. This is no longer so. Very early the stream of the black population started northward, but the increased foreign immigration of 1830 and later turned it back. It started south also but was checked by poor houses and worse police protection. Finally with gathered momentum the emigration from the slums started west, rolling on slowly and surely, taking Lombard street as its main thoroughfare, gaining early foothold in West Philadelphia, and turning at the Schuylkill River north and south to the newer portions of the city.

Thus to-day the Negroes are scattered in every ward of the city, and the great mass of them live far from the whilom centre of colored settlement. What, then, of this great mass of the population? Manifestly they form a class with social problems of their own—the problems of the Thirtieth Ward differ from the problems of the Fifth, as the black inhabitants differ. In the former ward we have represented the rank and file of Negro working-people; laborers and servants, porters and waiters. This is at present the great middle class of Negroes feeding the slums on the one hand and the upper class on the other. Here are social questions and conditions which must receive the most careful attention and patient interpretation.

Not even here, however, can the social investigator stop. He knows that every group has its upper class; it may be numerically small and socially of little weight, and yet its study is necessary to the comprehension of the whole—it forms the realized ideal of the group, and as it is true that a nation must to some extent be measured by its slums, it is also true that it can only be understood and finally judged by its upper class.

The best class of Philadelphia Negroes, though sometimes forgotten or ignored in discussing the Negro problems, is nevertheless known to many Philadelphians. Scattered throughout the better parts of the Seventh Ward, and on Twelfth, lower Seventeenth and Nineteenth streets, and here and there in the residence wards of the northern, southern, and western sections of the city is a class of caterers, clerks, teachers, professional men, small merchants, etc., who constitute the aristocracy of the Negroes. Many are well-to-do, some are wealthy, all are fairly educated, and some liberally trained. Here too are social problems—differing from those of the other classes, and differing too from those of the whites of a corresponding grade, because of the peculiar social environment in which the whole race finds itself, which the whole race feels, but which touches this highest class at most points and tells upon them most decisively.

Many are the misapprehensions and misstatements as to the social environment of Negroes in a great Northern city. Sometimes it is said, here they are free; they have the same chance as the Irishman, the Italian, or the Swede; at other times it is said, the environment is such that it is really more oppressive than the situation in Southern cities. The student must ignore both of these extreme statements and seek to extract from a complicated mass of facts the tangible evidence of a social atmosphere surrounding Negroes, which differs from that surrounding most whites; of a different mental attitude, moral standard, and all economic judgment shown toward Negroes than toward most other folk. That such a difference exists and can now and then plainly be seen, few deny; but just how far it goes and how large a factor it is in the Negro problems, nothing but careful study and measurement can reveal.

Such then are the phenomena of social condition and environment which this study proposes to describe, analyze, and, so far as possible, interpret.

FROM CHAPTER 5

14. The Seventh Ward, 1896.—We shall now make a more intensive study of the Negro population, confining ourselves to one typical ward for the year 1896. Of the nearly forty thousand Negroes in Philadelphia in 1890, a little less than a fourth lived in the Seventh Ward, and over half in this and the adjoining Fourth, Fifth and Eighth Wards.

***

The Seventh Ward starts from the historic centre of Negro settlement in the city, South Seventh street and Lombard, and includes the long narrow strip, beginning at South Seventh and extending west, with South and Spruce streets as boundaries, as far as the Schuylkill River. The colored population of this ward numbered 3621 in 1860, 4616 in 1870, and 8861 in 1890. It is a thickly populated district of varying character; north of it is the residence and business section of the city; south of it a middle class and workingmen's residence section; at the east end it joins Negro, Italian and Jewish slums; at the west end, the wharves of the river and an industrial section separating it from the grounds of the University of Pennsylvania and the residence section of West Philadelphia.

Starting at Seventh street and walking along Lombard, let us glance at the general character of the ward. Pausing a moment at the corner of Seventh and Lombard, we can at a glance view the worst Negro slums of the city. The houses are mostly brick, some wood, not very old, and in general uncared for rather than dilapidated. The blocks between Eighth, Pine, Sixth and South have for many decades been the centre of Negro population. Here the riots of the thirties took place, and here once was a depth of poverty and degradation almost unbelievable. Even to-day there are many evidences of degradation, although the signs of idleness, shiftlessness, dissoluteness and crime are more conspicuous than those of poverty.

The alleys[i] near, as Ratcliffe street, Middle alley, Brown's court. Barclay street, etc., are haunts of noted criminals, male and female, of gamblers and prostitutes, and at the same time of many poverty-stricken people, decent but not energetic. There is an abundance of political clubs, and nearly all the houses are practically lodging houses, with a miscellaneous and shifting population. The corners, night and day, are filled with Negro loafers—able-bodied young men and women, all cheerful, some with good-natured, open faces, some with traces of crime and excess, a few pinched with poverty. They are mostly gamblers, thieves and prostitutes, and few have fixed and steady occupation of any kind. Some are stevedores, porters, laborers and laundresses. On its face this slum is noisy and dissipated, but not brutal, although now and then highway robberies and murderous assaults in other parts of the city are traced to its denizens. Nevertheless the stranger can usually walk about here day and night with little fear of being molested, if he be not too inquisitive.[ii]

Passing up Lombard, beyond Eighth, the atmosphere suddenly changes, because these next two blocks have few alleys and the residences are good-sized and pleasant. Here some of the best Negro families of the ward live. Some are wealthy in a small way, nearly all are Philadelphia born, and they represent an early wave of emigration from the old slum section.[iii] To the south, on Rodman street, are families of the same character. North of Pine and below Eleventh there are practically no Negro residences. Beyond Tenth street, and as far as Broad street, the Negro population is large and varied in character. On small streets like Barclay and its extension below Tenth—Souder, on Ivy, Rodman, Salem, Heins, Iseminger, Ralston, etc. is a curious mingling of respectable working people and some of a better class, with recent immigrations of the semi-criminal class from the slums. On the larger streets, like

i. Alleys: "In the Fifth Ward only there are 171 small streets and courts; Fourth Ward, 88. Between Fifth and Sixth, South and Lombard streets, 15 courts and alleys." "First Annual Report College Settlement Kitchen," p. 6.

ii. Not too inquisitive: In a residence of eleven months in the centre of the slums, I never once was accosted or insulted. The ladies of the College Settlement report similar experience. I have seen, however, some strangers here roughly handled.

iii. It is often asked why do so many Negroes persist in living in the slums. The answer is, they do not: the slum is continually scaling off emigrants for other sections, and receiving new accretions from without. Thus the efforts for social betterment here have often their best results elsewhere, since the beneficiaries move away and others fill their places. There is, of course, a permanent nucleus of inhabitants, and these, in some cases, are really respectable and decent people. The forces that keep such a class in the slums are discussed further on.

Lombard and Juniper, there live many respectable colored families—native Philadelphians, Virginians and other Southerners with a fringe of more questionable families. Beyond Broad, as far as Sixteenth, the good character of the Negro population is maintained except in one or two back streets.[i] From Sixteenth to Eighteenth, intermingled with some estimable families, is a dangerous criminal class. They are not the low, open idlers of Seventh and Lombard, but rather the graduates of that school: shrewd and sleek politicians, gamblers and confidence men, with a class of well-dressed and partially undetected prostitutes. This class is not easily differentiated and located, but it seems to centre at Seventeenth and Lombard. Several large gambling houses are near here, although more recently one has moved below Broad, indicating a reshifting of the criminal centre. The whole community was an earlier immigration from Seventh and Lombard. North of Lombard, above Seventeenth, including Lombard street itself, above Eighteenth, is one of the best Negro residence sections of the city, centering about Addison street. Some undesirable elements have crept in even here, especially since the Christian League attempted to clear out the Fifth Ward slums,[ii] but still it remains a centre of quiet respectable families, who own their own homes and live well. The Negro population practically stops at Twenty-second street although a few Negroes live beyond.

We can thus see that the Seventh Ward presents an epitome of nearly all the Negro problems; that every class is represented, and varying conditions of life. Nevertheless one must naturally be careful not to draw too broad conclusions from a single ward in one city. There is no proof that the proportion between the good and the bad here is normal, even for the race in Philadelphia; that the social problems affecting Negroes in large Northern cities are presented here in most of their aspects seems credible, but that certain of those aspects are distorted and exaggerated by local peculiarities is also not to be doubted.

i. Gulielma street, for instance, is a notorious nest for bad characters, with only one or two respectable families.

ii. The almost universal and unsolicited testimony of better class Negroes was that the attempted clearing out of the slums of the Fifth Ward acted disastrously on them; the prostitutes and gamblers emigrated to respectable Negro residence districts, and real estate agents, on the theory that all Negroes belong to the same general class, rented them houses. Streets like Rodman and Juniper were nearly ruined, and property which the thrifty Negroes had bought was greatly depreciated. It is not well to clean a cess-pool until one knows where the refuse can be disposed of without general harm.

NOTES

1. Du Bois, "Criteria," 296.   2. Quoted in Wolfinger, *Philadelphia Divided*, 11.

BIBLIOGRAPHY

Byerman, Keith. *Seizing the Word: History, Art, and Self in the Works of W. E. B. Du Bois.* Athens: University of Georgia Press, 1994.

Du Bois, W. E. B. "Criteria of Negro Art." *Crisis* 32 (October 1926): 290–97.

———. *The Philadelphia Negro: A Social Study.* Edited by Elijah Anderson. Philadelphia: University of Pennsylvania Press, 1996.

Gross, Kali N. *Colored Amazons: Crime, Violence, and Black Women in the City of Brotherly Love, 1880–1910.* Durham: Duke University Press, 2006.

Horne, Gerald. *W. E. B. Du Bois: A Biography.* Westport, CT: Greenwood, 2010.

Hunter, Marcus Anthony. *Black Citymakers: How "The Philadelphia Negro" Changed Urban America.* Oxford: Oxford University Press, 2013.

Katz, Michael B., and Thomas J. Sugrue, eds. *W. E. B. Du Bois, Race, and the City: "The Philadelphia Negro" and Its Legacy.* Philadelphia: University of Pennsylvania Press, 1998.

Lewis, David Levering. *W. E. B. Du Bois: A Biography of a Race 1868–1963.* 2 vols. New York: Henry Holt, 2009.

Morris, Aldon. *The Scholar Denied: W. E. B. Du Bois and the Birth of Modern Sociology.* Oakland: University of California Press, 2017.

Rampersad, Arnold. *The Art and Imagination of W. E. B. Du Bois.* New York: Schocken, 1990.

Wolfinger, James. *Philadelphia Divided: Race and Politics in the City of Brotherly Love.* Chapel Hill: University of North Carolina Press, 2011.

Alain Locke, "Hail Philadelphia," *Black Opals* (1927)

Alain Locke was born in 1886 in South Philadelphia (2221 South 5th Street in the Whitman neighborhood) to middle-class parents. He graduated from Central High School and then attended the Philadelphia School of Pedagogy before transferring to Harvard University, from which he graduated with distinction, majoring in philosophy. He became the first African American to win a Rhodes Scholarship to study at Oxford University in 1907, earning a degree in literature. Locke later took courses in philosophy at the University of Berlin. He then returned to the United States in 1912 and took a teaching position in English and philosophy at Howard University in Washington, DC. He interrupted his teaching career for two years to return to Harvard to receive his PhD in philosophy before resuming teaching at Howard. He remained there with a brief pause until his retirement in 1952. He died in 1954.

Locke was one of the leading intellectuals of the twentieth century and was at the center of the Harlem Renaissance / New Negro movement. His anthology *The New Negro* (1925), which grew out of a special issue of the journal *Survey Graphic*, was a seminal text of the movement. Though he shared many of Du Bois's ideas, such as an embrace of Pan-Africanism and the belief in a Talented Tenth to lead the masses, Locke disagreed with Du Bois on other issues, maintaining that the power of Black art and culture was a better means to uplift the race and bring about change than through political action. He tended to be more accepted by the younger artists because of his belief in the power of the arts and his strong interest in Black folk culture. It is impossible to imagine the flowering of many of the great talents of the 1920s, '30s, and '40s, such as Langston Hughes, Jean Toomer, Zora Neale Hurston, Ralph Ellison, and Jacob Lawrence without him. Despite his conservatism in some ways, he was nontraditional in other ways, including being openly gay in an environment that was often hostile to such a lifestyle.

Though Locke is most often connected to Washington, DC, because of his long association with Howard University, his early years in Philadelphia helped shape his personality. The solidly middle-class Black upbringing he had experienced helped form his beliefs, and the education he received in his formative years prepared him well for the rigorous studies he would undertake. Central High School has long been regarded as one of the elite public schools in the country. Founded in 1836, it was, and remains, the only high school in the country that can administer BA degrees to its graduates.

"Hail Philadelphia" was written for the inaugural issue (Spring 1927) of the little Philadelphia-based magazine *Black Opals*. The magazine only ran four issues, but it had the involvement of many Philadelphia authors of the period, including writer/educator Arthur Huff Fauset as well as his half-sister Jessie, writer/educator Nellie Bright, poet Mae V. Cowdery, and poet/educator Idabelle Yeiser. The journal was praised by such venerable figures as Du Bois and poet Countee Cullen, who said it "is a venture we should like to see sweeping the country."[1] Locke envisions Philadelphia, which he depicts as the bastion of the Old Negro, as becoming the source of a new artistic spirit, one that "can break ground for the future without breaking faith with the past." It is not surprising that Locke would consent to write a piece praising the new journal, not nearly as radical in style or subject matter as the Harlem-based magazine *Fire!!* (1926). The contributors to *Black Opals* generally wrote works favoring "respectability, temperance, moral uplift, cultural improvement, family pride, and economic stability," genteel characteristics often associated with Locke's aesthetic tastes.[2]

Philadelphia is the shrine of the Old Negro. More even than in Charleston or New Orleans, Baltimore or Boston, what there is of the tradition of breeding and respectability in the race lingers in the old Negro families of the city that was Tory before it was Quaker. Its faded daguerotypes stare stiffly down at all newcomers, including the New Negro (who we admit, is an upstart)—and ask, 'who was your grandfather?' and failing a ready answer—'who freed you?'

I was taught to sing 'Hail Philadelphia' (to the tune of the Russian anthem) to reverence my elders and fear God in my own village.[3] But I hope Philadelphia youth will realize that the past can enslave more than the oppressor, and pride shackle stronger than prejudice. Vital creative thinking—inspired group living—must be done, and if necessary we must turn our backs on the past to face the future. The Negro needs background—tradition and the sense of breeding, to be sure, and it will be singularly happy if Philadelphia can break ground for the future without breaking faith with the past. But if the birth of the New Negro among us halts in the shell of conservatism, threatens to suffocate in the close air of self-complacency and smugness, then the egg shell must be smashed to pieces and the living thing freed. And more of them I hope will be ugly ducklings, children too strange for the bondage of barn yard provincialism, who shall some day fly in the face of the sun and seek the open seas.

Greetings to those of you who are daring new things. I want to sing a "Hail Philadelphia" that is less a chant for the dead and more a song for the living. For especially for the Negro, I believe in the "life to come."

NOTES

1. Quoted in Collins, "Black Opals," 1:133.
2. Quoted in West, "Philadelphia and the Harlem Renaissance," 263.
3. "Hail Philadelphia": a song written by Edgar M. Dilley for an alumni-sponsored contest by the University of Pennsylvania in 1895. It is sung to the tune of "God Save the Tsar!" The Song remains the official song of the University and is performed at events and functions.

BIBLIOGRAPHY

Collins, Kathleen. "Black Opals." In *Encyclopedia of the Harlem Renaissance*, edited by Cary D. Wintz and Paul Finkleman, 1:133. London: Fitzroy Dearborn, 2004.

Harris, Leonard. *The Philosophy of Alain Locke: Harlem Renaissance and Beyond.* Philadelphia: Temple University Press, 1989.

Harris, Leonard, and Charles Molesworth. *Alain L. Locke: The Biography of a Philosopher.* Chicago: University of Chicago Press, 2008.

Stewart, Jeffrey C. *"The New Negro": The Life of Alain Locke.* Oxford: Oxford University Press, 2018.

Washington, Johnny. *A Journey into the Philosophy of Alain Locke.* Westport, CT: Greenwood, 1994.

West, Sandra L. "Philadelphia and the Harlem Renaissance." In *Encyclopedia of the Harlem Renaissance,* edited by Aberjhani and Sandra L. West, 261–64. New York: Facts on File, 2003.

Jessie Fauset, from *Plum Bun: A Novel Without a Moral* (1929)

Jessie Redmon Fauset was born in 1882, in Fredericksville, Camden County, New Jersey, just across the Delaware River from Philadelphia. Her father was a minister in the African Methodist Episcopal Church, and, although not wealthy, he encouraged his precocious daughter to pursue her education. She attended the Philadelphia High School for Girls where she excelled. Still, because of racial prejudice she was denied admission to local Philadelphia colleges. She attended Cornell University but had to live off campus because of racial restrictions. Fauset was the only Black student at the school during her time there, yet she graduated with distinction. Fauset was able to obtain her MA degree from the University of Pennsylvania in 1919. She taught briefly at Fisk University and then in public schools in Washington, DC, for twelve years before moving to Harlem, New York, in 1919, and she became the literary editor for the NAACP's journal, *The Crisis,* from 1919 to 1926. In that role she helped usher in the Harlem Renaissance, being called a "midwife" of the movement by Langston Hughes.[1] The 1924 dinner honoring her first novel, *There is Confusion,* is often seen as one of the important milestones in the period.

She traveled to France in 1925, where she studied at the Sorbonne for six months. Soon after, she began teaching at DeWitt Clinton High School, in the Bronx, New York, where she continued to work until her retirement in 1944. In addition to teaching, Fauset published numerous poems and essays as well as three other novels, *Plum Bun* (1929), *The Chinaberry Tree* (1931), and *Comedy: American Style* (1933). *Plum Bun,* a novel about racial passing, is generally considered her best work. Her novels often speak of the absence of choice in her female protagonists' lives. During this time, in 1929, she married and resided in New York, but when her husband, Herbert Harris, died in 1958, she returned to Philadelphia, living with her stepbrother, Earl Huff Fauset, at 17th Street, near Berks Street, in North Philadelphia until her death in 1961.

Fauset, whose novels focus on the Black middle class, had a hard time finding publishers, who expected more sensational African American writing such as Claude McKay's *Home to Harlem* (1928). As one publisher remarked, "White readers just don't expect Negroes to be like this [middle-class]."[2] The semiautobiographical *Plum Bun*, set in North Philadelphia, New York City, and Paris, tells of the divergent approaches Angela Murray, her darker-complexioned sister Virginia, her light-skinned mother Mattie, and her darker-complexioned father Junius take to life because of their differing skin tones. Her mother, for example, takes weekly "excursions" in the White world. She likes visiting it, but the ambitious Angela longs to inhabit it, deciding to leave Philadelphia for New York City. Her drab, ordinary neighborhood in the city of her birth is described by terms such as "tiny" and "little" and as having "no mystery, no allure," typifying the stultifying middle-class African American life she seeks to avoid.[3] However, as Cheryl Wall suggests, she does not see the value that is suggested in the name of the street, Opal, on which she had lived.[4]

Once in New York, she decides to pass for White, changing her name to Angèle Mory and becoming the mistress of a White man, Roger Fielding, whom she thinks of as "a blond, glorious god," but who ultimately leaves her. She wins an art scholarship but refuses it when an openly African American woman is rejected because of her color. Outing herself as Black, she moves to Paris, where she reencounters an old friend, Anthony Cross, a light-complexioned Black who also, as his name suggests, had been passing. Unable to be together earlier because of their problems with racial identity, now, more reflective and mature, their relationship offers the suggestion of happiness for the couple. Literary critic Deborah McDowell, who edited the novel, states that "within this tapestry, the passing plot constitutes just one thread, albeit an important one, woven into the novel's over-arching frame, that of the *bildungsroman*, or novel of development."[5] The novel is a subtle excoriation of the pretentiousness of middle-class Black society and the lunacy of Black self-hatred due to racism.

CHAPTER 1

Opal Street, as streets go, is no jewel of the first water. It is merely an imitation, and none too good at that. Narrow, unsparkling, uninviting, it stretches meekly off from dull Jefferson Street to the dingy, drab market which forms the north side of Oxford Street. It has no mystery, no allure, either of exclusiveness or of downright depravity; its usages are plainly significant,—an unpretentious little street lined with unpretentious little houses, inhabited for the most part by unpretentious little people.

The dwellings are three stories high, and contain six boxes called by courtesy, rooms—a "parlour," a midget of a dining-room, a larger kitchen and, above, a front bedroom seemingly large only because it extends for the full width of the house, a mere shadow of a bathroom, and another back bedroom with windows whose possibilities are spoiled by their outlook on sad and diminutive back-yards. And above these two, still two others built in similar wise.

In one of these houses dwelt a father, a mother and two daughters. Here, as often happens in a home sheltering two generations, opposite unevenly matched emotions faced each other. In the houses of the rich the satisfied ambition of the older generation is faced by the overwhelming ambition of the younger. Or the elders may find themselves in opposition to the blank indifference and ennui of youth engendered by the realization that there remain no more worlds to conquer; their fathers having already taken all. In houses on Opal Street these niceties of distinction are hardly to be found; there is a more direct and concrete contrast. The satisfied ambition of maturity is a foil for the restless despair of youth.

Affairs in the Murray household were advancing towards this stage; yet not a soul in that family of four could have foretold its coming. To Junius and Mattie Murray, who had known poverty and homelessness, the little house on Opal Street represented the *ne plus ultra*[6] of ambition; to their daughter Angela it seemed the dingiest, drabbest chrysalis that had ever fettered the wings of a brilliant butterfly. The stories which Junius and Mattie told of difficulties overcome, of the arduous learning of trades, of the pitiful scraping together of infinitesimal savings, would have made a latter-day Iliad, but to Angela they were merely a description of a life which she at any cost would avoid living. Somewhere in the world were paths which lead to broad thoroughfares, large, bright houses, delicate niceties of existence. Those paths

Angela meant to find and frequent. At a very early age she had observed that the good things of life are unevenly distributed; merit is not always rewarded; hard labour does not necessarily entail adequate recompense. Certain fortuitous endowments, great physical beauty, unusual strength, a certain unswerving singleness of mind,—gifts bestowed quite blindly and disproportionally by the forces which control life,—these were the qualities which contributed toward a glowing and pleasant existence.

Angela had no high purpose in life; unlike her sister Virginia, who meant some day to invent a marvelous method for teaching the pianoforte, Angela felt no impulse to discover, or to perfect. True she thought she might become eventually a distinguished painter, but that was because she felt within herself an ability to depict which as far as it went was correct and promising. Her eye for line and for expression was already good and she had a nice feeling for colour. Moreover she possessed the instinct for self-appraisal which taught her that she had much to learn. And she was sure that the knowledge once gained would flower in her case to perfection. But her gift was not for her the end of existence; rather it was an adjunct to a life which was to know light, pleasure, gaiety and freedom.

Freedom! That was the note which Angela heard oftenest in the melody of living which was to be hers. With a wildness that fell just short of unreasonableness she hated restraint. Her father's earlier days as coachman in a private family, his later successful, independent years as boss carpenter, her mother's youth spent as maid to a famous actress, all this was to Angela a manifestation of the sort of thing which happens to those enchained it might be by duty, by poverty, by weakness or by colour.

Colour or rather the lack of it seemed to the child the one absolute prerequisite to the life of which she was always dreaming. One might break loose from a too hampering sense of duty; poverty could be overcome; physicians conquered weakness; but colour, the mere possession of a black or a white skin, that was clearly one of those fortuitous endowments of the gods. Gratitude was no strong ingredient in this girl's nature, yet very often early she began thanking Fate for the chance which in that household of four had bestowed on her the heritage of her mother's fair skin. She might so easily have been like her father, black, or have received the melange which had resulted in Virginia's rosy bronzeness and her deeply waving black hair. But Angela had received not only her mother's creamy complexion and her soft cloudy, chestnut hair, but she had taken from Junius the aquiline nose, the gift of some remote Indian ancestor which gave to his face and his eldest daughter's that touch of chiselled immobility.

It was from her mother that Angela learned the possibilities for joy and freedom which seemed to her inherent in mere whiteness. No one would have been more amazed than that same mother if she could have guessed how her daughter interpreted her actions. Certainly Mrs. Murray did not attribute what she considered her happy, busy, sheltered life on tiny Opal Street to the accident of her colour; she attributed it to her black husband whom she had been glad and proud to marry. It is equally certain that that white skin of hers had not saved her from occasional contumely and insult. The famous actress for whom she had worked was aware of Mattie's mixed blood and, boasting temperament rather than refinement, had often dubbed her "white nigger."

Angela's mother employed her colour very much, as she practised certain winning usages of smile and voice to obtain indulgences which meant much to her and which took nothing from anyone else. Then, too, she was possessed of a keener sense of humour than her daughter; it amused her when by herself took lunch at an exclusive restaurant whose patrons would have been panic-stricken if they had divined the presence of a "coloured" woman no matter how little her appearance differed from theirs. It was with no idea of disclaiming her own that she sat in orchestra seats which Philadelphia denied to coloured patrons. But when Junius or indeed any other dark friend accompanied her she was the first to announce that she liked to sit in the balcony or gallery, as indeed she did; her infrequent occupation of orchestra seats was due merely to a mischievous determination to flout a silly and unjust law.

Her years with the actress had left their mark, a perfectly harmless and rather charming one. At least so it seemed to Junius, whose weakness was for the qualities known as "essentially feminine." Mrs. Murray loved pretty clothes, she liked shops devoted to the service of women; she enjoyed being even on the fringe of a fashionable gathering. A satisfaction that was almost ecstatic seized her when she drank tea in the midst of modishly gowned women in a stylish tea-room. It pleased her to stand in the foyer of a great hotel or of the Academy of Music[7] and to be part of the whirling, humming, palpitating gaiety. She had no desire to be of these people, but she liked to look on; it amused and thrilled and kept alive some unquenchable instinct for life which thrived within her. To walk through Wanamakers'[8] on Saturday, to stroll from Fifteenth to Ninth Street on Chestnut, to have her tea in the Bellevue

Stratford,[9] to stand in the lobby of the St. James'[10] fitting on immaculate gloves; all innocent, childish pleasures pursued without malice or envy contrived to cast a glamour over Monday's washing and Tuesday's ironing, the scrubbing of kitchen and bathroom and the fashioning of children's clothes. She was endowed with a humorous and pungent method of presentation; Junius, who had had the wit not to interfere with these little excursions and the sympathy to take them at their face value, preferred one of his wife's sparkling accounts of a Saturday's adventure in "passing" to all the tall stories told by cronies at his lodge.

Much of this pleasure, harmless and charming though it was, would have been impossible with a dark skin.

In these first years of marriage Mattie, busied with the house and the two babies had given up those excursions. Later, when the children had grown and Junius had reached the stage where he could afford to give himself a half-holiday on Saturdays, the two parents inaugurated a plan of action which eventually became a fixed programme. Each took a child, and Junius went off to a beloved but long since suspended pastime of exploring old Philadelphia, whereas Mattie embarked once more on her social adventures. It is true that Mattie accompanied by brown Virginia could not move quite as freely as when with Angela. But her maternal instincts were sound; her children, their feelings and their faith in her meant much more than the pleasure which she would have been first to call unnecessary and silly. As it happened the children themselves unconsciously solved the dilemma; Virginia found shopping tiring and stupid, Angela returned from her father's adventuring worn and bored. Gradually the rule was formed that Angela accompanied her mother and Virginia her father.

On such fortuities does life depend. Little Angela Murray, hurrying through Saturday morning's scrubbing of steps in order that she might have her bath at one and be with her mother on Chestnut Street at two, never realized that her mother took her pleasure among all these pale people because it was there that she happened to find it. It never occurred to her that the delight which her mother obviously showed in meeting friends on Sunday morning when the whole united Murray family came out of church the previous Saturday, because she was finding the qualities which her heart craved, bustle, excitement and fashion. The daughter could not guess that if the economic status or the racial genius of coloured people had permitted them to run modish hotels or vast and popular department stores her mother would have been there. She drew for herself certain clearly formed conclusions which her subconscious mind thus codified:

First, that the great rewards of life—riches, glamour, pleasure,—are for white-skinned people only. Secondly, that Junius and Virginia were denied these privileges because they were dark; here her reasoning bore at least an element of verisimilitude but she missed the essential fact that her father and sister did not care for this type of pleasure. The effect of her fallaciousness was to cause her to feel a faint pity for her unfortunate relatives and also to feel that coloured people were to be considered fortunate only in the proportion in which they measured up to the physical standards of white people.

One Saturday excursion left a far-reaching impression. Mrs. Murray and Angela had spent a successful and interesting afternoon. They had browsed among the contents of the small exclusive shops in Walnut Street; they had had soda at Adams' on Broad Street and they were standing finally in the portico of the Walton Hotel[11] deciding with fashionable and idle elegance what they should do next. A thin stream of people constantly passing threw an occasional glance at the quietly modish pair, the well-dressed, assured woman and the refined and no less assured daughter. The door-man knew them; it was one of Mrs. Murray's pleasures to proffer him a small tip, much appreciated since it was uncalled for. This was the atmosphere which she loved. Angela had put on her gloves and was waiting for her mother, who was drawing on her own with great care, when she glimpsed in the laughing hurrying Saturday throng the figures of her father and of Virginia. They were close enough for her mother, who saw them too, to touch them by merely descending a few steps and stretching out her arm. In a second the pair had vanished. Angela saw her mother's face change—with trepidation she thought. She remarked: "It's a good thing Papa didn't see us, you'd have had to speak to him, wouldn't you?" But her mother, giving her a distracted glance, made no reply.

That night, after the girls were in bed, Mattie, perched on the arm of her husband's chair, told him about it. "I was at my old game of playacting again to-day, June, passing you know, and darling, you and Virginia went by within arm's reach and we never spoke to you. I'm so ashamed."

But Junius consoled her. Long before their marriage he had known of his Mattie's weakness and its essential harmlessness. "My dear girl, I told you long ago that where no principle was involved, your passing means nothing to me. It's just a little joke; I don't think you'd be ashamed to acknowledge your old husband anywhere if it were necessary."

"I'd do that if people were mistaking me for a queen," she assured him fondly. But she was silent, not quite satisfied. "After all," she said with her charming frankness, "it isn't you, dear, who make me feel guilty. I really am ashamed to think that I let Virginia pass by without a word. I think I should feel very badly if she were to know it. I don't believe I'll ever let myself be quite as silly as that again."

But of this determination Angela, dreaming excitedly of Saturdays spent in turning her small olive face firmly away from peering black countenances was, unhappily, unaware.

NOTES

1. Lewis, *When Harlem Was in Vogue*, 121.

2. Quoted in Lewis, *When Harlem Was in Vogue*, 124.

3. Rottenberg, "Jessie Fauset's *Plum Bun*," 268.

4. Wall, *Women of the Harlem Renaissance*, 78.

5. Fauset, *Plum Bun*, xv.

6. *Ne plus ultra*: the ultimate example.

7. Academy of Music: opened in 1857 and located at 240 South Broad Street in Center City. It is the oldest opera house in the United States used for its original purpose.

8. John Wannamaker established a chain of department stores, starting in Philadelphia in 1877. The original store was located at 1300 Market Street, a building now occupied by Macy's Center City.

9. City, Bellevue Stratford: The hotel was constructed in 1904 and stands at 200 S. Broad Street at the corner of Walnut Street in Center City. It is now called the Bellevue and is part of the Hyatt chain.

10. The St. James is a twelve-story hotel constructed in 1901 and located at 1226–32 Walnut Street in Center City.

11. The Hotel Walton was an eleven-story building constructed in 1896. It was located at the southeast corner of Broad and Locust Streets. The hotel was renamed the John Bartram Hotel before being demolished in the early 1960s.

BIBLIOGRAPHY

Fauset, Jessie. *Plum Bun: A Novel Without a Moral*. Edited by Deborah E. McDowell. Boston: Beacon, 1990.

Jones, Sharon L. *Rereading the Harlem Renaissance: Race, Class, and Gender in the Fiction of Jessie Fauset, Zora Neale Hurston, and Dorothy West*. Westport, CT: Greenwood, 2002.

Lewis, David Levering. *When Harlem Was in Vogue*. New York: Penguin, 1981.

McClendon, Jacquelyn Y. *The Politics of Color in the Fiction of Jessie Fauset and Nella Larsen*. Charlottesville: University of Virginia Press, 1995.

Pfeiffer, Kathleen. "The Limits of Identity in Jessie Fauset's *Plum Bun*." *Legacy* 18, no. 1 (2001): 79–93.

Rottenberg, Catherine. "Jessie Fauset's *Plum Bun* and the City's Transformative Potential." *Legacy* 30, no. 2 (2013): 265–86.

Wall, Cheryl. *Women of the Harlem Renaissance*. Bloomington: Indiana University Press, 1995.

Alice Dunbar-Nelson, "By Paths in the Quaker City" (Unpublished, 1932?)

Alice Dunbar-Nelson (née Moore) was a poet, short story writer, and journalist, born to middle-class interracial parents in New Orleans, Louisiana, in 1875. She was one of the few Black women at the time to obtain a college degree, graduating from Straight College (which later merged with Dillard University in New Orleans). Although strongly attracted to women, Dunbar-Nelson married three times, including her first marriage to famed African American poet Paul Laurence Dunbar. About 1895, she moved North, living for a time in Boston, New York City, Washington, DC, before settling in Wilmington, Delaware. She moved to Philadelphia in 1932 when her third husband, Robert J. Nelson, joined the Philadelphia Athletic Commission. While in the city, she belonged to numerous social organizations and book societies. She died in the city in 1935.

Dunbar-Nelson is a significant writer who played a role in the Harlem Renaissance and in the events leading up to it. Since she was aging and in ill health by the time she moved to Philadelphia, she did not write a great deal when she was in the city. However, "By the Paths in the Quaker City" is an interesting piece, one that suggests she was experimenting in a type of journalistic fiction utilized earlier by such writers as Stephen Crane and Eric Walrond. "By Paths in the Quaker City" is a manuscript piece probably written about 1932; it is used by permission of the University of Delaware, where Dunbar-Nelson's papers are collected.

Dunbar-Nelson's sketch seems to be set in an automat (short for automatic), a type of mechanized, waiterless restaurant that originated in Europe and was popularized in America by Philadelphian Joseph Horn and Frank Hardart from New Orleans. The precursor to our modern fast-food restaurants, the first successful Horn and Hardart automat in America was opened on 818 Chestnut Street in 1902.[1] Soon there were many Horn and Hardart automats opened nationally, at one time forty in New York City alone. Dunbar-Nelson, writing about an automat in Center City, Philadelphia, captures the wide appeal of the restaurant. The quick service, inexpensive cost, and modern appearance attracted a crosscurrent of the population from different social classes, but they were especially popular, as can be seen in this sketch, with the poorer class. Dunbar-Nelson shows an admiration for these hardy folks who manage to survive in the harsh Depression years.

—

"By Paths in the Quaker City"

High noon in a robot restaurant. Your nickels are your waiters and bring your sandwich or coffee to your hand. Far east on a side street off Market, where there are workingmen in caps and grimy coats, the derelict aged, and undersized girls from little shops or factories, pitiful in makeshift finery and thin shoes. Endless streaming in and out of a restless, hurried throng. Tables seat four and sometimes six; oftimes strange luncheon companions. Men stand at counters, feet resting on the rails, and churlishly wolf their sandwiches and coffee.

Here at this white topped table are four, two women, a man and myself. The two women are old, but there is at least twenty years difference between them. Some secret fear of the pitiful aged makes them avert their eyes from each other. The one not so old gulps her tea hastily, and fingers something in her lap. It is a brown paper bag, from which she draws forth tiny scraps of bread, which she eats with shame-faced haste, looking around fearfully. When her tea is gone, she thrusts some hard ends of bread back into the paper sack, rolls it into a small parcel under her arm, and rising swiftly, departs without a backward glance. Her black dress eddies about her shabby ankles; her straw hat nods defiance at the chill wind.

The man laughs. He is blue-chinned, red-nosed. His collar is open and innocent of a tie. He has had trouble navigating the cup of black coffee to his mouth without disaster.

The other one is an ancient crone, toothless, seamed, wrinkled, wispy-haired. She sips coffee, and eats hunks of raisin bread, which she boldly breaks from a loaf in her lap. She confides in me that she bought a fine loaf of raisin bread for six cents, and "T'will last me three meals with me coffee. Good nourishing bread." She nods her head, and the loosely tied bow of black ribbon on her nondescript hat waves a joyous affirmation.

The thin little girl who brings a plate of beans to the table draws away scornfully from the aged dame. She smiles toothlessly, unabashed by snubs, and waves her hunk of raisin bread. But the aroma of the beans draws the corners of her mouth and she pauses. Her hand trembles, her eyes glisten, her head poses as if to swoop upon the plate over which the thin girl picks daintily. Then the old soul draws back, wipes her moist mouth with the back of her hand, and gives the whole table a benevolent smile. "Nothing like good raisin bread and coffee for a square meal," she announces triumphantly.

NOTE

1. Nepa, "Automats."

BIBLIOGRAPHY

Alexander, Eleanor. *Lyrics of Sunshine and Shadow: The Tragic Courtship and Marriage of Paul Laurence Dunbar and Alice Ruth Moore: A History of Love and Violence Among the African American Elite.* New York: New York University Press, 2001.

Alice Dunbar-Nelson Papers. Special Collections, University of Delaware Library, Newark, Delaware.

Bendix, Trish. "Queer Women History Forgot: Alice Dunbar-Nelson." *GO Magazine*, March 22, 2017. https://gomag.com/article/queer-women-history-forgot-alice-dunbar-nelson/.

Dunbar-Nelson, Alice. *The Works of Alice Dunbar-Nelson.* 2 vols. Edited by Gloria Hull. Schomburg Library of Nineteenth-Century Black Women Writers, 1988.

Hull, Gloria. *Color, Sex and Poetry: Three Women Writers of the Harlem Renaissance* (Bloomington: Indiana University Press, 1987).

Hull, Gloria, ed. *Give Us Each Day: The Diary of Alice Dunbar-Nelson.* New York: W. W. Norton, 1984.

Nepa, Stephen. "Automats." *Encyclopedia of Greater Philadelphia.* https://philadelphiaencyclopedia.org/essays/automats-2/.

Decline, Racial Turmoil, and the Development of the Post-Industrial City (1950–1999)

By the 1950s, Philadelphia had acquired the dubious reputation of being the dirtiest city in the country, and it was notorious for its odorous drinking water. Whites continued their exodus to the suburbs while the number of incoming Blacks rose, growing to 375,000 in 1950, a 40 percent increase over the previous decade. These newcomers mostly crowded into poorer areas of North, West, and South Philadelphia.[1] Blacks and Whites both had high levels of home ownership though there were still unofficial limitations on where Blacks could live. When these "rules" were violated by African Americans, Whites reacted, sometimes with subtle pressure and other times with violence. Meanwhile, Whites tended to migrate to Northeast Philadelphia and the city's suburbs. Realtors and the city and suburban politicians often reinforced this housing segregation. As a result, between 1940 and 1960, the Black population in North Philadelphia "grew from twenty-eight to sixty-nine percent"[2] while White expansion to the Philadelphia suburbs expanded by 85 percent.

The two reformist Democratic Mayors Joseph Clark (1952–56) and Richardson Dilworth (1956–62) broke up sixty-seven years of Republican rule in the city and made attempts to lessen segregated housing patterns. They saw an opportunity in 1953 when the Pennsylvania Railroad tore down the Broad Street Station, including the "Chinese Wall," a large stone viaduct separating Center City from North Philadelphia. Unfortunately, many Black residents were forced to leave their homes, including in areas such as Society Hill and

Eastwick (located in the far southeastern section of the city), where almost twenty thousand people were evicted for new construction projects. In addition, a crosstown expressway that would have destroyed the Black community along South Street was also proposed. Even though the expressway was never completed, the plans caused a serious disruption in South Philly's Black community.[3] On the other hand, when Blacks tried to integrate areas considered "White," violence often occurred. In largely White Fishtown, for example, in North Philly in 1966, "a crowd of 150, mostly teenagers, burned an African-American effigy."[4] William Gardner Smith in his novel *South Street* provides an example of these tensions between the South Street neighborhood and the Grays Ferry area in South Philadelphia that simmered for more than a decade.

The job situation was also troubling for African Americans. After the soldiers came back from World War II, many Blacks who had civilian work lost their jobs. Manufacturing and other work for African Americans virtually disappeared. Newspaper advertisements blatantly stating "Whites only" were posted by the early 1950s. A state-sponsored survey found that 90 percent of state businesses would not hire Blacks for management or sales work.[5] Whites clung tenaciously to jobs they held, and incidents broke out when their dominance was challenged. In response, African Americans turned to their own organizations, such as the NAACP and the National Urban League, as they slipped into poverty. Meanwhile, when Mayors Clark and Dilworth tried to change the situation, they were often stifled by business leaders and the city's Republican Party.

The 1950s, however, did show some gains for Black Philadelphians. As Matthew J. Countryman points out, "Anti-discrimination laws opened up to African American workers large numbers of jobs from which they once had been excluded."[6] Unfortunately, these laws alone were not enough to bring about meaningful change. They needed to be coupled with the more militant political activism that came in the following decade led by local leaders such as Leon Sullivan and Cecil B. Moore, who employed "black nationalist traditions as collective action and self-reliance."[7] Moore, head of the local NAACP chapter, had a confrontational style that alienated him not only from Whites but also from many moderate Black leaders; nevertheless, he was a revered figure of the working class, and he remains a legendary figure in the community, in part for his success in desegregating the formerly all-White Gerard College in the 1960s.[8]

By 1964, these more muscular manifestations of resistance were on display when a major insurrection occurred in North Philadelphia (at Twenty-Second Street and Columbia—now Cecil B. Moore Avenue), started by a false rumor that police had beaten a pregnant African American woman. Mayor James Tate ordered almost two thousand police into the area derisively labeled by police as "the jungle." By the early to mid-1970s, the Black Panthers grew mounting support within the city and had violent conflicts with the police, led by then police commissioner Frank J. Rizzo, and the Black community reached a new high, as seen when the police clashed with the Panthers and Rizzo discussed using machine guns on the rioters.[9] Mumia Abu-Jamal discusses the frequent police skirmishes with Panthers in his essay, "A Panther Walks in Philly" (see section 4).

Philadelphia, like many Northern and Midwestern cities in the last decades of the twentieth century, was in a period of retrenchment. Health care and education replaced traditional sources of income, such as manufacturing, finance, and real estate; however, almost 40 percent of the labor source for these more lucrative positions did not live in the city. Many Black city residents were left with lower-paying jobs in the hospitality and retail sectors. Unemployment among African Americans rose to an alarming 17 percent. Meanwhile, city services declined precipitously, and the population fell by almost 25 percent.

The decline in revenues led to budget deficits, causing layoffs of city workers, many of whom were African Americans. In this poor economy, crime was on the increase, causing a desire by some residents, particularly Whites, for a law-and-order mayor.[10] Enter the former police commissioner Frank J. Rizzo, a highly polarizing figure, who was mayor between 1972 and 1980. Rizzo opposed desegregation, cut city services further, and was accused of allowing the targeting and intimidation of Blacks.[11] He was generally a reviled figure by African Americans, and with the emergence of the Black Lives Matter movement in 2019, the statue of him that had long hailed outside of the Municipal Services Building in Center City was among the first to be taken down. One accomplishment during Rizzo's tenure, though not through his initiative, was the completion of the African American Museum in 1976. It is the nation's first museum funded and built by a city that was designed to preserve Black history. The museum, affiliated with the Smithsonian, is located at 701 Arch Street in Center City. Rizzo's strongarm tactics met with strong resistance from African Americans and liberal groups, leading to the election of

Democratic mayor William J. Green in 1980 and then the city's first Black mayor W. Wilson Goode (1984–92).

Goode had several successes during his time as mayor. He instituted an anti-graffiti Mural Arts Program responsible for the creation of hundreds of works of art, described by Sonia Sanchez in her poem "10 Haiku (for Philadelphia Murals)" (see section 4). The city's largest building, One Liberty Plaza, was completed in 1987. Goode also attempted, not always successfully, to defuse some of the simmering racial tensions in the city. His tenure, however, is most likely to be remembered for one drastic action he took: the bombing of the radical group MOVE's headquarters. The group was formed in 1972 and had frequent run-ins with the police, including a deadly shoot-out in 1978. In 1985, there was a violent clash in which eleven MOVE members, including five children, were killed when the police bombed the building on Osage Avenue in West Philadelphia.[12] Sonia Sanchez and John Edgar Wideman powerfully record the incident, Sanchez in her poem "elegy (for MOVE and Philadelphia)" and Wideman in his novel *Philadelphia Fire*.

Another troubling occurrence in the city in these years was the crack cocaine epidemic during the 1980s and '90s. Crack brought to light the endemic racism, poverty, unemployment, and undereducation that had been festering for years in the city's poor neighborhoods. Crack was not the first drug to take hold of the city. Heroin was a plague in the 1960s and '70s, especially when Vietnam War veterans came back to the city with their drug habit; however, crack cocaine was frighteningly addictive. "Crack cocaine reached epidemic proportions in Philadelphia between 1989 and 1991, a period that saw some 500 dealers indicted by federal, state, and local authorities."[13] It was particularly deadly in the area called "The Badlands," a stretch of decaying buildings that ran from Front Street to Germantown Avenue and from Huntington Street to Alleghany Avenue in North Philadelphia. The devastation caused by the drug can be witnessed in Alexs Pate's novel *Losing Absalom*.

Mayor Ed Rendell's term (1992–2000) brought a generally less turbulent period to the city and was a time of growth. During Rendell's time in office, the Pennsylvania Convention Center opened in 1993, and the Kimmel Center, home of the Philadelphia Orchestra, was constructed, opening in 2001. The New Freedom Theater, a center for Black culture in the city, received a new building across from Temple University in North Philly in 2001. New homes for the city's sports teams, the Flyers (hockey), the 76ers (basketball), the

Phillies (baseball), and the Eagles (football), were all completed in these years in South Philly.[14] However, Rendell had to deal with his own scourge during his time in office: the deadly AIDS epidemic. The city had been hit hard by HIV-AIDS, and its place is memorialized in the popular film *Philadelphia* (1993), starring Tom Hanks and Denzel Washington. Although Philadelphia has made great strides in reducing the danger from the infection, as of 2013, the city was still suffering from its effects: "The per capita rates of new HIV infections are three times the national average, with roughly 700 to 800 newly reported cases in the city each year."[15]

NOTES

1. Wolfinger, *Philadelphia Divided*, 179–80.
2. "Civil Rights in a Northern City."
3. Simon, *Philadelphia*, 81–88; Clark and Clark, 669–71.
4. Simon, *Philadelphia*, 96.
5. Wolfinger, *Philadelphia Divided*, 206–7.
6. Countryman, *Up South*, 6.
7. Countryman, *Up South*, 10.
8. Willis, *Cecil's City*, 68–75, 146–50; Countryman, *Up South*, 83–179.

9. Clark and Clark, "Rally and Relapse," 676–77; Simon, *Philadelphia*, 98–99.
10. S. Griffin, *Philadelphia's Black Mafia*, 67–78.
11. Simon, *Philadelphia*, 99–103.
12. Simon, *Philadelphia*, 104–6.
13. Puckett, "Era of Drug Destruction."
14. Simon, *Philadelphia*, 108.
15. Gordon, "HIV Positive Extra."

BIBLIOGRAPHY

"Civil Rights in a Northern City: Philadelphia." https://northerncity.library.temple.edu/exhibits/show/civil-rights-in-a-northern-cit.

Clark, Joseph S., Jr. and Dennis J. Clark. "Rally and Relapse, 1946–1968." In *Philadelphia: A 300-Year History*, edited by Russell F. Weigley, 649–703. New York. W. W. Norton, 1982.

Countryman, Matthew J. *Up South: Civil Rights and Black Power in Philadelphia.* Philadelphia: University of Pennsylvania Press, 2006.

Gordon, Elena. "HIV Positive Extra in 'Philadelphia' Reflects on Film's 20th Anniversary." https://www.wbur.org/hereandnow/2013/12/23/philadelphia-twentieth-anniversary.

Griffin, Sean Patrick. *Philadelphia's Black Mafia: A Social and Political History.*

Dordrecht, Netherlands: Kluwer Academic, 2003.

Puckett, John L. "An Era of Drug Destruction: From Heroin to Crack Cocaine." West Philadelphia Collaborative History. https://collaborativehistory.gse.upenn.edu/stories/era-drug-destruction-heroin-crack-cocaine.

Simon, Roger D. *Philadelphia: A Brief History.* Revised and updated ed. Philadelphia: Temple University Press, 2017.

Willis, Arthur C. *Cecil's City: A History of Blacks in Philadelphia, 1638–1979.* New York: Carlton Press, 1990.

Wolfinger, James. *Philadelphia Divided: Race and Politics in the City of Brotherly Love.* Chapel Hill: University of North Carolina Press, 2007.

William Gardner Smith, from *South Street* (1954)

William Gardner Smith (1927–1974) was a novelist and journalist who was born in South Philadelphia, growing up in the South Street area "in family homes on Ninth Street, Wilder Street, and Twentieth Street."[1] He attended Benjamin Franklin High School located in Center City. Smith wrote four novels that serve as a bridge, *South Street* in particular, between the realistic social protest novels that were in vogue in the 1940s and '50s and the more militant Black Nationalist writing that was to emerge in the 1960s. Smith, abhorring the racism he witnessed in the United States, lived abroad much of his life, mostly in France, with two visits to his home country written about in his nonfiction book *Return to Black America*.

South Street has long been considered Philadelphia's most bohemian area. As Edward Mauger and Bob Skiba state, South Street "marked the southern edge of the original city. Since Quakers viewed theater as a 'waste of God's time,' the theaters were built on the south side of the street, technically outside the city limits."[2] Since South Street had such a "bad" reputation, it was thought of as an unfashionable part of town, largely populated by Jewish immigrants in the late nineteenth century. The western borders of the street were the center of a significant African American community at the time of Smith's novel, when the area was becoming a "contact zone—a place where different ethnicities and social classes interacted."[3] It is a distinct region, a thin vein separating Center City from South Philadelphia. Its business areas brought together many ethnicities, creating "a heterogeneous shopping strip."[4] However, the neighborhood had already begun its decline by the time Smith's novel was published, hastened by talk of destroying South Street to make way for a new eight-lane expressway.

At the heart of Smith's novel are the three Bowers brothers. Their lives have been shaped by the death of their father, who was murdered for voting in a primary election in the South. The sons have moved North but are still haunted by their father's death. The oldest, Claude, who is thirty, is admired by everyone in the community. He is a natural leader, but he is tired of the responsibilities that come with it and wants to be defined not by his race but simply as a man. He marries a White musician, Kristin, but is still tormented by his perceived obligations to his race. Michael, who is twenty-seven, is a militant, who despises all White people and desperately wants Claude to leave Kristin and return to the community in South Street and lead the fight against the neighboring Whites, largely Irish, who live in adjoining Grays Ferry⁵ in South Philadelphia. Philip, the youngest, is only twenty-three. He is too sensitive to deal with racial tensions and sees himself as a coward. The lives of the three brothers and those around them intertwine throughout the novel; the one thing uniting them is the lure of South Street and its sense of community. Whether they embrace the neighborhood where they are from or try desperately to avoid it, they all feel, as Claude does, "the pull of South Street."

—

BOOK 4, CHAPTER 7

One evening, while out alone, walking, Claude felt again the pull of South Street—the need, if only for the evening, to go back to the old loved neighborhood and see the old, familiar faces, and the old, familiar bars.

He walked along South Street, peered into a few of the bars and into the *Postal Card*, then turned into Broad and walked to Lombard Street, and down the stairs to the *Showboat*. Same place: smoke-filled, the people, the oval bar. Claude took a seat at the bar and ordered a whiskey from the Bartender, who was standing eating an apple. The Blues Singer went onto the platform. She sang: the same unforgettable voice, the same emotion.

Claude noticed Michael, sitting alone at a table far to his left, looking quite haggard and withdrawn. Claude felt sudden compassion for his brother, and a sudden desire to talk to him. He got off his stool and went back to Michael's table.

"Hello, Michael. May I sit here?"

Michael looked up at him; there seemed to be a struggle inside of him, for a moment, before he said, "Help yourself." Claude sat down, made a few idle remarks: How was Michael getting along? How was the organization? How was Margaret? Michael answered in monosyllables.

They were quiet for awhile. Claude laughed, "It's like a funeral. I'm not quite dead yet."

"You are to the rest of us!" Michael said.

Claude sipped his drink, lighted a cigarette. The *Showboat*. He remembered that first day home, after his trip to Africa, sitting here in this club, listening to the Blues Singer, talking to—to whom had he been talking?—Lil, the girlfriend of Slim. Also the Old Man, who was sitting now across the room, talking to three attractive girls.

Michael, across from him, was studying Claude's face.

"How did you happen to come down here tonight?" he asked Claude.

"I was out walking and I felt a sudden urge to see 'the folks' again." Claude laughed. "Can't stay away from them for too long at a time."

"It's kind of a new urge, isn't it?"

"No."

"And . . . your darling wife? Where is she?"

"At home."

"She doesn't . . . object to these urges of yours, to get back among your own people?"

Claude smiled. "Still the same old Michael."

"*I* won't change!"

"That's nothing to boast of."

Claude smoked. Michael watched his face. Michael struggled with himself before he could speak again.

"Claude." His voice was softer.

"Yes."

He leaned forward suddenly and touched Claude's arm. "Claude, it's not too late. Come back to us! Join our organization!"

Claude shook his head. "No, Michael. For one thing, your group has no focal point. It's only negative. There's little constructive to it."

"You see, you're probably right!" He seemed eager now. "The group does flounder. That's why we need you in it!"

Claude smiled. "Even if I am a 'leader' of which Negroes must 'beware'?"

Michael said, "It was . . . well, I was trying to hurt you, you know that. Besides, it's not too late for you. I have a feeling there's a struggle inside you—either side can still win. I want *us* to win, Claude. Will you work with us?"

"No. I've had enough of it. I'm tired, Michael. I accept this weariness as either strength or weakness, whichever you want to call it. But I'm tired. I want to be a plain, ordinary human being for awhile."

Michael said, "There are fourteen million of us with brown skins who want to be human beings for awhile!" Claude felt the blow; Michael saw that he felt it.

Michael pursued, leaning further toward his brother, "Claude, we need leaders. We are a people who, God knows, have had a rough time; there's a battle none of us want any part of, a war, we're under attack! We can spare no one!"

And then, softer still, more pleadingly, almost desperately, Michael said, "Claude, listen—you have a name! When you speak, the people rally around you. They have confidence in you; you've won enough victories for us in the past to merit any confidence! You've learned! You have no right to withhold your experience from the rest of us. We need you!"

Softly, Claude said, "Michael, you waste your breath . . ."

"Claude! Claude! I am no leader! I play a game! You called me 'puppy' once—well, I know it, I knew it that night, it's why I was so furious! I play a game, I try, but I'm not a leader! You are! It's *you* we need!"

Claude did not answer. He finished his drink and stood up. "I'm going home, Michael," he said. "I hope I see you soon again."

BOOK 5, CHAPTER 17

Philip walked whistling down the street, near the neighborhood of Grays Ferry.

The stone was in the air.

The youth who had thrown it, the stone, did not dislike Philip; did not know him, as a matter of fact. But several months ago, at the beginning of spring, he had been standing, with some others, on a street corner, minding his business, when a group of Negroes had come running up the street, from the neighborhood of South Street, and fallen upon them. All of the white youths had been beaten savagely—for no reason, as far as they could see. And this youth—rather a shy youth, with red hair and freckles—had never forgotten or forgiven it. Today, standing alone, again minding his own business, he had seen Philip—a Negro—come walking down the street. Memory and hatred had shot through him; memory and hatred had stared out of his eyes. From the gutter, he had picked up a large, jagged-edged stone; he had waited until Philip was opposite; then he had thrown it with all his strength.

The stone struck Philip at the temple. A jagged edge cut through into the vein. Philip fell. Blood poured from the vein.

The youth, across the street, was frightened when he saw the blood. He had not really expected the stone to strike its mark; he had thrown it as an expulsion of energy and resentment. He saw the blood and, frightened, looked around to see if anyone had seen him. Seeing no one, he ran around the corner and home. "What's the matter?" his mother asked as he raced panting into the house. "Nothing, nothing," he said, trying to control his breathing. His heart was pounding with fear. "You seem in a mighty big hurry," his mother said. "Just a little exercise." He picked up a newspaper and sat down in a chair and, hands trembling, tried to read.

Philip lay on the pavement, his face in the pool made by his own blood.

BOOK 5, CHAPTER 22

Walking alone, late that night, when South Street was relatively still, Claude felt a great calm and only a slight sadness. Occasionally, someone passed—an old man with white hair; couples chuckling, despite the world, alive, living, conscious unconsciously of the wind and the moon and the stars; a youth, with pork-pie hat and wide-legged trousers, fighting with clothes and a tone of voice his private universal battle against fear and hatred and the white-humped whale from which all evil sprang.

Claude breathed deeply, walking, and thought of an old man endlessly carrying bags of coal and a youth with law books and an ideal and people singing gospel songs and a brother, harmless, who had died. He thought of South Street, great blood vein of a people: thought of gaping dark doors and narrow halls and children who must one day grow up; thought of a hundred years and the years before and a slave who had died and a lie that had been born; thought of laughter and sad eyes, of lidded pain and rage, of dances in youth, of life lessons learned; thought of a million unsung deeds of bravery; thought of community; thought of love.

He felt now, walking, not sad at all; and not happy, either—but alive, and strong, and part of a wonderful people, and with something in this life of use to perform. Which was enough. Who, on earth, had more? And those other things? those mocking stars overhead? . . . endless, baffling Time and endless, terrifying Space? One could, should, be aware of them, in wonder and in awe. But one could not live in their contemplation; one could not live according to their all-paralyzing commentary. One lived—whether one wanted to or not—in the bounded time and the bounded space of one's life and one's own world, within the bounded nature of one's spiritual core. The thing to do was to accept this, without tears, with strength, dignity and, sometimes, defiance. Man was and always had been only Man; for him, there were crosses to bear, and pains to endure, and seemingly pointless struggles to wage—while the almighty stars laughed overhead. And the thing to do was to laugh back at the stars. The thing to do was to laugh with upraised shaking fist and head held high. The thing to do was to feel with all one's fibers the charging wonder and mystery of Life, to confront both the hard and the soft, and to wrestle straining with the Angels and wrestle with the self. Battle lost or battle won: this had no importance. The thing was to wrestle; the thing was to feel; the thing was to laugh with the upheld head.

Give back, then, to the beloved Kristin, her necessary world of music, of the song. For him? This was his blooded world, his cross, his love, his challenge—South Street.

NOTES

1. Rotella, *October Cities*, 143.
2. Mauger and Skiba, *Philadelphia*, 63.
3. Gottlieb, "South Street."
4. Rotella, *October Cities*, 137.

5. Grays Ferry: an area in South Philly traditionally inhabited by the Irish, but now more than 50 percent African American.

BIBLIOGRAPHY

Bryant Jerry H. "Individuality and Fraternity: The Novels of William Gardner Smith." *Studies in Black Literature* 3 (Summer 1972): 1–8.
Bush, Joseph Bevans. "On Re-Calling William Gardner Smith: Writer and Friend." *Philadelphia Tribune*, August 30, 1977, 21.
Gottlieb, Dylan. "South Street." *Encyclopedia of Greater Philadelphia*. https://philadelphia encyclopedia.org/essays/south-street/.
Hodges, LeRoy S., Jr. *Portrait of an Expatriate: William Gardner Smith, Writer*. Westport, CT: Greenwood, 1985.

Mauger, Edward, and Bob Skiba. *Philadelphia: Then and Now*. London: Pavilion, 2015.
Rotella, Carlo. *October Cities: The Redevelopment of Urban Literature*. Berkeley: University of California Press, 1998.
Von Mossner, Alexa Weik. *Cosmopolitan Minds: Literature, Emotion, and the Transnational Imagination*. Austin: University of Texas Press, 2014.
Wolfinger, James. *Philadelphia Divided: Race and Politics in the City of Brotherly Love*. Chapel Hill: University of North Carolina Press, 2011.

Fran Ross, from *Oreo* (1974)

Fran Ross was born in Philadelphia in 1935 to an African American mother and a Jewish father. She graduated from Temple University in 1956. After working briefly in Philly for the *Saturday Evening Post*, she moved to New York City, where she was employed as a proofreader. She published her novel

Oreo (an ethnic slur describing "someone who is black on the outside and white on the inside") in 1974. Ross also published articles in several journals before briefly writing material for comedian Richard Pryor. She died of cancer in 1985.

The loose plot of *Oreo* revolves around the classical myth of Theseus, founder of Athens, who performed many heroic deeds. This legend is satirically transposed on the present-day Oreo (birth name Christine Clark), a Black-Jewish girl seeking her father, who had disappeared when she was a child. It is a challenging work, one often filled with inside jokes and extremely experimental, mixing in classical as well as pop culture references, and utilizing a farrago of both Black Vernacular English and Yiddish to make a comic stew. Yet despite the novel's quirkiness, the book has won a loyal, if somewhat small, audience, one far in excess to when it was first published.

In *Oreo* Ross shows an excellent understanding of the places she's lived most of her life, New York City and Philadelphia, and is able to point out very nuanced distinctions between the two, including the uniqueness of hoagies, Philly cheesesteaks, mustard pretzels, and drinking water. In the sections given below, Ross demonstrates her keen wit in hilarious descriptions of the Philadelphia transit system (SEPTA, Southeastern Pennsylvania Transportation Authority) and the Amtrak ride to New York City.

—

FROM CHAPTER 3, "HELLENIC LETTERS"
Cincinnati

My Worst School Assignment: Mr. Storch, criminally insane English teacher, told our class that we should get to know our city more intimately. "I volunteer to fuck Market Street," whispered Joey Hershkowitz, class clown. This was my assignment: to do a first-hand report on all the statues in center city, from river to river, from Vine to Pine. Yes, he did mean fist hand. Yes, "river to river" did refer to our beloved Schuylkill and our renowned Delaware. Yes, Vine Street is not exactly cheek by jowl with Pine Street. Yes, it was the dead of winter. Yes, I did freeze my *kishkas*.[1] Yes, Storch is probably still at large in the Philadelphia school system.

New York

Advantages Philadelphia Has Over New York: Fairmount Park (more than four times bigger and better than Central Park). The park's colonial houses: Strawberry Mansion,[2] Lemon Hill,[3] Belmont Mansion.[4] The weeping cherry trees of George's Hill,[5] the Playhouse in the Park,[6] Robin Hood Dell.[7] Hoagies (more than four times better than heroes). Steak sandwiches (they don't make them here the way they do at home: layers of paper-thin beef smothered in grilled onions; melted cheese, optional; catsup, yet another option!). People who wait for you to get off the subway before they try to get on. Smoking on the subway platform. Row houses.[8] The Philadelphia Orchestra. Mustard pretzels *with* mustard (in New York—would you believe?—they sell mustard pretzels *plain*). Red and white police cars so you can shout, "Look out, the red devil's coming!"

Things I Miss About Philadelphia That Are Long Gone: Woodside Amusement Park.[9] The Mastbaum movie theater.[10] The Chinese Wall. Schuylkill Punch (no soup in the country is as chunky, as stick-to-your-ribs as the witches' brew we called water). The raspy spiel of a huckster named Jesus.

FROM CHAPTER 7, "PERIPHETES"[11]

The subway concourse at Thirtieth Street

Oreo knew that there were several stiff trials ahead before she reached the official starting of her overland journey, the Waiting Room of Thirtieth Street Station. The first and second trials came together: the Broken Escalator and the Leaky Pipes. Countless previous travelers had suffered broken ankles and/or Chinese water torture as they made their way between the subway and Thirtieth Street Station. With the advent of wide-heeled ugly shoes, which replaced hamstring-snapping spike heels, much of the danger had been taken out of the Broken Escalator's gaping treads. Much—in fact, all—of the movement had been taken out of the B.E. almost immediately after it began its rounds. Thus it had had a life of only two minutes and thirty seconds as a moving staircase before it expired to become the Broken Escalator of Philadelphia legend. Oreo had prepared for this leg of the journey by wearing sandals, which provided firm footing on the treads of the B.E. and also served as a showcase for her short-toed perfect feet.

The Leaky Pipes filled the traveler's need for irritation, humiliation, irrigation, and syncopation. According to the number of drops that fell on the traveler from the Leaky Pipes, he or she was irritated, humiliated, or irrigated. These degrees were largely a function of the Pipes' syncopation. With a simple one, *two*, three, *four*, a few even simpler souls would be by the drops of the offbeat. One who fell victim three or four times to this rhythm could safely be said to have passed beyond the bounds of irritation and into the slink of humiliation. The unlucky ones were those who got caught in a *one,* two, three, *four,*—, six, seven, eight. They would end up soaking wet by the time they got to the foot or the head (depending on their direction) of the Broken Escalator. Ninety percent of those caught by the *one,* two, three, *four,*—, six, seven, eight were white. They just couldn't get the hang of it. Black people were mostly caught by the normal, unsyncopated *one,* two, *one,* two—it was so simple, they couldn't believe it.

Oreo stood at the top of the B.E. and closed her eyes. She did not want to be distracted by looking at the drops. She just listened. She was in luck. The Pipes were in the one, *two,* three, *four* phase. She opened her eyes and observed that the drops (*two* and *four*) hit the same side of the B.E. on every other tread. It was a simple matter then to make her way down along the dry side, leaping over the treads on which the drops fell to avoid lateral splash. She did so hastily—and just in time too, for the Pipes switched into a different cycle just as her sandal hit the last tread, and one drop narrowly missed her exposed heel.

The third trial was suffering through the graffiti of Cool Clam, Kool Rock, Pinto, Timetable, Zoom Lens, and Corn Bread[12] (the self-styled "King of the Walls," who crowned his *B* with a three-pronged diadem). It was not considered fair to squint and stumble along the passageway to the station. No, the fully open eye had to be offered up to such xenophobic, no-news lines as

DRACULA AND MANUFACTURERS HANOVER SUCK

the polyphonic perversity of

BABE LOVES
BILL & MARY & LASSIE & SPAM

the airy, wuthering affirmation of

CHARLOTTE & EMILY LIVE!

the Platonic pique of

SOCRATES THINKS HE KNOWS ALL THE QUESTIONS

Oreo stared at these writings, a test of her strength. So intense was her concentration that at first she paid little notice to a tickle at her right shoulder. She felt it again and whirled to look into the eyes of a lame man she had passed near the Babe-Bill-Mary-Lassie-Spam graffito. One of the foil-wrapped pack-ages from her duffel-bag lunch was in his hand. He had been picking her pocket! She reached out to grab it but ducked when she saw the man's arm go around in a baseball swing. There was a *whoosh!* as molecules of air bumped against one another, taking the cut her head should have taken. Strike one. With the count 0–1, she noticed that the bat was a cane. She ducked again for strike two. "Well, aint this a blip!" Oreo said aloud, finally getting annoyed. She grabbed the cane and gave the man a mild *hed-blō*. She did not want to strike a lame old man with a full-force *hed-krac*. When the old pickpocket saw the look in her eye, he turned and ran down the passageway at Olympic speed. He was really hot*footing* it, honey. He was really picking them up and putting them down! Because of her backpack, Oreo did not catch him until he neared the end of the passageway. Felling him with a flying *fut-kik*, she pressed on his Adam's apple with his cane and he promised he would not try to get up until she gave him leave.

She asked him his alias and his m.o. Perry[13] recounted how he had gone to a hardware store and asked for a copper rod. The proprietor brought it to him, saying they were having a special on copper rods that day and that he was entitled to a fifteen percent discount. Perry, caviling emptor, who had read in the papers that the discount was supposed to be twenty percent, took the rod and racked up the storekeeper's head with it. He paid not a copper but, rather, copped the copper before the coppers came and he had to cop a plea. He had taken the rod home, sheathed it in wood, crooked one end, and brazenly decorated the other end with a brass ferrule. With this cupreous cudgel and a fake limp, he had been lurking in the subway concourse, prey-ing on unwary commuters, rampaging up and down the passageway.

"So why haven't I read about this in the papers?" Oreo asked. "We're only a stone's throw from the *Bulletin* building."

"Oh, I just started fifteen minutes ago. You were my first victim, not count-ing the hardware guy."

Oreo helped Perry up off the ground, advising him that better he should be home waiting for his social security check. She confiscated his cane and admonished him that the way of the cutpurse was hard and drear. He wasn't convinced. Then she said, "I can sum up your ability as a *gonif*[14] in one word."

"What's that?"

"Feh!"[15]

He was convinced.

***

Oreo on the train

She had passed through the Finding a Seat phase and was now in the state of Hoping to Have the Seat All to Myself. She took off her backpack and put it on the overhead rack. As each potential seatmate came down the aisle, Oreo gave a hacking cough or made her cheek go into a rapid tic or talked animatedly to herself or tried to look fat, then she laid her handbag and walking stick on the adjoining seat and put a this-isn't-mine expression on her face. But these were seasoned travelers. They knew what she was up to. Since most of them were in the pre-Hoping to Have the Seat All to Myself phase, they passed down the aisle, avoiding the eyes of the *shlemiels*[16] who were Hoping to Have Someone Nice to Talk to All the Way to New York. As the train filled, the hardened travelers knew that was pie-in-the-sky to hold down a double seat, and each of them settled down to the bread-and-butter business of Hoping My Seatmate Will Keep His/Her Trap Shut and Let Me Read the Paper and the even more fervent Hoping No Mewling Brats Are Aboard.

One young blond had been traipsing up and down the aisles for five minutes. Oreo's first thought when she saw him was that he was almost as good-looking as she was, and she enjoyed watching the other passengers watch him. On this trip, the young man stopped in front of her with arms akimbo, resigned, and said, "All right, honey, I've checked, and next to me, you're the prettiest thing on this train, so we might as well sit together. Give these Poor Pitiful Pearls something to look at."

Oreo smiled appreciatively at his *chutzpah* and moved her handbag and cane off the seat.

Before he sat down, he put a black case, about the size of a typewriter, on the overhead rack. He tried to move Oreo's backpack over, but it wouldn't budge. "Is this yours?" he asked.

Oreo nodded.

"What's in it—a piece of Jupiter?"

Oreo laughed, "No, my lunch. On Jupiter it would weigh more than twice as much—between skatey-eight and fifty-'leven pounds."

"Good, good. I see I can talk to you."

By the time the train pulled into North Philadelphia, Waverley Honor—"Can you *believe* that name?" he said. "In this case Honor is a place, not a code, thank God!" knew eight things about Oreo. "Okay, that's enough about you. Now go ahead, ask me what I do."

"What do you do, Waverley?" Oreo said dutifully.

"Are you ready for this?" He paused. "I'm a traveling executioner."

Oreo did the obligatory take.

"See that black case?" Waverley pointed to the overhead rack.

Oreo nodded. "It looks like a typewriter case."

"Guess what's in it."

"A small electric chair," Oreo said, playing straight.

"Good guess. No, a typewriter."

"Oh, shit," said Oreo.

Waverley placated her. "But it *was* a good guess. It's my Remington electric. Carry it with me on special jobs. It's a Quiet-Riter."[17]

"So tell me, already, and cut the crap," said Oreo.

Waverley explained that he was a Kelly Girl,[18] the fastest shift key in the East among office temporaries. Whenever a big corporation was having a major shake-up anywhere on the eastern seaboard, Waverley got the call to pack his Remington.

"Yes, but what exactly do you do?" asked Oreo.

"I thought you'd never ask." He moved closer to Oreo so that their conversation could not be overheard. "My last job was typical. I get the call from Kelly, right? They say, 'So-and-so Corporation needs you.' So-and-so Corporation shall be nameless, because, after all, a boy can't tell *everything* he knows." He paused for the laugh. "But believe me, honey, this is a biggie. I mean, you can't fart without their having something to do with it. Anyway, I show up at the building—one of those all-glass mothers. I flash my special pass at the guard. I wish I could use that identification card on all my jobs—absolutely *adorable* picture of me. Anyway, I take the back elevator to the fifty-second floor. The receptionist shows me to my cubicle. A man comes in a minute later with a locked brief-case. He opens it and explains the job. It's straight copy work. What I am doing is typing the termination notices of four hundred top executives. Off with their heads! That's why I call myself the traveling executioner. I mean, honey, most of those guys had been with that company since 1910, and they don't know *what* the fuck is going to hit them in their next pay check." He raised his eyebrows, an intricate maneuver involving a series of infinitesimal ascensions until the brows reached a plateau that, above all, tokened a pause for a rhetorical question. "Can you believe that? Well, my *dear*, the work was *so* mechanical and *so* boring that I *insisted* on having a radio the second day. So while I was decapitating these mothers from Scarsdale and Stamford and Darien, I was digging Aretha and Tina Turner and James Brown. Talk about ironic. While Tina is doing her thing on 'I Want to Take You Higher,'[19] I'm lowering the boom on these forty-five-thousand-a-year men. Made me feel just *terrible!* I really sympathize with upper-income people, honey. They're just *my* kind of minority."

NOTES

1. *Kishkas* (Yiddish), guts.

2. Strawberry Mansion was built around 1783 and located at 2450 Strawberry Mansion Drive. The mansion received its name in the 1850s when farmers sold strawberries and cream there. It also has given its name to the neighborhood around it, east of Fairmount Park in North Philadelphia.

3. Lemon Hill is a mansion built around 1800 and located near Fairmount Park at 1 Lemon Hill Drive.

4. Belmont Mansion was built in the eighteenth century and located at 2000 Belmont Mansion Drive in Fairmount Park. It is now the location of the Underground Railroad Museum.

5. South Georges Hill is located at the Fairmount Park Conservancy.

6. The Playhouse in the Park was a tent theater that operated in the summer between 1952 and 1979 in Fairmount Park.

7. Robin Hood Dell was a concert venue operated in Fairmount Park from 1935 to the 1970s. The Robin Hood Dell East is now known as the Dell Music Center. The Robin Hood Dell West is now known as the Mann Center for Performing Arts, built in 1976.

8. Row Houses: The predominant architectural structure in Philadelphia is the row house. The form is practical, relatively inexpensive, and can be adapted to the owner's tastes and budget. Although many cities have row houses, "Philadelphia's unique combination of original city planning, expansive geography, and the simultaneous trend of speculative building" lent itself to the structure (Caspar, "Row Houses").

9. Woodside Amusement Park was located in West Philadelphia at 3910–18 Conshohocken Ave. It operated from 1897 to 1955.

10. The Mastbaum was a large and luxurious movie theater located at North 20th Street and Market Street in Center City. It operated from 1929 to 1958.

11. Greek mythology, Periphetes (also known as Corynetes) was the son of Hephaestus, who fashioned weapons for the gods. Periphetes had one eye and always carried a cane, which he sometimes used as a walking stick and other times used as a club to strike unsuspecting travelers. When Theseus was accosted by Perphetes, Theseus took the club and killed the bandit with it.

12. Corn Bread: Philadelphia is known for its graffiti artists. Perhaps best known is Corn Bread (Darryl McCray), born in the Brewerytown area in North Philadelphia in 1953.

13. Perry: short for Periphetes.

14. *Gonif* (Yiddish): a dishonest person.

15. Feh: a Yiddish expression of disgust.

16. *Schlemiels* (Yiddish): foolish, incompetent people.

17. Quiet-Riter: a portable typewriter manufactured in the 1950s.

18. Kelly Girl: now called Kelly Services, an office staffing agency for temporary workers that was started in 1946 by William Russell Kelly.

19. "I Want to Take You Higher": 1969 song written by Sylvester (Sly Stone) Stewart. Tina Turner recorded it in 1970. It was a hit for both her and Sly and the Family Stone.

BIBLIOGRAPHY

Caspar, Amanda. "Row Houses." *Encyclopedia of Greater Philadelphia*. https://philadelphia encyclopedia.org/essays/row-houses/.

Johnson, Mat. "'*Oreo*': A Satire of Racial Identity, Inside and Out." *NPR*, March 7, 2011.

Mullen, Harryette. Afterword to *Oreo*, by Fran Ross, 213–30. New York: New Directions, 1974.

Senna, Danzy. "An Overlooked Classic About the Comedy of Race." *New Yorker*, May 7, 2015.

David Bradley, from *South Street* (1975)

David Bradley was born in 1950 and raised in Bedford, Pennsylvania, a small community about two hundred miles west of Philadelphia. He attended the University of Pennsylvania, where he graduated with honors and then was awarded a scholarship to attend the University of London, where he received his MA in English. *South Street* is his first novel. His second, *The Chaneyville Incident* (1981), won the PEN/Faulkner Award in 1982. This complex historical novel discusses slavery and its continuing impact on America. Bradley has worked as an editor and as a professor of creative writing at, among other schools, Temple University and the University of Oregon. In addition to his two novels, he has published numerous book reviews and essays.

The South Street in Bradley's novel picks up the later period of the street's history after the 1950s depiction by William Gardner Smith. The street underwent a transformation in the late 1950s when a crosstown expressway was proposed but never built, largely because of strong community resistance by such leaders as George T. Dukes and Alice Liscomb, who formed the Citizens Committee to Preserve and Develop the Crosstown Community.[1] However, as a result of the plan, "merchants closed up, leaving rows of vacant store fronts. In the 1970s, an alternative culture, lured by the low rents, began to filter into the area."[2] When the plan for the expressway failed, many Whites moved into the area, and the street eventually became the lively destination we know today, filled with restaurants, music clubs, and bars—as well as sex shops—and a favorite of visitors to the city. All this, however, came at the expense of the once-thriving Black community that had been living there.

Bradley's *South Street* reflects the period just before the beginning of the area's gentrification. His South Street is still one that Whites would speed through as quickly as possible, a place to be feared. There is a clearly defined boundary separating South Street and Center City.[3] The Black inhabitants, the struggling poet Adlai Stevenson Brown, the drunkard Jake, the aging prostitute Big Betsy, the bartender Leo, and the others who inhabit Bradley's South Street are based on people he had encountered while visiting his favorite bar as an undergraduate at Penn. Many of the characters may be down on their luck, but they are treated with humor and compassion by Bradley. As a result, they rise above the stereotype of ghetto dwellers and become human beings who arouse and maintain the reader's interest. They speak of their lives in a vernacular that rings true. The city is alive, and despite the poverty of the area, the spirit of the inhabitants is a revitalizing force, the reason why the better-off Brown moves from his more affluent section of the city to South Street in an attempt to improve his writing by getting in touch with his people. South Street itself is personified as a silent but living witness to all that happens within its domain. The first selection included here, the opening of the novel, reflects the sense of community of this often-dysfunctional family that bands together at Lightnin' Ed's bar, when they think a White intruder has killed one of their own. The comical misunderstanding over the word "cat" illustrates the different worlds in which Whites and Blacks sometimes dwell.

—

FROM CHAPTER 1, "LIGHTNIN' ED'S"
The street lay like a snake sleeping; dull-dusty, gray-black in the dingy darkness. At the three-way intersection of Twenty-second Street, Grays Ferry Avenue, and South Street a fountain, erected once-upon-a year by a ladies' guild in fond remembrance of some dear departed altruist, stood cracked and dry, full of dead leaves and cigarette butts and bent beer cans, forgotten by the city and the ladies' guild, functionless, except as a minor memorial to how They Won't Take Care Of Nice Things. On one side of South Street a chain food market displayed neat packages of precooked food sequestered behind thick plate glass—a nose-thumbing temptation to the undernourished. On the other side of South Street the State Liquor Store showed back-lit bottles to tantalizing advantage and proclaimed, on a sign pasted to the inside of the window, just behind the heavy wire screening, that state lottery tickets were on sale, and that you had to play to win.

There was no one on the corner where Grays Ferry met Twenty-second and Twenty-second met South: the police, spying any of the local citizens, assumed they were there to rob the liquor store or the food market, and ran the duly convicted offender away. But a little way downtown, near the junction of a nameless alley and South Street, was a dim entranceway, a hole in the wall with a thick wooden door hanging open, and out of it came belches of heavy-beating jukebox music and stale tobacco smoke.

The traffic light at the intersection changed. A flood of cars accelerated away from the corner, their lowered headlights reflecting in pools of the soft tar of the street. One set of headlamps, undimmed, lanced ahead, raking over the fronts of dingy brown-brick buildings and glinting in the eyes of a big black alley cat, scruffed and scarred from a thousand battles-royal. Blinded, the cat darted into the street and was caught beneath the rear wheel of the last car in the string. The car swerved slightly and pulled over to the curb and the driver, a balding man dressed in baggy gray slacks and a blue coat-sweater, got out, "What on earth did I hit?" he muttered, looking around.

"Oh, God, George!" said the woman in the right front seat. "It was probably just a bump in the street. There's enough of them, Lord knows. Why don't they *do* something about the streets in this neighborhood?"

"It couldn't have been a bump in the street," George said. "The front wheel didn't hit it and the back wheel did. I just hope it wasn't a child."

"A child? At this time of night? It was probably just a dog or a cat. Or a rat," she added, looking around with a shudder.

"What's wrong?" demanded a sleepy voice from the back seat.

"Your father's trying to convince himself he's a murderer because he ran over a dog or something."

"Daddy, did you kill a dog?"

"Be quiet, Stacey," said George. "If it was a dog or something, then I want to make sure it isn't lying injured somewhere to go mad."

"*You're* mad, George. Here we are sitting in the middle of this . . . this . . . *place*, about to be robbed or knifed or . . . worse, and all you're worried about is a stray dog."

"Cat," said George, who had walked around to the back of the car, where he could see the mangled body dripping red blood and yellowish intestines on the pavement.

"Good God!" exclaimed the woman, leaning out her window and staring at the mutilated mass. "Did it scratch the paint?"

"Daddy," Stacey said accusingly, "you *are* a murderer."

"George, let's get out of here. That cat smells terrible. This whole neighborhood smells terrible. It's giving me the willies." George looked up and down the street, hands on hips. Then he turned and began to walk toward the open doorway beside the alley. "George? George! Where are you going? Don't you dare leave us alone."

"Just right here, Martha. Somebody may want to do something." He walked on. Behind him he heard the windows being rolled up and door locks being engaged. He smiled to himself. Then he looked around at the dilapidated buildings and the overflowing garbage cans and the dark shadows, and he stopped smiling.

Leo, the two-hundred-and fifty-eight-pound owner-bartender-cashier-bouncer of Lightnin' Ed's Bar and Grill, looked up from the glass he was polishing to see a one-hundred-and fifty-eight-pound white man walk into his bar. Leo's mouth fell open and he almost dropped the glass. One by one the faces along the bar turned to stare at the single pale face, shining in the dimness. "Yes, sir, cap'n," Leo said uneasily, "what can we be doin' for you?"

George looked around nervously. "I, ah, had a little accident. I, ah, ran over a cat in the street, and I, uh, don't know what to do about it."

"Whad he say?" a wino at the far end of the bar, who claimed to be hard of hearing, whispered loudly.

The jukebox ran out and fell silent just as somebody yelled to him, "Paddy[4] says he run over some cat out in the street." The sound echoed throughout the bar. Conversation died.

"Goddamn!" said the wino.

Leo leaned over the bar, letting his gigantic belly rest on the polished wood. "Yeah?" he said to George. "Didja kill him?"

"Oh, yes," George assured him. "I made certain of that."

"Whad he say?" demanded the deaf wino.

Leo stared at George. "You pullin' ma leg?"

"Of course not," George snapped. "I ran over a cat in the street. Right outside."

"Well," said Leo, "there's a pay phone over there you can use to call the cops. But listen, was it right out in front a here?"

George nodded.

"Well, listen, cap'n, seein' as you're in trouble anyways, you think you could maybe drag him down the street a ways 'fore the cops get here? All that fuzz[5] hangin' round out front, bad for business, you know what I mean?"

"Whad he say?" demanded the wino.

"Look," George said, "I don't want to call the po . . . the cops. There's no need for that. The car isn't damaged. All I wanted was I ran over this cat and it's all smashed and it's lying right next to the sidewalk and I wanted a shovel or something to move it and put it in a garbage can or something."

Lightnin' Ed's knew a rare phenomenon—complete silence. It lasted for a long ten seconds before Leo sighed. "Whad he say?" demanded the deaf wino.

The answer was a multivoiced rumble. "He says he killed this cat on the street an' he wants a shovel so's he can hide him in a garbage can."

"Ain't that just like a fuckin' paddy?" said Big Betsy the whore.

"Look a here, cap'n," said Leo. "I don't want no trouble. This ain't like Alabama, you can't just go around hittin' and runnin' an' tossin' bodies into garbage cans."

"Solid!" said a rat-faced man who clutched a beer bottle. "You tell this sucker somethin', Leo 'fore I lay this bottle upside his head."

"Look," George said, spreading his hands and looking down the long row of hostile faces, "It was just one stray al—"

"Will you listen to the honky muthafucka," snapped a dark-skinned man wearing a black beret. "Listen to him! Cocksucker probly cheered when they offed[6] Malcolm an' cried buckets over Bobby Kennedy. We oughta waste the muthafucka, that's what I say."

"You got it, brother," said the rat-faced man, brandishing the beer bottle.

"What'd he say?" demanded the deaf wino.

"Buddy," said Leo, "if I was you, I'd split."

George looked at him in confusion. "But it was only an alley cat."

"Look," Leo said, "I'd just as soon kick the shit outa you maself, but I got ma business to be thinkin' about an' I can't . . . Whad you say?"

"I said it was just an alley cat."

"We oughta string the muthafucka up an' cut his pasty balls off," the man in the black beret was saying. "That'd teach 'em they can't be comin' 'round here runnin' the People down in the street like we was animals."

"Amen, brother," said the rat-faced man.

"Hold it, people," Leo said, waving his big arm. "It wasn't nothin' but an alley cat."

"An *alley* cat?" said Big Betsy, the whore. "Then what the hell'd he wanna go makin' out like he done killed somebody for?

"He's crazy," Leo said.

"Shit," said the man in the black beret, "he's a goddam muthafucka pale-faced honky."

"That's what I said," Leo snapped, and went back to polishing glasses.

George stood by the bar, looking around and realizing that nobody was paying any attention to him any more except for the man in the black beret, who looked up from his gin occasionally to glare and snarl and mutter something under his breath. "Hey," George said finally.

Leo looked up at him. "What you want now?"

"What should I do about the cat?"

"Damn if I know," said Leo. "It ain't my cat."

"It's in front of your bar."

Leo regarded him sourly. "You drinkin' somethin', cap'n, or you just causin' trouble?"

George looked at him for two seconds and then backed hastily out of the bar. When he reached the car he had to tap on the window four times before his wife would let him in.

"George where have you *been*? Why, Stacey and I could have been raped five times while you were in there? Let me smell your breath."

"I thought they were going to kill me," George said softly, staring through the windshield at the street. Suddenly he came to life, twisted his head, stared at Martha. "For a minute I honestly thought they were going to kill me." He shook his head as if to clear it and began fumbling with his seat belt, trying to buckle it with shaking hands.

"Of course they were," Martha told him. "They'd do it in a minute and think nothing of it. They aren't normal. Look at this neighborhood. Just *look* at it! I don't know why they live like this. I swear I don't."

George started the car and pulled away from the curb. As the car accelerated, turned the corner, vanished into the night, the bloody remains of the cat dropped off the fender and onto the street.

FROM CHAPTER 4, "TUESDAY"

South Street slept, slumbering in alleyways and apartments and furnished rooms and burned-out storefronts and in the steamy boudoirs upstairs in the Elysium Hotel, snoring peacefully in a vast choral blend of soprano, alto, tenor, bass; in the light snores of children, in the heavy exhalations of fat, drunken men. The police route car made its leisurely tour, trolling slowly eastward, turning at the river, and speeding back along Pine Street to the all-night pizza joint that was only too happy to treat cops to free coffee and Cokes, out of civic appreciation and a desire for additional protection. Except for the squad car nothing much moved on South Street; the stumbling winos had found their homes for the night, and the whores had long since gone off duty and sent their customers home or out to be mugged and, occasionally, murdered in a secluded side street. But one shadow did move, steadily, slowly, east, toward the Delaware and the lightening sky.

Brown crossed the asphalt expanse of Broad Street against the light, plunging through the strip of commercial prosperity, gratefully regaining the quiet rotting of South Street. He had hurried crossing Broad; now he resumed his heavy, plodding pace. He had been walking for hours, ever since the intimate lighting of Frankie's Place on Rittenhouse Square[7] had gone up, signaling closing time, pushing Brown out onto the street like toothpaste out of a tube. He had walked west at first, crossing the Schuylkill by the Walnut Street Bridge, then, on the west bank, turning north to walk up past the walls of the zoo, to cross the idle tracks of the Penn Central. Then he had walked south on Fortieth Street and through the never-locked gate of the Woodland Cemetery[8] to sit on a tombstone and stare for a while at the stars and the river, while sobriety sneaked up on him. He had walked past the Veterans Hospital, across the University Avenue Bridge, up Grays Ferry Avenue, and finally to South Street. It had felt strangely comforting, as if he had given in to the pull of gravity. Stepping onto South Street Brown had been tense and expectant, anticipating some magic transformation of the night and of himself; walking eastward he reached out around him with his fatigue- and alcohol-dulled senses, searching in the silence for some half-remembered rhythm, some dimly recalled melody, sniffing the air for an aromatic blend of all the odors of the night. But the silence had remained dull and random, and the smells of sweat and garbage and gasoline and wine and grease and asphalt had hung as separate and distinct stenches. Brown walked on, growing more and more sad, more and more sober. Finally he reached the end of South Street and still there was nothing beyond the simple realities of night and street and buildings and Delaware River. In a few minutes the delivery trucks would begin to move and the taxis would start to stream out of the Grays Ferry lot and the busses like mechanical cows would trundle forth from their barns and it would be morning.

Brown turned away from the river, walked back along South as far as Seventh Street, then walked north to Market and on west to the donut shop

between the Reading Terminal[9] and City Hall. He sat at the counter and consumed half a dozen donuts, three cups of coffee, rose, paid, and despondently
descended the concrete stairway to the Market Street subway. He sat on a
slatted wooden bench and waited, his eyelids drooping. The train came. Brown
stepped on, took a seat amid the curious mixture of people riding to
early-morning jobs. It was far too early for office workers—these were maids
bound for Thirtieth Street Station to take the Penn Central commuter trains
to the big expensive houses in the tiny expensive towns along the Main Line,
or for Sixty-ninth Street and the busses to Delaware County. Brown relaxed,
content to let the train carry him westward, beneath the Schuylkill. He left
the subway at Fortieth and Market, climbing the steps to the denuded corner
that already burned in the heat. He crossed Market and headed south. He
reached the tall building, passed beneath the broad awning, opened the heavy
door, crossed the luxurious lobby, entered the elevator, and rose effortlessly
upward. He opened and closed the apartment door with great care and headed
directly for the bar. He picked up a nearly full bottle of scotch and carried it
out onto the balcony.

Brown stood looking out over the city, drinking from the bottle. His eyes
followed a bus as it moved down Spruce Street, crawling an inch, stopping
while it swallowed a few small dots and spit out a few others, then crawling
on an inch, two inches, before stopping again. Brown wondered about the
bus's destination: either it was a forty-two, bound for Independence Hall,
or it was a forty, bound for Front and South. When the bus reached
Thirty-third and Spruce it did not turn but continued on across the river.
Brown's eyes followed it as it creeped across the bridge and dipped down
onto South Street. Brown stared after it as it gradually lost itself in traffic,
stood gazing into the smog long after the bus was lost to sight. Suddenly the
whiskey he had drunk turned to acid in his stomach. He dropped the bottle
and spun toward the living room, losing his footing and falling to his knees
on the carpet. Lips pressed tightly together, Brown struggled to his feet,
hung on the railing of the balcony, trying to decide if he could make it to the
bathroom or should simply stay there, waiting for the sour vomit to rise. But
as suddenly as it had come, the spasm passed, and Brown hung on the railing gulping at the clotted air. Gradually he stopped trembling. Brown took
a deep breath and bent over carefully and picked up the bottle. It was almost
empty—the liquid was on the balcony concrete, vanishing before the sun.
Brown looked at the bottle. Then he leaned over the railing, opened his

fingers, and let the bottle fall away, twenty-four stories, to shatter beyond recognition in the street below.

NOTES

1. Gottlieb, "South Street."

2. Mauger and Skiba, Philadelphia, 63.

3. Rotella, October Cities, 174–75.

4. Paddy: an Irishman. It is a derivative of Patrick.

5. Fuzz: slang for the police.

6. Offed: murdered.

7. Rittenhouse Square is a park and the surrounding affluent area around it is located in Center City.

8. Woodland Cemetery: the Woodland is a cemetery that opened in 1840 and is still operating. Located in West Philadelphia, the cemetery is now a National Historic Landmark District.

9. Reading Terminal: an indoor farmers' market that opened in 1893. It is located on Arch Street in Center City. It got its name because it was built under the tracks of the terminal for the Pennsylvania and Reading Company.

BIBLIOGRAPHY

Babb, Valerie. *A History of the African American Novel*. Cambridge: Cambridge University Press, 2017.

Blake, Susan, and James A. Miller. "The Business of Writing: An Interview with David Bradley." *Callaloo* 7 (1984): 19–39.

Gottlieb, Dylan. "South Street." *Encyclopedia of Greater Philadelphia*. https://philadelphiaencyclopedia.org/essays/south-street/.

Mauger, Edward, and Bob Skiba: *Philadelphia: Then and Now*. London: Pavilion, 2015.

Rotella, Carlo. *October Cities: The Redevelopment of Urban Literature*. Berkeley: University of California Press, 1998.

Smith, Valerie. "David Bradley." In *Dictionary of Literary Biography*, vol. 33, *Afro American Fiction Writers After 1955*, edited by Thadious M. Davis and Trudier Harris, 28–32. Detroit: Gale, 1984.

Joseph Beam, from "Brother to Brother: Words from the Heart" (1986)

Joseph Beam was born in Philadelphia in 1954. He had been involved in activist movements since his days at Franklin College in Indiana. After graduating, he returned to Philadelphia and worked in the gay/lesbian bookstore Giovanni's Room. He also began sending articles to many publications, including *Philadelphia Gay News*, edited by Mark Segal. He joined numerous organizations, such as the National Coalition of Black Lesbians and became editor of its journal, *Black/Out*. He also edited the pioneering anthology *In the Life*, in which "Brother to Brother" was included. The book is the first collection of writings by gay Black men. He had begun work on a second anthology, *Brother to Brother*, before his death from AIDS-related illness in 1988. The book was completed by his friend, the writer Essex Hemphill, and Beam's mother, Dorothy, and published in 1991 by Alyson Publications.

Philadelphia has had a fairly sizable gay population since at least the 1930s. On April 25, 1965, more than 150 people were denied service at Dewey's, a local coffee shop and diner at 219 South 17th Street in Philadelphia, near Rittenhouse Square, a popular meeting place for gays. The protest, shortly before the famous Stonewall uprising in New York City, was one of the key moments in the Gay Liberation Movement.

Beam makes only one brief but significant mention of Philadelphia in his essay, to Spruce Street, probably because he wanted to universalize his experience. The Spruce Street mentioned in Beam's essay is the Philadelphia equivalent of Castro Street / District in San Francisco and Christopher Street / Greenwich Village in New York, both of which Beam references. Spruce Street includes the William Way LBGT Community Center, 1315 Spruce Street, founded in 1975, at this location since 1997. The Center is within the so-called Gayborhood area (11th and Broad, Pine and Chestnut). The heart of Gayborhood is the Washington Square West area. Gayborhood also includes Giovanni's Room Bookstore, founded in 1973, at 12th and Pine since 1979. If it was Beam's intention to universalize the gay experience, he has undoubtedly succeeded, as he captures the struggles and loneliness many gays endure. One of the key concepts in the essay is the importance of home, and how Black gays often lack a sense of community.

Despite this gay presence in Philadelphia, Beam yearns for more of a sense of community with all Black people, straight and gay, male and female. Additionally, he dreams of a time when homophobia is gone and gays can be treated with dignity and respect by all people. Then gays can freely publicly display themselves without repercussion, showing their healing and supportive bonds with one another, brother to brother. Beam's work has helped to bring his vision closer to fruition.

⁓

. . . what is most important to me must be spoken, made verbal and shared, even at the risk of having it bruised or misunderstood.

I know the anger that lies inside me like I know the beat of my heart and the taste of my spit. It is easier to be angry than to hurt. Anger is what I do best. It is easier to be furious than to be yearning. Easier to crucify myself in you than take on the threatening universe of whiteness by admitting that we are worth wanting each other.[i]

I, too, know anger. My body contains as much anger as water. It is the material from which I have built my house, blood red bricks that cry in the rain. It is what pulls my tie and gold chains taut around my neck, fills my penny loafers and my Nikes, molds my Calvins and gray flannels to my torso. It is the face and posture I show the world. It is the way, sometimes the only way, I am granted an audience. It is sometimes the way I show affection. I am angry because of the treatment I am afforded as a Black man. That fiery anger is stoked additionally with the fuels of contempt and disposal shown me by my community because I am gay. *I cannot go home as who I am.*

When I speak of home, I mean not only the familial constellation from which I grew, but the entire Black community: the Black press, the Black church, Black academicians, the Black literati, and the Black left. Where is my reflection? I am most often rendered invisible, perceived as a threat to the family, or am tolerated if I am silent and inconspicuous. I cannot go home as who I am and that hurts me deeply.

Almost every morning I have coffee at the same donut shop. Almost every morning I encounter the same Black man who used to acknowledge me from across the counter. I can only surmise that it is my earrings and earcuffs that have tipped him off that I am gay. He no longer speaks, instead looks disdainfully through me as if I were glass. But glass reflects, so I am not even that. He sees no part of himself in me—not my Blackness nor my maleness. "There's nothing in me that is not in everyone else, and nothing in everyone else that is not in me."[ii] Should our glances meet, he is quick to use his *Wall Street Journal* as a shield while I wince and admire the brown of my coffee in my cup.

I do not expect his approval—only his acknowledgement. The struggles of Black people are too pervasive for us to dismiss one another, in such cursory fashion, because of perceived differences. Gil Scott-Heron[1] called it "dealing in externals," that is, giving great importance to visual information and ignoring real aspects of commonality. Aren't all hearts and fists and minds needed in this struggle or will this faggot be tossed into the fire? In this very

i. Bruised or misunderstood: Lorde, Audre. *The Cancer Journals.* Argyle, NY: Spinster's Ink, 1980.
ii. Not in me: Baldwin, James. *Village Voice*, vol. 29, no. 26, p. 14.

critical time everyone from the corner to the corporation is desperately needed.

> . . . [Brother] the war goes on
> respecting no white flags
> taking no prisoners
> giving no time out for women and children
> to leave the area
> whether we return their fire
> or not
> whether we're busy attacking each other
> or not . . .[i]

If you could put your newspaper aside for a moment, I think you, too, would remember that it has not always been this way between us. I remember. I remember the times before different meant separate, before different meant outsider. I remember Sunday school and backyard barbeques and picnics in the Park and Avenue and parties in dimly lit basements and skateboards fashioned from two-by-fours and b-b and . . . I remember. I also recall secretly playing jacks and jumping rope on the back porch, and the dreams I had when I spent the night at your house.

But that was before different meant anything at all, certainly anything substantial. That was prior to considerations such as too light/too dark; or good/bad hair; before college/army/jail; before working/middle class; before gay/straight. But I am no longer on the back porch; I want to play with my jacks on the front porch. There is no reason for me to hide. Our differences should promote dialogue rather than erect new obstacles in our paths.

On another day: I am walking down Spruce/Castro/Christopher Street on my way to work. A half block away, walking towards me, is another Black gay man. We have seen each other in the clubs. Side by side, and at the precise moments that our eyes should meet, he studies the intricate detail of a building. I check my white sneakers for scuff marks. What is it that we see in each other that makes us avert our eyes so quickly? Does he see the same

---

i. Or not: Blackwomon, Julie. *Revolutionary Blue and Other Fevers*. Philadelphia: self-published, 1984. (Distributed by Kitchen Table: Women of Color Press, P.O. Box 908, Latham, New York).

thing in me that the brother in the donut shop sees? Do we turn away from each other in order not to see our collective anger and sadness?

It is my pain I see reflected in your eyes. Our angers ricochet between us like the bullets we fire in battles which are not our own nor with each other.

The same angry face, donned for safety in the white world, is the same expression I bring to you. I am cool and unemotive, distant from what I need most. "It is easier to be furious than to be yearning. Easier to crucify myself in you . . ." And perhaps easier to ingest than anger until it threatens to consume me, or apply a salve of substitutes to the wound.

But real anger accepts few substitutes and sneers at sublimation. The anger-hurt I feel cannot be washed down with a Coke (old or New) or a Colt 45; cannot be danced away; cannot be mollified by a white lover, nor lost in the mirror reflections of a Black lover; cannot evaporate like sweat after a Nautilus workout; nor drift away in a cloud of reefer smoke. I cannot leave it in Atlantic City, or Rio, or even Berlin when I vacation. I cannot hope it will be gobbled up by the alligators on my clothing; nor can I lose it in therapeutic catharsis. I cannot offer it to Jesus/Allah/Jah. So, I must mold and direct that fiery cool mass of angry energy—use it before it uses me! *Anger unvented becomes pain, pain unspoken becomes rage, rage released become violence.*

Use it to create a Black gay community in which I can build my home surrounded by institutions that reflect and sustain me. Concurrent with that vision is the necessity to repave the road home, widening it, so I can return with all I have created to the home which is my birthright.

II

Silence is what I hear after the handshake and the slap of five; after the salutations what's happenin'/what's up/how you feel; after our terms of endearment: homeboy, cuzz, "girlfriend," blood, running buddy, and Miss Thing. I can hear the silence. When talking with a "girlfriend," I am more likely to muse about my latest piece or so-and-so's party at Club She-She than about the anger and hurt I felt that morning when a jeweler refused me entrance to his store because I am Black and male, and we are all perceived as thieves. I will swallow that hurt and should I speak of it, will vocalize only the anger, saying: I should have bust out his fuckin' windows! Some of the anger will be exorcised, but the hurt, which has not been given voice, prevails and accumulates.

Silence is a way to grin and bear it. A way not to acknowledge how much my life is discounted each day—100% OFF ALL BLACK MEN TODAY—EVERY DAY! I strive to appear strong and silent. I learn to ingest hatred at a geometric rate and to count (silently) to 10 . . . 10 thousand . . . 10 million. But as I have learned to mute my cries of anguish, so have I learned to squelch my exclamations of joy. What remains is the rap.

My father is a warm brown man of seventy, who was born in Barbados. He is kind and gentle, and has worked hard for me so that I am able to write these words. We are not friends; he is my father, I am his son. We are silent when we are alone together. I do not ask him about his island childhood or his twelve years as a janitor or about the restaurant he once owned where he met my mother. He does not ask me about being gay or why I wish to write about it. Yet we are connected: his past is my present, our present a foundation for the future. I have never said to him that his thick calloused hands have led me this far and given me options he never dreamed of. How difficult it is to speak of my appreciation, saying: Dad, I love you. *I am here because of you, much deeper than sperm meeting egg, much deeper than sighs in the night, I am here because of you.* Our love for each other, though great, may never be spoken. It is the often unspoken love that Black men give to other Black men in a world where we are forced to cup our hands over our mouths or suffer under the lash of imprisonment, unemployment, or even death. But these words, which fail, are precisely the words that are life-giving and continuing. They must be given voice. What legacy is to be found in our silence?

***

III

***

I dare myself to dream of us moving from survival to potential, from merely getting by to a positive getting over. I dream of Black men loving and supporting other Black men, and relieving Black women from the role of primary nurturers in our community. I dream, too, that as we receive more of what we want from each other that our special anger reserved for Black women will disappear. For too long have we expected from Black women that which we could only obtain from other men. I dare myself to dream.

I dream of a time when it is not Black men who fill the nation's prisons; when we will not seek solace in a bottle and Top papers;[2] and when the service is not the only viable alternative to high civilian employment.

I dare myself to dream of a time when I will pass a group of brothers on a corner, and the words "fuckin' faggot" will not move the air around my ears; and when my gay brother approaches me on the street that we can embrace if we choose.

I dare to dream that we are worth wanting each other.

IV

Black men loving Black men is the revolutionary act of the eighties.

At eighteen, David could have been a dancer: legs grown strong from daily walks from his remote neighborhood to downtown in search of employment that would free him from his abusive family situation. David, soft-spoken and articulate, could have been a waiter gliding gracefully among the tables of a three-star restaurant. David could have performed numerous jobs, but lacking the connections that come with age and race, the Army seemed a reasonable choice. His grace and demeanor will be of little importance in Nicaragua.

Earl is always a good time. His appearance at parties, whether it's a smart cocktail sip or basement gig, is mandatory. He wakes with coffee and speed, enjoys three-joint lunches, and chases his bedtime Valium with Johnny Walker Red. None of his friends, of which he has many, suggest that he needs help. His substance abuse is ignored by all.

Stacey is a delirious queen, a concoction of current pop stars, bound eclectically in thrift store threads. His sharp and witty tongue can transform the most boring, listless evenings. In private, minus the dangles and bangles, he appears solemn and pensive, and speaks of the paucity of role models, mentors, and possibilities.

Maurice has a propensity for white people, which is more than preference—it's policy. He dismisses potential Black friendships as quickly as he switches off rap music and discredits progressive movements. He consistently votes Republican. At night he dreams of razors cutting away thin slivers of his Black skin.

Bubba and Ray had been lovers for so long that the neighbors presumed them to be brothers or widowers. For decades their socializing had been done among an intimate circle of gay couples, so when Ray died Bubba felt too old to venture [to] the new gay scene. Occasionally he has visitors, an equally old friend or a much younger cousin or nephew. But mostly he sits, weather permitting, on the front porch where, with a can of beer over ice, he silently weaves tales of "the life" in the thirties and forties. Yet there isn't anyone who listens.

Bobbi, a former drag queen, has plenty of time to write poetry. Gone are his makeup and high heels since he began serving his two-to-five year sentence. He had not wanted to kick that bouncer's ass; however, he, not unlike the more macho sissies clad in leather and denim, rightfully deserved admittance to that bar. Although he has had no visitors and just a couple of letters, he maintains a sense of humor typified by the title of a recent set of poems: *Where can a decent drag queen get a decent drink?*

Paul is hospitalized with AIDS. The severity of his illness is not known to his family or friends. They cannot know that he is gay; it is his secret and he will expire with it. Living a lie is one thing, but it is quite another to die within its confines.

Charles is a ventman³ with beautiful dreads. On days when he is not drinking and is lucid, he will tell you how he winters on the south side of the square and sleeps facing the east so that he wakes with the sun in his eyes. He is only an obstacle to passersby.

Ty and Reggie have been lovers since they met in the service seven years ago. They both perform dull and menial jobs for spiteful employers, but plan to help each other through college. Ty will attend first. Their two-room apartment, which is neither fashionably appointed nor in a fashionable neighborhood, is clearly a respite from the madness that awaits outside their door. They would never imagine themselves as revolutionaries.

Black men loving Black men is the revolutionary act of the eighties, not only because sixties' revolutionaries like Bobby Seale, Huey Newton, and Eldridge Cleaver dare speak our name; but because as Black men we were never meant to be together—not as father and son, brother and brother—and certainly not as lovers.

Black men loving Black men is an autonomous agenda for the eighties, which is not rooted in any particular sexual, political, or class affiliation, but in our mutual survival. The ways in which we manifest that love are as myriad as the issues we must address. Unemployment, substance abuse, self-hatred, and the lack of positive images are but some of the barriers to our loving.

Black men loving Black men is a call to action, an acknowledgment of responsibility. We take care of our own kind when the night grows cold and silent. These days the nights are cold-blooded and the silence echoes with complicity.

NOTES

1. A paraphrase of the first line of singer/ musician Gil Scott-Heron's song "Brother" (1970).

2. Top papers: rolling papers used with tobacco or marijuana to make cigarettes or joints.

3. A ventman is a street person who lived near a hot vent. It particularly refers to a person who lived for years on the sidewalk of 34th and Spruce near Irvine Auditorium on the University of Pennsylvania campus.

BIBLIOGRAPHY

Brownworth, Victoria A. "Road to Stonewall: Joe Beam." *Philadelphia Gay News*, June 6, 2019.

Fullwood, Steven G., and Charles Stephens, eds. *Black Gay Genius: Answering Joseph Beam's Call*. New York: Vintage, 2014.

Gastic, Billie. "Beam, Joseph Fairchild (30 Dec. 1954–27 Dec. 1988)." Oxford African American Studies Center, 2013. https://doi.org/10.1093/acref/9780 195301731.013.35187.

Manley, Lauren Elisabeth. "Do You Live on Spruce Street or Are You Straight? The Boundaries of Philadelphia's Gayborhood and the Production of Queer Identities." MA thesis, City University of New York, 2014. https://www.visitphilly.com/articles /philadelphia/essential-lgbt-sites-things -to-do-philadelphia/.

Sonia Sanchez, "elegy (for MOVE and Philadelphia)" (1987)

Sonia Sanchez (born Wilsonia Benita Driver) is a poet, fiction writer, playwright, activist, and academic. She was born in Montgomery, Alabama, in 1934 and later moved to New York City, where she pursued her schooling at Hunter College (BA in political science) and took postgraduate courses in creative writing at New York University. She has worked at several universities, including San Francisco State College, where she taught the first course on Black Studies at a predominantly White institution. She taught at Temple University from 1977 until her retirement in 1999. She is currently poet in residence at Temple.

Sanchez is best known for her poetry, often on subjects of social justice, Black history and culture, and motherhood. She had been associated for a time with the Nation of Islam and the Black Arts Movement in the 1960s and '70s. She has published a collection of short stories, several plays, children's books, and multiple volumes of poetry, including *Shake Loose My Skin: New and Selected Poems* (2000) and *Morning Haiku* (2010). Sanchez was appointed the first poet laureate of Philadelphia in 2012 and has won numerous awards, including the American Book Award for her volume of poetry *Homegirls and Handgrenades* (1985) and the Wallace Stevens Award from the Academy of American Poets (2018).

"elegy (for MOVE and Philadelphia)" is a free-verse poem detailing the police bombing of the headquarters of the radical MOVE group in 1985 and was published in 1987 in her collection *Under a Soprano Sky*. MOVE, an anarchist group, was founded in 1972 and had had serious confrontations with authorities since its inception until these tensions culminated in the decision by Wilson Goode, the city's first African American mayor, to bomb the building on 6221 Osage Avenue (called Osage Street in the poem) in West Philadelphia to drive the MOVE members out of their headquarters. This action resulted in the death of six of the MOVE members and five of their children. As Laurene Munyan observes, the poem "focuses particularly on the tragic impact that the bombing had on black Philadelphia because of perceptions of MOVE as part of the Black Power movement."[1] Sanchez's mournful poem, written in the cadences of a sermon, carries with it images of a lynching as David Kieran points out.[2] The poem was so powerful and so painful for her to perform and for her audience to hear that Sanchez did not read it aloud for several years.

—

1.
philadelphia
    a disguised southern city
squatting in the eastern pass of
colleges cathedrals & cowboys
philadelphia, a phalanx of parsons
and auctioneers
    modern gladiators
easing the delirium of death from their shields
while houses burn out of control.

2.
c'mon girl hurry on down to osage st
they're roasting in the fire

smell the dreadlocks and blk/skins
roasting in the fire.

c'mon newsmen and tvmen
hurryondown to osage st and
when you have chloroformed the city
and after you have stitched up your words
hurry on downtown for sanctuary
in taverns and corporations

and the blood is not yet dry.

3.
how does one scream in thunder?

4.
they are combing the morning for shadows
and screams tongue-tied without faces
look, over there, one eye
escaping from its skin
and our heartbeats slowdown to a drawl
and the kingfisher calls out from his downtown capital need rest
and the pinstriped general reenlists
his tongue for combat
and the police come like twin seasons of drought and flood.
they're combing the city for life liberty and
the pursuit of happiness.

5.
how does one scream in thunder?

6.
hide us O lord
deliver us from our nakedness.
exile us from our laughter

give us this day our rest from seduction
peeling us down to our veins.

and the tower was like no other.   amen.
and the streets escaped under the
cover of darkness   amen.
and the voices called out from
their wounds   amen.
and the fire circumcised the city   amen.

7.
who anointeth the city with napalm?   (I say)
who giveth this city in holy infanticide?

8.
beyond the mornings and afternoons
and deaths detonating the city.
beyond the tourist roadhouses
trading in lobotomies
there is a glimpse of earth
this prodigal earth.
beyond edicts and commandments
commissioned by puritans
there are people
navigating the breath of hurricanes.
beyond concerts and football
and mummers³ strutting their
sequined processionals.
there is this earth. this country. this city.
this people.
collecting skeletons from waiting rooms
lying in wait. for honor and peace.
one day.

NOTES

1. Munyan, "Elegy."

2. Kieran, "Remembering Lynching," 41–42.

3. Mummers: The Mummers Parade is held
annually in Philadelphia on New Year's Day. It

was first held in 1901 and continues to today. Revelers come in costumes. Many pantomime Black people, and although blackface and racist caricatures have been banned from the parade since 1964, unfortunately, this tradition continues.

BIBLIOGRAPHY

Burton, Jazmyn. "Philadelphia Names Sonia Sanchez First Poet Laureate." *Temple Now*, January 23, 2012.

Evans, Mari, ed. *Black Women Writers (1950–1980): A Critical Evaluation*. Garden City, NY: Anchor Press / Doubleday, 1984.

Kieran, David. "Remembering Lynching and Representing Contemporary Violence in Black Arts Poetry." *Journal of the Midwest Modern Language Association* 41, no. 1 (2008): 34–45.

Munyan, Laurene. "Elegy (for MOVE and Philadelphia)" *Encyclopedia of Greater Philadelphia*. https://philadelphiaencyclopedia.org/essays/elegy-for-move-and-philadelphia.

Sanders, Kimberly, and Judson Jeffries. "Framing MOVE: A Press' Complicity in the Murder of Women and Children in the City of (Un) Brotherly Love." *Journal of African American Studies* 17, no. 4 (December 2013): 566–86.

Becky Birtha, "Route 23: 10th and Bigler to Bethlehem Pike" (1987)

Rebecca Lucille (Becky) Birtha was born in Hampton, Virginia, in 1948, but has lived much of her adult life in the greater Philadelphia area. She identifies as being an African American, a lesbian, a feminist, an adoptive parent, and a Quaker. Birtha has published two collections of short stories, *For Nights Like This One: Stories of Loving Women* (1983) and *Lovers' Choice* (1987); a book of verse, *The Forbidden Poems* (1991); and three children's books, *Grandmama's Pride* (2005), *Lucky Beans* (2010), and *Far Apart, Close in Heart* (2017). Birtha attended the Philadelphia High School for Girls and holds a BS in Child Studies from the State University of New York at Buffalo and an MFA from the Vermont College of Fine Arts. She has worked as a teacher, a librarian, and a representative for an adoption agency. Birtha has won numerous awards for her writing, including a fellowship from the Pennsylvania Council on the Arts, a grant from the National Endowment of the Arts, a Pushcart Prize, and a Lambda Literary award. Her work tends to focus on relationships between women, mothering and childlessness, and the challenges faced by poor people and women of color.

Much of Birtha's fiction has a strong Philadelphia flavor to it, as exemplified by "Route 23: 10th and Bigler to Bethlehem Pike" (from *Lovers' Choice*). The story concerns a proud woman, Leona Mae Moses, who leads her freezing children on an all-night wintry bus ride after her landlord refuses to provide adequate heat. The story is marked by Birtha's stark portrayal of poverty and her poignant depiction of a loving mother who will do whatever it takes to provide for her family.

Route 23 began as the Germantown trolley line sometime prior to 1877. It has had many iterations since then. At the time the story was written, Route 23 was a streetcar line traversing the length of the city, going through such diverse neighborhoods as South Philly, Chinatown, Center City, Germantown, North Philly, West Mt. Airy, and Chestnut Hill. The line extended almost fourteen miles and took more than ninety minutes before arriving at the final destination. Tenth and Bigler was the southern terminus of the line, while the intersection of Germantown Avenue and Bethlehem Pike Loop was the northern terminus. Buses replaced the trolleys in 1992, and the southern terminus is now the intersection of 11th and Market Street in Center City, but the northern terminus remains the same. The heavily trafficked route, the longest in the SEPTA bus system, is the perfect choice to exhibit the racial, ethnic, and economic diversity of the city.

—

Ain't no reason for you to be gaping at me. I pay my taxes, just like everybody else. And it just don't make no sense. The mayor and all them city council men sitting up in all them little offices over in City Hall, ain't never been cold in they life. And me and my little ones freezing to death up on Thirteenth Street.

Last time I was down to City Hall to try to talk to one of them men, heat just pouring out the radiator in that office. I had to yell at Kamitra and Junie not to touch it, scared they was gonna burn theyself. Man I'm talking to done took off his jacket and drape it over the back of his chair. Wiping his forehead off with his hanky, talking bout "No Miz Moses, we can't do nothing for you. Not a thing. Not as long as you living in a privately-own residence and you not in the public housing. . . ."

I'm thinking how they only use them offices in the day time. Ain't nobody in em at night. And my babies is sleeping in the kitchen, ever since the oil run out two weeks ago and they ain't deliver no more. Landlord claim he outta town.

Hasan, my baby here, he don't hardly even know what warm is. He so little he can't remember last summer. All the others had colds all winter. Noses ain't stopped running since last October. And Kleenex just one more thing I can't afford to buy em. Scuse me a minute.

—I know, Junie. I see it. Yeah, I see the swings. Can't get off and play today. Too cold out there. Maybe so, honey. Maybe tomorrow, if the sun come out. Lamont, let your sister have a turn to sit by the window now.—

Don't you be thinking I'm homeless, cause I ain't. You ever seen a bag lady with all these kids? These here shopping bags is just a temporary measure. Like I said, I live up on Thirteenth Street. Seventeen hundred block. North.[1] Top floor. You don't believe me you go look. My name on the mailbox: Leona Mae Moses. And all the rest of the stuff belong to us is right where we left it. The kids is got other clothes, and we got beds and dishes and all the same stuff you got in your house. We ain't planning to make this no permanent way of life. Just till this cold spell break.

—Cherise, honey, would you get the baby bottle out that bag you got up there? Right next to that box of Pampers. And you and Lamont gonna have to get off and get some more milk. Next time we come up to the A & P. Junie, get your hands away from that buzzer. We ain't there yet. We got to go all the way up to Chestnut Hill, and then turn around and come back down. Anyway, it's Kamitra turn to ring the bell this time.—

Ain't nobody got no call to stare at me like I'm some kinda freak. My kids got the same rights as other people kids. They got a right to spend the night someplace warm and dry. Got a right to get some sleep at night. Last night, along about eleven o'clock, when the man on the radio say the temperature gone down to fifteen below, he didn't have to tell me nothing. The pipes is froze, and the wind lifting the curtains right up at the windows in my kitchen, And my little girl crying, "Mama, I'm cold." Air so icy I can see a little cloud come out her mouth, every time she cry.

—Kamitra, sugar, don't sing so loud. Mama trying to talk. Anyway, other people on here besides us. They don't want to be bother listen to all that racket.—

You got kids? Well, think a minute what you would do if you was in my place. Last night I'm trying so hard to think what to do, feel like my head gonna split wide open. Nobody in my building ain't got no more heat than we do. I don't know no neighbors got enough space for all of us. They be sleep anyway. All my people still down south.

Kamitra crying done waked up the others, too. Then all of em crying they cold. I ain't crazy yet, but I like to went crazy last night trying to think what I'm gonna do. I just kept thinking theys got to be some place in this great big city that I can carry these children to, where it's warm, where it stay warm, even in the middle of the night. And then it come to me.

"Mama, where we going?" the kids is all asking. I just tell em to hush and go get they blankets and towels and sweaters and stuff. Comb everybody hair and dress em real warm. Start packing up some food to last us for a couple days. "Mama, what we gonna do? Where we taking all this stuff?" And Junie, he tickle me. Say, "Mama, we can't go no place. It's dark outside."

I just hush em all up and hustle em down to the corner. Little ones start crying again, cause even with all them layers on, they ain't warm enough for no fifteen below. Lamont done lost his gloves last week, and Cherise just got one a my scarf wrap around her head, cause it ain't enough hats to go round. Ain't a one of em got boots. Cherise still asking me where we going, while we standing at the corner, waiting. I tell em, "Mama got a surprise for you all. We taking a trip. We going on a nice, long ride."

—Get outta that bag, Kamitra. You can't have no more crackers. Mama gonna fix you some tuna fish for supper, pretty soon. What's the matter, Junie? You gotta pee? You sure? Well then, sit still. Lamont, next time we come up to our corner, I want you to take him in to the bathroom, anyway. It don't hurt to try.—

I guess that explain howcome we here. We intend to stay here, too, right where we at, up till the weather break. Or the oil come. Whatever happen first. It ain't no laws against it. I pay my taxes to keep these things running, just like everybody else. And I done paid our fare. The ones under six rides for free, just like the sign say. I got enough quarters here to last us a long time.

My kids is clean—all got washed up at the library just this morning. And look how nice and well-behave they is. I ain't got nothing to be ashamed of.

I hope your curiosity satisfied, cause I really ain't got no more to say. This car big enough for all of us. You better find something else to gawk at. Better look on out the window, make sure you ain't miss your stop.

—Cherise, sugar, we at the end of the line again. Go up there and put these quarters in the man box. No, Junie. This trolley gonna keep running all night long. Time just come for the man to turn the thing around. We ain't getting off. This trip ain't over yet.

NOTE

1. The address is in North Philadelphia.

BIBLIOGRAPHY

Blumgart, Jake. "SEPTA's Route 23: A Window on Philadelphia." *Philly Voice*, April 22, 2015. https://www.phillyvoice.com /septa-route-23-a-window-on -philadelphia/.

Brownsworth, Victoria. "The Other Tongue: Poet Becky Birtha Gives Voice to the Experience of Parenting." *Advocate* (April 23, 1991): 78.

Mark, Rebecca. "Becky Birtha." In *Contemporary Lesbian Writers of the United States: A Bio-Bibliographical Critical Sourcebook*, edited by Sandra Pollack and Denise D. Knight, 53–56. Westport, CT: Greenwood, 1993.

Bebe Moore Campbell, from *Sweet Summer: Growing Up With and Without My Dad* (1989)

Elizabeth Bebe Moore was born in North Philadelphia in 1950. She graduated from the Philadelphia High School for Girls and received a BS in Education from the University of Pittsburgh. Moore Campbell's five novels all feature a gripping narrative, which made them bestsellers, while also adding elements of social justice. They include *Your Blues Ain't Mine* (1992), inspired by Emmitt Till's murder in 1955, *Brothers and Sisters* (1994), which explores the aftermath of the Rodney King beating, and *72 Hour Hold* (2005), on mental illness, a longstanding concern of the author. She also wrote two children's books as well as dozens of periodical articles. She lived most of her adult life in Los Angeles, where she died of brain cancer in 2006.

Sweet Summer is a memoir of Moore Campbell's divided time between her mother and her father. During the school year, young Bebe lived in North Philadelphia with her mother, grandmother, aunts, and female teachers. She went to Logan Public School, located in a historic building from the 1920s. The Logan district, where the school is situated, is in the uppermost part of North Philadelphia. The school, and the area itself, was largely Ukrainian and Jewish when Bebe was a student. She received a top-notch education, particularly from the tough, but caring, Mrs. Bradley. Her all-female family and teachers, called the "Bosoms" by the young girl, raised her to be a proper, well-brought-up young lady. Her mother had won a scholarship, and the family expected her to follow in this tradition. When she threatens to use an imaginary knife on her teacher one day, it is the height of humiliation for the family. Bebe also has a growing-up experience, learning of the institutional racism within the school walls.

In the summer, Bebe went to North Carolina to spend time with her father, who did not let his confinement in a wheelchair limit his life. Here, Bebe lived a more relaxed and unstructured life, not under the constant watch of her elders. Despite the pain of her parents' separation, and being an only child brought up in two very different worlds, the young girl grew up with a deep sense of family and culture and of being loved fiercely.

⁓

CHAPTER 5

The red bricks of 2239 North 16th Street melded into the uniformity of looka-like doors, windows and brownstone steps. From the outside our rowhouse looked the same as any other. When I was a toddler, the similarity was unset-tling. The family story was that my mother and I were out walking on the street one day when panic rumbled through me. "Where's our house? Where's our house?" I cried, grabbing my mother's hand.

My mother walked me to our house, pointed to the numbers painted next to the door. "Twenty-two thirty-nine," she said, slapping the wall. "This is our house."

Much later I learned that the real difference was inside.

In my house there was no morning stubble, no long johns or Fruit of the Loom on the clothesline, no baritone hollering for keys that were sitting on the table. There was no beer in the refrigerator, no ball game on TV, no loud cussing. After dark the snores that emanated from the bedrooms were subtle, ladylike, little moans really.

Growing up, I could have died from overexposure to femininity. Women ruled at 2239. A grandmother, a mother, occasionally an aunt, grown-up girl-friends from at least two generations, all the time rubbing up against me, fixing my food, running my bathwater, telling me to sit still and be good in those grown-up, girly-girl voices. Chanel and Prince Matchabelli wafting through the bedrooms. Bubble bath and Jergens came from the bathroom, scents unbroken by aftershave, macho beer breath, a good he-man funk. I remember a house full of 'do rags and rollers, the soft, sweet allure of Dixie peach and bergamot; brown-skinned queens wearing pastel housecoats and worn-out size six-and-a-half flip-flops that slapped softly against the wood as the royal women climbed the stairs at night carrying their paperbacks to bed.

The outside world offered no retreat. School was taught by stern, old-maid white women with age spots and merciless gray eyes; ballet lessons, Sunday school and choir were all led by colored sisters with a hands-on-their-hips attitude who cajoled and screeched in distaff tongues.

And what did they want from me, these Bosoms? Achievement! This desire had nothing to do with the pittance they collected from the Philadelphia Board of Education or the few dollars my mother paid them. Pushing little colored girls forward was in their blood. They made it clear: a life of white picket fences and teas was for other girls to aspire to. I was to *do* something. And if I didn't climb willingly up their ladder, they'd drag me to the top. Rap my knuckles hard for not practicing. Make me lift my leg until I wanted to die. Stay after school and write "I will listen to the teacher" five hundred times. They were not playing. "Obey them," my mother commanded.

When I entered 2B—the Philadelphia school system divided grades into A and B—in September 1957, I sensed immediately that Miss Bradley was not a woman to be challenged. She looked like one of those evil old spinsters Shirley Temple was always getting shipped off to live with; she was kind of hefty, but so tightly corseted that if she happened to grab you or if you fell against her during recess, it felt as if you were bouncing into a steel wall. In reality she was a sweet lady who was probably a good five years past her retirement age when I wound up in her class. Miss Bradley remained at Logan for one reason and one reason only: she was dedicated. She wanted her students to learn! learn! learn! Miss Bradley was halfway sick, hacking and coughing her lungs out through every lesson, spitting the phlegm into fluffy white tissues from the box on her desk, but she was *never* absent. Each day at three o'clock she kissed each one of her "little pupils" on the cheek, sending a faint scent of Emeraude home with us. Her rules for teaching children seemed to be: Love them; discipline them; reward them; and make sure they are clean.

Every morning she ran a hygiene check on the entire class. She marched down the aisle like a stormtrooper, rummaging through the ears of hapless students, checking for embedded wax. She looked under our fingernails for dirt. Too bad for you if she found any. Once she made David, a stringy-haired white boy who thought Elvis Presley was a living deity and who was the most notorious booger-eater in the entire school, go to the nurse's office to have the dirt cleaned from under his fingernails. Everybody knew what was under David's fingernails was most likely dried-up boogies and not dirt, but nobody said anything.

If she was death on dirt and earwax, Miss Bradley's specialty was head-lice patrol. Down the aisles she stomped in the black Enna Jettick shoes,[1] stopping at each student to part strands of blond, brown or dark hair, look-ing for cooties. Miss Bradley would flip through plaits, curls, kinks—the woman was relentless. I always passed inspection. Nana put enough Nu Nile[2] in my hair to suffocate any living creature that had the nerve to come tipping up on my scalp. Nu Nile was the official cootie killer. I was clean, wax-free, bug-free and smart. The folder inside my desk contained a stack of spelling and arithmetic papers with As emblazoned across the top, gold stars in the corner. Miss Bradley always called on me. She sent me to run errands for her too. I was her pet.

When Mrs. Clark, my piano teacher and my mother's good friend, told my mother that Logan Elementary School was accepting children who didn't live in the neighborhood, my mother immediately enrolled Michael and later me. "It's not crowded and it's mixed," she told a nodding, smiling Nana. The fact that Logan was integrated was the main reason Michael and I were sent there. Nana and Mommy, like most upwardly mobile colored women, believed that to have the same education as a white child was the first step up the rocky road to success. This viewpoint was buttressed by the fact that George Wash-ington Carver, my neighborhood school, was severely overcrowded. Logan was just barely integrated, with only a handful of black kids thrown in with hordes of square-jawed, pale-eyed second-generation Ukrainians whose immi-grant parents and grandparents populated the neighborhood near the school. There were a few dark-haired Jews and aristocratic-looking WASPs too. My first day in kindergarten it was Nana who enthusiastically grabbed Michael's and my hands, pulling us away from North Philly's stacked-up rowhouses, from the hucksters[3] whose wagons bounced down the streets with trucks full of ripe fruits and vegetables, from the street-corner singers and jitterbugs who filled my block with all-day doo-wahs. It was Nana who resolutely walked me past the early-morning hordes of colored kids heading two blocks away to Carver Elementary School. Nana who pulled me by the hand and led me in another direction.

We went underground at the Susquehanna and Dauphin subway station, leaving behind the unremitting asphalt and bricks and the bits of paper strewn in the streets above us. We emerged at Logan station, where sunlight, bril-liant red and pink roses and yellow chrysanthemums, and neatly clipped lawns and clean streets startled me. There were robins and blue jays flying overhead. The only birds in my neighborhood were sparrows and pigeons. Delivering me at the schoolyard, Nana firmly cupped my chin with her hand as she bent down to instruct me. "Your mother's sending you up here to learn, so you do everything your teacher tells you to, okay?" To Michael she turned and said, "You're not up here to be a monkey on a stick." Then to both of us: "Don't talk. Listen. Act like you've got some home training. You've got as much brains as anybody up here. Do you know that? All right now. Make Nana proud of you."

A month after I returned from Pasquotank County,[4] I sat in Miss Bradley's classroom on a rainy Monday watching her write spelling words on the blackboard. The harsh sccurr, sccurr of Miss Bradley's chalk and the tinny sound the rain made against the window took my mind to faraway places. I couldn't get as far away as I wanted. Wallace, the bane of the whole class, had only moments earlier laid the most gigunda fart in history, one in a never-ending series, and the air was just clearing. His farts were silent wonders. Not a hint, not the slightest sound. You could be in the middle of a sentence and then wham! bam! Mystery Funk would knock you down.

Two seats ahead of me was Leonard, a lean colored boy from West Philly who always wore suits and ties to school, waving his hand like a crazy man. A showoff if ever there was one.

I was bored that day. I looked around at the walls. Miss Bradley has decorated the room with pictures of the ABCs in cursive. Portraits of the presidents were hanging in a row on one wall above the blackboard. On the bulletin board there was a display of the Russian satellite, *Sputnik I*, and the American satellite, *Explorer I*. Miss Bradley was satellite-crazy. She thought it was just wonderful that America was in the "space-race" and she constantly filled our heads with space fantasies. "Boys and girls," she told us, "one day man will walk on the moon." In the far corner on another bulletin board there was a Thanksgiving scene of turkeys and pilgrims. And stuck in the corner was a picture of Sacajawea.[5] Sacajawea, Indian Woman Guide. I preferred looking at Sacajawea over satellites any day.

Thinking about the bubble gum that lay in my pocket, I decided to sneak a piece, even though gum chewing was strictly forbidden. I rarely broke the rules. Could anyone hear the loud drumming of my heart, I wondered, as I slid my hand into my skirt pocket and felt for the Double Bubble? I peeked cautiously to either side of me. Then I managed to unwrap it without even rustling the paper; I drew my hand to my lips, coughed and popped the gum in my mouth. Ahhh! Miss Bradley's back was to the class. I chomped down hard on the Double Bubble. Miss Bradley turned around. I quickly packed the gum under my tongue. My hands were folded on top of my desk. "Who can give me a sentence for 'birthday'?" Leonard just about went nuts. Miss Bradley ignored him, which she did a lot. "Sandra," Miss Bradley called.

A petite white girl rose obediently. I liked Sandra. She had shared her crayons with me once when I left mine at home. I remember her drawing: a white house with smoke coming out of the chimney, a little girl with yellow hair like hers, a mommy, a daddy, a little boy and a dog standing in front of the house in a yard full of flowers. Her voice was crystal clear when she spoke. There were smiles in that voice. She said, "My father made me a beautiful dollhouse for my birthday."

The lump under my tongue was suddenly a stone and when I swallowed, the taste was bitter. I coughed into a piece of tablet paper, spit out the bubble gum, and crumpled up the wad and pushed it inside my desk. The center of my chest was burning. I breathed deeply and slowly. Sandra sat down as demurely as a princess. She crossed her ankles. Her words came back to me in a rush. "Muuuy fatha made me a bee-yoo-tee-ful dollhouse." Miss Bradley said, "Very good," and moved on to the next word. Around me hands were waving, waving. Pick me! Pick me! Behind me I could hear David softly crooning, "You ain't nothin' but a hound dog, cryin' all the time." Sometimes he would stick his head inside his desk, sing Elvis songs and pick his boogies at the same time. Somebody was jabbing pins in my chest. Ping ! Ping! Ping! I wanted to holler, "Yowee! Stop! as loud as I could, but I pressed my lips together hard.

"Now who can give me a sentence?" Miss Bradley asked. I put my head down on my desk and when Miss Bradley asked me what was wrong I told her that I didn't feel well and that I didn't want to be chosen. When Leonard collected the homework, I shoved mine at him so hard all the papers he was carrying fell on the floor.

Bile was still clogging my throat when Miss Bradley sent me into the cloakroom to get my lunchbox. The rule was, only one student in the cloakroom at a time. When the second one came in, the first one had to leave. I was still rummaging around in my bookbag when I saw Sandra.

"Miss Bradley said for you to come out," she said. She was smiling. That dollhouse girl was always smiling. I glared at her.

"Leave when I get ready to," I said, my words full of venom.

Sandra's eyes darted around in confusion. "Miss Bradley said . . ." she began again, still trying to smile as if she expected somebody to crown her Miss America or something and come take her picture any minute.

In my head a dam broke. Terrible waters rushed out. "I don't care about any Miss Bradley. If she messes with me I'll . . . I'll take my butcher knife and stab her until she bleeds." What I lacked in props I made up for in drama. My balled-up hand swung menacingly in the air. I aimed the invisible dagger toward Sandra. Her Miss America smile faded instantly. Her eyes grew round and frightened as she blinked rapidly. "Think I won't, huh? Huh?" I whispered, enjoying my meanness, liking the scared look on Sandra's face. Scaredy cat! Scaredy cat! Muuuy fatha made me a bee-yoo-tee-ful dollhouse. "What do you think about that?" I added viciously, looking into her eyes to see the total effect of my daring words.

But Sandra wasn't looking at me. Upon closer inspection, I realized that she was looking *over* me with sudden relief in her face. I turned to see what was so interesting, and my chin jammed smack into the Emeraude-scented bosom of Miss Bradley. Even as my mind scrambled for an excuse, I knew I was lost.

Miss Bradley had a look of horror on her face. For a minute she didn't say anything, just stood there looking as though someone had slapped her across the face. Sandra didn't say anything. I didn't move. Finally, "Would you mind repeating what you just said, Bebe."

"I didn't say anything, Miss Bradley." I could feel my dress sticking to my body.

"Sandra, what did Bebe say?"

Sandra was crying softly, little delicate tears streaming down her face. For just a second she paused, giving a tiny shudder. I rubbed my ear vigorously, thinking, "Oh, please . . ."

"She said, she said, if you bothered with her she would cut you with her knife."

"Unh, unh, Miss Bradley. I didn't say that. I didn't. I didn't say anything like that."

Miss Bradley's gray eyes penetrated mine. She locked me into her gaze until I looked down at the floor. Then she looked at Sandra.

"Bebe, you and I had better go see the principal."

The floor blurred. The principal!! Jennie G., the students called her with awe and fear. As Miss Bradley wrapped her thick knuckles around my forearm and dutifully steered me from the cloakroom and out the classroom door, I completely lost what little cool I had left. I began to cry, a jerky, hiccuping, snot-filled cry for mercy. "I didn't say it. I didn't say it," I moaned.

Miss Bradley was nonplussed. Dedication and duty overruled compassion. Always. "Too late for that now," she said grimly.

Jennie G's office was small, neat and dim. The principal was dwarfed by the large brown desk she sat behind, and when she stood up she wasn't much bigger than I. But she was big enough to make me tremble as I stood in front of her, listening to Miss Bradley recount the sordid details of my downfall. Jennie G. was one of those pale, pale vein-showing white women. She had a vocabulary of about six horrible phrases, designed to send chills of despair down the spine of any young transgressor. Phrases like "We'll just see about that" or "Come with me, young lady," spoken ominously. Her face was impassive as she listened to Miss Bradley. I'd been told that she had a six-foot paddle in her office used solely to beat young transgressors. Suppose she tried to beat me? My heart gave a lurch. I tugged rapidly at my ears. I longed to suck my thumb.

"Well, Bebe, I think we'll have to call your mother."

My mother! I wanted the floor to swallow me up and take me whole. My mother! As Jennie G. dialed the number, I envisioned my mother's face, clouded with disappointment and shame. I started crying again as I listened to the principal telling my mother what had happened. They talked for a pretty long time. When she hung up, ole Jennie G flipped through some papers on her desk before looking at me sternly.

"You go back to class and watch your mouth, young lady."

As I was closing the door to her office I heard her say to Miss Bradley, "What can you expect?"

"Ooooh, You're gonna get it, girl," is how Michael greeted me after school. Logan's colored world was small, and news of my demise had blazed its way through hallways and classrooms, via the brown-skinned grapevine. Everyone from North Philly, West Philly and Germantown knew about my crime. The subway ride home was depressing. My fellow commuters kept coming up to me and asking, "Are you gonna get in trouble?" Did they think my mother would give me a reward or something? I stared at the floor for most of the ride, looking up only when the train came to a stop and the doors hissed open. Logan. Wyoming. Hunting Park. Each station drew me closer to my doom, whatever that was going to be. "What can you expect?" I mulled over those words. What did she mean? My mother rarely spanked, although Nana would give Michael or me, usually Michael, a whack across the butt from time to time. My mother's social-worker instincts were too strong for such undignified displays; Doris believed in talking things out, which was sometimes worse than a thousand beatings. As the train drew closer to Susquehanna and Dauphin I thought of how much I hated for my mother to be disappointed in me. And now she would be. "What can you expect?"

Of me? Didn't Jennie G. know that I was riding a subway halfway across town as opposed to walking around the corner to Carver Elementary School, for a reason: the same reason I was dragged away from Saturday cartoons and pulled from museum to museum, to Judimar School of Dance[6] for ballet (art class for Michael), to Mrs. Clark for piano. The Bosoms wanted me to Be Somebody, to be the second generation to live out my life as far away from a mop and scrub brush and Miss Ann's[7] floors as possible.

My mother had won a full scholarship to the University of Pennsylvania. The story of that miracle was a treasured family heirloom. Sometimes Nana told the tale and sometimes my mother described how the old Jewish counselor at William Penn High School[8] approached her and asked why a girl with straight Es (for "excellent") was taking the commercial course. My mother replied that Nana couldn't afford to send her to college, that she planned to become a secretary. "Sweetheart, you switch to academic," the woman told her, "You'll get to college." When her graduation day approached, the counselor pulled her aside. "I have two scholarships for you. One to Cheyney State Teacher's College[9] and the other to the University of Pennsylvania." Cheyney was a small black school outside of Philadelphia. My mother chose Penn. I had been born to a family of hopeful women. One miracle had already taken place. They expected more. And now I'd thrown away my chance. Michael, who was seated next to me on the subway and whose generosity of spirit had lasted a record five subway stops, poked me in my arm. "Bebe," he told me gleefully, "your ass is grass."

Nana took one look at my guilty face, scowled at me and sucked her teeth until they whistled. My mother had called her and told her what happened and now she was possessed by a legion of demons. I had barely entered the room when she exploded. "Don't. Come. In. Here. Crying." Nana said, her voice booming, her lips quivering and puffy with anger. When Nana talked in staccato language she was beyond pissed off. Waaaay beyond. "What. Could. Possess. You. To. Say. Such. A. Thing? Embarrassingyourmotherlikethatinfrontof *those people!*" Before I could answer she started singing some

Dinah Washington song, real loud. Volume all the way up. With every word she sang I sank deeper and deeper into gloom.

Later that evening, when my mother got home and Aunt Ruth, Michael's mother, came to visit, the three women lectured me in unison. The room was full of flying feathers. Three hens clucking away at me, their breasts heaving with emotion. Cluck! Cluck! Cluck! How could I have said such a thing? What on earth was I thinking about? Cluck! Cluck! Cluck! A knife, such a, a *colored* weapon.

"But I didn't do anything," I wailed, the tears that had been trickling all day now falling in full force.

"Umph, umph, umph," Nana said and started singing. Billie Holiday this time.

"You call threatening somebody with a knife nothing?" Aunt Ruth asked. Ruth was Nana's middle girl. She was the family beauty, as pretty as Dorothy Dandridge or Lena Horne. Now her coral lips were curled up in disdain and her Maybelline eyebrows were raised in judgment against me. "They expect us to act like animals and you have to go and say that. My God."

Animals. Oh. Oh. Oh.

My mother glared at her sister, but I looked at Aunt Ruth in momentary wonder and appreciation. Now I understood. The unspoken rule that I had sensed all of my life was that a colored child had to be on her best behavior whenever she visited the white world. Otherwise, whatever opportunity was being presented would be snatched away. I had broken the rule. I had committed the unpardonable sin of embarrassing my family in front of *them*. Sensing my remorse and shame, Mommy led me out of the kitchen. We sat down on the living room sofa; my mother took my hand, "Bebe, I want you to go to your room and think about what you've done. I don't understand your behavior. It was very hard for me to get you in Logan." She drew a breath. I drew a breath and looked into the eyes of a social worker. "I'm extremely disappointed in you."

I didn't go straight to my room. Instead I sneaked into Michael's room, which overlooked Mole Street, the tiny one-sided alley of narrow rowhouses that face the backyards of 16th Street. Michael had usually played on the "back street." Alone in Michael's room with the window open. I could hear Mr. Watson, our neighbor, hollering at one of his kids. Why had I said what I said? What had possessed me? Then I remembered "Muuuy fatha made me a bee-yoo-tee-ful dollhouse for muuuy birthday." Something pinched me inside my chest when I heard those words. Pain oozed from my heart like a tube of toothpaste bursting open, going every whichaway. Blue-eyes kept yapping away with her golden hair and her goofy white smile. Who cared what her fatha did? Who cared? I couldn't help it. When she came into the cloakroom I got mad all over again. When I said I had a knife, she looked just like Grandma Mary's chickens. Scared. And my chest stopped hurting. Just stopped.

Mr. Watson's baritone voice was a seismic rumble echoing with the threat of upheaval, violence. His words floated over Mole Street and into the bedroom window. Whoever was in trouble over there was really gonna get it. None of this "go to your room" stuff. None of this corny "I'm disappointed in you" stuff. Mr. Watson was getting ready to beat somebody's ass.

Adam's. He was the youngest and one of my playmates. I could tell by his pleading voice. "Please, Daddy. I won't do it anymore, Daddy. I'm sorry, Daddy."

Michael came into the room. "What are you doing?" he whispered.

"Shhh. Adam's getting a whipping."

"You better go to your room before Aunt Doris comes upstairs."

"Shhhh."

My playmate's misery took my mind off my own. His father's exotic yelling hypnotized me. From downstairs I could hear the hens, still clucking away. Michael and I sat quietly, not making a sound. Mr. Watson's voice sounded so foreign coming into our house. For a moment I pretended that his anger was emanating from Michael's bedroom, and I remembered how only last year he got mad and ran after all of us kids—Jackie, Jane and Adam, his own three, and me. His face was covered with shaving cream and he held a razor in one hand and a thick leather belt in the other. I don't recall what we had done, but I remember him chasing us and yelling ferociously, "This belt's got your name on it too, Miss Bebe!" And I recall that I was thrilled when the leather grazed my hiney with the vengeance of a father's wrath.

My mind drifted back a few years. The memory was vague and fuzzy. When I was four or five I was playing on Mole Street when my ten-year-old neighbor, a boy named Buddy, asked me to come inside his yard. He was sitting on an old soda crate. "Come closer," he told me. "Wanna play doctor?"

"Uh, huh."

"You can examine me."

I told my mother, prattling on about the "game" I had played. She sat me down on her bed. "Did he touch your private parts."

"Nope." Why was Mommy's face so serious?

"Did you touch his?"

"I touched his zipper." Had I done something wrong?

Nana went into hysterics, singing and screeching like a wild woman. "Mother, just calm down," Mommy told her.

Mommy was cool, every inch the social worker; she took my hand and we walked down the street to Buddy's house. He was in his yard making a scooter out of the crate. "Buddy," my mother said softly. When he saw the two of us, he dropped his hammer. "Buddy, I want to talk with you."

My mother questioned him. Calmly put the fear of God in him. Warned him of penalties for a repeat performance. And that was that. Not quite. Weeks, maybe months later, my father came to visit me, one of his pop-in, no-real-occasion visits. My mother, my father and I were sitting in his car and she told him about my playing doctor. His leg shot out in wild, uncontrollable spasms. His face became contorted and he started yelling. Nana's screeching paled in contrast. This was rage that my mother and Nana could not even begin to muster. And it was in my honor. This energy was for my avengement, my protection. Or should have been. But the sound of his fury frightened me. I remember angling away from my father, this man who was yelling like an animal in pain. I leaned toward my mother, and she put one arm around me and with her other hand tried to pat my father's shoulder, only he snatched away. He leaned forward and started reaching for his chair. "I may not be able to walk, goddammit, but I can tear that little son of a bitch's ass up."

My mother kept talking very softly, saying, "No, no, no. It's all right. He's just a kid. I took care of it. It's okay." I leaned away from my father's anger, his determination. He frightened me. But the rage was fascinating too. And after a while, when my father was shouting only a little, I moved closer to him. I wanted to see the natural progression of his hot words. If he snatched his wheelchair out of the backseat and rolled up to Buddy's house, what would he do? What would he do in my honor? My mother calmed my father. His shouting subsided. I was relieved. I was disappointed.

"Hey"—I suddenly heard Michael's persistent voice—"ain't you glad Mr. Watson ain't your father?" I felt Michael's hands, shaking my shoulder, "Ain't you?"

I didn't answer; I was thinking about Miss Bradley, Jennie G., Aunt Ruth, Nana, and Mommy. All these women with power over me. I could hear Mrs. Watson telling her husband that enough was enough and then the baritone telling her he knew when to stop and Adam letting out another feeble yelp. "Muuuy fatha made me a bee-yoo-tee-ful dollhouse." Maybe my mother would write my daddy and tell him how bad I had been. Maybe he would get so mad he would get into his car and drive all the way to Philly just to whip my behind. Or tell me he was disappointed in me. Either one.

The Bosoms decided to forgive me. My mother woke me up with a kiss and a snuggle and then a crisp, "All right, Bebe. It's a brand-new day. Forget about yesterday." When I went to get a bowl of cereal that morning, my aunt Ruth was sitting in the kitchen drinking coffee and reading the newspaper. She had spent the night. "Did you comb your hair?" she asked me.

I nodded.

"That's not what I call combed. Get me the comb and brush."

She combed out my hair and braided it all over again. This time there were no wispy little ends sticking out. "Now you look nice," she said. "Now you look like a pretty girl, and when you go to school today, act like a pretty girl. All right?"

I nodded.

Last night Nana had hissed at me between her teeth. "If you want to behave like a little *heathen*, if you want to up there acting like a, a . . . *monkey on a stick . . . well*, thenyoucangotoschoolrigharoundthecornerandI'llwalkyouthere andI'llwalkyoubackhomeandI'llcomeandgetyouforlunchyou*behave*yourself!" But today she was sanguine, even jovial, as she fixed my lunch. She kissed me when I left for school.

On my way out the door my mother handed me two elegant letters, one to Miss Bradley and the other to Jennie G., assuring them that I had an overactive imagination, that I had no access to butcher knives or weapons of any kind, that she had spoken to me at length about my unfortunate outburst and that henceforth my behavior would be exemplary. These letters were written on her very best personalized stationery. The paper was light pink and had "D.C.M" in embossed letters across the top. Doris C. knew lots of big words and she had used every single one of them in those letters. I knew that all of her *i*s were dotted and all of her *t*s were crossed. I knew the letters were extremely dignified. My mother was very big on personal dignity. Anyone who messed with her dignity was in serious trouble.

I was only five when an unfortunate teller at her bank called her by her first name loud enough for the other customers to hear. My mother's body stiffened when she heard, "Doris, oh Doris," coming from a girl almost young enough to be her child.

"Are you talking to *me*, dear?" Her English was so clipped, her words so razor sharp she could have taken one, stabbed the teller and drawn blood. The girl nodded, her speckled green eyes wide and gapping, aware that something was going on, not quite sure what, and speechless because she was no match at all for this imperious little brown-skinned woman. "The people in *my* office all call me *Mrs. Moore.*"

And she grabbed me by the hand and we swept out of the bank. Me and Bette Davis. Me and Claudia McNeil. People stepped aside to let her pass.

So I knew my mother's letters not only would impress Miss Bradley and Jennie G. but also would go a long way toward redeeming me. After Miss Bradley read the note she told me I had a very nice mother and let me know that if I was willing to be exemplary she would let bygones be bygones and I could get back into her good graces. She was, after all, a dedicated teacher. And I had learned my lesson.

My mother wrote my father about the knife incident. I waited anxiously to hear from him. Would he suddenly appear? I searched the street in front of the school every afternoon. At home I jumped up nervously whenever I heard a horn beep. Finally, a letter from my dad arrived—one page of southpaw scribble.

Dear Bebe,
Your mother told me what happened in school about the knife. That wasn't a good thing to say. I think maybe you were joking. Remember, a lot of times white people don't understand how colored people joke, so you have to be careful what you say around them. Be a good girl.

Lots of love,
Daddy

The crumpled letter hit the edge of the wastepaper basket in my mother's room and landed in front of her bureau. I picked it up and slammed it into the basket, hitting my hand in the process. I flung myself across the bed, buried my face into my pillow and howled with pain, rage and sadness. "It's not fair," I wailed. Ole Blondie had her dollhouse-making daddy whenever she wanted him. "Muuuy fatha . . ." Jackie, Jane and Adam had their wild, ass-whipping daddy. All they had to do was walk outside their house, look under a car, and there he was, tinkering away. Ole ugly grease-monkey man. Why couldn't I have my daddy all the time too? I didn't want a letter signed "Lots of love." I wanted my father to come and yell at me for acting like a monkey on a stick. I wanted him to come and beat my butt or shake his finger in my face, or tell me that what I did wasn't so bad after all. Anything. I just wanted him to come.

NOTES

1. Enna Jettick shoes were a quality line of women's dress shoes popular from the 1920s through the 1960s. The name is a play on the word "energetic."

2. Nu Nile: created by Murray's Popular Products in 1925 and still popular today, the produce is a "hair slick dressing pomade" used to style hair.

3. Hucksters are peddlers who sell small items, often thought of as questionable quality.

4. Pasquotank County: located in the northeastern corner of North Carolina.

5. Sacajawea was a Lemhi Shoshone Indian guide who assisted Lewis and Clark on the Western Expedition in the early nineteenth century.

6. Judimar School of Dance: Marion Cuyjet, a classically trained ballet dancer, opened her school to teach young Black ballerinas in 1948 in Center City.

7. Miss Ann: a condescending white woman.

8. William Penn High School was a public high school located at 1333 North Broad Street in North Philly. It was opened in 1973 and closed in 2010.

9. Cheyney State Teacher's College: The school was begun as the African Institute in 1837, before being renamed the Institute for Colored Youth. The building is still standing at 915 Bainbridge Street in the Seventh Ward. The school in the city was closed in 1902 and reopened as Cheyney State University, a teacher-training college, located in West Chester, Pennsylvania. Cheyney State became the first historically Black university.

BIBLIOGRAPHY

Campbell, Jane. "An Interview with Bebe Moore Campbell." *Callaloo* 22, no. 4 (Fall 1999): 954–72.

Memmott, Carol. "Best Seller Bebe Moore Campbell Dead at 56." *USA Today*, November 27, 2006.

Mukhergee, Bharati. "The South Had All the Laughter: *Growing Up with and Without My Dad*, by Bebe Moore Campbell." *New York Times*, June 11, 1989, BR 47.

Satz, Martha. "I Hope I Can Teach a Little Bit: An Interview with Bebe Moore Campbell." *Southwest Review* 81, no. 2 (Spring 1996): 195–213.

John Edgar Wideman, from *Philadelphia Fire* (1990)

John Edgar Wideman was born in Washington, DC, in 1941. He is a well-renowned author of numerous novels, short story collections, memoirs, and essays. Wideman was raised in Pittsburgh but attended the University of Pennsylvania, where he was winner of a Rhodes Scholarship. Some of his writings include the memoir *Brothers and Keepers* (1984), the novels from The Homewood Trilogy (*Damballah, Hiding Place*, and *Sent for You Yesterday* 1985), and most recently the short story collection *American Histories* (2018). Wideman has taught at a number of universities, including the University of Massachusetts Amherst, the University of Wyoming, the University of Pennsylvania, and Brown University, where he is a professor emeritus. His awards include a MacArthur Foundation Fellowship, a PEN/Faulkner Award for Fiction, an American Book Award for *Philadelphia Fire*, and a PEN/Malamud Award for Excellence in the Short Story.

Philadelphia Fire, Wideman's eighth novel, is a complex work that operates along several historical planes, but its inspiration comes from the tragic bombing of the MOVE group headquarters on 6221 Osage Avenue in the Cobbs Creek area of West Philadelphia on May 13, 1985. The action, ordered by Mayor W. Wilson Goode, killed eleven people, and the resulting fire devastated a once-stable Black neighborhood. The novel is "written in three interconnected sections—sometimes an essay, sometimes in African-American idiom, sometimes in parables reminiscent of folktale or mythology."[1] The novel has several narrative threads, including one that is partly autobiographical, relating Wideman's recollections upon first hearing about the bombing while lying in bed with his wife, Judith. One strand of the novel involves the search for a child who was rumored to have survived the fire. For more on the bombing, see the poem "elegy (for MOVE and Philadelphia)" by Sonia Sanchez, included here.

⁓

FROM PART TWO

On May 13, 1985, in West Philadelphia, after bullets, water cannon and high explosives had failed to dislodge the occupants of 6221 Osage Avenue, a bomb was dropped from a state police helicopter and exploded atop the besieged row house. In the ensuing fire fifty-three houses were destroyed, 262 people left homeless. The occupants of the row house on Osage were said to be members of an organization called MOVE. Eleven of them, six adults and five children, were killed in the assault that commenced when they refused to obey a police order to leave their home. A grand jury subsequently determined that no criminal charges should be brought against the public officials who planned and perpetrated the assault.

Pretend for a moment that none of this happened. Pretend that it never happened before nor will again. Pretend we can imagine events into existence or out of existence. Pretend we have the power to live our lives as we choose. Imagine our fictions imagining us.

***

A Monday night in bed. Push-button scanning of all available channels, flipping, clicking, twenty-nine cable options and none satisfactory so you choose them all and choose none, cut and paste images, you are the director, driver, pilot, boss hoss, captain, the switch is in your hand. Or rather you grip the remote-control gadget with a desperate love-hate possessiveness that melds it to your palm. Your toy. Your game. Part of the fun of the game is the woman beside me who claims she doesn't enjoy clicking around the channels, who's screaming even as she silently indulges my flashes forward and flashes backward and fast shuffles and digital displays popping and muting, exploring every function the gun in my hand allows. She screams without uttering a sound: Don't touch that dial. And in a way I don't. We're in bed. The Sony's ten feet away. I can round first base and scoot into second and slide through a cloud of dust into third without getting my uniform dirty. A city burns on the screen. Any large city. Anywhere in America. CNN Cable News Network. Row houses in flames. Rooflines silhouetted against a dark sky. Something's burning. We watch. Wonder whose turn it is now. Whole city blocks engulfed. It must be happening in another country. A war. A bombing raid. We're watching a Third World shantytown where there's no water, no machines to extinguish a fire. Flames, true to metaphor, do leap and lick. The sky retreats, jerks away like a hand from a hot stove. We are curious. We are impatient for the voice-over to tell us what to think. Where? When? Why? What? We'd be on the edge of our seats if we were on seats and not lounging in our waterbed in Laramie at 9:05 PM with nothing better to do than play this spin-the-bottle sweepstakes of the dial. But here it was, a jackpot consuming all our attention. Philadelphia.

Philadelphia.

West Philly. Osage Avenue

Shit. We used to live in West Philly. On Osage Avenue. Osage can you see by the night's early firelight. Our old row house somewhere in there, down in the darkness of the silhouette's belly. Long camera shots preferred, sustained. Aerial views, probably from a copter. Perhaps the blaze is too hot to approach any other way.

Details are skimpy. Or we've missed them this time round. They'll return because news is cycled and recycled endlessly on this network. What we don't know always carries the potential to harm us, and we know just enough to believe that, so we stay tuned for further developments. Now, we bring you a word from our sponsor. But such courteous, ponderous, time-consuming transitions are a thing of the past. Cut. Cut to whatever, wherever with electronic speed. Warp drive. Chiquita and her banana shoved in your face faster than you can rub the smoke from your eyes. What'd he say? The announcer. Sixty-second and Osage? Powelton Village?[2] That's not Powelton. Too far west for Powelton, isn't it? But the conversation has switched to a woman pulling the oars of a rowing machine. Where's she going? What's she wearing? A miracle fabric or did somebody paint the bitch, brush a shiny second skin over her big boobs and tight butt mashed down into a funny valentine on the bicycle seat of the rowing machine? Do you receive one like her with each purchase? There's the price, sixty twice, then the number you must call to order right away.

Somebody's talking who doesn't know Philly.

Pneumatic woman's gone faster than I could punch her away with my magic twanger. A set of bamboo pots and pans, watertight, indestructible and a wok thrown in free if you call now. Which is May 13, 1985, the day after Mother's Day. I remember that. Remember it as well as I recall the lump of remote-control device in my sweaty palm.

We're both riveted. The channel riveted. We are all set in stone. Judy stops telling me. Don't touch that dial. She's having it her way this once without a fuss or fight. We both wonder what the fuck's going on. Why is Philadelphia burning? How do I know what she's thinking? Why do I assume I do? Her left breast, the one closest to me, or closer, since it's one of a pair, slouches brown nubbed and complacent, doing its own thing. If I touched it or bit it, would I learn what it was thinking? Sexy, I think it's sexy now, paying no afternoon to itself. Leaving me to make something of it. Whatever. Wherever. Many colors. Many ages coded in this plump breast that is part of this woman, part of a scene which included the image of a city where we once lived, burning, somewhere, for some reason. Burning in other bedrooms. In other cities, international coverage. I heard later from a friend who said he saw it same moment, same day in Japan. Instantaneous satellite spy-in-the-sky transmission everywhere. So much happening at once. Impossible to keep up. Even if you spin the dial till the colors run together and the tigers melt chasing each other's tails. But Sambo's[3] always caught in the middle of the ring. Puzzled. Appalled by the unforeseen consequences of his good intentions.

In the stillness of our bedroom her breast registers as deep silence. She sighs, extension of the breast, the breast under which she hides in a cage of ribs her heart. One of my ribs, so they say. Never thought to ask which one. To claim it. Many colors. Years coded. Flashing across the screen of this dark room. Forward and backyard. On my desk a snapshot of her at fourteen, sweater girl. Pointy, warrior bra that pulls her tits high on her chest. Saluting what? Patient for decades, waiting to relax into this natural, perfect, nubby pout. Flesh after all. Sighs when unbound. Rib bones delicate as rib bones when I trace them with my fingertip and she is fragile as the straw where you might stash eggs for safekeeping and why not think of her chest as a nest, her breasts pouched there for whatever subtle reasons. She is a tree full of nests. Nests of spun light. Nimbus. Swirls of light in branches if you are melancholy and can't sleep and walk Philly streets at night, look up and you'll see what I mean, you'll see wreaths of light, halos in bare branches above the streetlamps. Painterly swirls symmetrically gathering light, spinning it, casting it. Her dark hair used to be long enough to cover her breasts. Now it only reaches the first swell where the flesh softens and understands exactly what it's supposed to do next. Furrows below her shoulders, bones joined at her throat. I pull her silver-threaded hair forward so it drapes the first soft swelling. I run my finger up and down, up and down, curling the ends, learning the texture of fleece, the insistence of flesh beginning to pile up and form a breast. She was younger once and so was I and our whole history's contained in glances. In leftovers and new puzzling mounds and creases that we can't work into other stories. Once upon a time. This time, this age when we huddle under the covers and imitate ourselves as children playing in other rooms, other cities. All over again. Safe the way our children once were safe. Leftovers and remnants and day-old goods tasting stolen and better than ever some nights. Other nights the edginess, the anger, the sense of loss, the fear, so I flip-flop, ply the channels like a ghost, waiting for something to watch.

That's how I learned about the Philadelphia fire.

NOTES

1. Bray, "Whole City Seen the Flames."
2. Powelton Village is a historic district in the University City area in West Philadelphia.
3. "Sambo" is an offensive term once used to describe a Black person. It is especially known through the children's book *The Story of Little Black Sambo*, written by Scottish author Helen Bannerman in 1899.

BIBLIOGRAPHY

Bray, Rosemary L. "The Whole City Seen the Flames." *New York Times*, September 30, 1990.

Carden, Mary Paniccia. "'If the City Is a Man': Founders and Fathers, Cities and Sons in John Edgar Wideman's 'Philadelphia Fire.'" *Contemporary Literature* 44, no. 3 (Autumn 2003): 472–500.

Dubey, Madhu. "Literature and Urban Crisis: John Edgar Wideman's *Philadelphia Fire*." *African American Review* 32, no. 4 (Winter 1998): 579–95.

Eschborn, Ulrich. "'To Democratize the Elements of the Historical Record': An Interview with John Edgar Wideman About History in His Work." *Callaloo* 33, no. 4 (Fall 2010): 982–98.

Hogue, W. Lawrence. "Radical Democracy, African American (Male) Subjectivity, and John Edgar Wideman's *Philadelphia Fire*." *MELUS* 33, no. 3 (Fall 2008): 45–69.

Maney, J. Bret. "Philadelphia Fire." *Encyclopedia of Greater Philadelphia*. https://philadelphiaencyclopedia.org/essays/philadelphia-fire/.

Otter, Samuel. *Philadelphia Stories: America's Literature of Race and Freedom*. Oxford: Oxford University Press, 2010.

Richard, Jean-Pierre. "Philadelphia Fire, or the Shape of a City." *Callaloo* 22, no. 3 (Summer 1999): 603–13.

Elaine Brown, from *A Taste of Power: A Black Woman's Story* (1992)

Elaine Brown was born in North Philadelphia in 1943. She is a writer, musician, activist, and former Black Panther Party chairperson. Brown grew up in poverty but because of her grades was able to attend the prestigious Philadelphia High School for Girls. She attended Temple University for one semester before moving to California, where she joined the Black Panther Party in 1968 and in 1974 was appointed its leader by Huey Newton after he fled to Cuba to escape murder charges. Brown left the party in 1978 and made a brief run for the Green Party nomination for president in 2008. She currently lives in Oakland, California. In addition to *A Taste of Power*, Brown has also authored *The Condemnation of Little B: New Age Racism in America* (2002).

The section from *A Taste for Power* included here details Brown's growing-up years doing many "White" activities, such as studying ballet, theater, and classical music; however, she felt more at home hanging with her friends on York Street. The family later moved to the low-rent James Weldon Johnson Housing Project, in North Philly, first opened to tenants in 1940. This move, according to Brown's mother, allowed the family to be safe from "rats, roaches, and 'niggers.'" In her teen years, when Brown was attending the Philadelphia High School for Girls, she met her father, a wealthy doctor turned politician, who lived in the expensive Wissahickon Creek section of Northwest Philly. Despite the lure of a better life, the independent young Elaine remained true to her roots as "a North Philly girl."

FROM CHAPTER 3, "WE ARE THE GIRLS WHO DON'T TAKE NO STUFF"
At first it seemed a small miracle had occurred when my mother decided to move from York Street, out of the house that was my grandmother's, where we had lived for as long as I could remember.

We were moving into a place of our own, a lone-bedroom apartment in the James Weldon Johnson Housing Project, a barrackslike public-housing complex in another part of North Philadelphia, at 25th and Norris streets. It was close enough for me to remain tied to Barbara and Nita but not far enough from York Street.

To my mother, the important thing about our apartment in the Projects was that it had concrete floors and metal doors. They would restrain the entry of rats, roaches, and "niggers," she told me.

Harm was locked out as we were locked inside, alone, together. We seemed also to be locked in even poorer days than on York Street. We often ate hoe cakes[1] or cereal for dinner, except on my mother's paydays, when we would eat out, mostly at the Horn & Hardart Automat. In between paydays, we were often hungry behind our steel doors and concrete walls.

The government's "relief" program for the poor was beneath my mother's dignity. She did not believe in asking anybody for anything, telling me it was better to steal or starve than beg. We did not need anyone at all, including our "newsy" new neighbors, she said, confirming us as one against the world.

On my thirteenth birthday, however, my mother opened the doors to our Projects haven so that I could have a party. All my friends from York Street were invited. My mother brought me the outfit I demanded: a charcoal-gray felt skirt with a pink poodle embroidered on it, a pink blouse, a gray cinch belt, gray suede bucks, and pink knee socks.

Barbara and I went down onto Susquehanna Avenue to buy records for the party with the ten dollars my mother had given me. We bought "Sister Sookie Done Gone"[2] and some "sides" by Hank Ballard[3] and LaVerne Baker.[4] I ended up with a total of ten new records, "78's" and the new, plastic "45's," records of songs made popular on the radio of Georgie Woods,[5] "the man with the goods, coming to you from Phila-ma-del-phi-yea-aah!"

Despite the fact that my cinch belt curled at my now-chubby waist, or that I still wore an undershirt and not a brassiere, or that I did not have my period, I was elated by the prospect of becoming a teenager. I was not only going to be a real teenager, I was going to have a party, and a whole lot of boys were going to be there.

Once a few of my girl friends started arriving, my mother went out. She did it because she trusted me, she said. Most parents would have stayed at home under the circumstances, she reminded me, and plopped themselves in the middle of their kids' parties. After my mother left, Barbara and I substituted the regular light bulbs with the colored ones my mother had bought for the occasion, and put out the hot dogs and potato salad my mother had prepared.

All the "youngbloods" from the "Avenue" arrived in a pack. The Avenue was the street gang that controlled the territory that included 21st and York Streets. They had named the gang after Susquehanna Avenue, the main street running through the territory. Even though I now lived in Norris Street gang territory, I was, in spirit, part of life on York Street, part of the Avenue.

Having survived the dangerous trek into Norris Street territory, the members of the Avenue sauntered into my place wearing their "do-rags," scarves wrapped about their heads to hold their processed hairdos in place. They concealed half-drunk bottles of white port wine and lemon juice concoctions under their coats. Each fellow carried himself with one hand stuffed into his pant pocket, pulling his sharply pressed khaki pants above his ankles, his other hand remaining free to swing back and forth as he walked, leaning to one side. They all wore black nylon "pimp" socks, and black leather, ankle-high shoes called "old men's comforts." To me the fellows were, in a word, "cool."

My other girl friends came in small groups, each one making an entrance. Every girl's hair was freshly "pressed," and most of them had on tight skirts and cinch belts, with bobby socks and loafers, or else bucks and large hoop earrings implanted in their pierced ears. It was going to be the "toughest" party ever, I thought as everyone arrived—not ruined like Barbara's had been months before.

We had been in her whitewashed basement, at 2057 West York Street, on New Year's Eve. Everyone was anticipating "French-kissing" at midnight. When the midnight countdown rolled around, Barbara's father—one of the few in the neighborhood—clicked on the turned-out lights from the top of the cellar stairs. Mr. Moses Benjamin Taylor III was a member of the NAACP and a very religious man who everyone knew did not suffer too much foolishness.

Boys quickly tried to hide wine bottles, and girls started straightening their rumpled blouses, somewhat thankful for their reprieve to adjust the tissue stuffed against little breasts.

"All right, boys and girls," Mr. Taylor announced with church propriety as he began walking down the basement stairs, Bible in hand. "Close your eyes and say with me, please: 'Our Father which art in heaven . . .'"

Barbara cried for three solid days after that, for which her mother, Mattie, whipped her good with the cord of an iron. Barbara was inconsolable, however. She vowed to never, ever speak to her father again.

My party would, of course, be different: better. My mother had gone out for the evening, so we could carry on as we wanted. We could smoke our Chesterfields and Camels out in the open, and even sip from the boys' wine bottles. Everybody could "grind" tight, up against the wall, boys' stiff penises pressing against girls' thighs. Boys could even feel girls up and down.

I was a good hostess. After I served the food, I played disc jockey, and even did "the slop"[6] to get everybody started. Then I waited, slow-dance record after slow-dance record. I waited through the Spaniels' "Peace of Mind,"[7] through "Cherry Pie,"[8] through "Nightowl."[9] I waited for some "do-ragged" boy to tag my hand to dance slow, to grind. It never happened. I was not once asked to slow-dance.

I retired in tears to a concrete corner. From there, I watched Barbara slow-dancing and Nita slow-dancing and everybody else slow-dancing through a haze. In the blur of things, I certainly had no ability to realize that my mother had returned, everybody but me swooning to the Five Satins crooning "In the Still of the Night."[10] I certainly did not hear what she was saying to me when she called out in horror upon entering our bedroom: "Elaine! I said get in here! Somebody's had sexual intercourse in this bed!"

I walked heavily into the room to listen emotionlessly to whatever diatribe she was about to issue forth. I had had enough for one evening.

"I'm not going to have it," she shouted at me, standing in the doorway. "Who did this?!" she demanded, as I tried to figure out how she could have known such a thing.

"Look at this stain," she continued, pointing to the center of the disheveled bed. "It's semen! How could you let this happen? I gave you a party. I bought the food *and* cooked it. And I *trusted* you! I work like a dog every day to try to give you things and you let this happen. Look! There's even a pubic hair right here! Look at it!"

As she spoke, I contemplated what semen might look like, and tried to imagine somebody really doing "it." I wondered who had done it when I had not even had one slow-dance.

"I do not appreciate this shit. Not one bit," she went on. "I want everybody out of this house right now!"

"That sure is cold," I heard some of the boys mumble in the living room as everyone began easing out the door. I did not care about any of it, or certainly any of them. I had only one concern: that I had not once been asked to slow-dance.

Barbara and her cousin Kathy, who lived on 18th Street, and our other close friend, Carol Hollins, from 20th Street, stayed behind to help me clean up the mess, to wash the "process" grease stains off the walls and sweep the concrete floors. They also tried to help me figure out who had "fucked" in my mother's bed, which was also mine.

A few months later, I thought it might have been Nita who had done "it" in our bed. She casually announced to Barbara and me one day that she was pregnant. I felt betrayed. It was not because she was pregnant or that she had actually "gone all the way" and had not told any of us about it.

I wanted to know what it was like: where did the "dick" actually go. She never got around to filling us in, because she was busy making wedding plans.

Nita's mother had recently been born again as a Jehovah's Witness and had ordained, therefore, that no child of hers would have any babies out of wedlock. Within a month or so after Nita's announcement to us, she got married, in what reminded me of a Tom Thumb wedding ceremony, where children play grownups. Nita's pregnancy and forced marriage forced her out of her house, out of junior high, out of York Street, and out of our lives forever at the age of thirteen, gone to dwell in the house of her teenage husband, a member of the Avenue.

With Nita's pronouncement, the first loss of virginity I knew of, the big question of "doing it" began to permeate our daily lives. Then, in midsummer, Carol Hollins forged the next step in our trail.

"Girl, that shit hurt. I bled like a dog," Carol told Barbara and me one summer afternoon when we were sitting around her house.

"But how did you do it? Who with?" Barbara asked boldly.

"You ever hear of 'Snake' from the Valley?" Carol said.

"No, you didn't fuck somebody from the *Valley*, Carol!" I screamed.

It was a violation of gang territorial laws to have any dealings whatsoever with gang members from other territories. After all, despite my own move into Norris Street, we were all Avenue girls. It was important to understand the nuances of North Philly gang life. It was critical to one's survival—a concept that was my standing priority. First of all, gang members were boys. Although there were a few rough groups of girls who might claim to be a gang, girls were, at best, support groups for boys' gangs or, at least, girl friends of gang members.

I had actually heard of only one girls' gang in North Philly. The terrible Toasties were teenage girls who ran around assaulting other girls who had light skin, long hair, or "good" hair, or who wore "six-button bennies," double-breasted coats. Their practice was to surround a girl with long hair and cut it off; or walk past a victim and, with razor blades secreted between their fingers, slap a girl across the face, leaving a bloody opening a lifetime would never close.

The Toasties were extinct as far as we knew by the time we became teenagers. Anyway, none of us—not Barbara, or Nita, or Kathy, or Carol, or I—none of us was or ever had been intimidated by girls on the streets of North Philly. *We are rough! We are tough! We are the girls who don't take no stuff!* Instead, no matter how white I was at school, I was still of the stuff of York Street and I could deal with any girl on the streets of North Philly. If

some tough bitch even looked in my direction with a confrontational attitude, I put on my ugliest ghetto attitude and became the aggressor. I would
get directly into her face, ask the bitch who the fuck she was looking at, and
drop my fist to my side. No, none of us was afraid of any girl on the streets of
North Philly. The boys were another matter.

Boys' gangs literally controlled life in our various North Philly neighborhoods, and most boys claimed gang membership. They walked in packs and
generally terrified everybody with their very presence. They boastfully paraded
clothing or insignia or tattoos or other symbols of their gang membership.
They had to "stand" for their gang at all times, alone or not, inside or outside
their territory, the latter being a very dangerous proposition.

A "blood" caught outside his territory was subject to getting shot or
stabbed just for being there. Moreover, territory was complicated to compre-
hend. Since what territory a gang controlled depended on how hard a gang
fought to maintain or expand it, its boundaries could shift at any given
moment. Some gangs' territories stretched as much as eight square blocks;
some, like that of the Avenue, were contained within four square blocks;
others, like Carmac and Diamond, incorporated only a single street corner.
Given the high density of people in our neighborhoods, however, significant
numbers of people were affected by gang activity. The gangs stole from people,
robbed houses, took over house parties, punished enemies, and, worse,
warred. If a gang war was "called" by a "war council," hundreds of gang members from the two opposing gangs would gather in a vacant lot or open area
in some designated territory to battle it out with designated weapons until
death or the police ended the battle.

There were many rules for girls about how to relate to a gang and its
members. One of the most abiding was that girls living in one gang territory did not so much as hold a conversation with a member of another
gang. When Carol told us who "broke her cherry," we knew she was flirt-
ing with death.

"No, you didn't fuck somebody from the Valley!" Barbara echoed.

"Not only is he in the Valley," Carol continued dramatically, "he's the
leader of the Valley!"

Carol was the bravest girl we knew. We waited with open mouths for her
to bestow the next morsel on us.

"Yeah, child," she went on, "we 'macked'[11] for a long time."

"Where were you?"

"Right here, in my house," she said, laughing off the riskiness of the whole affair.

We shrieked with responsive laughter and passed around a Chesterfield cigarette, held by a bobby pin.

"He took off my skirt and then he took off his pants."

We were breathless.

"Then he got on top of me and pushed it in. Girl, I cried. I screamed my head off. then all this blood came out of me."

"Oooh!" we moaned, turning our heads away from Carol in disgust. Barbara and I vowed to *never*, ever do it.

***

I was finally on my mother's side. She was right. We were nothing! I had no business worrying about my color. It was nothing compared to being nothing at all. I had to work, to fight, to become something other than nothing. I had finally learned that, firsthand.

It was with this awareness that I entered the ninth grade at the Philadelphia High School for Girls. I was not the bastard reject of my father, neither black nor white, a faceless, disembodied misfit who had no place of her own. I was my mother's well-rounded, beautiful, perfect daughter, who was outside and above everybody else on the entire, uncaring planet.

The Philadelphia High School for Girls, or Girls High, was the perfect haven for a perfect girl. To attend, one either had to have a high I.Q. or pass an entrance test. I was not required to take the entrance examination. Girls High was located at 17th and Spring Garden streets, just four blocks from the special school I had attended only two years before.

A replicated statue of the *Winged Victory*, or Nike, the Greek goddess of victory, overwhelmed the hallowed entrance hall of Girls High. We entering girls were taught to silently salute her every day, even though her symbolism may have been lost on most freshman psyches. All freshmen were sure of only one thing, that we were the *crème de la crème*, the smartest girls in Philadelphia and among the smartest in the country.

Girls High was, we learned from day one, the first school of higher learning for women in the United States. It was one hundred years old when I entered in 1957, and steeped in a thousand traditions; and I was part of its two hundredth class. It was an elitist center, the purpose of which was to hone its daughters into the world's movers and shakers.

The Gothic structure of Girls High encased marble floors and marble walls. The old marble seemed to echo the footsteps and arcane academic chatter of girls past, joined by our own as we went to and from classes. I was enrolled in Latin, as were many in my class who thought Spanish or French beneath them. We wore understated Ivy League garb, spoke in tight-lipped, nasal "Eastern" tones, and looked down our noses at anybody who was not a student at Girls High, with the exception of the boys at our brother school, Central High. We conjugated verbs and declined nouns in Latin and in English, and gracefully dressed ourselves in prudery and pretension.

I became a solid-A student in Latin and English, maintained a high grade in history and decent grades in math and science. I rarely, if ever, went to gym class, considering it, like typing—which I refused to take—too plebeian. Since Girls High operated on an honor system, it was presumed by my word that I was present in all classes, which satisfied that minor requirement. In any event, by the end of the ninth grade, I had developed such a reputation I would never have been challenged.

I was considered rather arrogant by my peers and somewhat rebellious and argumentative by my teachers. My English teacher went so far as to give me a final grade of B, because she said I did not behave like an A student. Over the year, she argued when I assailed her over the grade, I had called out to speak rather than raising my hand, deferred doing most daily homework in reliance on my final test grade, and questioned nearly every statement she had made. I accepted her argument in the end because her grade did not matter to me. I was moving on course, becoming better than white, soaring above everybody, a superior, singular, independent, unattached being who needed no one, including a father.

I had, however, taken note of his political posters plastered all over Philadelphia during that time. He was running for Congress on the Republican ticket. Waiting for my bus to go to school, I had caught glimpses of his enlarged poster face, distorted by North Philly dirt and graffiti, and by PUSSY and FUCK YOU scrawled across his nose and chin. He was handsome, I saw, without giving thought to him at all. I was passingly sorry when he lost the election, though it, and surely he, meant nothing to me at all, I maintained.

His face in person, on the other hand, was different. It was my face, my eyes, my lips, my nose, the face of my father. I did not know what to call him when he touched me from arm's length for the first time I knew about. He and my mother had arranged it. It was in the beginning of my tenth-grade year at Girl's High. He was proud of me, proud of my grades, proud of everything I had become, my mother told me. He wanted to develop a relationship with me, she said.

I had to meet him at his office, a neat, brownstone, two-story structure in a clean pocket of North Philadelphia. No patients were there when I opened the double door, the top half of which was made of stained glass. He opened the door of his inner office as I was about to sit down in the outer one. He was not much taller than I. His brown skin and mine matched. He had some freckles and wavy hair. He was indeed very handsome, I felt, as he finally embraced me.

"Your mother has been telling me everything about you over the years, you know," he said, studying me.

I was speechless, trying to figure out whether I looked like the most beautiful girl in the world to him. Was my tailored clothing proper? I wondered. Could he see that I really did look like him?

"You've grown into quite a young lady," he continued in a rather formal way, showing me to an office chair across from his desk, on which he sat. His suit was brown, accented by his highly polished, expensive-looking brown shoes and stark-white shirt, the cuffs of which bore his initials.

He told me about "our" family, most of which my mother had, of course, already told me. He emphasized how special our bloodline was, pointing out specifically that I was the image of his sister Clarissa, who had been perhaps the very first colored woman to graduate from Wellesley College. I decided that was where I would go to college; it was, after all, among the preferred colleges for Girls High girls. He asked me about my grades, my life in school, my friends. He said other things to which I paid little attention, I was so dazzled by his handsome face and beautiful eyes and smart appearance. Before I left, after about an hour, I let him know that I accepted the secrecy of our meeting, and he let me know we could continue to see each other in this way.

I did not want to return to my mother. I did not want to return to our latest apartment in another part of Tioga,[12] or to our room. I wanted to start over, to start life over with that fine, refined colored man who was my real and only father, who wanted me in his life. I was noncommunicative with my mother that afternoon. I told her nothing about it, not even my impressions.

She was incapable of understanding, I felt. She did not really know him, or me. We, my father and I, were alike, I concluded that day. We were one—not my mother and I—but *he* and I.

As I walked from the bus stop to his office for my next visit, about a week later, I determined to convince him to take me into his life on a full-time basis. The details were unclear to me. I imagined we could stay together in a small apartment, probably in Germantown, where I could take care of myself, or something, while he maintained his other life with his wife and adopted daughter on Lincoln Drive.[13] I did not think of my mother at all.

"How does your mother really feel about your seeing me?" he asked early on.

"It doesn't matter, does it?" I responded conspiratorially.

He smiled. I knew he could understand that I would leave her and her lower-class ways and her North Philly attitudes and her numbers and her poverty if he would just say the word. I would leave her for him, forever.

"It has, you know."

I looked bewildered.

"I see she hasn't told you. Of course not. You see, we've always wanted you in our family, but she wouldn't have it."

I remained blank, not comprehending.

"I mean," he continued, "you are, after all, the only child any of us, my brother and sisters, has ever had; and we wanted you to live with your aunt in Chicago, a fine woman, whose husband is a prominent attorney there . . ."

"As my mother and father?"

"Well, yes. But your mother has always stood in the way," he said with little-subdued acrimony. "Now, of course, I'm not sure what we can do. So I just want to see you whenever possible."

"I guess I'd like that, too," I said rather idiotically, wrestling with the shock of everything he had just calmly told me, at once ashamed of my designs to leave my mother and angry with my mother for concealing so much from me.

As he continued speaking, mostly about how much like his family I was. I began to wonder why he had waited so long to see me, to tell me. Then I wondered what he wanted me to do. Then I tried to imagine life with *his* family. Then I wondered what he thought my mother should have done, or been, to me. Then I remembered what my mother had asked me to do.

We had no food and no money, because my mother's payday was on Monday and it was the weekend. She had instructed me, more times than I had listened, to try to get $10 from him.

Nearly an hour had passed. It seemed time to leave.

"By the way," I asked him casually, and somewhat embarrassed, "could you let me have ten dollars for some school books." My mother had told me to make it seem as if the request was for me personally. I smiled at him flirtatiously.

"Is that what your mother told you to ask me?" he said, suddenly very cold.

"Uh n-no," I stuttered.

"You tell your mother if she wants money from me to take me to court like she does every month. Has the gall to try to get a bench warrant for my arrest. Every damn month! Tell her don't *ever* again send you to get money out of me!"

Tears filled my eyes as they widened with shock and shame.

"But it's only ten dollars, and we need the money for food!" I cried out, surprising myself.

"That's what *she* says," he responded passionlessly. "She's got a job. She can handle everything. You just tell her what I said. And tell her not to try to play games with me anymore!"

I checked my tears and transformed myself. I became a Girls High girl, or maybe a North Philly girl. "As far as I'm concerned, *you* are the one playing games," I stated firmly, looking directly into his dark brown eyes. "But don't worry about me asking you for a cent again," I said in my most arrogant tone. "You don't have to worry about me again!"

I was holding the outer office door open, and he was looking at me in disbelief.

"As a matter of fact, I don't want to see you again!" I screamed. "I'd rather see you dead. And when you die, I'll spit on your grave!" I bellowed, borrowing language from some old movie, it seemed. I slammed the Dutch door, cracking the stained-glass mosaic.

It was the last door I would have to close, I thought, as I walked back to the bus stop, less damaged than determined. My mother and I, alone, would survive in his world, in "their" world, whoever they were, and without their help. That weekend, we ate eggs and hoe cakes with dry eyes and knowing expressions that we needed no one at all anymore.

NOTES

1. Hoe cakes: small pancakes made from cornmeal and popular in the South. Also called Johnny Cakes.

2. Sister Sookie Done Gone: "Sister Sookey" was a song performed by the Philly doo-wop group the Turbans in 1955.

3. Hank Ballard (born John Henry Kendricks, 1927–2003) was a songwriter and a rhythm-and-blues singer for the Midnighters. He wrote Chubby Checker's 1960 hit song, "The Twist."

4. LaVerne Baker (1929–1997) was a rhythm-and-blues singer with hits such as "Tweedle Dee" (1955).

5. Georgie Woods: a civil rights activist and a popular radio broadcaster beginning in Philadelphia in 1953 until 1994 for stations WHAT and WDAS. Known as "the guy with the goods," Woods coined the term "blue-eyed soul" describing white performers who sang in a soul style.

6. "The slop" is a couples' dance that involved no touching that was popular in the 1950s. It was introduced on the *Bandstand* TV show, aired out of Philadelphia starting in 1952. The show was later renamed *American Bandstand* when Dick Clark began hosting it in 1956.

7. Peace of Mind: "(You Gave Me) Peace of Mind," a 1956 song performed by the Spaniels.

8. Cherry Pie: a doo-wop song recorded by Marvin & Johnny in 1954.

9. Nightowl: "Nite Owl" was performed by Tony Allen and the Champs in 1955.

10. "In the Still of the Night": hit song by the Five Satins from 1956.

11. Macked: to sexually proposition.

12. Tioga is an area in North Philadelphia, sometimes called Nicetown-Tioga. It now is more than 85 percent African American.

13. Lincoln Drive links Northwest Philly to Center City.

BIBLIOGRAPHY

Elaine Brown (website). https://www.elaine brown.org.

See, Carolyn. "Book Review: An Insider's Look at the Black Panther Party; *A Taste of Power: A Black Woman's Story.*" *Los Angeles Times*, January 4, 1993.

Spencer, Robyn C. "Engendering the Black Freedom Struggle: Revolutionary Black Womanhood and the Black Panther Party in the Bay Area, California." *Journal of Women's History* 20, no. 1 (2008): 90–113.

Wallace, Michele. "*A Taste of Power: A Black Woman's Story.*" *New York Times*, January 31, 1993, BR, 7.

Alexs D. Pate, from *Losing Absalom* (1994)

Alexs Pate was born in Philadelphia in 1950. He has taught at the University of Minnesota and is now president and CEO of Innocent Classroom, which strives to eliminate racial stereotypes through teaching. He has published five novels, including *Amistad* (1997), based on the screenplay written by David Franzoni for the Steven Spielberg film. Most recently, he has published the nonfiction book *The Innocent Classroom: Dismantling Racial Bias to Support Students of Color* (2020).

Losing Absalom, Pate's first novel, is set in a crime-ridden section of North Philadelphia (Whither Street is a made-up location) and reflects the drug epidemic plaguing many urban neighborhoods in the late 1980s and into the '90s. Absalom Goodman has struggled hard and is reflecting on his life as he lies in a hospital bed while suffering from brain cancer. He questions whether his efforts to improve the lives of his family have failed. His son has moved away from the community and now works in White corporate America. His daughter, Rainy, is involved with Dancer, a local drug dealer. The excerpt included here focuses on Dancer and his interactions with the neighborhood youths. Pate's skill in the novel is demonstrated through the humanizing of his characters, no matter how questionable some of their actions are. Though the message in the novel is often bleak, it still resounds with a hope that it is possible to make some sense out of the tragedy in the characters' world. The book received the Minnesota Book Award and was named Best First Novel by the Black Caucus of the American Library Association.

⁓

FROM CHAPTER 5

Whither Street, which ran east to west, was a poseur, always in masquerade. It changed like the Nile from one end to the other. You could find Whither Street in white middle-class Wynnfield in West Philly and you could find Whither Street in the spare meanness of white working-class Fishtown. In between was the dense blackness of North Philadelphia that Dancer knew so well.

In the 2500 block of West Whither Street, as in most of North Philadelphia, the surface of the summer sunlight that reflected hope was deceiving. The internal hemorrhage of unemployment, the open flow of drugs, and governmental indifference all added to the gradual deterioration that was affecting the neighborhood.

As Dancer looked over Spider's shoulder he could see people going into Benson's store down at the corner. The neighborhood still had a corner store. But Benson, like other merchants, had to try everything, iron bars, bullet-proof glass, chicken wire—in an attempt to make his establishment safe from misguided, wounded, hopeless rage. The middle-class fire that sustained Absalom and Green and their neighbors had given birth to melancholy. It joined the gush of sad life that lived in North Philly, adding enough apathy to make it dangerous. To the eye, Whither Street offered an alternative to abject crime and poverty. In reality, Whither Street had succumbed to it.

Dancer kept Spider standing on the stoop—none of his boys ever actually crossed the threshold. That was Rainy's rule and it was fine with him. He didn't trust most of the guys he knew in this tight, compressed North Philadelphia community. In the business of their lives, the code demanded distance, strength, and swift action. If someone was doing you wrong—messing with your lover or cheating you out of money—the response was generally quick and extreme. What used to be settled with fists could now quickly result in death.

Behind Spider, in the midday sunlight, Whither Street was now alive. A block of Spike Lee colors and people. Children played in the middle of the block, while a group of men gathered in front of a green 1980 Nova, gesturing, their heads buried under the hood. Down the block near Twenty-fifth Street, the paper man stopped his car in front of Doc's house to collect. Newspaper delivery was no longer safe for children, but too lucrative to go to older teenagers, so the paper was now delivered by an adult. On Friday nights and Saturday afternoons, with his private driver (and bodyguard), he slowly rolled down the street in a 1979 red Buick, stopping to collect at every house that took the daily paper.

Dancer saw a group of teenagers standing on the corner directly across the street from him. They were listening to rap music on a large portable tape player. It was a sleek black box, the size of a saxophone case, with a sound that was as powerful as his own expensive stereo system. But this morning they were subdued, the volume hung low. Dancer could still feel the bass line rippling across the street; it tunneled under the drooping asphalt and resurfaced under his nose. It circled his head and forced it to bob. He shook it off. It was too early to be acting like that. Still he couldn't completely ignore the call. The bass was a deadly killer wave of funk, seeking a victim.

***

The young men nodded and grunted to Dancer, who waved back, joking, "Yo homes, why don't y'all kill *that* noise, it's too early for that kind of mess." Dancer smiled a big smile as he screamed across the street. They knew that he wasn't completely joking.

One of them yelled back, "It's never too early, homeboy."

"So, what's up?" Dancer turned his attention to Spider, who had been standing there the entire time. Dancer opened the screen, took a step outside, and tried to focus on Spider. He liked the boy. Spider was one of the few who could actually hold a reasonable conversation when he wanted to.

Even Dancer was dismayed at the plight of the younger generation. Although he exploited them, they made him sad. He couldn't understand what they were going to do with their lives. They were like a lost tribe, wandering in circles, hoping that when they got where they were going, they would know it. It angered Dancer that none of these kids ever talked about *becoming* anything. Nobody ever talked about dreams. Their lives were spent mostly with their heads down, rocked out, or jamming to the bumping rhymes of the pervasive hip hop air.

Two weeks before, Dancer had talked with a group of nine- and ten-year old boys in front of Benson's store, at the corner. The main theme of the conversation was how they didn't think Martin Luther King was so important. One kid had turned to Dancer and in a true homeboy stance—hands in his blue sweatshirt pockets, hood up and shadowing his face—said, "Shit, man, tell me one motherfuckin' thing King did. That's old-time bullshit. You old folks believe the hype, but I ain't down for that shit."

Dancer was stunned. Okay, so it was a rocked-out world and education was a joke. But you still had to know *something.* "Why don't you pick up a book? That's what you need to do before you come out here talking about Martin Luther King," he told them.

Dancer didn't have any children and what he was seeing didn't make him want any. No one seemed to be going anywhere. Some folks talked about Jesse Jackson and the Black Muslim leader, Louis Farrakhan, but there was no one representative that everyone believed in. They breathed apathy like air.

Even though he lived among them and did business with them, Dancer tried to distinguish himself. He placed himself among the teachers, artists, entertainers, and the steady professionals who kept the race moving forward—he just went at it differently. He could not see working nine to five every day for twenty thousand dollars a year for the rest of his life. He needed time to think and time to have fun. Selling drugs had come to him as an answer, and it had proven very lucrative.

The only problem was the people he came in contact with. At one end of the drug business, there were lots of young people who had nothing going for themselves except a tour on the rock pile. And at the other end were a small group of ruthless, greedy bankers, Italians or Panamanians, or Jamaicans.

Spider had worked for Dancer for about seven months. During the second week of employment with Dancer, Spider had asked for a loan. Dancer didn't trust him. He asked Spider, whose given name he still didn't know, to give him a good reason why he should loan him money. Spider told Dancer that his little sister (who turned out to be a complete fabrication) needed to go to an eye specialist or she would lose her sight. The explanation was long and obviously well thought out. He had impressed Dancer, and in turn had gotten what he wanted.

"Yo, man, I need my stash for the week. Now." Spider stared coldly at Dancer.

"Why? What's up?" This was completely out of the usual. No one ever got a week's product in advance. Each of the people who sold crack for Dancer met him in an approved place, every other day. That was Dancer's way of making sure that they were never tempted to take the drugs or the money and run.

"Nothing's up, Dance, I just want the whole stash." Spider held a single-dip cone of vanilla ice cream, which he now slid between his thin red lips. Dancer saw his tongue dart out, scoop some of the ice cream from the cone, and slip quickly back into his mouth.

Dancer fought against a growing suspicion. He didn't want to be paranoid of everything. "You got the money?"

Spider shuffled his feet and looked around. "I'll give it to you next week at the Sunday spot."

"Spider, I don't know what the fuck is up, but you better get right, homeboy." Across the street, the music had changed as Public Enemy's "Yo, Bum Rush the Show,"[1] ripped the air. But the music began to fade as the boys headed down Whither Street toward Twenty-sixth.

Spider sucked in a chest full of air. "Look Dancer, things are changing man. I got to get the shit and get in the wind."

Now Dancer's mind was completely clear. Spider's eyes had exploded with terror. Something had unhinged his composure. Suddenly everything started moving with incredible speed. A long black BMW turned the corner at Stillman. Dancer looked past Spider to see who was driving, but the window was opaque. Spider quickly twisted around to see the car.

Dancer felt a pressure building around them. "What's going on, Spider?"

"I don't know, man. I don't know." Spider was almost crying. "I don't know anybody driving a car like that."

The BMW sat in the middle of the street, right in front of them. It stole the sunlight and recast it black-yellow. Dancer couldn't help but admire it. He would have gotten one if Rainy hadn't objected. She didn't like BMWs. She thought they were too common, especially among successful dealers. Sometimes she called them Black Man's Wheels.

The red Buick, loaded with old undelivered papers stacked in the back seat, blocked the narrow street. With cars parked on either side, there was barely enough room to drive a large car down the street. The paper man exited the last house on the block, got in his car, sat there a moment counting money, then slowly pulled away, across Twenty-five Street, and into the next block.

"Spider, I'm not giving you shit until I know more about what's going on. Now, does this have anything to do with BuckTeeth Rodney?" The words had barely left his mouth when the rear window of the car began to drop. From where Dancer stood, he could see nothing inside the car. Suddenly he felt queasy.

Spider started unconsciously bouncing up and down on the balls of his feet. "Forget it, man, forget it. I got to jet, man." He turned to the street.

Now Dancer saw something in the open window of the car. It was the flash of gold trim around a pair of sunglasses. Then he saw the gun. From the barrel it looked to be an automatic machine pistol, the newest rage, holding more status than an Uzi. He immediately slammed the door shut and dove for the floor.

He heard the burst of popping sounds, *pata, pata, pata, pata,* from the street and the tearing of the aluminum screen door. Behind him he heard the maple wood stairs leading upstairs resound in three loud *whacks*. Dancer looked up to see Half-Dead approaching the vestibule. *"Down,"* Dancer screamed. "Get the fuck down!" Half-Dead immediately crumpled into a ball of bones and black skin.

Through the closed door, they heard the car take off down the street. Suddenly Dancer began shaking. Tremors riveted his body as he clutched a coat that had fallen from the coat rack just inside the door. He held it tightly, eyes closed. It was totally silent outside. No cars going by, no children playing, nothing. It was as still as Whither Street could be on a Saturday afternoon.

Half-Dead sprang out of his crumpled crouch. He stood over Dancer, who had pulled the coat over his head. "Who the fuck was it, man? Did you see who it was? Damn. I don't believe this shit." Half-Dead was straining in his skin. All of his senses were pushing him to action, but he didn't know what to do. He needed Dancer to direct him.

Dancer heard the words coming to him from above. He knew he had to get up, but he didn't want to. His body was still shaking. For a second, he forced his body to be still just to make sure he had not been shot. He felt no blood, no wetness. Everything seemed all right. But he wasn't sure he could actually stand up. If Half-Dead wasn't standing over him, he would have crawled into the crevices of the hardwood floors and stayed there forever. He wanted to stay in the safe feeling of his fetal crouch, it was dark and warm. But Half-Dead's eyes burned holes through the coat. Abruptly he flung the coat off.

"Dead, man," he started, as he pulled his heart back into his body. "This goddam black Beamer pulls up and sits there a minute, then bam." Dancer felt lighter than air. "They tried to kill me, man." He was pacing now. "Why would somebody try to off me?"

"Maybe Rodney's crazier than I thought he was." Half-Dead stared into Dancer's face.

"It just don't make sense." Dancer jerked his hands into the air. There had never been any trouble, no hassles. Before him, the neighborhood had been open to freelancers. "What the fuck does this mean?" He fought to keep his nerves from fleeing into the hot North Philadelphia air, screaming.

He and Half-Dead looked at each other as they heard sirens closing distance quickly. Half-Dead cautiously walked to the front door. As he looked outside, he talked to Dancer.

"Are you okay?"

"Yeah, I'm okay, I think."

"Well you better thank your lucky stars, homeboy." Half-Dead's voice added extra weight and fell to the floor around Dancer. He turned back to face Dancer. "Your boy Spider ain't okay at all. He's wacked out."

"What?" Dancer collapsed into the couch.

"Blew him away. You know, man, I don't think they wanted you at all. If they wanted you, they could of got you. You said they waited out there a bit. They was probably trying to wait for you to let the youngboy walk so they could get to him."

"You think?"

"Don't really matter, they got him and you're still bookin'." Half-Dead leaned against the wall, surveying the scene. There was no broken glass, but the screen had holes in it, the wooden door that Dancer had slammed had three half-inch holes in it, and the stairs held the bullets. "By the way, home, I hope you got your dope put away. They gonna want to see what was up in here."

"You're right," Dancer had sat dazed listening to Half-Dead. He heard the cars approaching outside and jumped to a new terror. He ran around the room quickly gathering up the two pipes, a set of small, empty plastic bags, and other paraphernalia and raced into the basement, where his small supply of rock cocaine was also hidden. Under the cellar stairs in the original stones used for the foundation, Dancer had created a small compartment. He put everything away.

As he rushed through the dining room, Absalom stared at him. Though his vision was blurred, he felt the panic swelling within the house. And yet, he was powerless. A thought occurred that at such a time, in his own house, there was no one there who loved him. Who even knew him.

Hurrying back up the steps, Dancer walked to the front door. Half-Dead was sitting quietly in the living room. Obviously he wanted to be left out of it.

Dancer opened the door on a terrible mess. Spider had gone up in pieces and his red blood ran down the gray cement steps into the crevices separating the blocks of concrete sidewalk. There the blood, nearing the end of its journey, soaked into the dirt. But enough blood remained—a stain on the cement that Rainy would eventually have to scrub away. Alongside the flowing blood, Dancer saw the thick, slow-moving stream of melting ice cream, white and sweet. Where the two streams met, the river was pink. He turned his head away.

But instinctively, against his better judgment, he turned quickly back to see Spider face down, sprawled across his front steps. Part of his head was missing. Dancer looked up, seeking some relief, only to find a wall of people pressing forward.

Breaking from the crowd, a fair-skinned black woman of about forty-five threw herself across the street toward Spider's body. "They shot my baby. They shot my baby. No. Please, Robert. Don't die, baby." She cradled Robert's lifelessness in her arms, looking up to Dancer. She had just left the corner store when she had heard the shots. Her radar had gone up and led her to her son's murdered body.

"Why did they shoot my Robert? Why?

"I don't know, ma'am. I don't know. We was just standing here talking."

"They didn't have to kill him," She cried a flowing barrage of tears, that ended in sentences. "My baby didn't have to die."

Dancer was stunned, drawn into a place where he felt full and empty at the same time, where he felt deeply, but found no facility to communicate it. "We were just standing here. He was eating the ice cream cone." As he looked down, he saw the flecks of cone spotting the stoop and the back of the boy's T-shirt. He looked back to the woman who was sobbing. "He was all right. Spider was all right. I liked him."

NOTE

1. "Yo! Bum Rush the Show" was Public Enemy's debut album (1987).

BIBLIOGRAPHY

Griffin, Barbara L. J. "*Losing Absalom* (Review)." *MELUS* 23, no. 2 (1998): 216.
Link, Katherine. "'Illuminating the Darkened Corridors': An Interview with Alexs Pate." *African American Review* 36, no. 4 (Winter 2002): 597–609.
"Literature and Life": The Givens Collections of the University of Minnesota. https:// video.tpt.org/video/tpt-documentaries -literature-and-life-givens-collection/.
"Losing Absalom (Review)." *Publishers Weekly*. https://publishers.weekly.com/978 1566890175.

Lorene Cary, from *The Price of a Child* (1995)

Lorene Cary was born in Philadelphia in 1956. She attended the exclusive St. Paul's boarding school in New Hampshire and then received her undergraduate and graduate degrees from the University of Pennsylvania as well as an MA in English literature from the University of Sussex in England. She currently teaches creative writing at the University of Pennsylvania.

Cary has published numerous works, including an acclaimed memoir of her experience at St. Paul's, *Black Ice* (1991); the historical novel *The Price of a Child* (1995); a novel of contemporary Black middle-class life, *Pride* (1995);

and *If Sons, Then Heirs* (2011), about a Black family that has migrated to Philly from the South in an attempt to escape a family tragedy. She has also published a young adult book, *Free*, in 2005 about the Underground Railroad and another memoir, *Ladysitting: My Year with Nana at the End of Her Century* (2019), as well as composing the play *General Tubman* (2020).

The Price of a Child was chosen as the first selection for the citywide reading program One Book, One Philadelphia. The novel, set in Philadelphia in 1855, is based on the story of the real-life escape from enslavement by Jane Johnson, recorded in William Still's *The Underground Railroad* and included in this anthology (see section 2). Johnson, along with her two sons, was freed due to the actions of the Railroad. In *The Price of a Child*, Cary leavens her powerful, often poignant, story with touches of dark humor as she examines the lives of escaped slaves and free Blacks in antebellum Philadelphia. She creates a narrative in which Virginia (Ginnie) Pryor (later named Mercer Gray) escapes a life of bondage with the assistance of the Underground Railroad. Taken in by Eliza Ruffin, head of a female Abolitionist group, Mercer enjoys the privileges of wealth but also has to deal with the responsibilities of being an antislavery speaker, including eventually going to trial to confront her former master and to defend the abolitionist who helped free her.

To Mercer, perhaps the most immediate thing that freedom promises is the right to privacy, to not have her body examined like an animal. However, in Philadelphia, she learns that it is not only the slave owners of the South who look at her body as property and as something to be ogled. In Philadelphia, she is forced to produce her body as evidence at the trial to save White abolitionist Passmore Williamson, who was imprisoned for over three months. In addition, the genteel abolitionist women are also titillated by her body, excited to witness the physical abuses she has borne under slavery. It is interesting to compare their examination of her with the more sensitive querying of Harriet Jacobs about her life by the Black pastor and his wife in *Incidents* (see section 2). Mercer also learns that this promised freedom comes at a heavy cost, the painful separation from her child Bennie, still considered property and forced to remain in Virginia when she escaped slavery. At the end of the novel, Mercer receives a monetary gift sufficient to buy the freedom of a child. Unlike the real-life Johnson, who settled in Boston, Mercer then moves on to Canada, where she will continue her abolitionist work. The story of Jane Johnson is also depicted in the musical *Stand by the River* (2003) by Joanne and Mark Sutton-Smith.

—

At Delaware and Dock Streets,[1] the thing was in progress, and it was no mere quiet, secret, scuffling sneaking away, such as Tyree[2] had helped in before. This escape was a public exhibition.

From the driver's seat on the carriage, Tyree could see the dock and the ferry. A group of onlookers had already gathered at the wharf. Sharkey stood among them. Dockworkers had left their cartons of freight and were standing under the CAMDEN AND AMBOY sign on the warehouse. White smoke curled from the chimney behind the ferry's waterwheel. Up on the hurricane deck was William Still, the black cochairman of the Vigilance Committee. He stood motionless, with one arm outstretched to beckon a tall, brown-skinned woman, who sat a few feet in front of him. A girl and a boy huddled on the bench to her left. A well-dressed white man sat on her right. Still reached out to the woman as confidently as a gentleman ushering his lady into a coach. Downstream from the ferry, the Dock Street sewer spewed filth into the river. The stink of it clung to rotten holes in the wooden wharves, which sanitary commissioners had for years urged owners to replace with stone.

"Madam," he said, "I believe you are the woman we are looking for."

Passmore Williamson stood next to Still and spoke in a sharply enunciated tenor:

"You are entitled to your freedom according to the laws of Pennsylvania, having been brought into the state by your owner. If you prefer freedom to slavery, as we suppose everybody does, you have the chance to accept it now."

He stopped for a moment, while the white man to the woman's side made some objection. Then Williamson continued speaking loudly and with confidence:

"Madam, act calmly—don't be frightened by your master. You are as much entitled to your freedom as we are, or as he is."

"Ginnie, we have no idea who these persons are." Pryor waved his hand dismissively.

"Madam," Williamson continued, "you know who we are, I'm sure, and why we are here. Please be assured that the law will protect you."

"Get out of here. You don't have a ticket. You're harassing us. And you have no idea who I am."

"But remember, if you lose this chance you may never get such another."

"Listen, I've had enough of this meddling," said Pryor. "She knows about the law. Believe me, she knows the law. What she may not know is the mischief you people make—pulling in nigras who know no better, and then, a week or two later, the marshals of the United States of America have delivered them back to their rightful owners. Isn't that so?"

Ginnie did not move, although her upper body seemed poised to rise and her eyes moved from William Still's face to Passmore Williamson's and out to the onlookers.

"Madam," Still said, ignoring Pryor, "you may be certain that judges have time and again ruled in favor of cases like yours."

"I suspect you even turn a profit doing this," Pryor said, sounding at once confident and irritable.

To contradict him, Still looked at the woman and shook his head in a slow, deliberate motion. The Dock Street sewer belched out a load of filth. The plopping and trickling made an obscene noise in the unnatural silence on the wharf.

Tyree saw the woman's eyes travel up the dock. There was something magnificent about her stillness, something terrible about her utter isolation from them at that moment. He invited her gaze. If only she could know that they stood with her. If she could know that escape was possible, that it could happen if she would have it.

Stand, he thought, as if he could communicate with her. Only stand and you'll have it.

She looked his way. Her eyes were fierce. Tyree felt revolt inside him. Who, in God's name, would hold this woman? He examined the white man next to her. How did they dare?

For a moment, Tyree let himself feel his desire to wrap his arm around her shoulders and show her a safety she'd never known. Freedom was part of that safety, the most rudimentary safety, from men like the one who sat next to her, imperious. Freedom meant safety from whatever treatment he and his agents meted out, but, beyond that, other assurances: safety from being ogled as if the cords of vein, the muscle in her neck, and the depth of fear in her eyes were public fare, available free to passersby, as the sweating brown haunches of a horse were public or the udders of a cow, because horses and cows had no shame; or the fountain in the park, because fountains had no sense. Hungry hod carriers and stevedores gorged their eyes on her riveting fear. Even a dog would look away if stared at so long.

Tyree wanted to give her a life with curtains around it that she might close at will, so that these gathered people could not lick their lips with the excitement of her predicament or the exquisite sweep of her bosom. He wanted to keep her safe from the fugitive officers and kidnappers who came in the night.

But he wanted her freedom to mean more than that. He wanted to show her how full of promise and delight, how colorful with passion, a life lived free could be. Sitting in the sun, with sweat gathering in his armpits and under his hat brim, Tyree found himself full of yearning. Had he ever thought to imagine his own life as he had just imagined a free life for her?

Perhaps he had. He'd known it vaguely when he was fifteen years old, when he had worked weekends with his father from dawn to dusk. That had been an experiment at first, to prove that he could match the old man job for job on holidays home from the academy. But before he'd become Manny's[3] mule, then helper, and, finally, replacement, before his ascension into the tiny club of well-off colored men, those strange, resented, and perforce, resentful creatures making quarter-fortunes on the fringes of the modern manufacturing that had just begun to churn—before all that, for a moment, he had been a strapping boy-turning-to-man, with a molasses voice and ambition for his own burgeoning manhood.

The yearning threatened to spread into a woozy melancholy, unseemly for a man of Tyree's station and responsibilities. Instead, he made of the woman and the ferry; of Still, with his outstretched hand, and Williamson, finger in the air like a politician; and of the curling white smoke, a perfect daguerreotype, the colors turned to gray and the fugitive's dark-eyed fierceness at the center. It helped to quiet the yearning and keep himself patient.

FROM CHAPTER 7, "MAKE YOUR MARK"

Mercer and Zilpha[4] rose at dawn. The sky promised a fine day: dry, at least, with only a gentle wind. Walking weather, Zilpha called it, and good thing too, because Mercer had walking to do. Miss Eliza Ruffin's house was almost five miles away. Zilpha cautioned Mercer to leave at least an hour and a half to get there, and not to be late, repeating one of her favorite sayings: "You wanna know the difference between a nigger and a Negro? A half an hour."

Zilpha stirred the embers in the stove. The fire crackled into life as they washed and dressed in the dark. After tea and bread, Zilpha left to do her day's nursing work and Mercer began hanging the clothes she'd left to soak the night before.

The linen was heavy and wet. Mercer squeezed it with numb fingers and shook it hard. It snapped in the morning's silence, disturbing the birds who, having finished their loud first-light singing, had flocked to the slanting sun on the east-facing eaves of Gabriel's whitewashed cottage. Mercer snapped again and again. Each time, a cold spray of water wet her face. At first she tucked her chin, but then it came to her that her face took water better than her head. So she blinked and let the water fly, as she listened to the birds flutter with each crack of the fabric. Mercer felt the solidity of the brown earth under her feet and the contrast between her cold face and hands and her body, warm with exertion. The muscles of her back began to pull each time she raised her hands over her head. She did not think about her meeting.

Before noon, Mercer ate a soup of onions and potatoes. Then she took in the laundry. She sprinkled it and put on the finger covers that Zilpha had cut from old gloves over the years to protect the white linen from snags where her skin cracked around her nails or stains when it broke open and bled. Mercer ironed half the load by half past one. Then she banked the fire, closed the shutters, and pulled on a gray wool cape Harriet had given her. She was warm from the iron and the fire, and her palms were smooth and shiny from the starchy linen. She did not wash off the starch; her hands were too sore and dry.

Mercer walked fast. Harriet's letter, which she had successfully put out of her mind, came back to her. It reminded her, after a brief few weeks of serenity, of the fragility of her freedom. She felt herself becoming anxious. One fugitive wrote that the price of freedom was eternal vigilance. The Quicks had read her these things, but Mercer was beginning to know them for herself. She looked at the green-and-brown valley with vigilant eyes. Fields dotted with cabbage and kale and bright winter squash suddenly lost their safety. She was no longer protected from her pursuers but made conspicuous for them. She felt foolish to walk abroad on the open road with her long strides and powerful thighs, as if she were a citizen. Neat stone farms, springhouses, icehouses and smokehouses; corn cribs and barns; water wheels spinning in fast-running creeks; fat cows and black-and-white goats with teats full of milk, chickens and roosters and hens that laid tiny green-and-white eggs: these were other people's—white people's—resources, as they always had been, not a common wealth she could share. Behind the window curtains, slave catchers and kidnappers could be hiding; people who would aid and abet her capture; people who would watch and applaud, or would look on indifferently, or, pitying her, would only shake their heads, as they might if a neighbor's dog were hit by a dray. They'd shake their heads and suck their tongues through thin lips like a gash in their faces, and return, gratefully, to their money and milk-fed children, and even the most well-meaning of them would fall back on the rock-bottom fact of human intercourse: better you than me. By the time Mercer arrived at Eliza Ruffin's house, she was rigid with distrust.

A blond woman with a blunt face opened the door. Behind her came Eliza Ruffin, dressed in a brown dress cut simply from rich fabric. She was tall but slight. She advanced with both hands extended and took Mercer's cold and shiny bare hands in her own soft ones.

"I am very grateful to you for agreeing to meet me. We cast a wide net among our Vigilant friends, but we could not know whether you would respond—or even where you were," she said.

Eliza Ruffin led Mercer into the alcove of a dark-green parlor. They sat next to a small fire, and the housemaid took Mercer's cloak before going to make tea. After the bright-blue day, the parlor felt private and dark. Then Ruffin explained her interest, as president of the Ladies Anti-Slavery Society, in the welfare of fugitives, and especially female fugitives, and especially Mercer. But beyond that, Ruffin admitted: "I have another particular interest in your case, and it is this: Passamore Williamson is my dear cousin. He's been in Moyamensing Prison⁵ for close to a month now, and our lawyers cannot seem to get him out."

Mercer studied Ruffin's face for resentment or blame. She had clear brown eyes and lush, wavy hair. No doubt she was about to ask Mercer to do something to help Williamson. Mercer owed the man a great deal. But how much did she owe him? Was this woman with her clear-eyed welcome about to ask Mercer to go back? Maybe the anti-slavery people had had enough of doing good? Maybe Williamson had had enough of prison and figured it was time for a switch. Maybe it was Mercer's turn in the barrel.

"What we'd hoped," said Miss Ruffin, "was that the lawyers could have him purged of contempt. We'd hoped that by his asserting vigorously—and honestly, of course—that he was unable to produce you and your children in court, he would be freed.

"Well, but, naturally, he cannot make such testimony unless he is allowed to appear in court, and he cannot appear so long as the judge holds him in contempt. The legal complications go on, but that's the outline, the sketch of it all. The lawyers have been to the Pennsylvania Superior Court, but they've ruled against us, so there's an end to it. Or not really an end, as they always say, because lawyers never give up, like people with things to sell, I suppose."

She smiled a little.

Mercer smiled back warily, "What do you think I can do to help you?" she asked.

"Well, your Captain Pryor has said that you and your children were abducted—kidnapped, actually—and that Passmore and Mr. Still and the rest must stay to answer charges, and really, the charges are ridiculous: riot—riot, mind you—forcible abduction, assault and battery, that sort of thing. And for Passmore, it's worst, because he's white, and the law holds him more responsible than the others. Our lawyers, his lawyers, think that if you were to swear an affidavit, witnessed by some third or fourth disinterested party—we'd retain another lawyer for the purpose—that you left of your own free will and Passmore did not abduct you, why, then, that might help his case."

Flushed, she finished with an uncharacteristic flourish.

"What is an affidavit, Miss Ruffin?"

Eliza Ruffin seemed eager to explain that Mercer would not be required to do more than tell her version of the story to the lawyers, who would write it down and have her make her mark at the bottom. They would swear in court that it was she who had given the testimony and she who had signed it.

"It's a petition, really, that's all."

"But won't they want to see me in court?"

Impatience crept into Ruffin's voice. "At this point, as I've said, no one is asking you to do any more than file a petition."

"I'm not ungrateful, Miss Ruffin. I am very, very grateful. I'm grateful for what everyone has done. I'm grateful to you now for talking to me and for giving me the choice. But what I'm learning, Miss Ruffin, is that being free costs dear. Now, mind, it's not that I won't pay. I'm just trying to find out what all it's gonna cost this time."

"It is quite likely that having received your affidavit, the judge will want to see you produced. Passmore is in prison for failing to answer the writ of

habeas corpus. In other words, he has to stay in jail because he cannot produce your body."

"Produce my body."

"Yes. So you're quite astute to see that at some point, the people who have
claimed to have seen you may also be asked to—"

"Produce my body."

"Just so," Ruffin made a quick little sigh. "But at each step it is your decision. Filing an affidavit does not obligate you to appear in court sometime
later. You must know that."

Mercer knew nothing of the sort. What she knew was that with this affidavit business, she'd be jumping onto a moving train. She might be on it
already.

"I'll file the affidavit, Miss Ruffin."

Ruffin sighed again. Her clear eyes had been hiding the extent of her anxiety. "Excellent."

They drank their tea, and somehow, while they chatted, Mercer found
that she had agreed to return the next day at the same time to appear at Ruffin's anti-slavery meeting. Nothing was required of her, Ruffin said, except to
appear and, perhaps, to answer a few questions. The following day, some
anti-slavery friend, as Ruffin described him, would come to transport Mercer
to New York, where two lawyers would take her testimony. The men must be
able to swear that they'd seen her in New York, Ruffin said, in order to keep
Pryor and his agents from combing through Philadelphia's anti-slavery coalition and finding her and her children. Mercer agreed.

Refusing Ruffin's offer of a servant and gig[6] to take her home, she walked
briskly in the gray-and-blue dusk. Pryor had done what he could. Now she
would make her next move. The thought of action made her feel less at his
mercy and less at the mercy of courts and judges and laws and marshals and
officers who played by rigged sets of rules.

He run, he run, he run his best. He run right into the hornets' nest.

Could happen, she thought.

The Ladies Anti-Slavery Society meeting took place most weeks in a room
off the Quaker meetinghouse that the Society shared with a temperance
group. But because the temperance people had planned a special event for
this afternoon, the Ladies Society agreed to meet at Eliza Ruffin's house.
Harriet's letter had explained the group to Mercer, by way of convincing her

to visit Ruffin. The Ladies Society was not just an outgrowth of a men's group but their own proper organization. They were Negro and white women together, and one of the colored women was a cochairwoman (not, as Harriet explained often happened in mixed groups, the helper). In principle, they occasionally met in one of the members' houses, because they believed that women who worked together should not be ashamed to entertain each other in their homes (although in practice, they met at Eliza Ruffin's, and no one protested, or even took much notice, that they did not alternate). As opposed to many groups that abhorred slavery but cared little for equality, the Ladies Society believed that achieving the "elevation of the freemen" by fighting discrimination in the North was inseparable, as the promoters of the year's colored national convention put it, from "the great work of the slave's restoration of freedom." They sponsored lectures and informal talks and fairs like everyone else, but mostly they liked their abolition radical.

By the time Mercer arrived, a dozen women, four of them colored, were assembled in the upstairs parlor. They had arranged themselves in a half-circle around the table where Eliza Ruffin sat pouring tea. The late afternoon was sunny and cold, but Eliza Ruffin's fire was just the slightest bit warmer than the one she'd had lit the day before in the downstairs parlor. Two ruddy-faced women shared a large chair and talked loudly about the virtues of not eating red meat. They move on to the subject of vigorous exercise; then, in general language, and with giggles, to moderation in conjugal relations.

"Mr. Graham[7] has worked out quite a specific regimen, and he says without question that it will relieve debility."

"The Mr. Graham who makes the crackers?"

"The same, yes."

"Relieve or prevent?"

"Excuse me. Prevention, of course—as in all matters of health, our first concern—but the system relieves as well."

"Priscilla is a wonderful advertisement. You are the picture of health."

"She always was."

"Well, yes, I've been blessed. But this regimen—"

"This regimen, my eye. Beth put her finger on it. Priscilla has never been sick a day in her life. I know, you see, Priscilla. I was there when your mother, my aunt Ruth, fed your family a lovely, rare chop every morning, noon, and night. I never saw so much meat. Red, quite red. And kept you in the house by the hour. You were the picture of health then, and you're the picture of health now."

"Well, I say like Sojourner Truth said: 'Is God dead?'[8] What I mean is: Do Mr. Graham and these other people who presume to keep one alive forever, do they talk about the restorative powers of prayer. I've seen it, you know." She slapped her thigh several times. Merriment sneaked shamefully out of the room. The women, all but a couple, hung their head or else looked reverently at the speaker's ample thigh and the pudgy hand that patted it.

"They said I'd never walk. Some of you have prayed for me. Don't you remember? And I didn't have to give up meat to do it. The tender hand of God touched me right here."

Again she whacked the recovered thigh, harder. Mercer began to think it was taking a little too much punishment for a limb that had been ailing.

Eliza Ruffin moved to stand next to Mercer's chair, and the stout woman's hand settled in her lap. Then she introduced Mercer to the group, saying that she could not tell them Mercer's former name, or the circumstances of her liberation, or even how long she'd been out of the South. Some of them had guessed who Mercer was, and they would tell the others later. It pleased them, however, to strike a note of secrecy in their meetings and to remind themselves of the gravity of their actions.

"I can say, however, that this woman's courage has made an indelible impression on me, and I think I can also say that she'd be willing to inform us—from her own experience—about the institution we've all sworn to erase from this country."

They clapped, surprisingly quietly, and began to fuss over Mercer's chair and her tea and what to put into it and whether or not she wanted a cake.

To Mercer, these women were a curious lot, at once girlish and old-ladylike. A small copper-colored woman spoke to Mercer through teeth and lips that she barely moved as she talked, as if not to disturb them: "I think you'll find a dear, good friend in Eliza."

Then, for no apparent reason, she continued: "I was just telling someone the other day that the greatest wish of my life is quite simple: only to live quietly and modestly with a few dear friends and do good in the world and make others better and happier."

Mercer smiled at her. So what? she thought. I like rhubarb pie. Who the hell asked you? Her sudden irritation surprised her.

"Do you do this often?"

"Beg pardon?"

"Do you often come to talk to groups like ours?"

"Oh, no, I've—"

Eliza Ruffin cut her off with an apologetic look. "Mercer's just begun this sort of work, and"—she looked toward her deferentially—"if I'm not incorrect, Mercer, you're deciding whether or not the work suits you."

Mercer nodded, realizing that she was supposed to go along with this cloaking of her identity. But if these women were truly friends of the slave, why should she have to be so secretive? She turned back to her tea. It was milky and sweet. Mercer sipped out of a cup so thin that she suspected she might bite it through if she didn't take care.

"Well, I think it most important to make others better, and if they are happier in the process, so much to the good," said the copper-colored lady.

Mercer could tell that her sips were too noisy. She could tell that from how they looked at her.

"Of course one is happier if one is better."

"Well." It came from the redhead who'd earlier refused to moderate her red-meat consumption and had laughed loudest about limiting marital relations. "I must admit that I am very, very happy in the summer at the seaside, when I'm not engaged in any work at all and I'm not being of any service to anyone. Is that wicked? It is, isn't it?"

"Of course," said the colored woman from behind those taut lips, "'happy' is too simple a word. Being at the seaside makes us happy. A child eating a candy is happy. But making others' lives better, such as work with the downtrodden, brings a joy that is longer lasting and more profound."

The women shook their heads and moaned softly together. Well, Mercer guessed that that set her straight. Happy sneaked out of the room and joined merriment down the hall.

At risk of shattering her cup, Mercer finished her tea. Eliza Ruffin promptly refilled the cup.

How, then, did she go from sitting in their midst drinking tea to standing before them, turned, with her skirts raised to let them see the scars on her thighs? She would look back, just days later, and be unable to recall. She did remember how they strained with attention, how they asked her one question after another: Who had done this to her? For what transgression? How long was she beaten? With what object? How old was she when it happened?

What had she done about it? What did other slaves do about it? Did it bleed? How had she healed? How much of her body did the scars cover? Were all her people treated likewise? Was that why she'd run away, to avoid more beatings?

The room darkened as evening approached. They closed the shutters and lit the lamps. The lamplight bounced off their faces and onto her legs, still bared, suffusing the room with the glow of their curiosity.

Had a man done this to her? Had he done it to take her virtue? Had he forced her?

They filled their eyes with her. They rubbed their clean, white fingers against each other impatiently, as men rubbed themselves, absently, when a woman walked by.

The skin of Mercer's forearm was mottled and shiny where she'd once been scalded. Maybe they'd like to have a look at that too. Or maybe the toe where the nail had dropped off that winter before she'd started working in the kitchen with Suzy, when people lost whole toes from being out tending to the animals, but she'd lost only a nail and a tip.

They wouldn't want to hear about that, though, she figured. They wanted the knock-down-drag-out. That much she could tell. They wanted the horse whip and pony whip, the green sapling branch, the leather belt and bridle cord. They wanted the old man with nubs for fingers standing in the circle of blows. *Did you bleed?* They wanted a crazy-ass overseer and her on the ground, twitching and calling for Jesus? Why? Why did they want it so? *Did you bleed?* They wanted her crying and snotting into the clay, dirty, filthy, violated. Why? *Did you bleed?* They wanted Jackson Pryor[9] crooking his finger at her after dinner. Or better yet, beating her first. They wanted rape in the room with them—on her body, contained in her body, the better to keep them safe.

Did it hurt? Hurt bad? Did you bleed?

Mercer dropped her skirts. She had been looked at plenty.

Eliza Ruffin said, "I think we've asked enough of Mercer today."

They fetched her more tea and a little white cake with vanilla-butter icing. She ate it slowly and sat wanting more while they concluded their other business.

That night Zipha finished reading aloud the first book of Samuel. Mercer dreamt that God was calling Bennie, but Bennie did not know who was calling him.

NOTES

1. Delaware and Dock Street: in the Penn's Landing area of the Old City (Central City).

2. Tyree Quick is a free Black who aids Mercer and falls in love with her, despite being married. Tyree and Mercer have an affair, but separate by the end of the novel.

3. Manny Quick, Tyree's uncle.

4. Zilpha is Manny's sister, and therefore Tyree's aunt.

5. Moyamensing Prison opened in 1835 and was in operation until 1963. It was located at 1400 East Passyunk Avenue in South Philadelphia. The space is now occupied by an Acme supermarket.

6. A gig is a light, open, two-wheeled, horse-drawn carriage.

7. Sylvester Graham (1794–1851) was a Presbyterian minister and member of the Temperance Movement. He was a vegetarian and a believer in dietary reform. He did not invent the cracker that bears his name, but he did support use of a bread using whole grains.

8. In an address in Faneuil Hall in Boston in 1860, Frederick Douglass questioned the existence of a God that could allow African American suffering to continue. Sojourner Truth supposedly remarked, "Is God dead?" in response. There are questions about whether Truth said this, and, if so, when and where it took place.

9. Jackson Pryor is Mercer's former owner.

BIBLIOGRAPHY

Eberstadt, Fernanda. "Freedom Rider: *The Price of a Child* by Lorene Cary." *New York Times*, June 18, 1995, sec. 7, p. 12.

Furman, Jan. "*The Price of a Child*." (Review) *African American Review* 31, no. 3 (Fall 1997): 554–56.

Kolenda, Joanna. "Price of a Child (The)." *Encyclopedia of Greater Philadelphia.* https://philadelphiaencyclopedia.org /essays/price-of-a-child-the/.

Lorene Cary (website). https://www.lorene cary.com.

Mitchell, Angelyn. *The Freedom to Remember: Narrative, Slavery, and Gender in Contemporary Black Women's Fiction.* New Brunswick: Rutgers University Press, 2002.

Toni Cade Bambara, from "Deep Sight and Rescue Missions" (1996)

Toni Cade Bambara (born Miltona Mirkin Cade) was born in 1939 in Harlem, New York City. She was a fiction writer, filmmaker, social activist, and college professor. She graduated from Queens College (CUNY) with a BA in theater arts and English literature. She also received an MA from the same college. She worked as a social worker in New York for a few years until taking teaching positions at several universities. Beginning in 1986, Bambara taught script writing at the Scribe Video Center in Philadelphia. She died in Philadelphia in 1995.

Bambara left a rich legacy of two short story collections, *Gorilla My Love* (1972) and *The Sea Birds Are Still Alive* (1977); two novels, *The Salt Eaters*

(1980) and the posthumous *Those Bones Are Not My Child* (1999); and the collection *Deep Sightings and Rescue Missions: Fiction, Essays and Conversations* (1996), edited by her close friend Toni Morrison. She herself also edited two important collections, *The Black Woman: An Anthology* (1970), as Toni Cade, and *Tales and Stories for Black Folk* (1971). Her screenplays include *The Bombing of Osage Avenue* (1986); *Cecil B. Moore: Master Tactician of Direct Action* (1987); and *W. E. B. Du Bois: A Biography in Four Voices* (1995). Her work is often marked by a keen sense of humor, an ear for the vernacular, and a strong impulse toward social justice.

Although Bambara lived in Philadelphia for the last decade of her life, illness prevented her from writing much about her experiences in the city. The essay "Deep Sight and Rescue Missions," however, and the films on the bombing of Osage Avenue and on activist Cecil B. Moore give a good feel of how the city influenced her creative mind and continued to stir her sense of social justice. "Deep Sight and Rescue Missions" details a typical day in Bambara's Philadelphia life. She takes a crosstown bus ride through the city (the 23 route, also featured in Becky Birtha's story "Route 23" in this section), making several stops, where she interacts with a variety of members of the community while thinking about the concept of identity, especially as it manifests itself in Philly. She speculates about the inner thoughts of several of the people she sees and imagines them in literary or cinematic settings. She goes back to her apartment building, where she has a conversation with one of her neighbors before having a fitful night's sleep thinking about social issues and the emerging forms of discourse being used to address issues of assimilation, identity, and inequality. In this piece, Bambara uses her literary and cinematic skills to present a slice of ordinary Philadelphians' lives and to comment on the ever-changing politics of the city.

—

It's one of those weird winter-weather days in Philly. I'm leaning against the wall of a bus kiosk in Center City brooding about this article that won't write itself. Shoppers unselfconsciously divest themselves of outer garments, dumping wooly items into shopping bags. I'm scarfed to the eyes à la Jesse James, having just been paroled from the dentist. And I'm eager to get back to the 'hood where I've been conducting an informal survey on assimilation. The term doesn't have the resonance it once had for me. I'm curious as to why that is.

At the moment, gums aching, I'm sure of only four things: ambivalence still hallmarks the integrationist-vs.-nationalist pull in Amero-African political life; social and art critics still disrespect, generally, actual differences in the pluralistic United States and tend to collapse constructed ones instead into a difference-with-preference sameness, with Whites as major and people of color (POCs) minor; media indoctrination and other strategies of coercive assimilation are endemic, ubiquitous, and relentless as ever; and the necessity of countering propaganda and deprogramming the indoctrinated as imperative as ever. I'm sure also that I am not as linguistically nimble as I used to be when interviewing certain sectors/strata of the community, for I've just blown a gabfest on identity, belonging, and integration at the dentist's through an inability to bridge a gap between the receptionist, a working-class sister from the projects, who came of age in the sixties and speaks in nation-time argot, and the new dental assistant, a more privileged sister currently taking a break from Bryn Mawr, who speaks the lingo of postmodern theory.

Across from the bus stop is a new luxury high-rise, a colossus of steel and glass with signs announcing business suites for lease. I wonder who's got bank these days to occupy such digs. Philly is facing economic collapse. Paychecks for municipal workers are often weeks late. The hijacking of neighborhoods by developers, who in turn are being leaned on by the banks, which in turn are being scuttled by the robber barons, who in turn are being cornered by IRS investigators working for the Federal Reserve, whose covers have been pulled off by Black and Latino task forces, who in turn are harassed by Hoover's heirs. And while many citizens are angry about the S & L bailout being placed on the backs of workers one paycheck away from poverty and obscurity, they are even more distressed by cuts in social services that have pushed homelessness beyond the crisis point. I roam my eyes over the building, wondering if the homeless union would deem it media-worthy for a takeover.

In the lobby of the high-rise is a sister about my age, early fifties, salt-'n-pepper 'fro, African brass jewelry, a wooly capelike coat of an Andean pattern. She's standing by a potted fern, watchful. She seems to be casing the joint. I get it in my head that she's a "checker," a member of a community group that keeps an eye on HUD and other properties suitable for housing the homeless. A brisk-walking young sister emerges from the bank of elevators. Briefcase tucked smartly under one elbow, coat draped over the left Joan Crawford shoulder pad, hair straight out of a Vidal Sassoon commercial, the sister strides past the visitors-must-sign-in information counter, and the older woman approaches her. I search for a word, rejecting "accosts," "buttonholes," "pounces," and "confronts," but can't find a suitable verb for the decisiveness and intensity of the older woman's maneuver. Obviously strangers, they nevertheless make short shrift of amenities and seem to hunker down to a heavy discussion forthwith, the older sister doing most of the talking. She's not panhandling. She's not dispensing literature of any kind. She doesn't reach over to pin a campaign button on the Armani lapel. But she's clearly on a mission. What kind of scam, then, could it be? And if not a scam, what?

I now get it in my head that the older sister is Avey Johnson, sprung from the pages of Paule Marshall's 1983 novel *Praisesong for the Widow*. Avey, having rejected her deracinated life of bleached-out respectability in White Plains, New York, fashions a new life's work, taking up a post in buildings such as the high-rise to warn bloods of the danger of eccentricity and to urge them to (re)center themselves and work for the liberation of the people. I'm so certain it's Avey, I move away from the wall to go get in it. My daughter's voice chimes in my ear: "Mother, mind your own business." I head for the curb, muttering my habitual retort: "Black people are my business, sugar." A youngblood on a skateboard zooms by. His bulky down jacket, tied around his hips by the sleeves, brushes against my coat and stops me. The No. 23 bus is approaching. So is rush hour. And who knows how swiftly and mean the weather will turn any second. I board.

***

The No. 23 bus, heading for Chinatown, first cuts through a district that community workers call the Zone of Diminishing Options. In the three-block area around Race and Ninth street are pawnshops that also sell used clothes, labor-pool agencies advertising dishwasher jobs in the Atlantic City casinos, a very busy blood bank, a drop-in shelter, the Greyhound terminal, an army recruiting office, and a hospice center. While draft counseling in the Zone, I'd often think of opening a gun shop, if only to disrupt the perverse visual gag. And while in the Zone, I caught a third of a provocative independent black film called *Drop Squad*.[1] A community worker, cassette in hand, persuaded a pawnshop owner to play it on a set in the window.

Written by David Taylor, produced by Butch Robinson, and directed by David Johnson, *Drop Squad* is a satire about hijacking the hijacked. A nationalist organization puts the snatch on an assimilated corporate blood, straps him down in a chair in a red-black-and-green-draped community center, and proceeds to try to deprogram him. "You need to reacquaint yourself with you, brother," they tell him, assigning him to read Toni Morrison's *The Bluest Eye*.

They take turns changing a roll-call reveille: Soul Train, Garvey, Fannie Lou Hamer, W. E. B. Du Bois, Sharpeville, Billie Holiday, Frantz Fanon. They argue, threaten, cajole, insist, are determined to wake the brother up. He counters with equal passion for the individual right to be whatever and whomever he pleases. Frequently his arguments are sound, momentarily stumping his captors. But they are relentless in their campaign to call the brother home, to reclaim him for the collective mission of race recovery. Privileged as he has become through people's struggles, they argue that he has a debt both to himself and to his community blasted by drugs, violence, joblessness, homelessness, lack of access, and the politics of despair.

I reach Germantown. The Hawk, out now and bold, blows me toward the greengrocer on Chelten. Worker Khan Nguyen has been discussing assimilation for me with her customers, especially Vietnamese and African and East Indian Caribbeans new to the U. S. She reports that assimilation is synonymous with citizenship training. It's her take that while folks know that the intent of the training is to "domesticate" them, the emphasis on democracy and rights makes them "wildly expectant." Khan winks. She has not been tamed by the process. "It may be naïve of me," she says, warming to the subject, but the fact that "new immigrants take democracy more seriously" than it is generally practiced in a society built on theft and bondage, riddled by a white-supremacist national ideology, motivated by profit and privilege, and informed by fascist relations between classes, races, sexes, and communities of various sexual orientations, cultural heritages, and political persuasions, "means that, in time, they will become unruly." She leans on the phrase "in time," because I am frowning. I ask about citizenship as a bribe contract: we'll grant you citizenship, and in return you drop your cultural baggage and become "American," meaning defend the status quo despite your collective and individual self-interest. She repeats the phrase "in time," putting her whole body into it to drown me out. I stumble out of there, hugging a bottle of Jamaican vanilla extract (excellent wash for cleaning/deodorizing the refrigerator, by the by), hopeful.

I run into a young friend, Anthony (Buffalo Boy) Jackson, graffiti artist and comic-book-maker. I ask for his help, easing into the topic by explaining "assimilation" as I first encountered it in Latin (the changing of letters to make them sound in accord with letters nearby, i.e., *adsimilare* in Latin becomes *assimilare, excentricus* in Medieval Latin or *ekkentros* in Greek becomes *eccentric* in English) and bio (the process by which the body converts food into absorbable substances for the maintenance of the system). Before I can get to the sociopolitical meaning, Anthony is off and running with "system," recounting a middle-school field trip to a marsh in the New Jersey Pine Barrens. to study ecosystems. He loses me, but I chime in when I hear usable things like "symbiosis" and "parasites," and finally the ability of the amoeba to give alternate responses to its environment because of its shape-shifting ability.

"Hold it, Anthony, are you saying amoebas can transform the system? I mean, err-rahh, are they capable of collective action or are they basically loners?"

My friend is dancing and laughing at me. "The amoeba shall overthrow, right?" Big joke.

I walk him toward Burger King 'cause now he has an idea—the amoeba as mantua, shape-shifter ninja—and the tables are big enough to spread out on. I bring him back to my needs, and he tells me the issue is rip-off, not assimilation.

"Everything we do," he says, meaning breaking, scratching, rapping, dressing, "gets snatched up and we get bumped off." Which is why, he explains, he admires Spike Lee, because of Lee's control over the films and especially over the spin-offs that come out of Forty Acres and a Mule—CDs, books, T-shirts, mugs, caps, jackets. He ducks inside and shakes his head about me. I'm old enough to know what the deal is, and the deal is rip-off.

Down the block, toward Wayne Avenue, is a produce truck where people frequently gather to talk over the news of the day. Trucker Mr. Teddy, a blood from Minnesota, tells me that only Europeans were invited to become truly assimilated. "And assimilation went out when *Roots* came in and busted up the whole melting-pot con game." According to him, nobody's been melted—not Norwegians, not Germans, not Japanese, and definitely not Africans. He talks about the Swedes in the Midwest who, in reclaiming their heritage, particularly their seventeenth-century socialist tradition, have rejected assimilation. "Hmm," sez I, and venture to ask if these unmelted Amero-Europeans he speaks of reject as well their race/skin privileges, the socio-eco-political and psychic profits derived from U. S. apartheid. "Now that would be un-American." He chuckles and slam-dunks a cabbage into my bag.

Across the avenue in front of the newsstand where folks are lined up to buy lottery tickets, the daily floor show is in progress. It features an old white guy who shuffles along the strip panhandling from the newsstand, past the wall bordering the Super Fresh, past the Woolworth, to the area near the bank where vendors line the curbs all the way down to Germantown Avenue, where I got off the No. 23. Some black people derive great pleasure from helping a down-and-out white person. The same pleasure, I suspect, that film-buff friends of mine enjoy watching a wrecked Chet Baker[2] fall totally apart on screen in the docu *Let's Get Lost*.[3] There are always folks about, fingering the videotapes on the tables—today *Highlights of the Clarence Thomas-Anita Hill Hearings* is selling for eight dollars—who crack on the generous-minded who give money to panhandling whites. "Christian duty my ass! Let that ole cracker beg in his own neck of the woods." But the consensus notion is that Old Whiteguy is pretty much in his neck of the woods, that he lives, in fact in posh quarters on Wissahickon Avenue. Should anyone voice that, they are charged with being proracist, at least stereotypic in thinking that all white people are well-off. "Well-off or not," someone is saying as I reach the performing area, "he's getting fat off black people." That remark triggers a mention of Jim Crow, talking low, and slavery. So a few people make a point of jostling the old man. Should anyone object and call the behavior racist, as in reverse racism, that provokes still another discussion: that some in the race seem to live outside history and don't appreciate the fact that a race war is going on and that it wasn't bloods who declared it; whereupon statistics are ticked off about infant mortality, life expectancy, illiteracy, unemployment, and other aspects of the war. Meanwhile, Old Whiteguy is steadily collecting loose change, wending his way toward a sister who vends around our way only occasionally.

I don't know her name yet, but I admire her titles: Sam Yette's *The Choice*,[4] Chancellor Williams's *The Destruction of Black Civilization*,[5] and everything that Angela Davis ever published. Should a youth bedecked in gold try to get past her, she'll beckon her/him over and give a mini-workshop on black miners in South Africa, apartheid, and the international gold trade. Should a youngblood stroll by in a Malcolm T-shirt ("By Any Means Necessary") she will get very generous with her wares. Old Whiteguy is another matter.

"You want a what—a quarter!?!" she says. "I'll give you a quarter." Images of Old Whiteguy tied to two horses being lashed in opposite directions flood my dentist-traumatized brain. She looks him up and down and says quite seriously, "Hey, you used to be a young peckerwood,[6] so why ain't you president?" He grins his drooly grin, hand still stuck out. Book Sister turns to the incense seller in a crocheted cufi[7] at the next table. "Come get this clown before I'm forced to hurt him."

Before dark, I reach home, a co-op whose comfy lobby I'd thought would ensure me neighbors enough for a roundtable discussion on this article. But the lobby's empty. I drop in on my neighbor Vera Smith. She takes a hard line on both aggressive assimilationists and seemingly spaced denialists, folks quick to call behavior manifested by Book Sister and jostlers as racist, folks who swear that things are all right, or would be all right if Black people weren't so touchy, mean, and paranoid. I say something like "consciousness requires a backlog of certain experiences." Vera ain't going for it. From day one, she says, there's enough evidence around to peep the game and resist. "So it's a decision to be like that," she says. "And it takes a lot of energy to deny what's obvious." Denialists don't want to see, don't want to belong, don't want to struggle, says Vera, putting a pin in it.

We talk into the night about a lot of things. A first-generation U. S. Bajun, she shares with me her plan to have dual citizenship, from the U. S. which she automatically has, and from Barbados also. I'm profoundly pleased for her, and for us, for whenever a Br'er Rabbit slip-the-yoke[8] operation can be achieved, it puts another plank underfoot at home *base*.

I ride the elevator, thinking about people I've known growing up (not that all these years aren't my formative years) who worked tirelessly to maintain a deep connection with the briar patch and its ways of being. No matter where they journeyed in the world or what kinds of bribes they were offered to become amnesiacs, they knew their real vocation was to build home base, sanctuaries, where black people can stand upright, exhale, and figure out what to do about the latest attack. And so they kept faith with the church of their childhood, or the UNIA[9] or Father Divine[10] movement (both alive and well in Philly, by the by), or the family farm in Alabama, or the homestead in the Islands, sending money, cement, clothing, books, lumber, weapons, certain that home base is not where you may work or go to school, but where the folks are who named you daughter, daddy, mama, doctor, son, brother, sister, partner, dahlin', chile.

I rinse my ravaged mouth out with warm salt water and hit the keyboard. As my young friend said, the issue is rip-off. Invisibility is not a readily graspable concept for a generation that grew up on MTV, Cosby, Oprah, Spike Lee, Colin Powell, and black folks on soaps, quiz shows, and the nightly news. Not only are black folks ostensibly participating—so what the hell does invisibility mean?—but what is generally recognized at home and abroad as "American" is usually black. A hundred movies come to mind, but not their titles, sorry. For instance, the one about two lost young Euro-Ams who find themselves in what they think is a time warp, the terrain woefully fiftyish, but discover that they've landed in a Soviet spy school, in an American village erected for the purpose of training infiltrators to pass as "American." The two are enlisted to update and authenticate the place and the curriculum. Everything they present as "American"—music, speech, gesture, style—is immediately identifiable, certainly to any black spectator, as black.

As for alienation, or as Dr. Du Bois limned it in numerous texts, double-consciousness[11] and double vision, people coming of age in a period hallmarked by all-up-in your-face hip-hop and an assertive pluralism/multiculturalism as well don't see barriers as a policy as old as Cortez, as deadly as COINTELPRO,[12] as seductive as the Chris Columbus[13] hype chugging down the pike, and more solid than the Berlin Wall, given the system's monstrous ability to absorb, co-opt, deny, marginalize, deflect, defuse, or silence.

I don't know what goes on in classrooms these days, but in informal settings the advice of the Invisible Man's granddaddy, "Undermine 'em with grins,"[14] is inexplicable Tomism. The paradoxical paradigm of the Liberty paint factory episode in Ellison's novel, the necessity of mixing in black to concoct pure white, is just a literary joke thought up by some old-timey guy on an equally old-timey typewriter. The three aspects of alienation as traditionally experienced and understood by my elders, my age group, and the generation that came of age in the sixties—alienation from the African past (and present—Was there ever an American airline with direct flights to the motherland?), alienation from U.S. economic and political power, alienation from the self as wholly participating in history—don't register as immediately relevant.

I spend a fitful night fashioning questions to raise with myself in the morning. What characterizes the moment? There's a drive on to supplant "mainstream" with "multicultural" in the national consciousness, and that drive has been sparked by the emancipatory impulse, blackness, which has been the enduring model for other down-pressed sectors in the U.S. and elsewhere. A repositioning of people of color (POCs) closer to the center of the national narrative results from, reflects, and effects a reframing of questions regarding identity, belonging, community. "Syncretism,"[15] "creolization,"[16] "hybridization"[17] are crowding "assimilation," "alienation," "ambivalence" out of the forum of ideas. A revolution in thought is going on, I'm telling myself, drifting off. Modes of inquiry are being redevised, conceptual systems over-turned, new knowledges emerging, while I thrash about in tangled sheets, too groggy to turn off the TV.

NOTES

1. *Drop Squad* is a 1994 satiric film about a group of African Americans who kidnap other African Americans who are thought to be disloyal to the race and try to "deprogram" them. The DROP in the name stands for Deprogram-ming and Restoration Of Pride. Spike Lee was the executive producer of the film.

2. Chesney Henry "Chet" Baker Jr. (1929–1988) was a white American jazz trumpeter and vocalist known for his "cool jazz" sound.

3. *Let's Get Lost* is a film documentary by Bruce Weber made in 1988 about Chet Baker's life, including his debilitating heroin addiction.

4. Sam Yette (1929–2011) was an author, journalist, and photojournalist. In 1971, he published the controversial book *The Choice: The Issue of Black Survival in America*, claiming the United States government was secretly supporting genocidal actions against African Americans.

5. *The Destruction of Black Civilization* (1971–1974) was written by Chancellor Williams (1893–1992). It is a major Afrocentric text, positing that ancient Egypt was largely a Black civilization.

6. Peckerwood is a derogatory name for a White person, usually from the South.

7. A kufi (cufi) is a cap worn primarily by West African elders. In America, many African Americans wear it as a sign of cultural pride.

8. Brer Rabbit is a trickster figure derived from African folklore, who uses his intellect to defeat more powerful characters. He is a hero in African American folklore. To slip the yoke means to escape capture. Ralph Ellison wrote an essay "Change the Joke and Slip the Yoke" (*Partisan Review*, 1958).

9. The UNIA (The Universal Negro Improvement Association) is a Black Nationalist organization that was led by Jamaican/American Black Nationalist Marcus Garvey (1886–1940).

10. Father Divine (ca. 1876–1965) was an African American spiritual leader who founded the International Peace Mission Movement,

which reached its peak in the 1930s. The group's few remaining members treat Father Divine's mansion in Woodmont, located in the Philadelphia suburb of Gladwyne, as a shrine.

11. Double-consciousness is the famous phrase created by W. E. B. Du Bois in *The Souls of Black Folk* (1903). It describes the "twoness" many African Americans experience because of racial prejudice.

12. The Counterintelligence Program is a covert Federal Bureau of Investigation operation designed to discredit organizations, often by using illegal tactics, that it considered subversive to American interests. It operated from 1956 to 1971.

13. Chris Columbus hype: Pennsylvania-born filmmaker who directed such commercial hits as *Home Alone* (1990), *Mrs. Doubtfire* (1993), and several Harry Potter films. It could also refer to the myth of American's greatness established from its "discovery" by the explorer of the same name. North Christopher Columbus is also the name of a major boulevard leading to Penn's Landing. The name of the boulevard has drawn the ire of many residents of the city.

14. "Undermine 'em with grins": The quotation is from the first chapter of Ralph Ellison's novel *Invisible Man* (1952). The words are spoken by the narrator's grandfather while on his deathbed. The words and their potential meaning haunt the narrator throughout the novel.

15. Syncretism: the merging of once different religions, traditions, and ideologies.

16. Creolization is a blending of a colonial language and an indigenous one in a contact situation. It refers to the process of acculturation whereby Amerindian European, Amerindian, and African traditions are blended to create a new culture in the Americas.

17. Cultural hybridization is a blending of elements from different cultures. It is a process in which someone inhabits two identities often emanating from a situation of forced contact.

BIBLIOGRAPHY

Evans, Mari, ed. *Black Women Writers (1950–1980): A Critical Evaluation.* Garden City, NY: Anchor Press / Doubleday, 1984.

Goodnough, Abby. "Toni Cade Bambara, a Writer and Documentary Maker Dies at 56." *New York Times,* December 11, 1995, 10.

Holmes, Janet Linda. *A Joyous Revolt: Toni Cade Bambara, Writer and Activist.* Santa Barbara, CA: Praeger, 2014.

Holmes, Janet Linda, and Cheryl Wall, eds. *Savoring the Salt: The Legacy of Toni Cade Bambara.* Philadelphia: Temple University Press, 2007.

Tate, Claudia. *Black Women Writers at Work.* Chicago: Haymarket Books, 1983.

Diane McKinney-Whetstone, from *Tumbling* (1996)

Diane McKinney-Whetstone was born in West Philadelphia in 1953 and continues to live in the city. Her family had a successful catering business, and her father served as a state senator for two terms. McKinney-Whetstone holds a BA in English from the University of Pennsylvania. She has published six novels; the manuscript for her first, *Tumbling* (1996), was awarded a Pennsylvania Council on the Arts grant. She has taught in the University of Pennsylvania's creative writing program.

Like most of McKinney-Whetstone's works, *Tumbling* is set in Philadelphia, this time in the South Street / South Philly area in the 1940s and '50s, and reflects stories told to her by her parents. McKinney-Whetstone's novel explores the life of a middle-class couple, Noon, a god-fearing woman, and Herbie, her club-loving husband. Tensions, of course, exist between the two as their marriage remains unconsummated due to a dark secret in Noon's past, leading Herbie to seek physical pleasure from Ethel, a blues singer. Their lives change forever when a baby, named Fannie by Herbie, is left on their doorstep. Led by the Reverend Schell, the couple are encouraged to take the fledgling into their home and into the community. Later in the novel, the proposed crosstown expressway threatens this sense of community. McKinney-Whetstone provides an excellent insight into the sights, sounds, and smells of this Black neighborhood by creating a story that demonstrates the power of family and community love to help heal the wounds of the past. It is "a novel about the successful exercise of personal and communal will to resist and even reverse urban processes that threaten the integrity of individuals, the family, and the neighborhood."[1]

⁓

FROM CHAPTER 1

The black predawn air was filled with movement. Its thin coolness rushed through the streets of South Philly, encircling the tight, sturdy row houses. In 1940 the blocks were clean and close. The people who lived here scrubbed their steps every morning until the sand in the concrete sparkled like diamond pins. Then some went to work mopping floors and cooking meals for rich folks, or cleaning fish at the dock, or stitching fine leather shoes or pinch-pleated draperies at the factories on the north side. Some answered phones or crumpled paper for the government. Some tended house and nursed babies. A few were really nurses. One or two taught school. Unless it was the weekend. On the weekend the blocks came to life. They'd cram into Club Royale, where redheaded olives danced in gold-colored liquid. And the music flowed like bubbly. And brown faces laughed for real, not the mannered tee-hees of the workday, but booming laughs. And Sunday they shouted in church and felt the sweet release where grand hats rocked, and high heels stomped or went clickety-clack depending on how the spirit hit.

Right now they slept. Especially if they'd been at Club Royale earlier. They were in a heavy sleep as the moving air wrapped around their chimneys, and stroked their curtained windows, and slid down their banisters. It breezed past the church where the bricks were gray and jutted into the dark air and even shone from the dew that was just beginning to settle. It shimmied over Pop's, the corner store famous for its glass jars filled with sweet pickled pigs' feet. And then dipped past the funeral home owned by the Saunderses, where the Model T hearse was usually parked out front. It blew over the playground where a makeshift swing hanging with tufted, braided clothesline swayed to the rhythm of the dancing air. And then turned on through a short block where Cardplaying-Rose lived; the light from her basement meant that kings and queens and aces were slapping her fold-up table adorned with piles of red and green chips for quarters and dollars and IOUs. And then the night air moved all through Lombard Street and bounced up and down the long block where Noon and Herbie lived. Right now it caressed a brown cardboard box being slipped onto Noon and Herbie's middle step.

Noon was fast asleep this Saturday morning. Still two hours before her faithful church bells would give her the early risers' wake-up call. So she didn't hear quick swishes of leather against concrete rushing straight to her house.

Nor did she stir when the rustling sound got louder as sweaty palms shifted the box gently along the steps so that it wouldn't tip. But if Noon or anyone else on the whole of Lombard Street had been only half awake, she surely would have heard the singular whisper tinged with a sadness that was dark as the night. The air heard it, and swallowed it up, and whipped around the corner to push Herbie on home.

Herbie was wide-awake, walking through the streets as the air nudged him on. Heading in after a night of clapping to the beat, then hanging later at Royale because he'd heard Ethel might be coming back, then stepping outside of Royale and running right into Bow, the barber who cut hair at the end of Herbie's block, and having to suffer through a lecture about the wages of sin and ignorance, Herbie appreciated the way the moving air was at his back. He needed a push to get home. The red and white candy cane lamp in front of Bow's barbershop made Herbie mad again as he thought about Bow's finger wagging in his face and his voice all in his ear saying, "Boy, you got a good wife, stop trying to live the fast life, chasing women and hanging in those clubs."

He got some nerve, Herbie thought. He ought to be glad my sweet, pretty mama taught me to respect my elders, or I would have yanked his finger and told him to mind his own business. Herbie kicked at the air as he walked past Bow's. He didn't consider himself a woman chaser anyhow. There was his wife, Noon. And there was Ethel. At least there had been Ethel. He hadn't seen her in several months. But now the thought of her roundness filled his head, the way she moved like fire made the air crackle when she laughed. The thought warmed him as he pushed up Lombard Street toward home.

The air was moving faster now, impatiently, rushing ahead of Herbie and then doubling back to egg him on. He pulled his jacket closer and picked up his pace. His house was in the middle of a long block. For the past year he and his wife, Noon, lived here with people mostly like him who used to live in the South too. Georgia, South Carolina, Alabama, Mississippi. They brought their dialects, their gospel music and blues, their love for Jesus, children, and candied yams. A few had been here all along, so they said. Like Noon's pastor, Reverend Schell. "My daddy's daddy worked for Harriet Tubman," Reverend Schell was often heard to proclaim. The stories of the perilous journeys on the "Railroad" made for rich metaphor many a Sunday about making it to the promised land. Except that Herbie got it secondhand from Noon. He rarely went to church, didn't particularly care for Reverend Schell's dramatics, and had a few "railroad" stories of his own, as he was a redcap, a porter, at the Thirtieth Street train station.

The air was really dancing now, and whistling, and made Herbie step even faster. Noon would be asleep, he was sure of that. Just as well, he thought, with her problem and all when it came time for them to mix pleasures, just as well. When he thought about Noon, his guilt vibrated in his chest like a tuning fork sitting where his lungs should be. Good churchgoing woman she was. Didn't go to card parties or speakeasies. Content to take care of him and her church business and roast a turkey for somebody's wedding or fix chicken for the gathering after somebody's funeral or sew organza² dresses for girls for Easter. Nice things. He was almost sorry he was warmed by thoughts of Ethel. But then he pictured Ethel's lips, the thickness and redness, and her drooping eyes that always seemed to be moaning, "baby, baby," and he thought about Noon and her problem, and Bow's finger wagging in his face, and all he could do was say, "Damn," out loud to only the moving air.

The box sat patiently on the steps as Herbie approached his house. He might have tripped over it except that pink yarn fringes hung over the edges. They rippled in the breeze and startled the night as they moved. They startled Herbie too. "What the hell?" he murmured as he stopped sharply and nudged the box with his foot. He pulled back the pink covering. He peered into the box.

He stood straight up. He pulled at the end of his long, thin nose and rubbed his hand hard across his head. How many beers had he had at Royale? Only two, not even enough to make him miss a step, certainly not enough to make the night do a strangeness on his mind. He reached in his jacket pocket and snatched out a tin filled with red-topped stick matches. He struck a match and cupped his hands to protect the flame from the air that was circling him in wispy drafts. He leaned into the box guided by the fire. A baby. Damn sure was. Somebody had left a baby right here on his steps.

FROM CHAPTER 2

Afternoon came quickly on Saturdays in this part of South Philly. The morning melted from sunrise to afternoon while the neighbors scrubbed the steps outside and poured buckets of bleach and hot water through the back alleys. They shined their windows and did their in-the-house work and then shopped on Ninth Street or South Street or Washington Avenue. One to five was catch-up time: to wonder where the morning went, to sew, to fry hair with a hot comb and a tin of Royal Crown grease, to get in on a card game at Rose's, or a special-call choir rehearsal, to go to Bow's for a cut, Royale for a shot, Pop's for a hoagie, or a car ride to Eden[3] to put flowers on somebody's grave. This Saturday from one until five they crowded into Noon and Herbie's because news of the baby spread as quickly as the morning went.

Reverend Schell came, and Noon's choir member friends, the deacons, people from the block, from around the corner, Big Carl from Royale, and Herbie's buddies from the train station. Somebody brought in a crate of fried chicken, somebody else an army pot filled with potato salad; they brought spirits from the club, coffee from the church. One came with a cradle, another with a large wooden playpen, another with a bag filled up with baby clothes. They piled into the neat Lombard Street row house from the kitchen to the front steps. They sat along the arms of the couch and on the steps and the floor. They clapped and sang, danced worldly dances, prayed holy prayers, and chatted excitedly about the baby in the box.

"Just like that, huh? Box was just sitting on the steps, huh?" Reverend Schell asked, as he sipped at his steaming cup of coffee.

"Just sitting like it was waiting for me to see it," Herbie answered, drinking his chilled wine. "Might have tripped over it in the dark, but they had her all in pink that acted like a light as I was on my way up the steps. Then I picked her up and she started to cry, but I rocked her a little and she got quiet and content like she was just waiting for me to come and rock her."

"You thought about calling the police?" asked Dottie, who lived across the street.

"No need to call the authorities. That child is a gift from God," Reverend Schell boomed. "We got to learn how to handle our own affairs without always getting white folks to intervene."

"Wait a minute," Herbie said slowly. "You saying you think we should keep the chile."

"What else you gonna do with her? Where I come from, which is right here in Philadelphia born and raised, we take care of our own."

"But I thought they were stricter with the laws here in Philadelphia," Herbie said excitedly. Then he called into the dining room, where Noon and a roomful of women were passing the baby from hand to hand.

"Noon," he said, "come on in here. Your reverend is saying we should just keep the baby."

"It's been on my heart to suggest that," Noon spouted as she moved through the throng of people into the living room. "I know down Florida it happened to two families that I know of, somebody left children with them and the people just raised them as their own."

"Well, down in Mississippi," Herbie said, taking the baby from Noon, "everybody raised everybody else's children anyhow. At least it was that way with me since my mama died when I was seven and my daddy was a Pullman porter and away for stretches at a time. My brother and me got all the mothering we needed from any of a number of good-cooking women."

"So y'all in agreement then, right?" Reverend Schell looked from Noon to Herbie. "Y'all gonna keep the baby, right?"

Noon looked at Herbie and smiled, almost shyly. "I was gonna suggest it this morning, but I didn't know how'd you'd take to such a notion so suddenly, having the finances of a baby's upkeep thrust on you."

"You should have spoken it then," Herbie said. "I was thinking along the same lines, but I thought that was a suggestion that should come from you, you being the woman, and the baby's tending to being your responsibility." He moved in close to Noon and handed the baby back to her and then covered his wife's shoulders with his arms. "I just want you to be happy, Noon."

"Seems like it's settled to me," Reverend Schell said. "God bless the new parents."

"Still seem to me like the court or somebody official needs to be involved," Dottie countered. She rested her hand on Herbie's forearm and squeezed it lightly.

"Now let me say something to you, Sister Dottie," Reverend Schell bellowed, raising his hand high. "What's a bunch of white folks gonna do once they get their hands on this baby? They gonna turn her over to a foster family, and I'm telling you the Lord has already handpicked the family. Noon and Herbie have just had a blessing laid at their doorsteps. No need to be second-guessing the hand of God. Sometimes the Lord's work and man's work don't always mesh. And when that happens, I'm going with the Lord every time." He loosened his tie and cleared his throat for preaching.

Herbie reached up to Reverend Schell, who towered over him, grabbed Reverend Schell's cup, and put his arm around his shoulder. "Now Rev, you been a good pastor to my wife this past year that we been here in Philadelphia. And I promise, I do plan to visit you in the House of the Lord one of these Sundays. But Reverend, if you fixing to preach right here, and now, we got to trade off cups 'cause I'm sure gonna need some coffee and I do believe you could benefit from some wine."

The rooms from the kitchen to the front door exploded with laughter. These were downtown folks. Holy Ghost-filled to whiskey-inspired, bartender to deacon, jazz singer to choir member, the separations fell away when there was an occasion for a grand coming together such as this.

"I will say this," Cardplaying-Rose offered, "you won't have to worry 'bout that mother coming back for the chile. Whoever left that chile cared for her. They know just what they doing. Ain't coming back. No offense to you, Reverend, but I saw Queen of Hearts in my reading this morning. Means motherly love, they ain't coming back."

"Sister Rose, I agree the mother won't return, but my source is more reliable than a deck of cards. It's the word of God—"

Rev, Rev, Rev," Herbie cut in. "So what we got to do legally? I mean what about birth certificates?"

"First thing Monday morning"—Reverend Schell placed his hand on Herbie's shoulder as he spoke—"go down to City Hall, to the department that handles birth certificates. Tell them one of your relatives from down South left the baby for you to raise, and you want to do whatever paperwork you need to do so you don't get any of their undereyed looks when it's time for the chile to get enrolled in school. And you sure don't want to have to worry about anybody gathered here saying anything different. To intercede in the workings of God that way might bring damnation to us all. Am I right, Sister Dottie?" He looked over at his shoulder and squinted his eyes at Dottie.

"I was only saying that the law—"

"Damnation! Sister Dottie, am I right?" Reverend Schell cut her off.

"You right, Reverend," Dottie mumbled, trying to shake off the collected gaze of the roomful of people.

"Now you give me your Bible," Reverend Schell said, "and I'm gonna make it legal right now in the sight of God. That's what I love about my God, we don't have to wait till Monday morning to do our business with the Lord."

"Ain't it the truth," someone shouted, until sounds of agreement rippled through the whole house.

"Now, what you gonna call her?" Reverend Schell asked as he patted his breast pocket and then handed the Bible to Herbie. "Left my glasses home, but you can do this part. Just turn the gold-trimmed pages of this beautiful white leather Bible to the one marked 'Birth Certificate,' and you take this with you Monday, let them put their official stamp to it."

The memory of the early morning fell over Herbie like a wave as he moved his fingers over the thin, soft pages. He thought about the way the air felt at his back as he pushed up Lombard Street right before he stumbled upon the box. And then the eyes, as the air fanned the flame of the match and made the baby's eyes dance in the flickering light.

"Fannie!" he shouted. "Her name's Fannie. The name just came to me; it fits her too. That name all right by you, Noon?"

"Fannie it is," Noon answered.

"Just put it right there on the top of that page, then fill in the date and hand it here and let me put my scribble to it," Reverend Schell's voice was filled with jubilation.

They cheered and shouted. Reverend Schell prayed over the infant. Afterward they raised their cups filled with wine, or juice, or milk, or coffee, or vodka, or tea. The merriment even sifted out of the front door, onto the street, where even more people had gathered to hear about the baby in the box.

Noon's round face beamed as she sat propped in the deep green armchair. She ran her hand along the baby's hair and almost seemed to blush. "Fannie," she said again. "Who would've thought it? Noon and Herbie's baby girl named Fannie."

NOTES

1. Rotella, *October Cities*, 194.

2. Organza is a lightweight, sheer, plain-woven garment.

3. Eden Cemetery is located in Collingdale, Pennsylvania, about fourteen miles outside Philadelphia in Delaware County. It was founded in 1902 and is the oldest Black-owned cemetery in the United States. Some notable interments include Jessie Fauset, Octavius Catto, Frances Harper, James Forten, William Still, Marion Anderson, and Absalom Jones.

BIBLIOGRAPHY

Diane McKinney-Whetstone (website). https://www.mckinney-whetstone.com.
Funderburg, Lise. "*Tumbling.*" *New York Times*, June 9, 1996, 9.
Jabari, Asim. "*Tumbling.*" *Washington Post Book World*, May 26, 1996, 4.
Rotella, Carlo. *October Cities: The Redevelopment of Urban Literature.* Berkeley: University of California Press, 1998.
Russell, Margaret. "A Vanishing World: Review of *Tumbling.*" *Women's Review of Books* 13, nos. 10/11 (July 1996): 33.

John Edgar Wideman, from *The Cattle Killing* (1996)

The Cattle Killing conflates several narrative threads. One, from which the title of the book derives, concerns a South African legend. A dream voice advises the Xhosa people to sacrifice their cattle in an attempt to secure a better future. The narrator's dream, however, counsels them against such a killing, which, it is suggested, was implanted by the European enemy. Another major thread is set in 1793 plague-stricken Philadelphia and also shows the need for Blacks to stand up to European treachery. Two sections from this second part of the novel, set in Center City, are included here. The first excerpt involves an unnamed narrator, an itinerant Black preacher, who assisted Richard Allen during the yellow fever epidemic. Allen, to prove himself strong enough to be a leader, must be able to start a new church after the White church, St. George's, refuses to allow Blacks to pray where they wish. This incident is discussed further in the section from Allen's autobiography included in this anthology. The second excerpt is dictated by the blind wife of Dr. Thrush (the historical Dr. Rush) to the Black servant Kathryn and relates how White publisher Mathew Carey attempts to negate the selfless sacrifices that Blacks made in combatting the illness. Again, Allen challenges White prejudice, this time by countering Carey's false narrative by writing his own story, also included here. Wideman wrote about the epidemic in more detail in his short story "Fever" (1989).

—

FROM PART 2

Just as I sit beside you on this bed, speaking to you, the dead speak to me. I feel them as the song says drawing me on, drawing me on. I found Philadelphia, of course. Fought the fever. Met Richard Allen. Old Bishop Allen, dead now, but I see him, he sits on the side of his bed, head bowed, wondering if his God will follow him and Absalom Jones and their flock of dark sheep into the church they are building. Allen is struck—nay, dumbfounded—by the audacity of the task he's undertaken. No one can help him now. Not Absalom Jones. Not the men and women who have placed their faith entirely in him. Though his God is everywhere, sees everything, He's chosen to disappear into the quiet, somber chill of Bishop Allen's bedchamber.

The weight and pinch of Allen's heavy body bears down on the bed's wooden railing. His haunches spread. Pumpkin-colored feet protrude where he stares down past the nightshirt stretched over his knees. Weighty flesh, its liquids and stenches, the rot and sting of its hungers. He shuts his eyes to escape the room, the relentless complaints of his aging body.

He breathes slowly, an eternity between breaths, space for the body to be undone and tumble backward through its many births, the mothers, continents, seas, backward to the stillness of stone, the mud beneath stone that had never dreamed the light he closes his eyes against in this room in Philadelphia, light from the stubby candle in a dish of clay beside his bed.

Father. Father. The enormity of what he set in motion when he led his brethren from the white people's church engulfs him. A mantle of mourning, and he hadn't guessed till this moment the full burden on his shoulders. God had dwelt in the white people's church. Leaving it, he'd turned his back on God. With Satan's pride and scheming arrogance, he'd gathered other rebels around him, multiplied his own sin by leading them away from God's house.

God's house even though the whites had profaned it. He'd never felt God's presence in their church more surely than the morning the deacons of St. George's had ordered him up off his knees, back into a corner of a gallery they'd decided to assign to him and others like him, whose skin, the deacons said, bore the mark of Cain.[1] He'd pitied the church elders. They'd changed shape before his eyes, transformed by the evil clouding their hearts as they laid hands on him and his brethren at prayer. He was ashamed for them, the stewards of the church, his neighbors, men whose names he knew, men whose wives and children watched from the front pews as their men marched among us, disturbing the sanctity of our prayers, attempting to herd us into a corner, separate us from our fellow parishioners, treating us as if they didn't know us, our names, our families. As if they'd never heard God's commandments forbidding the outrage they were committing.

He needed God then. To show him why he shouldn't strike back, resist with all the strength in his body the evil of men forcing themselves betwixt him and his faith.

He needed God as counterweight to balance the evil of what was transpiring in the church. He saw fear in dark faces. Hate in white. The confusion of the children, the helplessness of a few faces unable to be either black or white if it meant they must act out the role to which their color doomed them. He needed God somewhere, somehow keeping track, weaving the ugliness of what was happening into some larger pattern, a tapestry whose myriad scenes he might never grasp but whose overarching design promised that God's hand was active in this, even this.

And what he'd needed had shone forth. A kind of lightness, giddiness when he'd risen to his feet from the boards of the church floor. A whispering in his ear. Yes. Yes. Lightness but also iron. His voice didn't tremble when he spoke to his brethren. He unclenched his fists, his heart. Now *he* was standing, touching people's shoulders, nudging, hugging, guiding, gathering, moving the others in a body, not to some shameful margin but out the church door, heads held higher than when they'd entered.

Yes. God was there. A rock he'd leaned on. Pushed into a corner by evil, the power of evil rampant, he'd found that the seeming absence of God was God's best proof. The pang of needing Him, the prospect of a world without Him, evil pressing down, no light, no hope, the impossibility of coping in such a world, where evil has the power to consume you, to consume the world—that pang of urgent need and utter desolation, that stab in the heart, reveals Him.

God surely there in the building white people had erected. His love imminent in the dumb, humble things of wood and tallow and cloth, even as His presence turns water to wine, wine to blood, changes minutes and hours spent inside the church to time without beginning or end. Yet in his stiff-necked pride he'd led his people away from a holy abode of grace. Away from Canaan, back into the wilderness from which God had brought them safely out. Away from an ark of safety into what. An unhallowed, unpaid-for house, so hastily constructed the green lumber of the benches sweats pitch.

Allen sat on the edge of his bed thinking these thoughts and might be sitting still except he heard a voice telling him something like a story.

You cannot lead, Allen, unless you turn your back on God's house. Unless you promise to deliver to the others what in your pride you saw fit to seek for yourself—a new beginning, a new tabernacle where the holy presence you deserted will reappear. Earth, Allen. The step into darkness, the leap. The others believed you, amened you, pledged to follow you, and now you cower in the gloomy chamber, sorry for yourself, frightened in the depths of your soul as you consider a simple truth. Is truth so unbearable. Are you uncertain now of your goal. Speak your fear aloud, Allen; will God indeed accompany you to this new house of worship you are abuilding.

In your anger, your fervor (or was in vanity, Allen, phrase-making; a desire to be praised even when you know you don't deserve it—the need to be viewed as a certain kind of man in spite of the fact you know you are not such a man), you never doubted you were sinned against when they tried to pen you like goats in the church's rear gallery, nor doubted that God would follow you and those others if you deserted St George's. In the righteousness of your grievance, the mean hypocrisy of the deacons, no ambiguity lurked. The actions of the church elders mocked God. You sought only justice, fairness, no more no less than the church was obliged to suffer you, unless it dishonored the covenant with the Almighty.

When you marched out, marched away, admit, Allen, in your secret heart you hoped the entire congregation, black and white, would rise and march with you in affirmation of God's law, the holy community of His Word. Then the procession would not have ended in some sticky green place but would have danced along the Philadelphia streets like a cleansing wind. When you arrived again at the sacred portal through which you had departed, swelled now to a multitude by the spirit no one could resist, you would pack the church, send up glad hosannas of great joy resounding in every corner of the land.

Pleasing perhaps even to God's ear, to His eye, as you knelt to thank Him for sundering us one from the other, black from white, rich from poor, man from woman, age from youth, so we might find ourselves, finally, so gloriously conjoined once more. As He intended. All creation worshipping Him, one flesh, under one roof.

The voice, the bright vision fades, Allen is alone again, an old man on his knees. God's absence confirmed by evil everywhere raging. The need.

He'd slid from the edge of the bed like some soulless cluster of dirt and stones loosed from a hillside when the earth shivers. Yes, His flock will gather at the new building, a blacksmith's shed horses had hauled to a vacant lot. But does he have the power to summon God. Do they. God promised him nothing. Yet Allen had coaxed his African brethren, prodded, enticed, harangued them as if surely, surely God would be waiting when they crossed over to the promised land.

In the darkness, the quiet of the room (pumpkin breath wheezing, part of the quiet, the figure against which the ground of quiet defines itself), he wishes to be a white man. Holds the wish long enough for it to become a wet intimacy his tongue traces inside his pursed mouth, inside his lower lip, against his teeth, the sour, vacant spaces where teeth once rooted. A wish he would whisper aloud—*wouldn't you be one of them if you could*—as a half-serious question to someone in the room, if there were someone he could trust, someone who could smile coldly, understand, and, never say anything to anyone about the bishop's confession. If that's what the thought was.

The thought curdles, a foulness up from his gut, compresses in his throat. He expels it, a hissing jet that buckles the candle flame, nearly extinguishing it. He stares at the pale, wrinkled stub, the mincing yellow tip.

He despises his duplicity. Despises the cowardice bringing him low. To this shameful impasse. A frightened soul begging for certainty, for supernatural assurance and signs. He would walk in God's way. He would be a warrior in the Lord's army, yet he holds back from the fray, petitions God to storm ahead, banners flying, clearing the field of enemies, of peril. He's prepared to sacrifice, to commit himself and his people to battle, but he's waiting for the clear blast of God's trumpet to lead him.

In his heart he does not wish to be white, to be one of them. He's the man he is. Not some other. Yet he is praying for an easier way than the way opening up for him. Why has he been orphaned in this strange land, in this unimaginable city. Divided first from others, then from himself. He does not secretly yearn to be one of the whites. No. No. He is praying for a lifting of the burden that crushes them all, black and white, in their tortured, bitter dealings one with the other. He cannot change what he is or they cannot change what they are, and he cannot pray to God to wipe white people off the face of the earth and also keep his heart free for Christ's mercy, Christ's love, so he is not wishing to be white, but if he calls on Heaven to purge whatever it is the whites fear and hate in him, must it also be a prayer for sweet annihilation.

He hears the mighty pounding of waves. On both sides of him like a million roaring horses the sea curls back, white underbelly and flashing green hooves, the roar and menace in check as he stands on a dry highway between steep canyon walls of churning water. God's will has opened this path through the sea and planted him here as a pilgrim, as witness, pioneer and point man, and he must summon his brethren to follow him, to trust this strait, dry, narrow way, but mist blinds, the sting of salt spray, the shrieking gulls, thunder of ponderous waves slamming against the thin air restraining them. He is perplexed, frightened, stunned by the tumult. Though his feet are on dry land and the miracle that brought him this far is undeniable, he falters, begs for a vision of the new world at the far end of this threatening path—the earth restored, flood receded, peace.

Like Lot's wife,[2] he is doomed if he turns around. With the eyes in back of his head he counts his people, names them, the meager column of African folk, women, men, children exiting through the church door. He shouts to send his voice above the roaring of furious waves. His people are behind him. If he doubts, if he halts again, the stony waters will come crashing down with the force of mountains.

He cannot hold the posture of prayer. He will not beg. He will not grovel. He will not forget what brought him to his resolve. Unwieldy saddles of meat, the groaning bones and grinding joints collapsed in a head beside the bed, he must refashion into a man. He is no thing of clay waiting for a spirit's breath. He must rise on his own two feet. Arise and go. Where, Allen. Where.

***

Five days blank except for wooden jottings—did this, did that, thus and so still is to be done—I've been reminded sternly that neither time nor peace of mind is mine to summon at will—and both are necessary, I find, to this writing affair.

A great commotion boils in the city—now that the worst horrors of the fever seem to have subsided, the town's appetite for scandal has revived full-blown—a letter authorized by a Mr. Mathew Carey attacks the Negroes who served so valiantly during the late calamity—at the height of the emergency Dr. Thrush's letters daily commended the work of black nurses who tended the dead from the city streets—now Mr. Carey impugns them—accuses the Negroes of charging—nay, extorting—piratous rates for their services—profiting heartlessly from the misery and helplessness of the afflicted.

Carey's bill of particulars against the city's Negroes, alleging blackmail, assaults, robbery, even murder, was recently published as a pamphlet and widely circulated—what's surprising is not that one unhappy soul would conjure up such a distorted picture—who knows how the plague damaged him, who could guess what wrongs, real or imagined, some black person committed against the author or he visited upon a Negro, or what personal grievance became transformed into general enmity toward an entire race— what shocks me is how many citizens, ignoring the evidence of their own eyes and ears, including many who themselves doubtless benefited from the charity and ministrations of the Negro nurses, have embraced Carey's libels as well.

I blush as I dictate this news, dear Kathryn—a hot flush of shame rises to my cheeks—*as well it should, milady*—it frightens and humbles me that we should have learned so little from our late season of suffering—God warned us, set the plague upon us to demonstrate our unworthiness, our weakness, our dependence on His divine mercy, and what use do we make of the lesson—as soon as danger passes, we turn like cowardly curs on the weak and helpless among us.

Two days ago an emissary from a Bishop Allen of the African Church— the Negroes call themselves sometimes by one name, sometimes by another—I could not pry a preference from our visitor—*Why have you never asked my preference*—arrived at our door seeking assistance from Dr. Thrush in this Carey matter—the Negroes believe they are in peril—*yes, yes, yes*— unless leading citizens such as Dr. Thrush step forward and publicly repudiate Carey's charges, the Negroes fear their community, already beleaguered, may be struck a fatal blow—Dr. Thrush summarized to me the contents of their letter—they say the fever hit hardest in those poor, crowded streets and alleys near the river, and that the rate of mortality in that district where most Negroes reside is far higher than anywhere else in the city—people there are starving today, they say, many too ill to work, with little or no work available for the able-bodied, families deprived of wage-earners by the fever's winnowing hand, hapless orphans no cradle but the cold ground—if only half of the Negroes' contentions are true, they have been mightily sinned against—I shudder at the cruel irony—those who suffered most, those who fought hardest to allay its blows, are now being blamed for the plague.

Though he never subscribed to the theory that Negroes from the West Indies brought the plague to our shores, Dr. Thrush himself was part of the chorus insisting upon the Negroes' immunity, thereby denying them assistance until he witnessed with his own eyes how the deadly tide of fever had swept through that neighborhood of hovels, warrens, cellars, of taverns and houses of sin where the poorest folk, Negroes the poorest of these, are trapped.

Now Mr. Carey's libels will imperil them even more—set them apart as pariahs, criminals—in my heart I believe we all, every one of us, must answer one day to our Maker for the un-Christian manner in which we have separated the black folk from ourselves—this latest episode one more instance of a habit so ingrained it has become second nature—I think of my worthy Kathryn—how but for fortune's smile she might be trembling in a cave by the river, helpless, afraid, awaiting the punishment Carey and his rabble are determined to exact.

Your people have a steadfast friend, dear Kate, in Dr. Thrush—you must recall the letter from him you read to me during the last week of September, when the bells mourning the dead tolled from dawn to dusk and hurried missives from my dear husband our sole communication for days at a time—the exacting, soul-wrenching work of saving the city removed all superficial distinctions among men, he wrote—my good husband and his dark angels of mercy welcomed—nay, implored—to attend the highest and lowest citizens—remember how he recounted in his delightful style a conversation with one of his favorite Negro nurses—I can recite his words exactly, an iron memory perhaps one benefit dropped on the scale to balance my lost sight. Huh! Mama. We black folks have come into demand at last.

Always one who judged me on merit, not birth or caste, Dr. Thrush confided to me his profound respect for the skill, patience and compassion he discovered in his black assistants, toiling side by side with them long into the seemingly endless nights—I did not remind him of your example, Kathryn, here in the bosom of his own household—I suspect his silence on your virtues when he waxes eloquent on the potential of the Negro race indicates how completely he regards you as a member of our family, inseparably one of us.

You may rest assured he will speak out for what is right—he will stand beside your people again in their hour of need—*one of us, you say. When there are two, will we still be one of you.*

NOTES

1. Cain was considered "marked" by God for killing his brother Abel (Genesis 4:1–18). Many Whites thought the dark complexion of people of African descent was a manifestation of this mark.

2. Lot's wife: The story of Lot's wife is told in Genesis 19. She was turned into a pillar of salt after disobeying God's order to not look back at the destruction of the city of Sodom.

BIBLIOGRAPHY

Birat, Kathie. "'All Stories Are True': Prophecy, History and Story in 'The Cattle Killing.'" *Callaloo* 22, no. 3 (Summer 1999): 629–43.

Birkerts, Sven. "The Fever Days." *New York Times*, November 3, 1996, sec. 7, 20.

Cryderman, Kevin. "Fire for a Ghost: Blind Spots and the Dissection of Race in John Edgar Wideman's 'The Cattle Killing.'" *Callaloo* 34, no. 4 (Fall 2011): 1047–67.

Lynch, Lisa. "The Fever Next Time: The Race of Disease and the Disease of Racism in John Edgar Wideman." *American Literary History* 14, no. 4 (2002): 776–804.

David Bradley, "The Station" (Previously unpublished, 1997)

Bradley's "The Station" is a meditation on the life and history of 30th Street Station (since 2020 formally titled the William H. Gray III South Street Station), the busy Amtrak, SEPTA, and New Jersey Transit Station located on 2955 Market Street in University City, which opened in 1933. It replaced the smaller Broad Street Station in Center City. The sketch is told through the voice of the personified station. Bradley's keen ear for the vernacular is again apparent. This is a previously unpublished work that was first aired on WHYY-TV-12 as part of the special First Person Philadelphia in 1997. Conceived and directed by Emmy-winning producer/director Glenn Holsten, the ninety-minute drama features a dozen separate monologues written by Philadelphia poets, novelists, and playwrights. Each is set in, and inspired by, a Philadelphia location and delivered by a local actor. I thank David for generously allowing me to publish it here, a "scoop" as he said.

—

Ma bestest time is the early bright, when light comes pourin' in through them East End windows, sweet as warm red clover honey, with a little taste tipped in. Light dances offa all this marble an' then whips up there ten stories to the ceilin', an' does the low-down get-down with all that gold—some calls it gilt, but I says it's gold; either way, it's a sight to see.

'Course, mornin' ain't always that spectacular. Some days, light drags in like bad breath and baggy britches—ain't got no shine to it, you know? Still, it sorta glows, soft an' pretty, like a pearl. An' then there's mornin's when the light's so weak it'd die if it had the strength, an' all you got to see by is these here 'lectric lights. They nice, all bronze an' fancy glass, but it ain't natural light, an' it draws attention to that there War Memorial.[1] No disrespect, but that is one depressin' statue. Forty-foot angel totin' a dead soldier like he was a sack a mail. Maybe that's just my attitude. Them weak-light mornin's make me blue.

But then somebody starts coffee brewin', an' the smell makes me want to knock ma Pappy over. Then the folks starts stumblin' in, lookin' for a cup of that good-to-last-drop, buyin' tickets an' the mornin' paper. Then a Big Voice say: NOW ARRIVING, TRACK NUMBER FOUR, TRAIN NUMBER TWELVE, MAKING STATION STOPS AT NEWARK AND NEW YORK. ALL ABO-ARD! Ain't nobody but this skinny white dude, got a loudspeaker slavin' for him, but in here it bounces an' booms around—sounds like the Voice of God. Then the clock hits five-ohfive, an' comes a rumble down below, an' a bong, bong, bong, an' a hiss, an' a screech, an' then ka-chunk, an' a thousand tons a iron settles down to rest, an' makes me feel full up. Tells me why I'm here. Tells me why I been here goin' on sixty-two years—some says sixty-seven, but I says sixty-two.

Some can't get with bein' one place all that time. They say it's borin'. Say I'm borin', too. Well, I says, trains is crazy. Number Twelve go North, she hardly slow for Trenton. She come back South she's Number Seventeen, or Number One Twenty-seven, or Number who-the-hell-knows, an' she not only stops at Trenton, she stops at Princeton Junction, too. That's how trains are. If they didn't run on tracks, no tellin' where they'd go. Used to be they'd try to keep to schedule. Then the government took over; now, these trains can roll in ten minutes late, an' still say they On Time. Ain't got no discipline. Don't show no respect, neither. The Betsy Ross[2]—they put her on in '76, for the Bicentennial—had the nerve to say to me, "Boy, are you still here?" I says, "Yeah, girl, I'm still here, an' it's a good thing for you, 'cause if wasn't, how you gone know when you done arrived?"

"I ain't playin'. If I ain't here, how folks gone know where a train gone stop? An' where folks gone wait when Number Whatever-She-Be-Callin'-Herself-This-Trip decide to be so late even the government got to admit it? Folks depends on me moren they depends on trains. Besides, what would I want to go someplace for? Plenty to see in here.

Look, there, at Mr. Metroliner—three-piece, button-down. Pays twice the money to save twenty minutes, an' the train half an hour late anyways. Leastways he got sense enough to spend the time gettin' a spit-shine. Gone get there late, but gone get there straight.

An' watch that Shoe Man work. Board a Health won't let 'em spit no more, so he got to use tap water, but that brush still go di-dee-swish, di-dee-swish, rag still go di-dee-whap, di-dee whap, an' he tell folks goin' by, "Can't make a dollar 'less your shoes shine, mister. Can't make a million 'thout a good hot wax!"

Now here come a College Kid, truckin' home a ton a books he ain't studyin' studyin', an' a duffle bag full a dirty threads for his Moms to wash. An' check the corner: a Hot Lip Couple, tongues so far down each other's throats their ears be clogged. They can't hear the Big Voice; first they know the train come in is when they feel that rumble through the floor and he gots to book it down the stairs, callin' love trash over his shoulder.

An' here come the Fambly, up the stairs, Mama, Papa, half-a-dozen kids, comin' to see Gram an' Gramps. They all huggin', smilin', cryin'. Gram's face lit up like early bright, Gramps sayin', They don't need no Red Cap, there ain't but fo'teen bags.

I pokes fun, but I loves these folks. An you know who I loves most? Ones like that gal yonder, vinyl garment bag an' train case she musta borrowed from her Grandmama, comin' in from East Jesus by way a' South Hell. All my years, I seen 'em come, boys an' girls, an' some that ain't sure yet; different sizes, different colors, cheap suitcases, cardboard cartons tied with twine, lookin' for they ain't sure what, an' their eyes be wide, tryin' to see everything at once, an' every one of 'em is certain they gone catch one fine big city break. Don't a one of 'em think they'll end up goin' back knocked up, knocked out, knocked galley-west.

Maybe I ain't never been nowhere, but I know what it's like to be all primed with promises. I was gone be an airport—land planes up on the roof. I was gone be a hospital—had three thousand square feet set aside. I was gone be a mortuary, bury the mistakes. An' I was gone be a chapel, too, to pray 'em into Heaven. I was gone be a lot of things. What I am is here.

An' don't tell me I come up short; I spent some dark decades findin' out what short's about, years when mornin' didn't make no nevermind because them windows was so damn dirty, and the coffee come from a roach coach, and over where the cops is now, there was this lunch counter, served day-old Tasteekake,[3] soft pretzels that was hard, an' hot dogs that laid on that roller-grill all day turnin' green—man, them dogs was nasty. An' there was all these pigeons flyin' around, an' you know what they'd do. Them days I actually felt sorry for that angel. But then Congress let 'em spend a hundred million bucks to fix things up, and now I'm clean, Jack. Clean as the board of health. Cleanern Congress, if what I hear is true.

Late dark be my worstest time. I guess I am gettin' old. Used to be, I didn't mind waitin' up for the midnight train—The Night Owl,[4] they calls her, now—but these days by eleven, I start to feelin' blue. I think 'bout nineteen hundred an' thirty-four, the year I started out; wasn't no darker year than that, stayed dark, too; took a war to get things hummin', which is about as dark as dark can get.

I think about the thousands gone—Vent Man, who panhandled the West Portico for twenty years, till they run him off, an' Sylvia, The Duck Lady,[5] God rest her foul-mouthed Tourette-Syndrome soul, an' three wars worth of soldier boys, some with girls who kissed 'em goodbye like there wasn't no tomorrow—which, for some there wasn't—an' some boys who didn't have girls, so the women tried to cheer 'em up—USO, an' Doughnut Dollies[6] an' the Ladies of the Night. An' the old Red Caps, not these wimps with handtrucks; brother men with coolie blood, could tote them fo'teen bags an' still keep a hand out for a tip.

And the scammers! Ain't got them no more, but once upon a time, you could get skunked in here in a deuce of ticks. I don't mean no lowdown jeffers;[7] I mean artists, could slip your roll out your sliders an' your stretcher wouldn't even know. There was one boy who'd lift your chimer, then ask you for the time a day, an' when you found your watch done walked, he'd say, "Why, Cuz, that's terrible; what is the world comin' to!" One day the Nabs caught his slick butt, took him out to Western Penitentiary[8] on the Broadway Limited.[9]

An' I think about trains—not these electrified, stainless steel, red-white-and blue, never-on-time government issue; the old trains, steam and diesel, Brunswick Green, True Black, Tuscan Red with Buff Yellow trim. Trains with names that sound like somethin'—the Broadway, the Silver sisters, Meteor,[10] Comet[11] an' Star,[12] triplets, but I knew how to tell 'em apart. An' The Liberty Limited.[13] Man, that train had class. Never late, that train; she had some discipline and pride. Just the name could get me goin'. It sounded like a train runnin' flat out. Liberty Limited, Liberty Limited, clickety-clack, ty-clack, ty-clack; clicketyclack, ty-clack, ty-clack; Course I never heard that. Down below, goin' slow over the points, she just go: ca-thunk, ca-thunk. But I used to dream about her runnin' free through open country . . . Man, I loved that train! And sometimes I'd think . . . well, it don't matter what I thought. They decommissioned her in '57.

Late dark come, I start thinkin' 'bout things like that. But I ain't really sad, you know? You get to be my age—which is sixty-two, thank you—you just glad you got your memories. Hell, you glad you still around. Stations do die, you know. But there's worse things than the wreckin' ball; ask Reading Terminal what it feels like to get turned into a Market. I ain't in no hurry, mind, and until it happens, I'll be gettin' all I can get, but when my time comes, I'ma be ready, 'cause the way I see it, there's got to be a last train, an' somebody got to ride it.

An' here she come a-rumblin' now, twenty minutes behind schedule—another on-Amtrak-time performance. Big Voice say, NOW ARRIVING, an' there they go, all the po' zoned out jaspers,[14] couldn't find a heifer would have 'em, so now they shaggin' it on the last train home. Time for me to get some shut-eye, be rested for the early bright, an' Number Twelve, at five-oh-five— if you fool enough to believe timetables.

But hold up. Here comes some boy a runnin'. I remember him! Come in a few years back, full of hope an' hot peppers. Now look at him: run down heels, shinyseat suit, bookin' it for the train back to East Jesus with his tail between his legs. Well, don't worry 'bout it, brother. Gone home. Get yourself together. Take a little time. Then come on back, give the big city another try. Odds are I'll be waitin'.

There he go, down the stairs. The Big Voice don't say nothin'; skinny white dude's in the union, so he clocks out on time. But I feel it in the marble, an' I hear it in the steel: NOW DEPARTING. ALL ABOARD. Amen.

NOTES

1. The War Memorial, dedicated to the 1,307 Pennsylvania Railroad workers who died in World War II, is located on the main concourse of the 30th Street Station. The twenty-eight-foot bronze statue depicts the archangel Michael lifting up the soul of a dead soldier. The statue is named *Angel of Resurrection*.

2. *Betsy Ross* was a train put on the Northeast Regional Amtrak service.

3. TASTYKAKE is a brand of snack foods. It originated in Philadelphia in 1914 and remains popular.

4. The *Night Owl* train operated along Amtrak's Northeast corridor between Washington and Boston. It ran from 1972 to 1995 and was the only Northeast Corridor train that offered sleeper service.

5. The Duck Lady was a rumpled-looking woman who made sounds like a duck and frequently was seen on the University of Pennsylvania campus and in West Philadelphia, among other places, in the 1970s. It was felt she may have had Tourette Syndrome.

6. The Doughnut Dollies were a group of American women who volunteered to serve during the Vietnam War through the Red Cross. They would provide snacks and entertain the troops.

7. Jeffers: a derogatory name for Black people.

8. Western Penitentiary, also known as State Correctional Institution, was a low to mid-level institution, and was located in Pittsburgh. It operated from the 1820s until 2017. The penitentiary held many Confederate prisoners during the Civil War years.

9. The *Broadway Limited* was operated by the Pennsylvania Railroad that ran between New York and Chicago from 1912 to 1995.

10. The *Silver Meteor* operates between New York and Miami. It began operations in 1939 and continues to operate today via Amtrak.

11. The *Silver Comet* began service in 1947 and ran from New York to Birmingham, Alabama. Service was phased out and ceased completely in 1969.

12. The *Silver Star* operates between New York and Miami. It shares many stops with the *Silver Meteor*, but makes additional stops, mostly in North Carolina.

13. The *Liberty Limited* was operated by the Pennsylvania Railroad and operated from Washington to Chicago from 1925 to 1957.

14. Jaspers are fools or simpletons.

Philadelphia in the Twenty-First Century and Beyond (2000 to the Present)

Recent years have brought increasing gentrification, which had begun in the 1960s and '70s. The influx of younger Whites has slowed the flight from the city, especially in Center City. Now, Philadelphia has the third-most-populated downtown area in the country. Increasingly, the downtown and surrounding neighborhoods of Society Hill, Bella Vista, and Old City, among other areas in the city, have seen the encroachment of young, often White, professionals, displacing the older, frequently African American, residents from their homes. Property taxes have increased, and the cost of living in these gentrified areas has skyrocketed. Old neighborhood ties were broken, and communities disintegrated. Gentrification also reduced the city's available affordable housing stock by 20 percent.[1]

Over the past fifty years, and increasingly in the twenty-first century, immigration has also grown at a rapid pace, causing the population to swell overall. The African American population has grown even faster. By the 1990s, non-Hispanic Whites became a minority in the city for the first time. In 2015, they made up 35 percent of the city's population, while non-Hispanic Blacks constituted 41 percent.[2] Despite the influx of Whites to certain areas, this demographic shift of the population is likely to continue.

One reason Whites have left the city is its generally weak public school system. Segregation within the system had long been widespread, although such practice technically had ended by 1881. Inevitably, however, most public schools were largely populated by Blacks, and Whites tended to go to the better-funded schools.[3] "In 2014, only 15 percent of public-school students were non-Hispanic whites, attending mostly all-white schools."[4] The 2008 recession also hit Philadelphia especially hard, reducing school resources even further. One encouraging note is a higher graduation rate for Black high school students, though the rate for Black males is still abysmal.

Public housing is one area of some improvement. Many of the older projects have been replaced with row houses. The Housing Choice Voucher Program (once known as Section 8) helped subsidize living space in market-rate units. By 2015, some eighty thousand people were housed in Pennsylvania Housing Authority programs.[5] Mayor John Street (2000–2008), the city's second Black mayor, implemented the Neighborhood Transformation Initiative, which improved some city conditions, including the creation of thousands of units of public housing. The plan met resistance, though, from those whose homes were allotted for demolition. During Street's time in office, money from increasing property taxes helped balance the city's budget. Homeownership among Blacks increased, but more than half of these owners ended up with subprime mortgage loans.

Michael Nutter (2008–16), the city's third Black mayor, had the misfortune of having the Great Recession occur during his first term in office. Unemployment rose, particularly among Blacks, and it has been slow to recover. Many of the jobs that are available are in the low-wage sector. Fiscal troubles curtailed some of Nutter's most ambitious projects, including increased funding for education and reducing crime. He was, however, able to make significant improvements in several areas of social service and increased housing.[6] He also reorganized the police force, helped improve the high school graduation rate, and took steps toward improving the environment.

Cherelle Parker became Philadelphia's fourth Black and first female mayor in 2024. She and future Philadelphia mayors face a daunting task. Many public officials devote much of their energy to Center City and other gentrifying areas to the detriment of the rest of the city. There remains a high percentage of the population who are unemployed and many who do work have low-paying jobs. Black unemployment rates are the highest in the city, as of August 2020, at 14.6 percent.[7] Despite some gains, interminable problems still exist with housing. Tight housing may have contributed to the deaths of twelve people, including eight children, in a three-story row house fire in the Fairmount section of the city in January 2022. The city is still one of the most segregated major cities in the country, resulting in occasional skirmishes with flash mobs beginning in the 2010s and continuing until today.[8] Tensions between the police and minority communities continue, as evidenced by the killing of a twenty-seven-year old Black man, Walter Wallace Jr., by police in West Philly in November 2020. Like many parts of the country, COVID-19 also presents a challenge. As of January 2022, more than 240,000 Philadelphians have caught the virus, and over 4,000 have died.[9]

These lingering problems are evident in several of the selections from this section. Major Jackson speaks of the drug and crime problems in the city in his poem "Euphoria." Asali Solomon also takes up these subjects in her short story "Secret Pool." The excerpt from Mat Johnson's novel *Loving Day* displays the deterioration that has taken place in the Germantown area of the city. And new problems keep arising, including the growing use of fentanyl in the city.[10]

Despite these problems, other works, such as Yolanda Wisher's poem "5 South 43rd Street, Floor 2" and Warren Longmire's poem "Brotherly Love" demonstrate the resilience of Philadelphians. They are tenacious, adaptable, and creative. They are survivors, having overcome many obstacles in their collective history. It will take a lot to break their spirit. The writings in this anthology are a testimony to their strength and resilience from the city's founding until today. To any who know the African American population of this city, there is no reason to believe this will not continue well into the future.

NOTES

1. Simon, *Philadelphia*, 109–11.
2. Simon, *Philadelphia*, 112.
3. Levenstein, *Movement Without Marches*, 128–32.
4. Simon, *Philadelphia*, 116.
5. Simon, *Philadelphia*, 117–18.

6. Simon, *Philadelphia*, 104–6.
7. Han and Grubola, "Action News Data."
8. Gottlieb, "South Street."
9. "Pennsylvania Coronavirus."
10. Whelan, "More Philadelphians than Ever Died."

BIBLIOGRAPHY

Gottlieb, Dylan. "South Street." *Encyclopedia of Greater Philadelphia*. https://philadel phiaencyclopedia.org/essays/south -street/.
Han, Nydia, and Heather Grubola. "Action News Data: Philadelphia-Area

Unemployment Numbers Show Gaps Between Certain Races." 6abc.com. https://6abc.com/unemployment -racial-disparities-race-jobs/6367493/.
Levenstein, Lisa. *A Movement Without Marches: African American Women and the Politics*

of Poverty in Postwar Philadelphia. Chapel
  Hill: University of North Carolina Press,
  2009.
"Pennsylvania Coronavirus Map and Case
  Count." *New York Times*, March 23, 2023.
  https://www.nytimes.com/interactive
  /2021/us/pennsylvania-covid-cases.html.
Simon, Roger D. *Philadelphia: A Brief History*.
  Revised and updated ed. Philadelphia:
  Temple University Press, 2017.

Whelan, Aubrey. "More Philadelphians than
  Ever Died of Overdoses in 2022, with
  Toll Especially Grim Among Black
  Residents." *Philadelphia Inquirer*,
  October 7, 2023. https://www.inquirer
  .com/health/opioid-addiction/overdose
  -deaths-philadelphia-2022-fentanyl
  -cocaine-opioid-crisis-20230927.html.

Major Jackson, from *Leaving Saturn* (2002)

Major Jackson was born in Philadelphia in 1969. He was raised in the city, going to the celebrated Central High School, and then earning degrees from Temple University and the University of Oregon. Jackson is currently the Richard A. Dennis Professor of English and University Distinguished Professor at the University of Vermont. He also serves as the poetry editor of the *Harvard Review*. He has written five books of poetry, the most recent being *The Absurd Man* (2020). He has won numerous awards, including the Cave Canem Poetry Prize for best first book of poetry, *Leaving Saturn*, which contains the poems anthologized here.

Jackson looks at Philadelphia from many angles in his poetry. "Urban Renewal ii" traces the city's history of both extreme wealth and poverty. It is framed as a pastoral place by founder William Penn, but it is also linked to disease. It is a tale of two cities, to continue the Dickens imagery that Jackson employs in the poem, depending upon one's race and social class. In the words of poet Al Young, in the foreword to *Leaving Saturn*, "The meaning of Philadelphia's and all the rest of the republic's flickering history is captured as only a poet can capture whole moments and epochs in the turn of a phrase or a line." Another poem, "Urban Renewal iv," touches on how the city has been made into a tourist site, especially in the Old City. As Amor Kohli writes, the poem "grapples with the exclusions that take place in the United States," particularly in Philadelphia.[1] "Euphoria" takes us to another section of the city, North Philadelphia, where the tourists are far less frequent. Here, a mother leaves her teenage son outside to protect her car while she enters a crack house; meanwhile the son has a sexual encounter with a young prostitute who is his own age. "Hoops" is about two men seeking to better themselves, one through basketball and the other through schooling, proving, as the poem states, *"There's more ways to skin. . . ."*

—

"URBAN RENEWAL II"

> Penn's GREEN COUNTRIE TOWNE uncurled a shadow in the 19th
>   century
> that descended over gridiron streets like a black shroud
> and darkened parlors with the predatory fog of prosperity
> as familiar as the ornate plot in a Dickens novel.
> The city breathed an incurable lung (TB in that time), trolleys
> clanged the city's despair. Workers in cotton mills and foundries
> shook heads in disbelief, the unfolding theme caked on ashen faces.
> Above mantels in gilded frames: tasseled carriages, silk bonnets,
> linen parasols echoing the silence of Victorian evil,
> the shade soldered to new empires as steam engines hissed,
> and brought this century's opening chapter to a creeping halt.
> Step on a platform in our time, the city's a Parthenon,
> a ruin that makes great literature of ghostly houses
> whose hulking skin is the enduring chill of the western wind.
> Stare back down cobbled alleys that coil with clopping horses,
> wrought-iron railings, to grand boulevards that make a fiction
> of suffering; then stroll these crumbling blocks, housing projects,
> man-high weeds snagging the barren pages of our vacant lots.

"URBAN RENEWAL IV"

Mama, unplug me, please[2]

MICHAEL HARPER, In the Projects

> From the LIBERTY BELL's glass asylum,
> tourists emerge convinced of a cracked republic,
> and for signs further join the edge of the human
> circle where you break-dance the bionic two-step.
> Democracy depends upon such literacy.
> Snapshots. Maps. The vendor's fist of stars and stripes—
> *She sewed pennants.* The public gallery of bronze statues
> whose Generals grimace frightened looks

at the darkening scenery. Your Kangoled[3] head spins
on cardboard, a windmill garnering allegiance.
Here prayed those who signed for Independence.
Break beats blasting your limbs to Market,
you're ghostbloom in the camera's flash,
so they call you FURIOUS ROCKER, CRAZYLEGS,—
The circle tightens like a colony, horse-and-carriages
hemming OLDE CITY to scraps of time;
squirrels pretremble then leap to bark.
Tourists ease on shades to enhance the dark.

"HOOPS"
Trees fall so I can play
ground with my ink.

DE LA SOUL[4]

I.
Bound by a falling CYCLONE
fence, a black rush streaks
for netless hoops, & one alone
from a distance, seeming to break

above the undulant pack, soars—
more like a Sunday SKYWALK,[5]
he cups the ball, whirls his arm,
swoops down a TOMAHAWK.[6]

Radar! Don't fly without me!
It's Big Earl who coughs, then downs
his bottle, a 40 oz. of OLDE E[7]
Laughter makes its rounds.

I cross a footpath of a city block,
a short rut that snakes between
a lush epitaph of dandelions
& weed-brush behind Happy

Hollow Courts;[8] the ghost
of a staircase echoes here: sign
of lives lived, of souls lost.
Mottled hues of graffiti lines

bombed on this wall, PHASE
says DON'T STOP THE BODY ROCK.
At gate's entrance, my gaze
follows Radar & his half-cocked

jump shot. All morning I sang
hymns, yet weighed his form:
his flashing the lane,
quick-stop, then rise like popcorn.

Now, elbows set a pair
of handlebars, he flicks his wrist,
the ball arcs through sunlight glare—
splashes the basket's

circle of air. A boom box bobs
& breaks beats on a buckling sea
of asphalt;—the hard,
pounding rhymes of BDP[9]

flooding a wall as a crowd
of hustlers toss craps, waging
fists, dollar bets, only louder—
& one, more enraged,

promises to pistol-whip
the punk who doesn't pay.
Doubling-down, he blows a kiss;
each dealer counts his days.

I turn from these highlights
as SPALDINGS[10] fly like meteors.
Radar dribbles near. I'm late
& before I say a word:

Shootin' more geometry?
We laugh, father Dave, coach
at St. Charles, once let me
play as a walk-on in hopes

I would tutor Radar. Not even
Pythagoras could awaken
in his head the elegance
of a triangle's circumference.

Four years later, he's off
on scholarship to UNC.
I'm to study Nabokov
at the state's university.

Proof of Pop-pop's maxim,
There's more ways to skin . . .
If the slum's our dungeon,
school's our Bethlehem.

Yet, what fate connects those dots
that rattle in hustler's palms
with Radar's stutter-step
& my pen's panopticon?[11]

It casts shadows dark
as tar as we begin
a full-court run. A brick
off the half-moon's side

—in waves, we sprint.
No set offence: his pass,

my bounce, his eloquent
lateral two-hand jam.

"EUPHORIA"
    Late winter, sky darkening after school.
    & groceries bought from Shop-Mart,
    My mother leaves me parked on Diamond
    To guard her Benz, her keys half-turned
    So I can listen to the Quiet Storm[12]
    While she smokes a few white pebbles
    At the house crumbling across the street.

    I clamber to the steering wheel,
    Undo my school tie, just as Luther Vandross
    Starts in on that one word tune, "Creepin.'"[13]

    The dashboard's panel of neon glows,
    And a girl my age, maybe sixteen or so,
    In a black miniskirt, her hair crimped
    With glitter, squats down to pane glass,

    And asks, *A date, baby? For five?*
    Outside, street light washes the avenue
    A cheap orange: garbage swirling
    A vacant lot; a crew of boys slap-boxing
    On the corner, throwing back large swills
    Of malt; even the sidewalk teeming with addicts,
    Their eyes spread thin as egg whites.

    She crams the crushed bill down
    Her stockings, cradles & slides her palm
    In rhythm to my hips' thrashing,
    In rhythm to Luther's voice, which flutters
    Around that word I now mistake for "Weep"
    As sirens blast the neighborhood &
    My own incomprehensible joy to silence.

Out of the house my mother steps,
Returned from the ride of her life,
Studies permanent cracks for half-empty vials,
Then looks back at bricked-over windows
As though what else mattered—
A family, a dinner, a car, nothing
But this happiness so hard to come by.

NOTES

1. Kohli, "'Life Ruptured,'" 185–86.

2. The lines are from Harper's poem "Debride-ment." Harper taught at Brown University from 1970 to 2016. He was the first poet laureate of Rhode Island.

3. Kangol is a British headwear company. The name combines the "K" from "silK," the "ANG" from "ANGora," and the "L" from "wooL." Founded in 1938, Kangol hats have been favorites of many hip-hop artists and their fans since the early 1980s.

4. De la Soul is an American hip-hop trio. The lyrics are from their song "I Am I Be" released on their album *Buhloone Mindstate* (1993).

5. To skywalk is to move laterally while in the air.

6. A tomahawk is a type of thunderous dunk thrown through the basket with a sharp downward thrust.

7. Olde English 800 is a brand of malt liquor often coming in 40-ounce bottles.

8. The Happy Hollow Recreation Courts are at 4800 Wayne Avenue in Germantown. Several NBA players started their careers here.

9. Boogie Down Productions, a hip-hop trio fronted by KRS-One (Lawrence Parker). The group originated in the Bronx and fused dancehall music, hip-hop, and reggae, and was active from 1986 to 1992.

10. For many years, the NBA used Spalding's basketballs. After the 2020–21 season, the league switched to Wilson basketballs because of contract problems with Spalding's.

11. Panopticon: a system created by eighteenth-century British philosopher Jeremey Bentham to observe all those housed in an institution, such as a prison or hospital, by one person. Though it would be impossible for one person to do this, the residents would not know who was being watched.

12. The Quiet Storm: a jazz-influenced radio format and form of contemporary rhythm and blues. The name was derived from the title song on Smokey Robinson's 1975 album with the same name.

13. "Creepin'" is a song from the rhythm-and-blues singer Luther Vandross's album *The Night I Fell in Love* (1985). The song was written by Stevie Wonder.

BIBLIOGRAPHY

Kohli, Amor. "'Life Ruptured Then Looped Back': Affiliation as Process in Major Jackson's 'Urban Renewal' Series." *MELUS* 35, no. 2 (Summer 2010): 177–98.

Major Jackson (website). https://www.major jackson.com.

Pardlo, Gregory. "About Major Jackson" *Ploughshares* 39, no. 1 (Spring 2013): 187–93.

Tursi, Alexandra. "Author Interview: Major Jackson." *Identity Theory*, Septermber 17, 2009. https://www.identitytheory.com /major-jackson.

Young, Al. Foreword to *Leaving Saturn: Poems*, by Major Jackson. Athens: University of Georgia Press, 2002.

Mumia Abu-Jamal, "A Panther Walks in Philly" (2004)

Mumia Abu-Jamal (Wesley Cook) was born in Philadelphia in 1954. He was a member of the Black Panther Party between 1968 and 1970. He later became a journalist, eventually becoming president of the Philadelphia Association of Black Journalists. He was a supporter of the radical MOVE organization. In 1982, Abu-Jamal was convicted for the 1981 murder of Philadelphia police officer Daniel Faulkner. Initially given the death sentence, the decision was overturned in 2001, and he is currently serving a sentence of life without parole. Many petitions have been filed on his behalf. While in prison, Abu-Jamal has published several works, including *Live from Death Row* (1996) and *Writing on the Wall: Prison Writings of Mumia Abu-Jamal* (2015). "A Panther Walks in Philly" is taken from *We Want Freedom: A Life in the Black Panther Party*, new edition (2016).

The chapter "A Panther Walks in Philly" is divided into two sections. The first part is a succinct history of the violence and racial prejudice inflicted upon Black residents of Philadelphia almost from the city's inception. The author relates such incidents as the Flying Horse Race Riots (1834), which took place near Seventh and South Streets, the burning of Pennsylvania Hall (1838), and the Christiana Resistance Riot (1851). The second half of the chapter discusses more recent acts of racial prejudice in the city, where Blacks routinely have been segregated into certain areas and generally forced to live in substandard conditions. In such an atmosphere Abu-Jamal maintains that it has been natural for the Black Panther Party and other Black resistance movements to find a home.

—

There is not perhaps anywhere to be found a city in which prejudice against color is more rampant than in Philadelphia. Hence all the incidents of caste are to be seen there in perfection. It has its white schools and its colored schools, its white churches and its colored churches, its white Christianity and its colored Christianity, its white concerts and its colored concerts, its white literacy institutions and its colored institutions.

—FREDERICK DOUGLASS (ca. 1862)[1]

i. McPherson, *The Negro's Civil War*, 259.

When Frederick Douglass made this comment, he had spent over two decades living in freedom. He was personally familiar with Rochester, New York, the coastal regions of Maryland, Boston, and England, where he secured the funds to legally purchase his freedom. As an editor, writer, and abolitionist speaker of some renown, he undoubtedly traveled further than many, perhaps most men, white or Black, of his time. Here was a man who was a deep thinker, a sharp speaker, and an astute observer of life, with a broad range of experience. One wonders, why would Philadelphia bring so foul a taste to his distinguished palette?

In Philadelphia one finds the perfect example of American ambivalence on race. It is formally a northern city, but as it virtually straddles the mythical Mason-Dixon line, it is, in many ways, a southern city as well. It boasts the historical distinction of being the nation's first capital, the site of the signing of both the Declaration of Independence and the Constitution, but also of sustained racial and ethnic rivalry, conflict, and repression.

Known worldwide as an almost mythical birthplace of liberty, the hope of freedom acted as a kind of psychic magnet, drawing the poor and oppressed from the class-bound aristocracies of Europe in rivers of emigration, as well as Black captives escaping from southern bondage and Black freedmen and women fleeing a humiliating and soul-sapping southern apartheid. The Philadelphia that the stalwart Frederick Douglass beheld with snarled contempt would more than double in size in half a century, rising from 650,000 people in 1860 to 1.5 million by 1914.[i]

It was a city of extremes, with pronounced differences in wealth, power, and influence. For although millions of Europeans came to the English colonies with visions of a land where streets were paved with gold, they found cities awash in staggering poverty, with wealth concentrated in the hands of a few. The cities of the colonial era had almshouses or poorhouses, but these were hardly sufficient. "It is remarkable," one citizen of Philadelphia said in 1748, "what an increase of the number of beggars there is about this town this winter."[ii]

A century later, although the white working class could find work in cities, their standard of living was miserable. In Philadelphia, they lived fifty-five to a tenement, one room per family. There were no toilets and no garbage

i. Zinn, *People's History*, 48.
ii. Zinn, *People's History*, 49–50.

collection, and fresh water or even fresh air was virtually nonexistent.[i] Many whites fought against their Black contemporaries, efforts to find work and tried to ensure they would not. Edward Abdy, a British visitor to Philadelphia in 1833, described the efforts of local Irish to remove Blacks from gainful employment. "Irish laborers were actively employed in this vile conspiracy against a people of whom they were jealous, because they were more industrious, orderly and obliging than themselves."[ii] While Abdy's report may be influenced by the longstanding and deep-rooted antipathy between the British and the Irish, his remarks present evidence of what seemed to be deep anti-Black feeling among the Irish both in Philadelphia and New York.

> Forty years ago a colored man appeared for the first time, as a carman in Philadelphia. Great jealousy was excited among that class of men; and every expedient was tried to get rid of a competitor whose success would draw others into the business. Threats and insults were followed by a report that he had been detected in stealing. The Quakers came forward to support him. They inquired into the grounds of the charge, and published its refutation. Their patronage maintained him in his situation, and encouraged others to follow his example. There are now plenty of them employed. At New York, a license cannot be obtained for them, and a black carman in that city is as rare as a black swan.[iii]

George Lippard is now forgotten, but before the work of Harriet Beecher Stowe stole the scene, he was the best-selling novelist in America. His 1844 novel *The Quaker City* told of a Philadelphia that was hideously violent, racist, and proud in its ignorance. He drew characters from the streets and headlines of the penny press, and one of his most memorable was an Irish rioter called Pump-Handle, who, in Irish-accented English, explained how he got his name:

> Why you see, a party of us one Sunday afternoon, had nothin' to do, so we got up a nigger riot. We have them things in Phil'delphy. Once

i. Zinn, *People's History*, 213.

ii. Forbes, E. *We Have No Country*, 191.

iii. Abdy, Edward. *Journal of Residence and Tour in the United States*. Quoted in Forbes, E. But We Have No Country, 191.

or twice a year, you know? I helped to burn a nigger church, two orphan asylums, and a school-house. And happenin' to have a handle in my hand, I aksedentally hit an old nigger on the head. Konsekance was he died. That's why they call me Pump-Handle.[i]

Lippard, although a novelist, used his skills as a radical journalist to draw accurate portrayals of the city where he lived and worked.

What were not fictional, but strictly factual, were the scores of racist riots against Black achievement, abolitionism, and Black freedmen and -women who lived in the city. Seven major mob attacks occurred between 1834 and 1838, among the most reported was the "Flying Horse Riot" of 1834. Radical and race historian Noel Ignatiev has written in his *How the Irish Became White*:

On a lot near Seventh and South Streets in Philadelphia, an entrepreneur had for some time been operating a merry-go-round called, "Flying Horses." It was popular among both black people and whites, and served both "indiscriminately." Quarrels (not necessarily racial) over seating preference and so forth were frequent. On Tuesday evening, August 12, a mob of several hundred young white men, thought to be principally from outside the area, appeared at the scene, began fighting with the black people there, and in a very short time tore the merry-go-round to pieces. The mob then marched down South Street, to the adjacent township of Moyamensing, attacked a home occupied by a black family, and continued in violence on the small side streets where the black people mainly lived. On Wednesday evening a crowd wrecked the African Presbyterian Church on Seventh Street and a place several blocks away called the "Diving Bell," operated by "a white man, and used as a grog shop and lodging house for all colors, at the rate of three cents a head." After reducing these targets to ruins, the rioters began smashing windows, breaking down doors, and destroying furniture in private homes of Negroes, driving the inmates into the streets beating any they caught. One correspondent reported that the mobs threw a corpse out of a coffin, and cast a dead infant on the floor, "barbarously" mistreating its mother. "Some arrangement, it appears, existed between the mob and the white inhabitants, as the

i. gnatiev, *How the Irish*, 124.

dwelling houses of the latter, contiguous to the residences of blacks, were illuminated, and left undisturbed, while the huts of the negroes were signaled out with unerring certainty."[i]

By midweek, when the fury had ebbed, several Blacks had been killed and two churches and at least twenty homes were destroyed. Hundreds of Blacks fled that part of town for other neighborhoods or sought refuge across the Delaware in New Jersey. This brutal violence, perpetrated by Irish gangs (many of them organized into the neighborhood fire companies), usually went unpunished. On the off chance that someone was arrested, Philadelphia juries duly acquitted them, especially when the victims were Black.[ii] The bloody and bitter feuds between the largely immigrant Catholics and the so-called nativists (other non-Catholic whites) often retreated when the target of local ire was a Black person or institution (such as a church). Then the nativist-Catholic divide would dissipate into whiteness against Blackness.[iii]

Three years after the terrorist violence of the Flying Horse Riot and the destruction of the Diving Bell, Pennsylvania Hall (built with Black and abolitionist money in Center City), Pennsylvania, was burned to the ground by several thousand whites who disapproved of Blacks and whites coming together to meet and discuss the heated issue of the day—slavery. The nativist commander of the Philadelphia militia, Col. August James Pleasonton, who witnessed Pennsylvania Hall being consumed by the flames, would later note:

There are serious apprehensions that the injudicious, to say the least, but as many think highly exciting and inflammatory proceedings of abolitionists, which have recently taken place here, and the disgusting intercourse between the whites and the blacks, as repugnant to all the prejudices of our education, which they not only have recommended, but are in the habit of practising in this very Abolition Hall, will result in some terrible outbreak of popular indignation, not only against the Abolitionists, but also, against the colored people.[iv]

i. Ignatiev, *How the Irish*, 125–226.
ii. Ignatiev, *How the Irish*, 55.
iii. Ignatiev, *How the Irish*, 134.
iv. Ignatiev, *How the Irish*, 134.

Pleasonton's view, aside from its elegant phrasing, could hardly be distinguished from the most uncouth Fenian[1] of the period.

As for the cops or firemen of the day, little help could be expected from that quarter. Both, to the extent they existed at all, were little more than the accretion of local, ethnic street gangs who used their positions to scam and threaten people for money. These street gangs, for whom the fire company or the police were but an instrument, had names like the Rats, the Bleeders, the Blood Tubs, the Deathfetchers, and the Hyenas.[i] It was for good reason that the American wit Mark Twain once quipped that people insured their homes, not against fires, but against the firemen. Failure to pay them might result in arson, a riot, or both!

This was the Philadelphia that Douglass loathed and perhaps feared.

It would be unfair and inaccurate to suggest that the anti-Black feeling in Philadelphia, or in other northern cities, for that matter, was the exclusive province of the white lower or working classes. At the highest levels of state and federal government, as well as in circles of wealth and influence, there was ample evidence of a pronounced antipathy for Blacks and of the fact that the popular rhetoric about "Philadelphia liberty" did not extend to them.

In 1837, a Pennsylvania constitutional convention overtly prevented Blacks from voting in the state.

At the time of the sensational Christiana Resistance[2] in nearby Lancaster Country, Pennsylvania, the *Philadelphia Bulletin* published an editorial that left no question as to whose side it defended in the conflict:

> Who is to prevail, the many or the few? The Old Saxon blood, which at vast sacrifice, founded these republics; or these African fugitives, whom we Pennsylvanians neither wish, nor will have? . . . Where the interests of two races come into collision, the weaker must yield, not merely as a matter of might, but according to our republican doctrines of right also. Among ourselves, we whites understand this, and act upon this . . ."[ii]

Nor did the official voice of the state of Pennsylvania differ, in essence, from that of the bigotry of the *Bulletin* on the issue of liberty for those

---

i. Ignatiev, *How the Irish*, 144.
ii. Forbes, E. *We Have No Country*, 150–51.

"African fugitives," in flight from bondage, who made their way to the "free" state. Margaret Morgan escaped from the slave system and fled to Pennsylvania in search of liberty. She found instead a state that spoke about freedom, but not for those who would seem to have need of it most—the enslaved.

When her capture by a Maryland slave-catcher was held to violate Pennsylvania's "personal liberty" laws, Maryland's attorney general argued that the Constitution did not apply to Blacks. For they, as slaves, he argued, were not a party to the national pact and thus were not contained under the Preamble "We, the People." Pennsylvania agreed with her sister state, admitting their adversary's claims. Lawyers for Pennsylvania took what one legal scholar called a feeble position:

> Pennsylvania says: Instead of preventing you from taking your slaves, *we are anxious that you should have them; they are a population we do not covet*; and all our legislation tends toward giving you every facility to get them; but we do claim the right of legislating upon this subject so as to bring you under legal restraint, which will prevent you from taking a freeman.[i]

As might be expected of a court composed predominantly of slave owners, the Supreme Court held for Edward Prigg, agent of the slave owner, and overturned Pennsylvania's "personal liberty" law as unconstitutional. For Margaret Morgan and her children—including her youngest, born into a "free" state—the Court's majority opinion meant a return to bondage.

The majority opinion in *Prigg v. Pennsylvania* (1842), penned by Justice Joseph Story of Massachusetts, made it clear that the state's claim to "personal liberty" applied to everyone, except slaves:

> The rights of the owners of fugitive slaves are in no just sense interfered with, or regulated by such a course. . . . But such regulations can never be permitted to interfere with or to obstruct the just rights of the owner to reclaim his slave, derived from the Constitution of the United States; or with the remedies prescribed by Congress to aid and enforce the same.

i. Irons, *People's History of the Supreme Court*, 152 (emphasis added).

Upon these grounds, we are of the opinion that the act of Pennsylvania upon which this indictment is founded, is unconstitutional and void. It purports to punish as a public offence against the state, the very act of seizing and removing a slave by his master, which the Constitution of the United States was designed to justify and uphold.[i]

The *Prigg* case would prove a harbinger of the judicial insults to come, among them, *Dred Scott v. Sanford*, decided nearly a decade later. The *Prigg* case was also a precursor of the infamous Fugitive Slave Law of 1850. Pennsylvania's lawyers betrayed Margaret Morgan, her five children, and thousands like her throughout the northern state. Instead of defending liberty, they defended comity between sister states and, by extension, the legality of slavery. Once again, the courts favored the illusion of human beings as property, as chattel, rather than the reality of humans yearning for liberty from base tyranny.

PHILADELPHIA MODERNITY

The Philadelphia of the mid twentieth century remained a conflicted, class-conscious, racially stratified city.

Black Philadelphia's population burgeoned, fueled in large part by the Great Migration which sent wave upon wave of a Black rural flood into urban centers like Pittsburgh, New York, Chicago, Boston, San Francisco, Seattle and Oakland. In these centers were established de facto Black Quarters, areas of containment and isolation, policed by law and social custom to minimize and restrict Black movement, mobility, and dispersal.

Ghettos are not natural growths, like bunions; they are legal constructs that are the fruit of the long-held beliefs and practices of segregation, and they survived its alleged death through restrictive covenants that forbade the selling of millions of units of housing to African Americans. This legal restriction had its equally effective corollary in social and customary practices of pricing property at rates that were prohibitive to the vast majority of the ghetto population.

Over the generations, central North Philadelphia, West Philadelphia, Southwest Philadelphia, and, to a lesser extent, small pockets of South Philadelphia became shorthand for Black Philadelphia. This did not mean these

i. Prigg v PA, 41 US 536, 625–26 (1842).

were the only places one found Black inhabitants, but it meant these areas were ones where Blacks dwelt in predominance.

Conversely, there were areas of the city, notably Northeast Philadelphia, East Oak Lane, Kensington, and South Philadelphia where Black folks walked, drove, or strove to live and work at their peril. To see Black homes marred by racist graffiti or firebombed by whites dwelling in neighboring homes was not an odd occurrence in the city with a name meaning Brotherly Love. Nor was it a rare occurrence for a Black pedestrian to be put to the chase for daring to walk in a "white" neighborhood.

These private, communal acts were echoed by official ones, done in the name of the city, by the police. Black Philadelphians came of age with the deeply felt knowledge that they could be beaten, wounded, or killed by cops with virtual impunity. The predominantly white police seemed like foreigners in a dark village who treated their alleged fellow citizens with the vehemence reserved for an enemy. For ghetto youth, this took the form of the police using the maddened self-hatred and regional antipathy between youth of various gangs to foment yet more hatred and violent reprisal. One favorite tactic they routinely utilized was to pick up a few youngsters from one gang, place them in a patrol car, drive them to enemy gang turf, let them out of the vehicle, and scream curses and insults against the enemy gang. To the young men left standing as the cop car raced off at breakneck speed, their choices were few and unenviable: stand and fight against the swarm of sworn enemies or run like the devil, hoping to get to safe territory before they got badly beaten, shot, or worse.

It was into this milieu that the Black Panther Party came into being in Philadelphia. Once the chapter was formed, other questions remained:

What would this new organization do?

How would we let folks know we existed?

What would be our focus?

These were but some of the challenges facing the group and met by the late spring of 1969:

With the renting, repair, cleaning, and painting of the storefront at 1928 West Columbia Avenue,³ the local party would have its first formal presence (odd apartments and private homes had sufficed previously), a reliable place where people could contact us. The time could not have been more perfect for our arrival, for the clear air, the bright sky blue, the very essence of the season of new life was upon us.

As soon as we had finished painting the walls (Panther powder blue, with black glaze adorning the moldings), affixed a few posters to the walls (Malcolm X, Che Guevera, Huey and Bobby, armed), and used pressure-sensitive letters to inscribe the inside of the fronting glass with the black, capital, gold-edged letters: YTRAP REHTNAP KCALB people began appearing at our door. What drew them was the bold letters blaring from the window: BLACK PANTHER PARTY.

That seemingly simple message drew in the young, the old, and those in the middle, from the cautious to the curious. Students came in, eager to sell the paper.

Even the established, like the real estate owner who rented the property to the Party and who owned properties all around the neighborhood took pains to demonstrate his nationalist credentials. He confided to us that he went to the historically Black college, Lincoln University, with the revered Kwame Nkrumah, the first President of the independent West African nation of Ghana.

But to have an office was not enough. The fledgling organization had to do something. After much thought, and a request from the national office, the captain ordered us to assemble at the State Building, at Broad and Spring Garden Streets, near the center of the city, to demonstrate for the freedom of the imprisoned BPP Minister of Defense, Huey P. Newton, who was facing murder charges stemming from a car stop and shoot-out in Oakland. The objective was to snag some publicity for the Party, and thus to inform the city's huge Black population of our presence.

The date is May 1, 1969, and between fifteen and twenty of us are in the full uniform of black berets, black jackets of smooth leather, and black trousers. As we assemble, a rousing chant of "Free Huey!" is raised. Leaflets are distributed to passerby, and we are able to inform some people of our presence and how to contact us.

Several of Huey's articles are read over the megaphones, and, before long, we have a somewhat rousing rally on our hands. Some of the excited kids from the nearby Ben Franklin High School cut their classes to attend the rally, and several papers are sold. Captain Reggie reads from Huey's "In Defense of Self-Defense," which noted, in part:

The heirs of Malcolm now stand millions strong on their corner of the triangle, facing the racist dog oppressor and the soulless endorsed spokesmen. The heirs of Malcolm have picked up the gun and taking first things first are moving to expose the endorsed spokesmen so the Black masses can see them for what they are and have always been.

The choice offered by the heirs of Malcolm to the endorsed spokesmen is to repudiate the oppressor and crawl back to their own people
and earn a speedy reprieve or face a merciless, speedy, and most timely
execution for treason and being "too wrong for too long."[i]

*Cameras went off like popcorn, but we had no real idea who the mostly white
photographers were. We assumed they were the press, but some had the unmistak-
able air of cops about them. It never dawned on us that some were FBI agents
building a file on us. Mostly, it was because, in an age of global revolution, it didn't
seem too extraordinary to be a revolutionary. Didn't America come into being by
way of the American Revolution?*

*Here we were, reading the hard, uncompromising words of the Minister of
Defense of the Black Panther Party at the State Building in the heart of the fifth
largest city in America, while red-faced, nervous, armed cops stood around on the
periphery of our rally . . . what did we think would happen? We thought, in the
amorphous realm of hope, youth, and boundless optimism, that revolution was
virtually a heartbeat away. It was four years since Malcolm's assassination and
just over a year since the assassination of the Rev. Martin Luther King, Jr. The
Vietnam War was flaring up under Nixon's Vietnamization program, and the
rising columns of smoke from Black rebellions in Watts, Detroit, Newark, and
North Philly could still be sensed—their ashen smoldering still tasted in the air.*

*Huey was our leader, and we felt, with utter certainty, that he spoke for the
vast majority of Black folks. He certainly spoke for us. We loved and revered him
and wondered why everybody else didn't feel the same way. Our job was to make
all see this obvious truth. His work moved us all deeply, and we believed we could
in turn move the world. This feeling motivated us to sell The Black Panther newspaper with passion and spirit, for Huey himself had written that "a newspaper is
the voice of the party, the voice of the Panther must be heard throughout the land."[ii]*

*We struggled daily to make it so. We got up early and didn't go to sleep until
late. For most of us, Party work was all that we did, all day, into the night. Our
little branch blossomed into the biggest, most productive chapter in the state and
one of the most vigorous in the nation.*

*A year after our rally, our branch sold 10,000 Party newspapers a week and
had functioning Party offices in West Philadelphia and Germantown. The Party*

i. Newton, *Revolutionary Suicide*, 90–91.
ii. *The Black Panther*, April 6, 1970, 17.

nationally sold nearly 150,000 papers through direct street sales and paid subscriptions per week. The Party was literally growing by leaps and bounds, both locally and nationally. From our original fifteen-odd members in the spring of 1969, a year later virtually ten times that number would call themselves members of the Black Panther Party of Philadelphia.

We spoke at antiwar rallies. We attended school meetings. We met with high school students. We met in churches. We worked with gangs and provided transportation to area prisons. Everywhere we went, we brought along the 10-Point Program and Platform of the Black Panther Party, as a guideline for our organizing efforts.

By any measure, we made an impressive beginning.

It was May 1969.

A young man named O. J. Simpson had just been named the number one NFL draft pick by Buffalo, a year after winning the Heisman for his performance as running back for University of Southern California.

The album Blood, Sweat and Tears (by the group Blood, Sweat and Tears) would win the best album Grammy.

The Oscar for Best Picture would be awarded to Midnight Cowboy.

The great Mohammad Ali had been stripped of his heavyweight boxing crown two years previous, and the championship was vacant.

The number one first-round draft pick for the NBA was a lanky, Afro-coifed youth named Lew Alcindor of UCLA, who went to Milwaukee.

In April, the US military had mobilized its biggest troop deployment of 543,400 soldiers.

In just three months, half a million young folks would gather in a remote corner of New York called Woodstock.

Shortly thereafter, a quarter million people would march in front of the White House demanding an end to the Vietnam War.

Before the month of May ended, a police raid in New Haven, Connecticut, would threaten the very stability of the Party.

Chairman Bobby Seale and Ericka Huggins would face murder charges. In all, eight Panthers would be arrested, and at least one would agree to turn state's evidence. If convicted, Seale would face the electric Chair.[4]

NOTES

1. A Fenian was a member of a nineteenth-century Irish or Irish American organization that espoused nationhood for Ireland.

2. The Christiana Resistance was an armed struggle by free Blacks and four enslaved fugitives against white law enforcement officials

who made a raid to recapture the fugitives. The raid took place in Christiana, Pennsylvania, on September 11, 1851.

3. 1928 West Columbia Avenue: the headquarters of the Black Panther Party, located in North Philadelphia. The section of Columbia Avenue from 33rd Street to Frankford Avenue has been renamed Cecil B. Moore Avenue in honor of the activist.

4. Face the electric Chair: Panther Alex Rackley, under torture, confessed to being a police informant. Panther George W. Sams Jr. testified that Seale had ordered him to kill Rackley. The charges were dropped after the jury could not reach a verdict.

BIBLIOGRAPHY

Faulkner, Maureen, and Michael A. Smerconish. *Murdered by Mumia: A Life Sentence of Loss, Pain, and Injustice*. Guilford, CT: Lyons Press, 2007.

Gay, Kathlyn. *American Dissidents: An Encyclopedia of Activists, Subversives, and Prisoners of Conscience*. Santa Barbara, CA: ABC-CLIO, 2018.

"A Life in the Balance: The Case of Mumia Abuu-Jamal." Amnesty International, February 17, 2000. https://www.amnesty.org/en/wp-content/uploads/2021/06/amr510012000en.pdf.

Rimer, Sara. "Death Sentence Overturned in 1981 Killing of Officer." *New York Times*, December 19, 2001.

Smith, Laura. "I Spend My Days Preparing for Life, Not for Death." *Guardian*, October 27, 2007.

Asali Solomon, "Secret Pool" (2010)

Born in West Philadelphia, Asali Solomon attended a neighborhood grade school and then the private Baldwin School in Bryn Mawr before graduating from Central High School. She received a BA from Barnard College in New York City and has a PhD in English from the University of California, Berkeley, and an MFA from the University of Iowa. She presently teaches English and creative writing at Haverford College, located just outside Philadelphia.

Solomon has written a short story collection, *Get Down* (2006), set in Philadelphia, as well as two novels, *Disgruntled* (2016) and *The Days of Afrekete* (2021), which are also situated in the city. "Secret Pool" is from the anthology *Philadelphia Noir* (Akashic Books, 2010). The University City Swim Club, at the center of the story, is located in the Garden Court neighborhood of West Philadelphia. First operated in 1964, the club is open to private members and, in addition to several pools, has a basketball court and a dining area. Currently, there are about 1,500 members; however, the cost is well beyond the means of most of the residents of the area. The story deals with tensions not only along class and racial lines but also over issues of gender and sexual preference. When a drowning occurs at the pool, the narrator, Nzingha, a teenager exploring her sexual orientation, is torn between loyalty to her friend and her brother.

—

I learned about the University City Swim Club around the same time things started disappearing from my room. First I noticed that I was missing some jewelry, and then the old plaid Swatch I'd been saving for a future *Antique Roadshow*. I didn't say anything to my mother, because they say it's dangerous to wake a sleepwalker. But then I felt like we were all sleepwalkers when Aja told me about the pool, hiding in plain sight right up on 47th Street in what looked like an alley between Spruce and Pine.

"You don't know about the University City Swim Club?" she said, pretending shock. It was deep August and I sat on the steps of my mother's house. Aja was frankly easier to take during the more temperate months, but since my summer job had ended and there were two and a half more weeks before eleventh grade, I often found myself in her company.

Aja Bell and I had been friends of a sort since first grade, when we'd been the only two black girls in the Mentally Gifted program, though there couldn't have been more than thirty white kids in the whole school. Aja loved MG because there was a group of girls in her regular class who tortured her. Then in sixth grade, I got a scholarship to the Barrett School for Girls and Aja stayed where she was. Now she went to Central High, where she was always chasing these white city kids. It killed her that I went to school in the suburbs with real rich white people, while her French teacher at Central High was a black man from Georgia. Despite the fact that I had no true friends at my school and hated most things about my life, she was in a one-sided social competition with me. As a result, I was subjected to Aja's peacocking around about things like how her friend Jess, who lived in a massive house down on Cedar Avenue, had invited her to go swimming with her family.

"Come off it, Aja. I just said I didn't know about it."

"I just think if you live right here . . . maybe your mom knows about it?"

"Look, is there a story here?"

"Well, it's crazy. There's this wooden gate with a towing sign on it like it's just a parking lot, but behind it is this massive pool and these brand-new lockers and everything. And it was so crowded!"

"Any black people there?"

"Zingha, why you have to make everything about black and white?"

"Maybe because people are starting all-white pools in my neighborhood."

She sighed. "There was a black guy there."

"Janitor?"

"I think he was the security guard."

I snorted.

We watched a black Range Rover crawl down the block. The windows were tinted, and LL Cool J's "The Boomin' System"[1] erupted from the speakers.

"Wow," I said, in mock awe. "That's boomin' from his boomin' system."

"So ghetto," said Aja.

"Um, because this *is* the ghetto," I said, though my mother forbade me to use the word.

"He spoke to me," Aja said suddenly. "The pool security guard. He wasn't that much older than us."

"Was he cute?" I asked without much interest.

"Tell you the truth, he's a little creepy. Like maybe he was on that line between crazy and, um, retarded."

I laughed and then she did too.

"So you been hanging out with Jess a lot this summer?" Jess, a gangly brunette with an upturned nose, was Aja's entry into the clique to which she aspired. But Jess sometimes ignored Aja for weeks at a time, and had repeatedly tried to date guys who Aja liked.

"Well, not a lot. She was at tennis camp earlier," Aja said, glancing away from my face. She could never fully commit to a lie. I imagined my older brother Dahani a couple of nights ago, spinning a casual yarn for my mom about how he'd been at the library after his shift at the video store. He said he was researching colleges that would accept his transfer credits. Dahani had been home for a year, following a spectacular freshman-year flameout at Oberlin. That memory led me to a memory from seventh grade, when Dahani said he'd teach me how to lie to my mother so I could go to some unsupervised sleepover back when I cared about those things. I practiced saying, "There *will be* parental supervision," over and over. Dahani laughed because I bit the inside of my cheek when I said my line.

"You mean the pool at the Y?" my mom asked me later that night. We had just finished eating the spaghetti with sausage that she had cooked especially for my brother. She had cracked open her nightly can of Miller Lite.

"Not that sewer," I said.

"Poor Zingha, you hate your fancy school and you hate your community too. Hard being you, isn't it?"

"Sorry," I muttered, rather than hearing again about how I used to be a sweet girl who loved to hug people and cried along with TV characters.

Dahani, who used to have a volatile relationship with our mother, was now silent more often than not. But he said, "I know what you're talking about, Zingha. Up on 47th Street." Then he immediately looked like he wanted to take it back.

"You been there?" I asked.

"Just heard about it," my brother said, tapping out a complicated rhythm on the kitchen table. When he was younger it meant he was about to go to his room. Now it meant he was trying to get out of the house. I wasn't even sure why he insisted on coming home for dinner most nights. Though of course free hot food was probably a factor.

"So what are you up to tonight?" my mother asked him brightly.

"I was gonna catch the new Spike Lee with Jason," he said,

My mother's face dimmed. She always hoped that he'd say, *Staying right here.* But she rallied. "You liked that one, didn't you, Zingha?"

I looked at Dahani. "Sure, watch Wesley Snipes do it with a white woman and stick me with the dishes."

"Oh, I'll take care of the dishes," my mother snapped, managing to make me feel petty. Turning to Dahani she asked, "How *is* Jason?"

"Just fine," Dahani said, in a tight voice. I followed his eyes to the clock above the refrigerator. "Movie starts at seven."

My brother kissed my mom and left, just like he did every night since he'd come home in disgrace. I went upstairs so I wouldn't have to listen to the pitiful sound of her cleaning up the kitchen. After that she would doze in front of the TV for a couple of hours, half waiting for Dahani to come home. She always wound up in bed before that.

I went up into my brother's room. I didn't find my things, but I helped myself to a couple of cigarettes I knew I'd never smoke, and an unsoiled *Hustler* magazine.

It happened after I had done the deed with a couple of contorting blondes who must have made their parents proud. I had washed up for bed and was about to put on my new headphones, which would lull me to sleep.

I realized that my Walkman was gone.

Understand this. I did not care about the mother-of-pearl earrings from my aunt that even my mother admitted were cheap. I did not care about the gold charm bracelet that my mother gave me when I turned sixteen—the other girls in my class had been collecting tennis racket and Star of David charms since they were eight. And of course the future value of nonfunctioning Swatches was just a theory. But Dahani, who had once harangued my mother into buying him seventy-five dollar stereo headphones, understood what my Walkman meant to me.

Every summer since eighth grade, the nonprofit where my mom worked got me an office job with one of their corporate "partners." I spent July and part of August in freezing cubicles wearing a garish smile, playing the part of Industrious Urban Youth. This summer it had been a downtown bank, where the ignoramus VPs and their ignoramus secretaries crowed over my ability to staple page one to two and guide a fax through the machine. If you think I was lucky I didn't have to handle French fries or the public, you try staying awake for six hours at a desk with nothing to do except arrange rubber bands into a neat pile. It was death.

Most of the money I made every summer went for new school uniforms and class trips. The only thing I bought myself that I cared about was the most expensive top-of-the-line Walkman. I had one for each summer I'd worked, and all three were gone. I turned on my lamp, folded my arms, and decided that I could wait up even if my mother couldn't.

The next day I hovered around the living room window waiting for Aja to appear on my block and also hoping that she wouldn't. I needed to tell someone about my brother. But on the other hand, Aja had the potential to be not so understanding. She had two parents: a teacher and an accountant who never drank beer from cans. They went to church and had a Standard Poodle called Subwoofer. It was true that sometimes we were so lonely that we told each other things. I had told her that I liked my brother's dirty magazines and she told me that she didn't like black guys because once her cousin pushed her in a closet and pulled out his dick. But whenever we made confessions like these, the next time we met up it was like those mouthwash commercials where couples wake up next to each other embarrassed by their breath. Besides, I didn't want her to pronounce my crack-smoking brother "ghetto," not even with her eyes.

He lied, he lied, he lied. Dahani, who used to make up raps with me and record them, who comforted me the one time we met our father, who seemed bored and annoyed, and once, back when we were both in public school, beat up a little boy for calling me an African bootyscratcher. *That* brother, said calmly, "I didn't take any of your stuff, Nzingha. What are you thinking?"

"I'm thinking: what the hell is going on? I'm thinking where are my Walkmans? I'm thinking: where are you all the time?"

"I'm out. You should go there sometimes." He laughed his high-pitched laugh, the one that said how absurd the world is.

"Okay, so you supposedly went to the movies tonight, right? What happens to Gator at the end of *Jungle Fever*?"[2] I asked.

"Ossie Davis shoots him."

"That's right. The crackhead dies. Remember that," I said.

"Crackhead?" Dahani sounded his laugh again. I didn't realize how angry I was until I felt the first hot tear roll down my cheek.

I stomped out, leaving his door open. That was an old maneuver, something we did to piss each other off when we lost a fight. But then I thought of something and went back in there. He wouldn't admit that he'd taken my things. But he agreed that if I didn't say anything to our mother, he'd take me to the pool. He could only take me at night after it closed, and only if I kept my mouth shut about going.

That night, a Friday, we made our mother's day by convincing her we were going to hang out on South Street together. Then, as it was getting dark, Dahani and I walked silently toward 47th Street. A clump of figures looked menacing at the corner until we got close and saw that they couldn't have been more than fifth graders. We slowed down to let a thin, pungent man rush past us. Even thought the night air was thick enough to draw sweat, the empty streets reminded me that summer was ending.

"Is anybody else coming?" I asked finally. "Jason?"

"I haven't seen that nigger in months. Ever since he pledged, he turned into a world-class faggot." Jason, my brother's best friend from Friends Select,[3] the only other black boy in his class, had started at Morehouse the same time my brother had gone to Oberlin.

"So it's just going to be us and the security guard?" I had worn a bathing suit under my clothes, but felt weird about stripping down in front of the character Aja described.

"Look," my brother said, "be cool, okay?"

"Cool like you?"

"You know, Nzingha, this is not the best time of my life either."

"But it could be. You could go back to school," I said, teetering on the edge of a place we hadn't been.

"It's not that fucking easy! Do you understand everything Mom's done for me already!"

"Don't talk to me like that."

"Let's just go where we're going."

We passed under a buzzing streetlight that could die at any moment. I had a feeling I knew from nightmares where I boarded the 42 bus[4] in the daytime and got off in the dark. In the dreams I heard my sneakers hit the ground and I thought I would die of loneliness.

We finally reached the tall wooden gate with its warning about getting towed. In a low voice that was forceful without being loud, Dahani called out to someone named Roger. The gate opened and Dahani nearly pushed me into a tall, skinny man with a tan face and eyes that sparkled even in the near dark.

"Hey man, hey man," he kept saying, pulling my brother in for a half-hug.

"What's up, Roger?" said Dahani. "This is my sister."

"Hey, sister," he said and tried to wink, but the one eye took the other with it.

I looked around. It was nicer than the dingy gray tiles and greenish walls at the Y pool, but to tell the truth, it was nothing special. I'd been going to pool parties at Barrett since sixth grade and I'd seen aqua-tiled models, tropical landscaping, one or two retractable ceilings. This was just a standard rectangle bordered by neat cream-colored asphalt on either side. There were a handful of deck chairs on each side and tall, fluorescent lamps. This is what they were keeping us out of?

A bunch of white guys with skater hair and white-boy fades drank 40s and nodded to a boombox playing A Tribe Called Quest[5] at the deep end near the diving board. Then nearby enough to hover but not to crowd, were the girls, who wore berry-colored bikinis. I thought of my prudish navy-blue one-piece. There was a single black girl sitting on the edge of the pool in a yellow bathing suit, dangling her feet in the water.

"Aja?" I called.

"Nzingha?" she replied, sounding disappointed.

Then I recognized Jess, who seemed not to see me until I was practically standing on top of her. Actually, this happened nearly every time we met. "Hey," she said finally. "I thought that was you." She always said something like that.

"What are you doing here?" Aja asked.

"My brother brought me."

"That's your brother?" Jess gestured with her head to Dahani, who stood with his hands in his pockets while Roger pantomimed wildly.

"You know him?" I asked. "He's down with my boys," she said. I tried not to wince. "Speaking of which, hey, Adam! Can you bring Nzingha something to drink."

We looked toward the end of the pool with the boys and the boombox. One of them, with a sharp-looking nose and a mop of wet blond hair sweeping over his eyes, yelled back: "Get it for her yourself!"

Jess's face erupted in pink splotches. "He's an incredible asshole," she said.

"And this is news?" said one of the other girls. She had huge breasts, a smashed-in face, and a flat voice. Suddenly I remembered the name Adam. Aja had a flaming crush on him for nearly a year, and then Jess had started going out with him on and off. Last I heard they were off, but now Aja liked to pretend she'd never mentioned liking him.

"I don't want anything to drink anyway," I said.

Aja asked if I was going to swim and I don't remember what I said because I was watching my brother walk down to the end of the pool where the boys were, trading pounds with wet hands. He reached into a red cooler and pulled out a 40. Roger stayed at the tall wooden gate.

"They think they're gangsters," Jess said, rolling her eyes in their general direction. "They call themselves the Gutter Boys. All they do is come here and smoke weed."

"That's not all," the girl with the smashed-in face said with a smirk.

"Is my brother here a lot?" I asked.

"I've only seen him once. But this is only the third time I've been here, you know, after hours."

My brother didn't seem interested in swimming. I didn't even know if he was wearing trunks. Instead he walked with a stocky swaggering boy toward the darkness of the locker room. *Don't go back there*, I wanted to scream. But all I did was stand there in my street clothes at the water's edge.

Adam cried out, "Chickenfight!"

"Not again," said smashed-in face. "I'm way too fucked up."

Adam swam over to us. "Look, Tanya, you'll do it again if you wanna get high later."

Tanya's friend murmured something to her quietly. Tanya laughed and said, "Hey, Adam, what about this?" Then she and her friend began kissing. At first just their lips seemed to brush lightly, and then the quiet girl pulled her in fiercely. I stepped back, feeling an unpleasant arousal. The boys became a cursing, splashing creature moving toward us. "Dayummm!" called Roger, who began running over.

"Keep your eye on the gate, dude!" yelled one of the boys.

"Okay, you big lesbians get a pass," said Adam when they finally broke apart. Then he turned to Jess. "What can you girls do for me?"

"I think we're going to stick with the chickenfight," said Aja, giggling. She still liked him. I could not relate.

While they sorted out who would carry whom, my brother emerged from the locker room. I waited until he and the stocky boy had parted ways before I began walking over.

"Dahani," I called in a sharp voice.

"You ready to go?" he asked. I examined him. He didn't seem jittery and he wasn't sweating. This was what I knew of smoking crack from the movies.

"What are you looking at?" he asked.

I glanced back at the pool, where Adam, laughing, held Jess under the water. Aja sat forlornly on the shoulders of a round boy with flame-colored hair waiting for the fight to start. "I'm ready to go," I said.

When Roger closed the gate the pool disappeared, and though "Looking at the Front Door"[6] sounded raucous bouncing off the water, I couldn't hear anything at all.

"Are you smoking crack?" I blurted.

Dahani came to a full stop and looked at me. "This is the last time I think I'm going to answer that dumb-ass question. No."

"Are you selling it?"

He sighed in annoyance. "Nzingha. No."

"But something isn't right."

"No, nothing is right," Dahani said. "But this is where I get off." We had reached my mother's house. He kept walking up the dark street.

It wasn't until a couple of nights later that Dahani didn't show up for dinner. My mother, who barely touched the pizza I ordered, kept walking to the front window and peering out.

When it began getting dark, I slapped my forehead. "Oh my God!" I said.

My mother looked at me with wild round eyes. "What?"

Without biting the inside of my cheek, I said, "I totally forgot. He said to tell you he wouldn't be home until really late."

"Where is he?"

"Don't know."

My mother folded her arms. "Thanks for almost letting me have a heart attack."

"Mom, he's a grown man."

"Nzingha," she said, "what is this thing with you and your brother?"

I didn't answer.

"You don't seem to realize that he's having a really hard time. I mean I'm the one stuck with loans from his year at college. I'm the one supporting his grown-ass now and I'm the one who's going to have to take out more loans to send him back. So what's *your* issue?"

"Nothing," I said. "Can I go upstairs?"

"You really need to change your attitude. And not just about this."

"Can I go upstairs?" I said again.

My mother and I sometimes had strained conversations. It was she and Dahani who had fireworks. But now she looked so angry she almost shook. "Go ahead and get the hell out of my sight!" And I did, hating this.

That night I wasn't sure if I was sleeping or not. I kept imagining the nightmare bright scene at the pool, those girls kissing, my brother disappearing into the back. Night logic urged me that I had to go back there. After my mother was in bed with her TV timer on, I climbed out of bed and dressed. Then excruciatingly, silently, I closed the front door. I plunged into darkness and walked the three blocks as fast as I could.

"Roger," I called at the gate, trying to imitate my brother's masculine whisper. I tapped the wood. There was a pause and then the tall gate wrenched open.

"Where's Dahani?" Roger said, waving me inside. His clothes were soaked and he was in stocking feet. "Oh God. You didn't bring Dahani?"

I felt my legs buckle, and only because Roger's sweaty hand clamped over my mouth was I able to swallow a scream. I had seen only one dead body in real life, at my great-grandmother's wake. Though with her papery skin and tiny doll's limbs, she'd never seemed quite alive. I'd never seen a dead body floating in water, but I knew what I was seeing when I saw Jess's naked corpse bob up and down peacefully. I ran to the water's edge near the diving board. There was a wet spot of something on the edge of the pool that looked black in the light.

Roger began pacing a tiny circle, moaning.

"Did you call 911?" I asked him.

"It was an accident. They're gonna think—"

"What if she's alive?" I said.

Roger suddenly loomed in front of me with clenched fists. "No cops! And she's not alive! Why didn't you bring Dahani?"

In the same way I knew things in dreams, I knew he hadn't done it. Not even in a Lenny in *Of Mice and Men*[7] way. But I needed to get away from his panic. I spoke slowly. "It's okay. I'll go get him."

"You'll bring him here?"

Before I let myself out through the tall gate, I watched Roger slump to the side of the pool and sit Indian style with his head in his hands. I took one last look at Jess. Later I wished that I hadn't.

I found myself at Aja's house. It was after midnight, but I rang the bell, hoping somehow that she might answer the door instead of her parents. I heard the dog barking and clicking his long nails excitedly on the floor.

Aja's dad, a short yellow man with a mustache and no beard, answered the door. "Zingha? Now you know it's too late. Does your mom know—"

"Mr. Bell, I really need to see Aja."

"Are you serious, girl?" Then he started pushing the door shut. The dog was going crazy.

"Aja!" I screamed.

Her mother appeared. She grabbed Subwoofer's collar with one hand and pulled him up short. He whimpered and I felt bad for him. All I'd ever known him to attack with was his huge floppy tongue.

"Shut up and get in here," she said.

Aja's father moved off to the side but he wasn't happy about it. "What the hell do you think you're doing?" he asked her.

"Quiet, you!" she responded. She was nearly a head taller than he was, with eggplant-colored lips and very arched eyebrows.

"Look, Nzingha," she said, "Aja's not here. We don't know where she is."

I shook my head frantically. "We have to find her! You don't know what's going on. There's a—"

"Stop talking and listen," she said, getting louder. "If anyone comes around asking where my daughter is, tell them the truth. That she has disappeared and that we are very worried. Mr. Bell will walk you home."

Mr. Bell fumed as he escorted me. "I guess there's no point in any more stupid fucking shit happening," he muttered. I didn't answer; he wasn't talking to me.

I let myself in as quietly as I had left, shocked by the thick silence of the house. I tried not to imagine Jess's closed eyes, her blood on the asphalt. I had to remind myself that she was dead, so she couldn't be as cold as she looked. I tried to tell myself that her floating body, Dahani, and Aja were in another world.

But the next morning I learned that my mother hadn't been home. She'd been down at the precinct with my brother.

By the time the police had arrived at the pool, Roger was nearly dead. He had tried to drown himself. He couldn't answer questions about Jess from his coma, but the police knew he hadn't done it.

It seemed to me, from what I managed to read before my mother started hiding the papers, that Jess's death had been an accident. But her dad was a lawyer and Aja was dragged back from an aunt's house in Maryland to do eighteen months in the Youth Detention Center. I went to visit her once that winter, in the dim, echoing room that reminded me of the cafeteria at our elementary school. I didn't tell my mother where I was going. She hadn't let me go to the trial.

Aja and I made painful small talk about how the food was destroying her stomach and about her first encounter with a bed bug. She said *fuck* more than usual and her skin looked gray.

Then she blurted, "I didn't do it."

"I know," I said.

"Things just got crazy." She told me about that night. Everyone had been drinking, including her, and Adam called for another chickenfight.

"First I fought that girl Tanya and I beat her easy. Then it was me and Jess. But I had won the time before, the night you came, you remember?"

I nodded, though I hadn't seen her victory.

"So she was really getting rough. And then she fucking—"

"We don't have to talk about this anymore," I said, trying to be the sweet girl my mother remembered.

"She pulled my top down. I kept telling them I wanted to stop. But they were yelling so loud. And Adam was cheering me on. It was so—" Aja's voice seemed to swell with tears, but her eyes remained empty.

"It doesn't matter," I said, and we were quiet for a moment. The din of the visiting room filled the space between us.

"But Jess was my best friend," she said. I had come to be good to her, yet I wanted to shake her by the shoulders until her teeth chattered.

My brother was able to convince the police that he hadn't done it. But he not only needed an alibi, he also had to rat out the Gutter Boys, with whom he'd apparently tried to go into business. Tried, I say, because he was such a crummy drug dealer that he had to steal to make up for what he couldn't sell. Dahani told the police what he knew about the small operation, and after that, a couple of Jeeps slowed down when he crossed the street, but he didn't turn up in the Schuylkill or anything. He got his old job at the video store back, but he got fired after a couple of months, and then our VCR disappeared. After two weeks in a row when he didn't come home, and my mom had called the police about sixteen times, she changed the locks and got an alarm system.

Sometime after that she looked at me over a new tradition—a second nightly beer—and said, "Nzingha, I know we should have talked about this as soon as I knew what was going on with your brother. But I didn't want to say anything because I know that you love him."

The scandal didn't break the pool. They held a floating memorial service for Jess and hired a real security company. The scandal did, however, break the news of the pool to the neighborhood. But at $1,400 a year, none of the black folks we knew could afford to join it anyway.

NOTES

1. LL Cool J's "The Boomin System" was a single from the hip-hop artist's album *Mama Said Knock You Out* (1990).

2. *Jungle Fever*: Spike Lee's 1991 film about an interracial relationship. In the film "Gator" Purify (played by Samuel L. Jackson), a crack addict, is shot and killed by his father, The Good Reverend Doctor Purify (played by Ossie Davis).

3. Friends Select is a Quaker college-preparatory school (grade school through high school) located in Center City.

4. The forty-two bus runs from Penn's Landing in South Philly to Wycombe, located in Bucks County, about forty-five minutes from the city. It is likely the bus Nzingha took to her suburban school.

5. A Tribe Called Quest was a hip-hop group fronted by main producer Q-Tip. They are considered pioneers in alternative hip-hop.

6. "Looking at the Front Door" is a 1990 song by the hip-hop group Main Source.

7. Lenny, a strong, but mentally challenged, character in John Steinbeck's 1937 novel, unintentionally kills a woman by breaking her neck.

BIBLIOGRAPHY

Salai Solomon (website). https://www.asali solomon.com.

Cha, Steph. "Review: Coming of Age with Asali Solomon's 'Disgruntled.'" *Los Angeles Times*, January 29, 2015.

McCarthy, Michael. "A Conversation with Asali Solomon." *Adroit Journal*, July 27, 2022. https://theadroitjournal.org/2022 /07/27/a-conversation-with-asali -solomon.

Sonia Sanchez, "10 Haiku (for Philadelphia Murals)" (2010)

"10 Haiku (for Philadelphia Murals)," contained in the collection *Morning Haiku* (2010), allows Sanchez to write in one of her favorite forms, having composed hundreds of haiku, tanka, and sonku. Sanchez believes that "the haiku form is inherently non-violent in its intent and structure and engenders beauty, serenity, and brief reflection."[1] "10 Haiku (for Philadelphia Murals)" celebrates the city's murals, a distinctive feature of Philadelphia; the organization Mural Arts Philadelphia has created more than 3,600 murals in the city since 1984. The group worked with Sanchez on one project entitled "Peace is a Haiku Song," which is located at 1415 Catherine Street (in the Hawthorne neighborhood in South Philadelphia) and was completed in 2013.

~

1.

Philadelphia roots
lighting these walls
with fireflies

2.

flowers stretched
in prayer on a
cornerstone wall

3.

> brownskinned
> children dancing
> with butterflies

4.

> these children's
> faces humiliate
> the stars

5.

> Philadelphia
> painted with
> blue hallelujahs

6.

> winter
> a warrior's face
> i hear our bones singing

7.

> in the open
> alley a galaxy
> of dreams

8.

> common ground
> is we, forever
> breathing this earth

9.

> hands
> in the green light
> saluting peace

10.
    even in the
    rain, these murals
    pause with rainbows.

NOTE

    1. "Peace Is a Haiku Song."

BIBLIOGRAPHY

"Peace Is a Haiku Song." Mural Arts Philadel-
    phia. https://www.muralarts.org
    /artworks/peace-haiku-song/?gclid=
EAIaIQobChMI6oPyq9ungQMV
4zjUARovDADCEAAYASAAEg
KRgfD_BwE.

Gregory Pardlo, "Philadelphia, Negro" (2012)

Gregory Pardlo was born in Philadelphia in 1967 but grew up in New Jersey.
He has authored *Totem* (2007), winner of the APR/Honickman First Book
Prize, and *Digest* (2014), awarded the Pulitzer Prize for Poetry in 2015. He is
also the author of *Air Traffic: A Memoir of Ambition and Manhood in Ameri-
can* (2018). In addition to his other awards, Pardlo won a Guggenheim
Fellowship in 2017.

    "Philadelphia, Negro" was first published in the periodical *Tin House*.[1]
The poem is in part a reflection of Pardlo's upbringing. Like many of his
poems, it is filled with allusions. The title, of course, is a tribute to W. E. B.
Du Bois's famous tome, *The Philadelphia Negro* (1899), a section of which is
included in this anthology. The speaker in the poem, in fact, makes a comment that as a youth living in Philadelphia, he "thought every American a
Philadelphia / Negro." The reference to aviation at the beginning of the poem
concerns Pardlo's father, an air traffic controller who was let go in 1981 during
Ronald Reagan's mass firings after the controllers went on strike. Pardlo's
father often makes an appearance in his poems. The referral to the TV miniseries *Roots* (1977) also connected him to his father and his heritage. Perhaps
it is also a sly nod to Questlove (Ahmir Khalib Thompson), the Philly-born
drummer and front man of the hip-hop band The Roots. The poem includes

many other Philadelphia references, including Georgie Woods, the Philadelphia DJ who coined the term "blue-eyed soul" in 1964; the southpaw Phillies
hurler Steve "Lefty" Carlton, who pitched for the team for more than a decade
and led them to the 1980 World's Championship; Sylvester Stallone's film
character Rocky Balboa climbing the steps of the Philadelphia Art Museum;
and Elton John's song "Philadelphia Freedom" (1975), inspired by Philly's
entry in World Team Tennis.

—

Alien-faced patriot in my Papa's mirrored aviators
that reflected a mind full of cloud
keloids, the contrails of Blue Angels[2] in formation
miles above the campered fields of Willow Grove[3]
where I heard them clear as construction paper slowly
tearing as they plumbed close enough I could nearly see
flyboys saluting the tiny flag I shook in their wakes.
I visored back with pride, sitting aloft dad's shoulders,
my salute a reflex ebbing toward ground crews in jumpsuits
executing orchestral movements with light. The bicentennial
crocheted the nation with the masts of tall ships and twelve-foot
Uncle Sams but at year's end my innocence dislodged
like a powdered wig as I witnessed the first installment
of *Roots*. The TV series appeared like a galleon on the horizon
and put me in touch with all twelve angry tines[4] of the fist
pick my father kept on his dresser next to cufflinks
and his Texas Instruments LED watch. I was not in the market
for a history to pad my hands like fat leather mittens. A kind
of religion to make sense of a past mysterious as basements
with upholstered wet bars and black-light velvet panthers, maybe,
but as a youngster I thought every American a Philadelphia
Negro, blue-eyed soulsters and southpaws alike getting
strong now, mounting the art museum steps together
like children swept up in Elton's freedom from Fern Rock[5]
to Veterans Stadium,[6] endorphins clanging like liberty
themed tourist trolleys unloading outside the Penn Relays,[7]
a temporal echo, and offspring, of Mexico City, where Tommie
Smith and John Carlos[8] made a human kinara[9] with the human

rights salute while my father scaled the Summit
Avenue[10] street sign at the edge of his lawn, holding a bomb
pop that bled tricolor ice down his elbow as he raised it like
Ultraman's[11] Beta Capsule in Flight from a police K (used to
terrorize suspicious kids). Your dad would be mortified too
if he knew you borrowed this overheard record of his oppression
to rationalize casting yourself as a revolutionary American
fourth-grader even though, like America, your father never lifted
your purple infant butt proudly into the swaddling of starlight
to tell the heavens to "behold, the only thing greater
than yourself!"[12] And like America, his fist only rose on occasion,
graceful, impassioned, as if imitating Arthur Ashe's[13] balletic serve,
so that you almost forgot you were in its way.

NOTES

1. Pardlo, "Philadelphia, Negro."

2. The Blue Angels is a flight formation squadron of the US Navy, which started in 1946.

3. Willow Grove is a suburb of Philadelphia in Montgomery County. It had an amusement park that operated from 1896 to 1976.

4. Tines are the teeth in the comb.

5. Fern Rock is a neighborhood in upper North Philadelphia.

6. Veteran's Stadium was the home of the Philadelphia Phillies baseball team and the Philadelphia Eagles football team from 1971 to 2003. It was located in South Philadelphia at 3501 South Broad Street.

7. The Penn Relays is the oldest and largest track and field competition in the United States. Since 1895 it has been held annually at the University of Pennsylvania's Franklin Field.

8. During the 1968 Olympic Games held in Mexico City, Smith and Carlos, two

American track and field winners, raised their fists in a Black Power salute during the medal ceremony.

9. A *kimara* is a seven-branched candleholder. It is used during the festival of Kwanzaa to hold the candles representing the seven principles of African Heritage.

10. Summit Avenue is located in Roxborough in Lower Northwest Philadelphia.

11. Ultraman: the Ultramen are technologically advanced beings who were once identical to humans. The Japanese franchise, begun in 1966, has spawned a very profitable series of TV shows, films, and videogames.

12. In the 1977 TV miniseries *Roots*, the child is held up to the sun.

13. Arthur Ashe (1943–1993) was an African American tennis player who won three Grand Slam singles titles.

BIBLIOGRAPHY

Alter, Alexandra. "Gregory Pardlo, Pulitzer Prize Winner for Poetry, on His Sudden Fame." *New York Times*, April 23, 2015, sec. C, 1.

Gregory Pardlo (website). https://gregory pardlo.com.

Martin, Kristen. "Gregory Pardlo, on Form, His Father and Not Writing a Book About Race." Literary Hub, April 9, 2018. https://lithub.com/gregory-pardlo -on-form-his-father-and-not-writing-a -book-about-race.

Paolino, Tammy. "Poems, Perspective and a
Pulitzer." *Courier Post*, June 12, 2105.
https://www.courierpostonline.com
/story/news/local/south-jersey/2015

/06/12/pulitzer-black-poet-gregory
-pardlo-rutgers/71069968.
Pardlo, Gregory. "Philadelphia, Negro." *Tin
House* 54 (Winter 2012).

Ayana Mathis, from *The Twelve Tribes of Hattie* (2012)

Ayana Mathis was born in Philadelphia in 1964 and attended the Philadelphia High School for Girls, a stellar school founded in 1848 and located at
Broad Street and Olney Avenue in the Logan section of North Philadelphia.
Mathis is also a graduate of the Iowa Writers' Workshop. Her first novel, the
widely praised *The Twelve Tribes of Hattie*, was a selection in Oprah's Book
Club 2.0. The sweeping scope of the novel examines the lives of a Black family
between 1925, when many migrated north to Philadelphia, to 1980. The main
protagonist, Hattie, arrived in the Germantown area of Philadelphia as part
of this Great Migration and was filled with hope, which is reflected in the
choice of her twins' names, Philadelphia and Jubilee. Like so many Black
migrants desperate to escape oppression in the South, Hattie looked at Philadelphia as representing a place of freedom and equality. This is reinforced
on her arrival at the train station, where she witnesses the civil interaction
between a Black customer and a White shop owner; however, the promise
of the North proves illusory as she soon encounters the harshness of life faced
by Black migrants and she loses her children to poverty and disease. She
begins to miss the sense of family and community that she had back home
and painfully learns to understand the reality of the segregation and the cruel
winters that await her up North. Hattie survives her ordeal with grit and courage, raising nine more children and a grandchild (with the two dead children
making up the twelve tribes), but she is left devoid of any sense of love and
tenderness. Mathis's second novel, *The Unsettled* (2023), is also partly placed
in Philadelphia.

FROM "PHILADELPHIA AND JUBILEE"

1925

Hattie Shepherd looked down at her two babies in their Moses baskets. The
twins were seven months old. They breathed easier sitting upright, so she had

them propped with small pillows. Only just now had they quieted. The night had been bad. Pneumonia could be cured, though not easily. Better that than mumps or influenza or pleurisy. Better pneumonia than cholera or scarlet fever. Hattie sat on the bathroom floor and leaned against the toilet with her legs stretched in front of her. The window was opaque with steam that condensed into droplets and ran down the panes and over the white wooden frames to pool in the dip in the tile behind the toilet. Hattie had been running the hot water for hours. August[1] was half the night in the basement loading coal into the hot water heater. He had not wanted to leave Hattie and the babies to go to work. Well, but . . . a day's work is a day's pay, and the coal bin was running low. Hattie reassured him: the babies will be alright now the night's passed.

The doctor had come around the day before and advised the steam cure. He'd prescribed a small dosage of ipecac[2] and cautioned against backward country remedies like hot mustard poultices,[3] though vapor rub was acceptable. He diluted the ipecac with a clear, oily liquid, gave Hattie two small droppers, and showed her how to hold the babies' tongues down with her finger so the medicine would flow into their throats. August paid three dollars for the visit and set to making mustard poultices the minute the doctor was out the door. Pneumonia.

Somewhere in the neighborhood, a siren wailed so keenly it could have been in front of the house. Hattie struggled up from her place on the floor to wipe a circle in the fogged bathroom window. Nothing but white row houses across the street, crammed together like teeth, and gray patches of ice on the sidewalk and the saplings nearly dead in the frozen squares of dirt allotted to them. Here and there a light shone in an upstairs window—some of the neighborhood men worked the docks like August, some delivered milk or had postal routes; there were schoolteachers too and a slew of others about whom Hattie knew nothing. All over Philadelphia the people rose in the crackling cold to stoke the furnaces in their basements. They were united in these hardships.

A grainy dawn misted up from the bottom of the sky. Hattie closed her eyes and remembered the sunrises of her childhood—these visions were forever tugging at her; her memories of Georgia grew more urgent and pressing with each day she lived in Philadelphia. Every morning of her girlhood the work horn would sound in the bluing dawn, over the fields and the houses and the black gum trees. From her bed Hattie watched the field hands dragging down the road in front of her house. Always the laggards passed after the first horn: pregnant women, the sick and lame, those too old for picking, those with babies strapped to their backs. The horn urged them forward like a lash. Solemn the road and solemn their faces; the breaking white fields waiting, the pickers spilling across those fields like locusts.

Hattie's babies blinked at her weakly; she tickled each one under the chin. Soon it would be time to change the mustard poultices. Steam billowed from the hot water in the bathtub. She added another handful of eucalyptus. In Georgia, there was a eucalyptus tree in the wood across from Hattie's house, but the plant had been hard to come by in the Philadelphia winter.

Three days before, the babies' coughs had worsened. Hattie threw on her coat and went to the Penn Fruit to ask the grocer where she might find eucalyptus. She was sent to a house some blocks away. Hattie was new to Germantown, and she quickly got lost in the warren of streets. When she arrived at her destination, bruised from the cold, she paid a woman fifteen cents for a bag of what she could have had for free in Georgia. "Well, you're just a little thing!" the eucalyptus woman said, "How old are you, gal?" Hattie bristled at the question but said that she was seventeen and added, so the woman would not mistake her for another newly arrived southern unfortunate, that she was married and her husband was training as an electrician and that they had just moved into a house on Wayne Street.[4] "Well, that's nice, sugar. Where's your people?" Hattie blinked quickly and swallowed hard, "Georgia, ma'am."

"You don't have anybody up here?"

"My sister, ma'am." She did not say that her mother had died a year earlier while Hattie was pregnant. The shock of her death, and of being an orphan and a stranger in the North, had driven Hattie's younger sister, Pearl, back to Georgia. Her older sister, Marion, had gone too, though she said she's come back once she'd birthed her child and the winter passed. Hattie did not know if she would. The woman regarded Hattie closely. "I'll come round with you now to look in on your little ones," she said. Hattie declined. She had been a fool, a silly girl too prideful to admit she needed looking in on. She went home by herself clutching the bag of eucalyptus.

The winter air was a fire around her, burning her clean of everything but the will to make her children well. Her fingers froze into claws around the curled top of the brown paper bag. She burst into the house on Wayne Street with great clarity of mind. She felt she could see into her babies, through their skin and flesh and deep into their rib cages to their weary lungs.

***

Thirty-two hours after Hattie and her mother and sisters crept through the Georgia woods to the train station, thirty-two hours on hard seats in the commotion of the Negro car, Hattie was startled from a light sleep by the train conductor's bellow, "Broad Street Station, Philadelphia!" Hattie clambered from the train, her skirt still hemmed with Georgia mud, the dream of Philadelphia round as a marble in her mouth and the fear of it a needle in her chest. Hattie and Mama, Pearl and Marion climbed the steps of the train platform up into the main hall of the station. It was dim despite the midday sun. The domed roof arched. Pigeons cooed in the rafters. Hattie was only fifteen then, slim as a finger. She stood with her mother and sisters at the crowd's edge, the four of them waiting for a break in the flow of people so they too might move toward the double doors at the far end of the station. Hattie stepped into the multitude. Mama called, "Come back! You'll be lost in all those people. You'll be lost!" Hattie looked back in panic; she thought her mother was right behind her. The crowd was too thick for her to turn back, and she was borne along on the current of people. She gained the double doors and was pushed out onto a long sidewalk that ran the length of the station.

The main thoroughfare was congested with more people than Hattie had ever seen in one place. The sun was high. Automobile exhaust hung in the air alongside the tar smell of freshly laid asphalt and the sickening odor of garbage rotting. Wheels rumbled on the paving stones, engines revved, paperboys called the headlines. Across the street a man in dirty clothes stood on the corner wailing a song, his hands at his sides, palms upturned. Hattie resisted the urge to cover her ears to block the rushing city sounds. She smelled the absence of trees before she saw it. Things were bigger in Philadelphia—that was true—and there was more of everything, too much of everything. But Hattie did not see a promised land in this tumult. It was, she thought, only Atlanta on a larger scale. She could manage it. But even as she declared herself adequate to the city, her knees knocked under her skirt and sweat rolled down her back. A hundred people had passed her in the few moments she'd been standing outside, but none of them were her mother and sisters. Hattie's eyes hurt with the effort of scanning the faces of the passersby.

A cart at the end of the sidewalk caught her eye. Hattie had never seen a flower vendor's cart. A white man sat on a stool with his shirtsleeves rolled and his hat tipped forward against the sun. Hattie set her satchel on the sidewalk, and wiped her sweaty palms on her skirt. A Negro woman approached the cart. She indicated a bunch of flowers. The white man stood—he did not hesitate, his body didn't contort into a posture of menace—and took the flowers from a bucket. Before wrapping them in paper, he shook the water gently from the stems. The Negro woman handed him the money. Had their hands brushed?

As the woman took her change and moved to put it in her purse, she upset three of the flower arrangements. Vases and blossoms tumbled from the cart and crashed on the pavement. Hattie stiffened, waiting for the inevitable explosion. She waited for the other Negroes to step back and away from the object of the violence that was surely coming. She waited for the moment in which she would have to shield her eyes from the woman and whatever horror would ensue. The vendor stooped to pick up the mess. The Negro woman gestured apologetically and reached into her purse again, presumably to pay for what she'd damaged. In a couple of minutes it was all settled, and the woman walked on down the street with her nose in the paper cone of flowers, as if nothing had happened.

Hattie looked more closely at the crowd on the sidewalk. The Negroes did not step into the gutters to let the whites pass and they did not stare doggedly at their own feet. Four Negro girls walked by, teenagers like Hattie, chatting to one another. Just girls in conversation, giggling and easy, the way only white girls walked and talked in the city streets of Georgia. Hattie leaned forward to watch their progress down the block. At last, her mother and sisters exited the station and came to stand next to her. "Mama," Hattie said. "I'll never go back. Never."

NOTES

1. August is Hattie's husband.

2. Ipecac is a medicine that induces vomiting.

3. Hot mustard poultices are made with mustard seed powder that is put in a heated wrapping and placed on the sick person's chest. It was a popular remedy for colds, congestions, and rheumatism into the twentieth century and is still used as a home remedy in some quarters.

4. Wayne Street: The author probably intends Wayne Avenue, located in Germantown.

BIBLIOGRAPHY

Ayana Mathis (website). https://www.ayana mathis.com.

Churchwell, Sarah. "*The Twelve Tribes of Hattie* by Ayana Mathis—Review." *Guardian*, February 8, 2013. https://www.the guardian.com/books/2013/feb/08 /twelve-tribes-hattie-mathis-review.

Wilkerson, Isabel. "Northern Passage." *New York Times*, January 6, 2013, BR sec., 1.

Ross Gay, "To the Fig Tree on 9th and Christian" (2013)

Ross Gay was born in Youngstown, Ohio, in 1974. He received a BA from
Lafayette College, an MFA from Sarah Lawrence, and a PhD in American lit-
erature from Temple University. He currently teaches at Indiana University.
Gay has published several books of poetry and essays. His poetry collection
Catalogue of Unabashed Gratitude was a finalist for the 2015 National Book
Award and won the 2016 National Book Critics Circle Award.

"To the Fig Tree on 9th and Christian" was originally published in the
May–June 2013 issue of *American Poetry Review*. Ninth and Christian is located
in South Philly in the neighborhood of Bella Vista and is in the heart of the
Italian Market area, the South Market Street Curb Market. The fig tree is a
hopeful sign; figs are a sign of fertility, and the tree is a hardy survivor, growing well beyond its normal Mediterranean environs, much like the tenacious
immigrants who live in the area. Despite the often hostile environment Philadelphia presents to its residents, a simple act such as eating figs can briefly
provide comity between strangers.

Tumbling through the
city in my
mind without once
looking up
the racket in
the lugwork[1] probably
rehearsing some
stupid thing I
said or did
some crime or
other the city they
say is a lonely
place until yes
the sound of sweeping
and a woman
yes with a
broom beneath
which you are now

too the canopy
of a fig its
arms pulling the
September sun to it
and she
has a hose too
and so works hard
rinsing and scrubbing
the walk
lest some poor sod
slip on the
silk of a fig
and break his hip
and not probably
reach over to gobble up
the perpetrator
the light catches
the veins in her hands
when I ask about
the tree they
flutter in the air and
she says take
as much as
you can
help me
so I load my
pockets and mouth
and she points
to the step-ladder against
the wall to
mean more but
I was without a
sack so my meager
plunder would have to
suffice and an old woman
whom gravity
was pulling into

the earth loosed one
from a low slung
branch and its eye
wept like hers
which she dabbed
with a kerchief as she
cleaved the fig with
what remained of her
teeth and soon there were
eight or nine
people gathered beneath
the tree looking into
it like a
constellation pointing
do you see it
and I am tall and so
good for these things
and a bald man even
told me so
when I grabbed three
or four for
him reaching into the
giddy throngs of
yellow-jackets sugar
stoned which he only
pointed to smiling and
rubbing his stomach
I mean he was really rubbing his stomach
like there was a baby
in there
it was hot his
head shone while he
offered recipes to the
group using words which
I couldn't understand and besides
I was a little

tipsy on the dance
of the velvety heart rolling
in my mouth
pulling me down and
down into the
oldest countries of my
body where I ate my first fig
from the hand of a man who escaped his country
by swimming through the night
and maybe
never said more than
five words to me
at once but gave me
figs and a man on his way
to work hops twice
to reach at last his
fig which he smiles at and calls
baby, *c'mere baby*,
he says and blows a kiss
to the tree which everyone knows
cannot grow this far north
being Mediterranean
and favoring the rocky, sun-baked soils
of Jordan and Sicily
but no one told the fig tree
or the immigrants
there is a way
the fig tree grows
in groves it wants,
it seems, to hold us,
yes I am anthropomorphizing
goddammit I have twice
in the last thirty seconds
rubbed my sweaty
forearm into someone else's
sweaty shoulder

gleeful eating out of each other's hands
on Christian St.
in Philadelphia a city like most
which has murdered its own
people
this is true
we are feeding each other
from a tree
at the corner of Christian and 9th
strangers maybe
never again.

NOTE

1. Lugwork: bicycle frames using steel tubes
combined with lugs, which are socket-like sleeves.

BIBLIOGRAPHY

Powell, Crystal. "An Interview with Ross Gay."
    Washington Square Review 40 (Fall 2017)
    https://www.washingtonsquarereview
.com/crystal-powell-an-interview-with
-ross-gay.

Yolanda Wisher, "5 South 43rd Street, Floor 2" (2014)

Yolanda Wisher is a poet, singer, and spoken word artist who was born in Philadelphia in 1976 and holds a BA in English and Black Studies from Lafayette College and an MA in creative writing from Temple University. She was chosen to be the third poet laureate of Philadelphia in 2016. Wisher is the author of *Monk Eats an Afro* (Hanging Loose Press, 2014), which contains "5 South 43rd Street, Floor 2," and is coeditor of *Peace Is a Haiku Song* (2013). In her poem Wisher perfectly captures the sounds, scents, and rhythms of life on a summer day on a street in West Philadelphia. The grittiness of life is evident, but so are the simple pleasures of inhabiting this multiethnic neighborhood. On such a blessed day, one can only "hold on to the moment / as if time is taking your blood pressure."

Sometimes we would get hungry for the neighborhood.
Walk up the sidewalk towards Chestnut Street.
Speak to the Rev holding the light-skinned baby,
ask his son to come put a new inner tube on my bike.
Cross Ludlow, past the mailbox on the corner,
Risqué Video, Dino's Pizza, and the Emerald Laundromat.
The fruit trucks tucked into 44th Street on the left,
house eyes shut with boards, fringes of children.
Once we went into a store sunk into the street,
owned by a Cambodian woman. She sold everything,
from evening gowns to soup. Over to Walnut and 45th,
where the Muslim cat sells this chicken wrapped in pita,
draped in cucumber sauce. The pregnant woman
behind the counter writes our order out in Arabic.
We grab a juice from the freezer, some chips,
eye the bean and sweet potato pies.

Back into the hot breath of West Philly, sun is setting.
The sky is smeared squash, tangerines in a glaze.
Three girls and one boy jump doubledutch. A white man
hustles from the video store with a black plastic bag.
We look for money in the street, steal flowers
from the church lawn. The shit stain from the wino
is still on our step. Mr. Jim is washing a car for cash.
John is cleaning his rims to Buju Banton.[1]
Noel is talking sweetly to the big blue-eyed woman.
Linda, on her way to the restaurant. The sister
in the wheelchair buzzes by with her headphones on.

One night, a man was shot and killed on this block,
right outside our thick wood door. But not today.
Today is one of those days to come home from walking
in the world, leave the windows open, start a pot of
black beans. Smoke some Alice Coltrane.[2] Cut up
some fruit, toenails. Hold on to the moment
as if time is taking your blood pressure.

NOTES

1. Buju Banton (Mark Anthony Myrie) is a Jamaican-born dancehall musician born in 1973. He has had an enormous popularity, but has been dogged by drug charges and anti-gay lyrics, such as in his song "Boom Boom Bye" (1992).

2. Alice Coltrane (1937–2009) was an American jazz pianist and composer. She was the wife of famous jazz saxophonist and composer John Coltrane, who lived in Philadelphia at 1511 North 33rd Street in North Philadelphia from 1952 to 1958.

BIBLIOGRAPHY

Fiske, Rachel. "Yolanda Wisher Is Here for Your Truth." *Title Magazine*, April 2017. http://title-magazine.com.
Timpane, John. "Yolanda Wisher Named Philly's Third Poet Laureate." *Philadelphia Inquirer*, February 6, 2016. https://www .inquirer.com/philly/news/20160205 _Yolanda_Wisher_named_Philly_s _third_poet_laureate.html.
"Yolanda Wisher." Poetry Foundation. https:// www.poetryfoundation.org/poets /yolanda-wisher.
Yolanda Wisher (website). https://www .yolandawisher.com.

Mat Johnson, from *Loving Day* (2015)

Mat Johnson was born in 1970 and grew up in the Germantown and Mount Airy sections of Philadelphia. He is the child of an African American mother and an Irish American father. Johnson holds a BA from Earlham College in Richmond, Indiana, and an MFA from Columbia University. He currently is the Philip H. Knight Chair of Humanities at the University of Oregon. He has written five novels, *Drop* (2000), *Hunting in Harlem* (2003), *Pym* (2011), *Loving Day* (2015), and *Invisible Things* (2022). He has also authored several graphic novels, including *Incognegro Renaissance* (2018). Johnson has won many awards, including the 2016 American Book Award for *Loving Day*. His writings often provide a satirical look at race in America.

Loving Day is set in Germantown, an area founded by Quakers and Mennonites, with an important place in American history, including often being considered the birthplace of the antislavery movement. Now largely African American, it is divided into two areas, Germantown and East Germantown, and is located in the Northwestern part of Philadelphia. Originally built as a pastoral area with many historic homes, parts of Germantown have fallen into disrepair. The setting of the story is one such dilapidated home, "an eighteenth-century estate in the middle of the urban depression of Germantown."

The protagonist in the story, Warren Duffy, is bequeathed the Loudin Mansion by his father. The home is an obvious play on the Loudoun Mansion at 4650 Germantown Avenue, built in 1801 and severely damaged by a fire in 1993. Warren is the mixed-race son of a recently deceased White father and a Black mother. Warren initially sees the mansion, now in a dilapidated condition, as a quick source of funds to help pay a settlement with his ex-wife. Over time, after returning to his roots and encountering a seventeen-year-old who turns out to be his daughter, Warren is forced to confront his own conflicted views of his heritage and of himself as a Black man often thought of by others as White because of his light complexion.

—

CHAPTER 1

In the ghetto there is a mansion, and it is my father's house. It sits on seven acres, surrounded by growling row houses, frozen in an architectural class war. Its expansive lawn is utterly useless, wild like it smokes its own grass and dreams of being a jungle. The street around it is even worse: littered with the disposables no one could bother to put in a can, the cars on their last American owner, the living dead roaming slow and steady to nowhere. And this damn house, which killed my father, is as big as it is old, decaying to gray pulp yet somehow still standing there, with its phallic white pillars and the intention of eternity. An eighteenth-century estate in the middle of the urban depression of Germantown. Before he died, my father bought the wreck at auction, planned on restoring it to its original state, just like he did for so many smaller houses in the neighborhood. Rescuing a slice of colonial history to sell it back to the city for a timeless American profit. His plan didn't include being old, getting sick, or me having to come back to this country, to this city, to pick up his pieces. This house is a job for a legion, not one person. It would kill one person. It did—my father. I am one person now. My father's house is on me. I see it from the back of the cab, up on its hill, rotting.

Donated by the Loudin family after the Depression, the mansion was used by the city as a museum until a fire that created repair costs beyond its means and interest. At one point in my life, decades before, I was a boy. As such, I knew this house. I used to ride the 23 trolley past its absurd presence and marvel at this artifact of rich white folks' attempt at dynasty. A physical memory of historic Germantown's pastoral roots, before the larger city of Philadelphia exploded past this location, propelled by the force of the industrial revolution. Most things from childhood get smaller with age, but Loudin Mansion towers, because now I have to take care of it. So I want to run. I sit passively in the taxi as I'm driven closer, but my thighs ache and my bowels are prepared to evacuate, and I want to open the door and run. I'll run. I'll run through North Philly if I have to, all the way downtown. Run along the highway back to the airport, then run away again from the whole damn country.

The white cabdriver makes no move to get out with me when he finally stops, just pops the trunk open with one button and with another relocks the doors after I open mine. That lock clicks hard. I'm on the street with my bags, and I can't get back inside. I'm not white, but I can feel the eyes of the few people outside on me, people who must think that I am, because I look white, and as such what the hell am I doing here? This disconnect in my racial projection is one of the things I hate. It goes in a subcategory I call "America," which has another subheading called "Philly." I hate that because I know I'm black. My mother was black—that counts, no matter how pale and Irish my father was. So I shall not be rebuked. I will not be rejected. I want to run but I refuse to be run off.

A kid walks by, about seventeen, not much younger than I was when I escaped this neighborhood. He looks up, and as I lift my bags I give him the appropriate local response, an expression that says I'm having a bad life in general and a headache right now. Welcome home. There are blocks around here where you can be attacked for looking another man in the eyes, and other blocks where you can be assaulted for not giving the respect of eye contact. I could never figure it, which blocks were which, until I realized these were just the excuses of sociopaths. The sociopaths, that's the real problem. The whole street demeanor is about pretending to be a sociopath as well, so that the real ones can't find you.

When I get to the porch, the front door opens. I can hear it creak before I see someone emerging from behind its paint-cracked surface. Sirleaf Day is carpeted in cloth. He's got a Kenyan dashiki, Sudanese mudcloth pants, and a little Ghanaian kente hat. It's like Africa finally united, but just in his wardrobe. Last time I saw him, he dressed the same, but he only had one leather medallion. Now he has enough to be the most decorated general in the

Afrocentric army. I give him a "Howyadoin," and the Philly salute, a hummingbird-like vibration of my forehead, the most defensive of nods. He gives me a hug. He hugs me like he knows I'm trying to get away.

"So you had your first divorce. That just means you a man now. Which kind was it? She stop loving you, or you stop loving her?"

"It wasn't like that," I tell him. Sirleaf grips me closer.

"Oh hell no. I hope it wasn't one of those where you both still love each other, but it's broke anyway. Those are the worse. My first, fourth marriages, they were like that. At least you didn't have any kids with her."

"Uncle Sirleaf, I really don't want to talk about—"

"Don't give me that 'uncle' mess. You're too old for that shit. And I'm way too young," he says, pushing me back for another look before pulling me in once more. "Your pop was waiting for you to come home, you know that? This house, it was going to be for you. You and your wife, your children. Bring you back to the community." Sirleaf's voice cracks with emotion. It makes me feel guilty for wanting to break free of his musky grasp. "And it did. You got to give that crazy honky that."

I look over Sirleaf's shoulder: there's a rusty Folgers Coffee can sitting on the porch, by the wall. It's there because my dad never smoked in a house. This can of ashes is full of cheap cigar butts, mixed with the cigarette butts of whoever visited. I know without looking inside it, because there was always a can like that on the porch of wherever my dad was living.

"He knew I wasn't coming back. He was just going to fix it up to sell it, like he always did." This gets him to release me, partially. He still holds my shoulders, pushes me back as far as he can to take a look at my face.

"Wasn't his fault you run off, was it? My daddy left me when I was four and gave me nothing but my stunning Yoruba[1] features. So stop bitching."

Sirleaf is a lawyer, a realtor, a griot, and a kook, and he's good at all of those things. My dad was his white friend, because they had the kook thing in common. For three decades, they would get together to sell a property or drink whiskey and get kooky together. My dad had his own realtor's license, but he wasn't good with most types of humans. Sirleaf is the people's man, knows everyone that matters in Germantown, from councilmen to people looking to buy their first homes. He speaks three languages: Street, Caucasian, and Brotherman.

Sirleaf's getting old and finally looks it. Some people age, and some just dehydrate. Sirleaf looks like someone let the water out and the creases dried in its absence. I can't imagine how old my dad must have looked. They were the same age but my father was one of those pasty Irish people with no melanin to protect his skin from time. He could barely manage enough pigment for a mole.

"We should really have a funeral," I tell him. "Or a memorial or—"

"He ain't want one, and we're going to respect that. You know your pop—he wasn't one to spend good money on a bunch of bullshit. His legacy, it's this house, this property. And it's you. Now let's look at your inheritance."

With great flourish, Sirleaf turns back to open the front door. But it's stuck. The wood's swelled and it takes a lot to jar, a lot of effort to protect so little. Hell's lobby waits on the other side. If my father's soul is left in the physical world, it's in the tools he left behind. Sandpaper, ladders, and scaffolding. Plaster and tarps, rollers and paint tins. At the back of my nose I can smell the Old Spice and Prell even though he hadn't used either since I was eleven. I will be buried here too, I just know, and then I fight that thought with the words I have been thinking in the days leading up to this moment: paint and polish. Paint it, polish the wood floors, tidy up whatever basic visual problems might get in the way of a buyer's imagination. Build on whatever my father managed in the months since he'd taken ownership. Use all the tricks he taught me. That's what I thought, packing to come back Stateside; that's what I thought waiting for the plane. That's what I tell myself now. Paint and polish. I even say it out loud.

"There ain't no roof," Sirleaf says back to me. "Go on, take a look at that jawn.[2] That shit's crazy. The wiring in here is, like, seventy years old. And exposed—I seen that old fuse box in the back pop sparks twice in the last hour. It's a miracle he didn't burn the place down running his power tools. I don't know how your pops lived up in this mess. Craig was one cheap bastard. No offense," and he wags his head at the shame of it.

I don't remind him about a childhood camped out in many a shelled home. My dad had been doing the same thing since my mother kicked him out, and that was twenty-seven years ago. I don't tell him about pissing in paint buckets and dumping it out the window.

"You sure you want to sleep here? I mean, what about Tosha's? They still in the house I sold them. Six bedrooms. Maybe you could stay there."

"I'll stop by, but I doubt her husband wants me under the same roof for an extended period."

"Up to you, but I'm out of here. This place creeps me out. You better see what you're dealing with on the second floor, before it gets dark. Power's iffy up there." He points to the stairs. I get the message that he wants me to go up. I also get the message that he's afraid to. That at least he understands the limits of his age. As he leaves, Sirleaf stares at his feet with every step, as if he's worried the old beams might give out on him.

"How soon can you get it listed?" I ask. He sighs. I've missed something.

"I told you. You can't sell this place the way it is, not without taking a huge loss. You can't sell it for the land; it's historic so it's hard to get permission to build on it. You going to have to pick up where your pop left off, and it's going to take awhile to get it together. At least, the basics. You got shoes to fill, boy," he tells me. I just happen to look down when Sirleaf says it. His shoes have at least two-inch heels on them. He catches me staring and says, "I'm engaged to this new jawn: young sister. She likes me tall."

"Sirleaf, look: I just got divorced. My comic-book shop, I had to sell it. I owe my ex half of that, but I'm still living off the money. Whatever we got to do, whatever we can get, let's just get it soon, okay? I don't care if we take a loss, I just want out."

"Yeah. Sure. Right. You seeing the same house I'm seeing, are you not? I mean, take a look around," he implores me. I don't need to do that.

"My ex is a lawyer. A really, really, good one. And she'll sue the living shit out of me if I don't pay back the money I owe her. I'm already late on the payments. You read my emails, right? I need that cash, man."

"Your ex isn't an American citizen, so she can't sue you here. I'm telling you, Warren, it might seem like a big deal to get sued, but that ain't your major problem right now. You got other things to worry about," and he lifts a mudcloth-adorned arm and motions in a slow sweep around the whole damned building.

Sirleaf is right; there is no roof. There are walls. It has floors. Just no real top. In my book, that barely qualifies it as a house, makes it more of a massive cup. I brave the stairs, shining a flashlight above me as I pace the hall of the second story. In most parts of the ceiling, there's nothing but blue tarp separating the interior from the elements. There are a few charcoaled beams in those rooms where my father hadn't knocked the remains of the fire damage down. In the master bedroom, there's a green canvas tent, the old Coleman tent my dad used when he took me on trips to the Pine Barrens and the Appalachian Trail. Now its yellow plastic spikes are nailed directly into the blackened, fire-ravaged hardwood. Instead of camping out in the room of the house least damaged, as I would have done, as any normal person would have done, my father took up residence in a room that looks like a hollowed out piece of charcoal. There's a tarp on the floor to match the one glimpsed through the burnt shingles above, but besides that, the space is nearly unprotected to the heavens. It's the nineteenth of August, about 80 degrees outside and 90 in this room. The windows up here are covered with brown paper, taped to the glass, but the sun's heat gets in anyway. This is the place he grew sick in. Made the decision to not go to the doctor in. Then died in. Quietly, of pneumonia. I always assumed he would die on the streets of Germantown itself, loud. Knocked over the head for being the wrong race in the wrong neighborhood in the wrong century.

In the gloom, I drag everything—the foldout table and chair, the lamp connected to the car battery, the propane grill, the five-gallon jugs of water, and eventually the tent itself—one by one downstairs to the dining hall, the least damaged room in the whole house. My father managed new drywall in here, matched and replaced sections of the crown molding, and had gotten as far as laying out cans of primer for painting. With the sliding doors to the hall closed, the room almost seems habitable.

I try to narrow my mind to the pragmatic nature of my next steps. I am exhausted and jet-lagged and need to set up camp. Tomorrow, for spending money, I will go draw cartoons at a convention. And all this lets me ignore that I am deconstructing the scene of my father's death and then lying down in it.

I hear a sound and am awake, and it happens so fast that I don't know if I've dreamt it. I'm not married anymore, there's no Becks in the bed next to me to ask if she heard something too. No Becky, who knows what to do because she's so much smarter than me that I can resent the truth and depend on it at the same time. No Becks, because I never grew up or wanted what grown folks want and that's my fault and I can accept that. No Becky, with her sallow Welsh flesh glowing in the moonlight, an image I loved because its contrast made my own pale flesh seem sable in comparison. I sink into the despair at that, at the reminder of my failure to meet the needs of the one person I was legally sworn to love, and even though it's been almost thirteen months now I feel how alone I am. Then I hear the sound again and suddenly all I feel is fear once more. It could be the settling of the house, the symphony of old wood doing its opening-night performance. There are no sounds of cars outside to hide acoustics. Another sound. I think. I don't know. So I stop breathing. When I was a kid I would lie in bed at night till my fear of an exploding bladder was greater than my fear of the ghosts I was sure I'd see on my way to the can. I remain still in my bed for a minute more before my fear congeals into self-consciousness: I'm a grown man scared of the dark. I get up to take a piss.

My feet are so loud on the creaking planks that it reminds me that real objects make real sounds, not negotiable ones. Around me, there are shadows, and there may even be ghosts too, but I am old enough to refuse to see them. In the bathroom, my urine hits the water in the bowl, and I look out the window into the gray of the night, the mist hovering over the grass. And then I see him.

He's sitting on the tall grass. In the dark. All alone. His legs folded under him. Just sitting there. My stream runs its course, but I still stand there. I can't move. I look at him, bald, black, ageless, clothes without distinction in the gloom, in the middle of the massive lawn between this mansion and the street, and I become as frozen as he is. I don't move because I'm too scared to. Even though I don't know why. Even though he's not moving. He doesn't seem to be looking at me, or at least his head isn't facing my exact direction. It's facing the front door. I think he's a ghost. I know he's a ghost. He stays there. A minute passes and he stays there. Maybe not a ghost. Ghosts come in and out, dissipate, are insubstantial by nature. So it's a man. And when I move to pull away from the window, his head snaps and he stares up at me.

Shooting down to a squat, I stay low till my legs begin to hurt. There's no phone. I have no phone, not in this country. Not in this house. I cannot call anyone even if I wanted to. No Becks. My father is dead. I am alone. My breath, it's so loud, and I try opening my mouth wider just to get the sound to stop taunting me.

I am a big guy, six four, weigh 225 naked, and I decide to act like I am a big man and I shoot upright, head for the room my father's work materials are in, go to grab the biggest thing I can find. This turns out to be a long wooden spear, an extension for a foam paint roller. I hold it with two hands. I am an African warrior! Who looks like a Celtic one. I grip it so hard my hands become even more white, adrenaline having replaced my blood. And then I go to the window. And I want him to see me. I want him to see my size. My determination, my intent. My lance. I look out the window.

And he's gone.

And for a second I'm even more scared. I want to be relieved, but now I'm incapable of it. Rod in hand, I check the other windows. I see nothing. I go upstairs for a better view, but no change. Germantown Avenue, past the fence, is without life. I stare out for minutes. Then more. Occasionally a car drives past along the chipped cobblestones, but otherwise it's empty, too late to come home and too early to drive out, which puts the time around four A.M. I stand there, on the second floor, in the burnt-out room of my father's. He chose it because it has the best view of the lawn, I realize. And when, many minutes later, I grow more tired than scared, I head back downstairs to lie down.

Tomorrow, which is today, I will go sit at a table in a large crowded room and smile at strangers, drawing pictures of their heads on muscle-bound bodies covered in leotards, and they will pay me cash. It is so absurd I laugh a little in my head, and I need that to get into my tent again, slide myself into the sleeping bag. Fear *that*, I remind myself. Fear social failure, you're better at it. I saw a crackhead, in the night, in Germantown. This hardly qualifies as a supernatural experience. I chuckle a bit, and go to zip up the tent, and then I see a person standing by my door.

She's a woman. She's not looking at me; she's looking up the stairs. My breath gets heavy again, but she keeps looking up there, not over at me. And she's a ghost. Not the dead kind. She's clothed in a dirty gown, the lingerie of a drug-addled seductress. She's a white woman, gaunt cheeks like bones around the dark hollows of her eye sockets. If she looks at me I will pee myself, I will shit myself on this very floor, and I will scream too. I don't care what she wants, I just don't want her to turn her head and look at me. She coughs. It keeps going, phlegm rising from behind her toenails with each convulsion till it gets to the back of her throat and jumps to her hand. It echoes through the house. It is more here than I am. There's a splatter and then she's gone.

When I hear the front door click behind her, I pull myself frantically from my bag and out of my tent and grab my spear and head for her. I am rage. I am anger. All the fear has been recycled. But I am caution, too, and when I reach the door I think there might be a pack of them out on the porch, the monsters, the rags falling from the skin, prepared to ambush me. So I let go of the handle.

I. Am back. In Philly.

Landing in an airport doesn't count. Sitting in a taxi can be done anywhere. This, this feeling, this, is *Philly*.

They want something from me. They must or they wouldn't be here. Do they think I'm white? Out of my element? Vulnerable? They want something and I have nothing. I am a man who has nothing, all this time meandering through life yet all I have is wounds. I have no treasure, and I never want to know what they'd take from me instead.

There is a tattered curtain over the entryway's left window and I pull it aside and the glass revealed is hand blown and old and distorted. But I see movement.

And I see them. I see the figures. A man and a woman. Staring at the house. Standing on the lawn. Walking. Walking backward. Staring at the house, walking backward. Away from me. Until they reach the fence to the street and float up, and over.

I keep staring and waiting for more, but there's nothing there. I keep staring though, until my breathing calms down, but nothing happens out there. When I turn around, I look through the shadows at this home. I look at the buckling floors. I look at the cracks in all the walls, the evidence of a foundation crumbling beneath us. I smell the char of the fire, the sweet reek of mold, the insult of mouse urine. I see a million things that have to be fixed, restored, corrected, each one impossible and each task mandatory for me to escape again. I see Sisyphus's boulder,[3] just with doors and beams. I can't take it so I look out the window once more, where nothing is coming to get me, because the neighborhood doesn't need to, because it knows I'm trapped and it has all the time in the world. Then I look back into the house.

And that's when I decide I'm going to burn the fucker down.

NOTES

1. The Yoruba are an African people located in southwest Nigeria and in Benin. It is also the name of their language.

2. Jawn: a uniquely Philadelphian word. Generally, it can be used as a substitute to refer to almost any person, place, or thing. As Don Nosowitz states, a *jawn* "is an all-purpose noun, a stand-in for inanimate objects, abstract concepts, events, places, individual people, and groups of people" ("The Enduring Mystery of 'Jawn' Philadelphia's All-Purpose Noun," Atlas Obscura, March 24, 2016).

3. Sisyphus's punishment for offending the Greek gods was to eternally push a boulder up a hill, only to have it fall back down when he reached the top.

BIBLIOGRAPHY

Dean, Michelle. "*Loving Day* by Mat Johnson Review—A High Energy Romp on Mixed Race Matters." *Guardian*, June 10, 2015.

De Greff, Dana. "*Loving Day*: Review." *Mosaic: Literary Magazine of the African Diaspora*, October 10, 2015.

Dreisinger, Baz. "Blackish in America." *New York Times*, June 7, 2015, BR, 1

Warren Longmire, "Brotherly Love" (2015)

Warren Longmire was born in North Philly and is a lifelong resident of the city. He is a poet, computer programmer, poetry editor for *Apiary Magazine*, and a three-time member of the Philadelphia Fuze's national slam. He's been published in numerous little magazines, including *Painted Bride Quarterly* and has two chapbooks *Ripped Winters* and *Do.Until.True*. You can find his writings, essays, videos, and sounds at https://alongmirewriter.squarespace .com and https://soundcloud.com/wclongmire.

"Brotherly Love" was first published in *Philadelphia Stories* (2015). The poem shows the city with all its paradoxes, dangerous yet comforting, ugly yet beautiful, Philadelphia leaves one waiting, disappointing even in its sports teams, but with its supporters never giving up hope. It is unique down to its toxic "Schuylkill punch" drinking water. It is resilient and tough, a place where even the mice look at you with disdain. If you can live here, you can survive anywhere.

——

Philly all the emo with none of the moshpit.
Philly free jazz in a trashbag.

Philly's a synthetic weave tumbleweed down 69th street.
Philly's Schuylkill punch brown and meek mill's[1] cadence for an
    anti-depressant.

Philly's a rust covered trolley rail used as a balance beam for cat
    sized rats.
Philly's a mouse that stands in the middle your living-room
    wondering what you staring at.

Philly's when the scent of urine feels comfortable.
Philly's a crackhouse where someone pulls out an ipod touch.

Philly's the seasoning left in potato chip bag, littered because
     fuck you.
Philly's bulletproof glass protecting blunt wrappers and raisinets.

Philly's a bed sheet ad for pet colonics.
Philly's four empty barber shops in a two block radius.

Philly is abandoned midnight unsafe even if desert.
Philly looks at anything but you as intensely as it can.

Philly is dubstep[2] basement row-home hot pagan light-show for
     nobody Philly.
Philly's a cafe a bored new jersey dreamed into existence.

Philly bucktoothed street with caution tape floss.
Philly flosses through beirut in a hooptee.[3]
Philly ain't no white car.
Philly For Sale sign.

Philly loose dutch tobacco[4] on the 23. Philly loose money. Philly is
     cheap.
Philly chirps. Philly speaks its first words. Philly lounges.

Philly is waiting.
Philly is waiting.
Philly is waiting and the teams choke.
The kids choke.

The fey smokers identical outside the whiskey bar chain smoke like
     it's new orleans downtown.
The buses weeze.

The roads are cracked and the sidewalk's [sic] grow flowerbeds
     beneath them.

Philly grows and shrinks. Screams "back door" but doesn't tell you
    to step down.
Doesn't speak. Gets cut. Names.
A paradox laughing at itself. The old friend with no money and a
    ugly mouth.

NOTES

1. Meek Mill (Robert Rihmeek Williams) is an American rapper born in 1987 in Philadelphia. Despite his musical success, he has had several run-ins with the legal system.

2. Dubstep is a type of electronic music that originated in South London in the early 2000s.

3. *Hooptee* is urban slang for an old car.

4. Dutch tobacco is loose tobacco used for cigarettes. There also may be a reference to dutchies, loose marijuana rolled inside Dutch Masters cigar wrappers to make joints or blunts.

Yvonne (Chism-Peace), "4951 Walnut Street" (2019) and from *Rosetta on the Bus,* "Momma House" (2019)

First poetry editor at two pioneer feminist journals, *Aphra* and *Ms.*, Yvonne (Chism-Peace) received NEAs (poetry/1974/1984), a Leeway (fiction/2003), a Pushcart Prize (vol. 6), and more. She is the author of the epic trilogy *Iwilla/ Soil, Iwilla/Scourge, Iwilla/Rise* (Chameleon). Forthcoming and recent publications appear in*Black in the Middle: An Anthology of the Black Midwest* (Belt), *From the Farther Shore* (Bass River Press / Calliope), *Rattle: Poets Respond* (6/21/2020), *Horror USA: California* (Soteira), *Is It Hot in Here Or Is It Just Me?* (Beautiful Cadaver Project), *Home: An Anthology* (Flexible), *Quiet Diamonds 2019/2018* (Orchard Street), *161 One-Minute Monologues from Literature* (Smith and Kraus), *Yellow Arrow Journal: Home, Event* (49.1), *Philadelphia Stories, Metonym, Dappled Things, Burningword Literary, Bryant Literary, Pinyon, Nassau Review, Bosque Press #8,* and *Foreign Literary #1.* Selected online publications can be found at https://www.lwill.com.

Many of Yvonne's poems are deeply rooted in Philadelphia, where she was born and has spent much of her life. She often documents forgotten or neglected places and people from the city's rich Black history. "4951 Walnut Street" is a double sonnet about renowned singer, actor and civil rights activist Paul Robeson. Many people do not realize that he spent his final years (1966–76) in West Philadelphia, at a Walnut Street house built in 1925. It was purchased in 1959 by Robeson's older sister, Marian Robeson Forsythe, and her husband, once a physician. The house and museum are now owned by the West Philadelphia Cultural Alliance. The poem was first published in *Moria*, Woodbury University, Los Angeles, California (December 1999).

"Momma House" is a sonnet about Sister Rosetta Tharpe (1915–1973), a guitarist, songwriter, and gospel singer who is seen as one of the important influences on both gospel and early rock and roll music. In 2011 a marker was placed at the corner of 11th and Master Streets in the Yorktown section of North Philadelphia to commemorate the modest rowhouse where Tharpe lived in a modest rowhouse from the mid-sixties until her death. She is buried in the city's Northwood Cemetery, where a headstone was not erected until many years after her death. The poem was first published in *Philadelphia Stories*.[1]

—

"4951 WALNUT STREET"[i]

I.

> Did he drink his breakfast coffee with cream
> Or black? Or was it green tea with lemon,
> No milk? Did he linger in his bedroom,
> On his tray another bloody headline?
> Or gentle hunger dared him stumble down
> To where Sister blurred with Salvation?
> Left him dirty dishes, her cooking done?
> Within liberty's forced decline.
> Laughter returns—What old childhood fun!
> Himself, a tired two-step, out of time.
> That was 1966. I had just blown
> Up my family, scholarship in hand, no plan
> But get-away sane. Thus, missed fortune
> Aligned our paths. I never met the great man.

II.

> Further back in '59, my folks tied down their youth
> To a simpler house arrest five blacks south
> From the great man's last resort. As a teen

---

i. Black-listed, his passport revoked, civil rights icon Paul Robeson spent his final years (1966–76) in a house built in 1911 and purchased in 1959 by his older sister, Marian Robeson Forsythe, and her husband, once a physician, in demolished Eastwick.

I had crisscrossed for years that urban
Avenue begging for my great church done
In the distance in the sunset like him—
A monument sublime.
We each return wounded to the womb.
Not his mother, but female, all the same,
To one spartan and poor Sister offered her home
With wallpaper and lace, that special perfume
Rising sickly-sweet. Not with innocence,
I, too, return, buying back my inheritance.
But all is well. Each heart, a museum.

FROM *ROSETTA ON THE BUS*, "MOMMA HOUSE"[i]

Touring is a kind of homelessness,
The price the body pays as the soul takes wing.
Fans brought to their feet, the faithful to their knees!
Yet meals on a tray in her lap left its sting.
Under the spinning stars on a midnight bus
Sleep came and washed away the heaviness
Of the heart. Sleep and the wisdom of dreams.
Miracle child with flowers in her voice
And in her fingertips unquenchable flames—
Did she ever have a choice?
Echoes awake and bend laggard legendry.
Momma, beloved Marie, a far galaxy.
The end of the line. Everybody's got one.
Same old same old. For decades, no tombstone.

i. In 2011, a marker at the corner of 11th and Mercer Streets in the Yorktown section of North Philadelphia was set to commemorate where Sister Rosetta Tharpe lived in a modest row house from the mid-sixties until her death in 1973. She is buried in Northwood Cemetery.

NOTE

1. Chism-Peace, "4951 Walnut Street," *Philadelphia Stories* (Winter 2020).

BIBLIOGRAPHY

"Yvonne Chism-Peace," Leeway Foundation.
    https://www.leeway.org/artists
    /yvonne_chism_peace.

Charles D. Ellison, "Philadelphia, Where Blackness Transcends,"
The Root (February 14, 2019)

Charles D. Ellison is an award-winning thought leader, political strategist, commentator, and advocacy expert, with nearly two decades of applied expertise in the arena of politics, public policy, campaigns and elections, crisis management, and emerging/digital media strategy. Ellison is the executive producer and host of *Reality Check*, a daily public affairs program on WURD (96.1FM / 900AM / wurdrradio.com in Philadelphia). He is also contributing editor for the *Philadelphia Citizen*, weekly Wednesday cohost on the nationally syndicated *Keepin' It Real with Rev. Al Sharpton*, and managing editor for ecoWURD.com, a publication covering the intersection of the environment, race, and income. His writings have been frequently featured in major publications such as the *Philadelphia Tribune*, TheRoot.com, the Forward, *Politico*, Pacific Standard, the *Daily Beast*, the *Washington Post*, and others. He is a regular analyst for numerous major metropolitan media outlets, including WVON-AM (Chicago), WHUR-FM (Washington, DC), KSRO-AM (California), and KDKA (Pittsburgh). He has appeared on MSNBC, CNN, NPR, FOX, CBS's *Face the Nation*, SkyTV, and elsewhere. More engagement at @ellisonreport on X (formerly Twitter).

"Philadelphia, Where Blackness Transcends" is a Valentine's day prose/poem. It is a clear-eyed celebration, a love letter to the city Ellison loves, warts and all. The essay expresses the unique character of the city for its Black residents. They have inextricably changed the city and the city in turn has changed them. The essay helps explain why Black Philadelphians love their city despite the abuse they have often seen at its hands. As Ellison states, "There are no boundaries to the blackness of Philly, the blackness that empowers you, protects you and never leaves. The blackness that brings you home and loves you back."

If we needed a Capital of Blackness, we'd make it Philadelphia.

Philly is the soundtrack to blackness, every facet of black life rolled into a hoagie of diasporic oneness. Every elastic, painful, ebullient chord, like Gerald Price's mystically floating fingers across piano keys at Zanzibar Blue, or young brothers freestyle battling elder cats on trumpet at Ortlieb's.[1]

There is an inexplicable richness, rawness and deeply embedded resistance. Six degrees of everything-is-black separation. In Philly, black is *Black* . . . with a capital "B." As not-this-side-of-the-tracks ethnic white as it is, Philly is the only place where you defiantly exhibit the infinite spectrum of your blackness, the many kaleidoscopic wonders in political fist-full flashes of dreadlocked glory, chiseled beards, homegirl scrappiness, old-school pulpit, trademark black Islamic swagger and a nonstop blend of sound, art and taste oozing through every asphalt, Fairmount Park vein.

There's power in its black cowboys on horseback, the gifted rage and misery in its soul and neo-soul, its Freedom Theater, its mural art. It is the only place you'd spot a car-sized Afro pick outside the main city government office building, just to piss white people off over Frank Rizzo, Philly's version of Confederate generals. Black Philly is mic-booming Black Israelites on Center City soapboxes and stone-faced, armed MOVE brothers staring down sweaty crimson-necked police on a humid Philthy day.

The Force pulling on her like a Jedi, my late grandmother—who just transitioned a few weeks ago at 92—couldn't fully explain why she picked Philly. But she knew "[t]here's no place as black as Philly," Mary laughed, half-chuckling through memories of a mourned exodus from Jim Crow Virginia, younger years in D.C. and then Philly, with kids and without much of an initial plan. Yet, it was something always stirring that gripped her like those heart-bursting, roof-shaking gospel solos you can find in any random North Philly church.

And, sometimes, when Philly police drop a bomb on your neighborhood or knock a handcuffed sister to the ground by the lock of her hair, or the public schools are so *hot* from no air conditioning that the kids miss weeks of school, that's OK, because "*we all we got.*"

"PHL" is nearly 44 percent black (the highest black population share of the top 10 most populous American cities), a colorful canvas of black imagination and grit; a 26 percent poverty rate where half of it is black. Still: black mayors? We've had *three*, each winning two full terms (even the one who ordered the bomb drop). Black politicians, community leaders and a city-wide organization class is business as usual. Black power principles are universally acknowledged, albeit scaled, regardless of neighborhood and class. There is a constant busyness to Philly's blackness, a constant need to start some shit, good or bad: from political firsts to the first black architect who designed everything from our iconic art museum to our central library.[2] There is the legendary Philly Black Mafia[3] that was more organized and elusive than its Italian and Irish peers of cinematic repute.

Half-a-million people make annual pilgrimage to our Odunde Festival,[4] symbol of Philly as capital of black spirit and black standards. We are a place of black *options*. We have the nation's oldest, largest and near daily black news-paper, *The Philadelphia Tribune*. We enjoy constant black-owned broadcast gems such as WURD,[5] the only one of its kind in Pennsylvania, and just a few like it in the nation. The oldest HBCU? That would be Cheyney University, struggling on the edges of town.

Mind you, none of this is perfect. But black Philadelphians are, as WURD President and CEO Sara Lomax-Reese reflects, " . . . heirs to revolutionary legacy."

"With all its flaws and hypocrisy, we were the place where the ideals for a free, egalitarian society were shaped," says Lomax-Reese. "This was an epi-center of the abolitionist movement." A place of promise and possibility for enslaved Africans, where heroes like Octavius Catto and William Still blazed the path for freedom firsts and "the fight to claim our basic humanity." Some-thing about Philly blackness refuses to accept second-class status and *less than*. Tired of sitting in the discarded pews of a white church, Richard Allen just started his *own thing*, creating the African Methodist Episcopal church. Philly gave life to organized black theology in America.

"Philly is a tough place to live, but black Philadelphians are some tough people," says Marilyn Kai Jewett, longtime journalist, marketing consultant and Yoruba priest. "We ain't afraid of nobody; it's been that way since this place was founded." Real African spiritual traditions thrive in Philly unlike anywhere else in the nation, many continuing to practice Yoruba and Ifa[6] tra-ditions to this day.

Yes, it is an unforgiving place, a clash of our best and worst. Black Philly is the birthplace of black middle-class Jack-and-Jillery.[7] But parasitic high poverty and bad environment permeates every social and economic indicator ever studied. Philly can make your blackness—or it can eat it alive.

Black prose is poetic and Biblical in a city of contradictions, Brotherly Love and Sisterly Affection. Black chests proudly rising as paradox, spawned from the city's 337-year history. It is a blackness of the good and bad happenings that consume it, of celebrations at the Dell[8] and living while black at the local Starbucks. The weathered and weathering blackness of streets with famous Philly black names and dreams gambled to fate. No wonder W.E.B. Dubois used it to pen his inaugural work *The Philadelphia Negro*, the first authoritative volume of American sociology.

"We are a town filled with black leadership," says Councilwoman Jannie Blackwell, who's [sic] late husband was Congressman Lucien Blackwell (D-Pa.). "There are a lot of black people involved in things that move the city forward. We are involved in all of the discussions to turn it around, on every major issue."

Michael Coard, civil rights lawyer and WURD host, is "*The Angriest Black Man in America,*" . . . and you can't pull that off anywhere else but in a city as black as Philly. "What makes us the blackest city in America? Octavius Catto's statue on City Hall grounds, one of the greatest voting-rights activists in history. Three black former mayors, a current black city council president,[9] a black police commissioner,[10] and a black sheriff."

The world mistakenly relegates Philly blackness to groupie gimmickry, but Philly is so much more than "Summertime" on Belmont Plateau,[11] the overused grease of footlong cheesesteaks at Broad and Erie[12] or *Made in America* concerts[13] on Ben Franklin Parkway. Of course, black Philly is proud of that. But we are so much more than our beloved Eagles, our blackness a bigger triple double than our Sixers, our issues so much deeper than freeing Meek Mill. We are aging, decaying symbols of imprisonment like Mumia Abu Jamal, and we are nail-solid activist lawyers like Cecil B. Moore, whose name is forever etched across a long strip of Philly avenue.

"This is home to countless sons and daughters of the diaspora," says State Rep. Joanna McClinton (D-Philadelphia). "We have the region's largest West African and Caribbean population, we have parents and grandparents who migrated from the segregated South looking for opportunities."

In Philly, our black goes *big*. Some of it is the Philly you know: from Uptown to Philly Sound; from countless names like Anderson, Abele, Scott,

Gray, Gamble, Huff, Stone, Tucker, Washington, LaBelle, Pendergrass, Morgan, Vanzant, Wideman, Delaney, and, yeah, (damn) Cosby, too. Philly is so black that folks like Ella, Sonia and Badu[14] stopped through for inspiration or stayed. There are no boundaries to the blackness of Philly, the blackness that empowers you, protects you and never leaves. The blackness that brings you home and loves you back.

NOTES

1. Zanzibar Blue, Ortlieb's: Zanzibar Blue was a jazz club that operated in Central City from 1990 to 2007. The owners, Robert and Benjamin Bynam, opened another jazz club, South Kitchen and Jazz Parlor, in 2015, at 600 North Broad Street in North Philadelphia. Ortlieb's is a restaurant and live music venue located at 847 North 3rd Street in North Philadelphia.

2. Central Library: Julian Francis Abele (1881–1950) was the first African American student to graduate from the University of Pennsylvania's Department of Architecture, and went on to a distinguished career, helping to design the Central Library, the Museum of Art, and the Widener Memorial Library at Harvard, among many others.

3. Philly Black Mafia: begun by Samuel Christian in 1968 and particularly active in the 1970s. See Sean Patrick Griffin's *Philadelphia's "Black Mafia": A Social and Political History* (2003) for more on this.

4. Odunde Festival: Created by Lois Fernandez in 1975, the Odunde Festival is an annual one-day event on the second Sunday in June. It is held in South Philadelphia and celebrates Black history and culture.

5. WURD: the AM radio station started operations as WFLN in 1958. After a number of owners and call numbers, the station took on the current talk format in 2002, aimed largely at a Black audience.

6. Ifa: spiritual beliefs largely practiced by the Yoruba people in Nigeria.

7. Jack-and-Jillery: Jack and Jill of America is an African American organization begun in 1938, designed to improve the lives of Black children and young adults through social and cultural activities. The first chapter was founded in

Philadelphia. The group was seen by some Blacks as being elitist.

8. The Dell: The Dell Music Center is located in Fairmount Park at 2400 Strawberry Mansion Drive.

9. Black city county president: Darrell L. Clarke is the Democratic representative from the 5th election district. He has been the council president since 2012.

10. Black police commissioner: Willie L. Williams (1988–1992).

11. Belmont Plateau: Located at 2075 Belmont Avenue in Fairmount Park, the plateau provides some of the best views of the city.

12. Broad and Erie: the location of Max's Steaks in Germantown.

13. Concerts: The annual two-day Made in America festival was started in 2021 in Philadelphia by rapper Jay-Z. The 2020 festival was canceled due to COVID-19, but it was renewed in 2021.

14. Anderson . . . Badu: Here, Ellison gives a shout out to some notable Black Philadelphians. Marian Anderson (1897–1992) was an opera singer, and she was the first African American to perform at the Metropolitan Opera in New York City in 1955. She performed at an open-air concert before a mixed-race audience at the Lincoln Memorial in 1939. Jill Scott (1972–) is a well-known singer-songwriter. William H. Gray III (1941–2013) was an important political figure who represented Pennsylvania's 2nd congressional district from 1979 to 1991. Kenneth Gamble (1943–) and Leon A. Huff (1942–) are a songwriting and production team responsible for dozens of rhythm-and-blues hits. Cynthia Dolores Tucker (1927–2005) was a politician and civil rights advocate. Ora

Washington (ca. 1899–1971) was a tennis and basketball star. Patti LaBelle (1944–) is a renowned rhythm-and-blues and soul singer. Teddy Pendergrass (1958–2010) was a well-known rhythm and blues and soul singer. Iyanla Vanzant (1953–) is a best-selling author and spiritual speaker. Martin Delaney (1812–1885) was an author, Black nationalist, army officer, and abolitionist. Ella Fitzgerald (1917–1996) was a jazz singer. Erykah Badu (1971–) is a neo-soul singer and songwriter.

APPENDIX A: ALTERNATE TABLE OF CONTENTS

BY GENRE

(Auto)Biographical: Alice, *Thomas Isaiah's Memoirs*; Joyce, *Confession of John Joyce*; Allen, *The Life, Experience, and Gospel Labours*; Jacobs, *Incidents in the Life of a Slave Girl*; Davis, *Diaries*; Still, *The Underground Railroad*; Moore Campbell, *Sweet Summer*; Brown, *A Taste of Power*.

Excerpts, Fiction: Webb, *The Garies and Their Friends*; Fauset, *Plum Bun*; Gardner Smith, *South Street*; Ross, *Oreo*; Bradley, *South Street*; Wideman, *Philadelphia Fire*; Wideman, *The Cattle Killing*; Pate, *Losing Absalom*; Cary, *The Price of a Child*; McKinney-Whetstone, *Tumbling*; Mathis, *The Twelve Tribes of Hattie*; Johnson, *Loving Day*.

Nonfiction Prose: Cato and Petitioners, "Letter of Cato and Petition by 'The Negroes Who Obtained Freedom by the Late Act'"; Jones and Allen, *Narrative of the Proceedings of the Black People*; Jones and Others, "Petition of the People of Color and Freemen of Philadelphia"; Forten, *Letters from a Man of Colour*; Forten and Parrott, "To the Humane and Benevolent Inhabitants of the City and County of Philadelphia"; Whipper, *An Address Delivered Before the Colored Reading Society*; Purvis, *Appeal of Forty Thousand Citizens*; Willson, *Sketches of the Higher Classes*; Harper, "An Appeal for the Philadelphia Rescuers"; Catto, *Our Alma Mater*; Still, "A Brief Narrative"; Du Bois, *The Philadelphia Negro*; Locke, "Hail Philadelphia"; Beam, "Brother to Brother"; Bambara, Deep Sight and Rescue Missions"; Abu-Jamal, "A Panther Walks in Philly."

Poetry: Sanchez, "elegy (for MOVE and Philadelphia); Sanchez, "10 Haiku (for Philadelphia Murals)"; Jackson, "Urban Renewal ii"; Jackson "Urban Renewal iv"; Jackson, "Euphoria"; Jackson, "Hoops"; Pardlo, "Philadelphia, Negro"; Gay, "To the Fig Tree on 9th and Christian"; Wisher, "5 South 43rd Street, Floor 2"; Longmire, "Brotherly Love"; Yvonne, "4951 Walnut Street"; Yvonne, "Momma House."

Short Fiction: Coppin, "Christmas Eve Story"; Dunbar-Nelson, "By Paths in the Quaker City"; Birtha, "Route 23"; Bradley, "The Station"; Solomon, "Secret Pool."

APPENDIX B: ALTERNATE TABLE OF CONTENTS

BY THEME

Black/White Interactions: Jones and Allen, *Narrative of the Proceedings of the Black People*; Jones and Others, Petition of the People of Color and Freemen of Philadelphia; Forten, *Letters from a Man of Colour*; Allen, *The Life, Experience, and Gospel Labours*; Purvis, *Appeal of Forty Thousand Citizens*; Webb, *The Garies and Their Friends*; Jacobs, *Incidents in the Life of a Slave Girl*; Still, *A Brief Narrative*; Still, *The Underground Railroad*; Fauset, *Plum Bun*; Smith, *South Street*; Bradley, *South Street*; Sanchez, "elegy"; Cary, *The Price of a Child*; Gay, "To the Fig Tree"; Solomon, "Secret Pool"; Mathis, *The Twelve Tribes of Hattie*; Johnson, *Loving Day*.

Drugs: Pate, *Losing Absalom*, Jackson, "Euphoria"; Solomon, "Secret Pool."

Education: Whipper, *An Address Delivered Before the Colored Reading Society*; Brown, *A Taste of Power*; Moore Campbell, *Sweet Summer*; Jackson, "Hoops."

Family: Mathis, *The Twelve Tribes of Hattie*; McKinney-Whetstone, *Tumbling*; Cary, *The Price of a Child*; Moore Campbell, *Sweet Summer*; Birtha, "Route 23."

Gender: Jackson, "Euphoria"; Moore Campbell, *Sweet Summer*; Brown, *A Taste of Power*; Fauset, *Plum Bun*, Jacobs, *Incidents in the Life of a Slave Girl*; Cary, *The Price of a Child*; Birtha, "Route 23"; Solomon, "Secret Pool"; Mathis, *The Twelve Tribes of Hattie*; McKinney-Whetstone, *Tumbling*.

Illness/Disease: Wideman, *The Cattle Killing*; Mathis, *The Twelve Tribes of Hattie*; Jones and Allen, *Narrative of the Proceedings of the Black People*.

Middle Class: Willson, *Sketches of the Higher Classes*; Webb, *The Garies and Their Friends*; Davis, *Diaries*; Still, "A Brief Narrative"; Du Bois, *The Philadelphia Negro*; Moore Campbell, *Sweet Summer*; McKinney-Whetstone, *Tumbling*.

Pride in the City: Wisher, "5 South"; Bradley, "The Station"; Longmire, "Brotherly Love"; Pardlo, "Philadelphia, Negro"; Yvonne, "Momma House"; Yvonne, "4951 Walnut Street"; Gay, "To the Fig Tree"; Sanchez, "10 Haiku"; McKinney-Whetstone, *Tumbling*; Locke, "Hail Philadelphia."

Public Transportation: Ross, *Oreo*; Birtha, "Routh 23," Bambara, "Deep Sight and Rescue Missions"; Still, "A Brief Narrative"; Bradley, "The Station."

Racial Violence: Abu-Jamal, "A Panther Walks in Philly"; Sanchez ,"elegy"; Webb, *The Garies and Their Friends*; Pate, *Losing Absalom*; Smith, *South Street*; Wideman, *Philadelphia Fire*.

Religion: Allen, *The Life, Experience, and Gospel Labours*; Jones and Allen, *Narrative of the Proceedings of the Black People*; Wideman, *The Cattle Killing*; McKinney-Whetstone, *Tumbling*.

Resistance: Jones and Others, Petition of the People of Color and Freemen of Philadelphia; Forten, *from a Man of Colour*; Purvis, *Appeal of Forty Thousand Citizens*; Harper, "An Appeal for the Philadelphia Rescuers"; Jacobs, *Incidents in the Life of a Slave Girl*; Cary, *The Price of a Child*; Still, *The Underground Railroad*; Sanchez, "elegy," Wideman, *Philadelphia Fire*; Abu-Jamal, "A Panther Walks in Philly"; Allen, *The Life Experience and Gospel Labours*.

Slavery: Jones and Others, Petition of the People of Color and Freemen of Philadelphia; Still, *The Underground*

Railroad; Cary, *The Price of a Child*; Harper, "An Appeal for the Philadelphia Rescuers"; Jacobs, *Incidents in the Life of a Slave Girl*; Forten, *from a Man of Colour*.

Working Class: Birtha, "Route 23"; Dunbar-Nelson, "By Paths in the Quaker City"; Mathis, *The Twelve Tribes of Hattie*; Du Bois, *The Philadelphia Negro*; Brown, *Taste of Power*; Bradley, *South Street*.

APPENDIX C: ALTERNATE TABLE OF CONTENTS
BY GEOGRAPHY

Center City (the central business district and the original area that made up the City of Philadelphia. It is bounded by South Street to the south, the Delaware River to the east, the Schuylkill River to the west, and Vine Street to the north. It includes such neighborhoods as Penn's Landing, Old City, Society Hill, Chinatown, and the Museum District.): Dunbar-Nelson, "By Paths in the Quaker City"; Wideman, *The Cattle Killing*; Allen and Jones, *Narrative*; Still, *The Underground Railroad*; Cary, *The Price of a Child*.

Germantown (northwestern Philadelphia): Mathis, *The Twelve Tribes of Hattie*; Johnson, *Loving Day*; Jackson, "Hoops."

North Philadelphia (north of Center City. Includes areas such as Fairmount, Fishtown, Northern Liberties, Strawberry Mansion.): Birtha, "Route 23"; Jackson, "Euphoria"; Brown, *A Taste of Power*; Moore Campbell, *Sweet Summer*; Yvonne, "Momma House"; Fauset, *Plum Bun*; Abu-Jamal, "A Panther Walks in Philly"; Pate, *Losing Absalom*.

South Philadelphia (bounded by South Street to the north, the Delaware River to the east and south and the Schuylkill River to the west. It includes such neighborhoods as Bella Vista, Grays Ferry, the Italian market, and Moyamensing. It became part of the city of Philadelphia, along with other jurisdictions in Philadelphia Country, when the Act of Consolidation was passed in 1854.): Sanchez, "10 Haiku"; Gay, "To the Fig Tree"; Du Bois, *The Philadelphia Negro*; Webb, *The Garies and Their Friends*; McKinney-Whetstone, *Tumbling*.

South Street (the boundary between South Philadelphia and Center City): Bradley, *South Street*; Smith, *South Street*; McKinney-Whetstone, *Tumbling*.

West Philadelphia (generally considered to reach from the western shore of the Schuylkill River, to City Avenue to the northwest, Cobbs Creek to the southwest, and the SEPTA Media/Elwyn Line to the south. It includes such neighborhoods as Southwest Philadelphia, University City, and Cobbs Creek.): Sanchez, "elegy"; Wisher, "5 South"; Yvonne, "4951 Walnut Street"; Wideman, *Philadelphia Fire*.

TEXT CREDITS

SECTION 1

Cato and Petitioners to the Pennsylvania Assembly, "Letter of Cato and Petition by 'The Negroes Who Obtained Freedom by the Late Act,'" *Freeman's Journal*, or *North-American Intelligencer* (Philadelphia), September 21, 1781.

Excerpts from Absalom Jones and Richard Allen, *Narrative of the Proceedings of the Black People, During the Late Awful Calamity in Philadelphia in the Year 1793; And a Refutation of Some Censures Thrown upon Them in Some Late Publications* (Philadelphia: Printed for the authors by William W. Woodward, at Franklin Head, No. 41 Chesnut-Street, 1794).

Absalom Jones and Others, *Petition of the People of Color and Freemen of Philadelphia—Against the Slave Trade to the Coast of Guinea to the President, Senate, and House of Representatives of the United States* (1799). Records of the U.S. House of Representatives, National Archives and Records Administration.

"Alice: Pioneer of Philadelphia," from Thomas Isaiah's *Eccentric Biography or Memoirs of Remarkable Female Characters, Ancients and Modern* (Worcester, MA: Isaiah Thomas, 1804).

Confession of John Joyce, alias Davis, Who Was Executed on Monday, the 14th of March, 1808. For the Murder of Mrs. Sarah Cross; With an Address to the Public and People of Color. Together with the Substance of the Trial, and the Address of Chief Justice Tilghman, on His Condemnation (Printed at No. 12 Walnut-Street, for the benefit of Bethel Church, 1808).

James Forten, "Series of Letters by a Man of Colour," in *Letters from a Man of Colour, on a late Bill before the Senate of Pennsylvania* (1813).

James Forten and Russell Parrott, *To the Humane and Benevolent Inhabitants of the City and County of Philadelphia, Address Delivered August 10, 1817* (1817).

Excerpts from William Whipper, *An Address Delivered in Wesley Church on the Evening of June 12, Before the Colored Reading Society of Philadelphia, for Mental Improvement* (Printed by John Young, 1828).

Excerpt from Richard Allen, *The Life, Experience, and Gospel Labours of the Rt. Rev. Richard Allen. To Which is Annexed the Rise and Progress of the African Methodist Episcopal Church in the United States of America. Containing a Narrative of the Yellow Fever in the Year of Our Lord 1793: With an Address to the People of Colour in the United States* (Printed by Martin & Boden, 1833).

Excerpts from Robert Purvis, *Appeal of Forty Thousand Citizens, Threatened with Disfranchisement to the People of Pennsylvania* (Printed by Merrihew and Gunn, No. 7 Carter's Alley, 1838).

Excerpts from Joseph Willson, *Sketches of the Higher Classes of Colored Society in Philadelphia* (Printed by Merrihew and Thompson, 1841).

SECTION 2

Excerpt from Frank J. Webb, *The Garies and Their Friends With an Introductory Preface by Mrs. Harriet B. Stow* (Printed by G. Routledge Co., 1857).

Frances Ellen Watkins Harper, "An Appeal for the Philadelphia Rescuers," *Weekly Anglo-African American*, June 23, 1860.

Excerpt from Harriet Jacobs, *Incidents in the Life of a Slave Girl: Written by Herself*, edited by L. Maria Child (Printed for the Author, 1861).

Excerpts from Judith Giesberg et al., eds., *Emilie Davis's Civil War: The Diaries of a Free Black Woman in Philadelphia, 1863–1865* (University Park: Pennsylvania State University Press, 2014).

Octavius Catto, *Our Alma Mater. An Address Delivered at Concert Hall on the Occasion of the Twelfth Annual Commencement of the Institute for Colored Youth, May 10th, 1864* (Published by the direction of the Alumni Association; Printed by C. Sherman, Son & Co., 1864).

Excerpt from William Still, *A Brief Narrative of the Struggle for the Rights of the Colored People of Philadelphia in the City Railway Cars* (Printed by Merrihew & Son, 1867).

Excerpts from William Still, *The Underground Railroad Record: Authentic Narratives and First-Hand Accounts* (Printed by People's Publishing Company, 1879).

Fanny Jackson Coppin, "Christmas Eve Story," *Christian Recorder* (December 1880).

Excerpts from W. E. B. Du Bois, *The Philadelphia Negro: A Social Study* (published for the University of Pennsylvania; printed by Ginn & Co., 1899).

Alain Locke, "Hail Philadelphia," in *Black Opals* (Spring 1927).

Excerpt from Jessie Fauset, *Plum Bun: A Novel Without a Moral* (Published by Frederick A. Stokes, 1929).

Alice Dunbar Nelson, "By Paths in the Quaker City." Unpublished. Alice Dunbar Nelson papers, University of Delaware Library, Newark, Delaware.

SECTION 3

Excerpts from William Gardner Smith, *South Street*, © 1954 by William Gardner Smith. Copyright renewed © 1982 by Mrs. William Gardner Smith, Rachel Elizabeth Smith, Claude Smith, and Michele Smith. Reprinted by permission of Farrar, Strauss, & Giroux, Inc. All rights reserved.

Excerpts from Fran Ross, *Oreo*. © 1974 by Frances D. Ross. Reprinted by permission of New Directions Publishing Corp. © 2018 by Fran Ross with an introduction by Marlon James. Reproduced with the permission of Pan Macmillan, through PLSclear.

Excerpts from David Bradley, *South Street*. Grossman Publishers, a division of The Viking Press, 1975. By permission of the author.

SECTION 4

INDEX

Abdy, Edward, 283
Abele, Julian Francis, 341n2
abolitionism
    Black-White interactions and, 236
    of churches, 13, 15
    colonization movement and, 44–47
    of freed slaves, 228
    Germantown as birthplace of, 322
    gradual approach, 6, 17–21, 28, 46
    growth of, 11–12
    opposition to, 15
    of Quakers, 3, 6, 12, 15, 28
    race riots and, 81–83, 284
    of women, 15, 88, 233, 235–39
    See also Underground Railroad
Abu-Jamal, Mumia:
    A Panther Walks in Philly," 8, 148, 281–92
Academy of Music, 139, 142n7
accommodationist philosophy, 125
Addison, Joseph: *Cato, a Tragedy*, 39, 43n5
African Americans
    Civil War service of, 74, 75, 95, 101–2, 115n8
    disfranchisement of, 3, 6, 15, 38, 49, 61–66,
        82, 286
    double consciousness of, 125, 248, 249n11
    gay community, 172–79
    Great Migration and, 77, 288, 311
    Harlem Renaissance and, 7, 77, 133, 135, 143
    homeownership among, 66, 272
    love for Philadelphia, 5, 337–38, 341
    as percentage of Philadelphia population, 2,
        14, 73, 79, 271, 339
    restrictions on free movement of, 39–42, 288
    stereotypes related to, 34, 61, 66, 165, 219
    wealth disparities among, 13–14
    World War I service of, 77
    See also Black-White interactions;
        discrimination; middle-class African
        Americans; racism; segregation; slavery
        and enslaved persons; working-class
        African Americans
African Episcopal Church, 13
African Institute*See* Institute for Colored Youth

African Methodist Episcopal (AME) Church, 13,
    22, 58, 122, 135, 339
African Presbyterian Church, 284
AIDS epidemic, 150, 173, 179
Alice (enslaved woman), 31–33
Allen, Richard
    criminal narratives and, 33–37
    Free African Society and, 6, 13, 22
    The Life, Experience, and Gospel Labours,
        57–60
    *Narrative of the Proceedings of the Black
        People, During the Late Awful Calamity in
        Philadelphia*, 13, 22–27
    *Petition of the People of Color and Freemen of
        Philadelphia—Against the Slave Trade to
        the Coast of Guinea*, 13, 28–30
    St. George's Church and, 21–22, 58–60, 258–61
    Underground Railroad and, 22
    yellow fever epidemic and, 6, 13, 21–27, 58,
        258
AME Church*See* African Methodist Episcopal
    Church
American Anti-Slavery Society, 15, 61
American Colonization Society, 44, 47
American Moral Reform Society, 14, 38, 48
American Revolution, 12, 17, 38, 39, 291
Anderson, Marion, 257n3, 341n14
antislavery movement*See* abolitionism
Aristotle, on education, 103
art
    Black Arts Movement, 180
    Harlem Renaissance and, 7, 77, 133, 135, 143
    murals, 8, 149, 306–8, 338
    racial uplift through, 125, 133
Ashe, Arthur, 310, 310n13
assimilation, 125, 241–45, 247, 248
automats, 143–44, 208

Baker, Chesney Henry "Chet," Jr., 246, 249nn2–3
Bambara, Toni Cade: "Deep Sight and Rescue
    Missions," 240–49
Bannerman, Helen: *The Story of Little Black
    Sambo*, 207n3